JOSEPH R MORICE
1632 WORCESTER DR
PITTSBURGH PA
15243

JOSEPH R. MORICE
PROFESSOR EMERITUS
DUQUESNE UNIVERSITY

LINCOLN THE PRESIDENT

SPRINGFIELD TO GETTYSBURG

VOLUME ONE

LINCOLN
THE PRESIDENT

SPRINGFIELD TO GETTYSBURG

VOLUME ONE

BY

J. G. Randall

PROFESSOR OF HISTORY
IN THE UNIVERSITY OF ILLINOIS

DODD, MEAD & COMPANY
NEW YORK

E457
.R2
vol. 1
cop. 2

COPYRIGHT, 1945,
BY DODD, MEAD AND COMPANY, INC.

ALL RIGHTS RESERVED
NO PART OF THIS BOOK MAY BE REPRODUCED IN ANY FORM
WITHOUT PERMISSION IN WRITING FROM THE PUBLISHER

PRINTED IN THE UNITED STATES OF AMERICA

To Ruth, whose unfailing help and interest illumined the labor of these pages.

gyt 9/28/00

OCT 05 2000

PREFACE

THE vastness of Lincoln literature is a bit misleading. It requires a very small space to enumerate the authors who have produced significant biographies of Lincoln—i. e., works above the level of campaign lives or superficial treatments. Lincoln is an easy subject for one who merely writes "another book" about him. The field is one in which the public has been tolerant of uncritical writing. But Lincoln is an extremely difficult subject if the motive and design be that of careful, critical investigation off the beaten path. Though the literature is voluminous, and though the more thoughtful works will live through the years, no one conversant with these matters would think of supposing that the claims have all been staked out and the fields fully tilled. As for Lincoln's presidency the themes are so challenging, the source material so massive, the problems so complex, that reëxamination and rewriting have become a necessity in our time.

The treatment here offered is conceived both as biography and as history. It has been found impossible to present Lincoln's background and his crowded years of leadership except by integration with contemporary movements and thought currents. If history is attempted, the standards of historical craftsmanship must not be neglected. Statements must be tied to reality, and this not merely by way of something to quote or cite, but in terms of tested and competent evidence. There is nothing cryptic about this. The principle is simple; it is the fulfillment of the principle with imperfect and conflicting material that comes hard. The muse is strict and exacting. Without submitting to these requirements one can dabble in history, but it is a field where the tyro falls short and the amateur betrays himself. This is not said with the least assumption of professionalism. It is simply a recognition of realities within which the author has had to work.

If sources are diligently reëxamined, then by the same token the product may become "revisionist." Even in a simple matter it is not easy after the passage of years to recover the true picture. If the past situation was complicated, if many factors went into its making, if observers at the time lacked full understanding or differed as to what it meant, and especially if it has become controversial, then an uncommon effort is needed to disengage reality from the accumulated deposit which the years have brought.

What happens over and over is that a certain idea gets started in association with an event or figure. It is repeated by speakers and editors. It soon becomes a part of that superficial aggregation of concepts that goes under the heading "what everybody knows." It may take decades before a stock picture is even questioned as to its validity. Evidence is then unearthed, some of it being first discovered, or brought to light after having been forgotten or neglected. Discoloring is corrected, partisan misrepresentation—perhaps accepted unawares by the public—is exposed, predilections and presumptions stripped away. Historical insight cuts through with a new clarity. In this process the historian does not claim to arrive at perfection, but he does hope by fresh inquiry to come nearer to past reality.

This is called "revision," but that suggests mere change or rewriting; a much better word for it would be historical restoration. Where a building belonging to a past age has disappeared or fallen into ruin, there is the process of studying available traces and records, examining the period, and gradually building up a "restoration" to show the structure as it originally stood. With a like motive the historian seeks out original records, excavates, so to speak, clears away unhistorical debris, and endeavors, if he can, to restore events and essential situations of the past.

Certain accepted ideas of Lincoln and his period will probably be upset in the following pages. This does not mean that the account has been prepared in an iconoclastic spirit, nor does it imply any claim of finality. The task has been undertaken in some trepidation and in contemplation of the difficulty of attaining authentic truth. New conclusions come not from preconception, assuredly not from a wish to overthrow or destroy. The historian searches; he presents his findings; if he works validly he destroys nothing except misconception and unfounded tradition. It is only so that scholarship can be constructive. Where *clichés* have become fixed in the popular mind the historian's finding may occasion surprise or even dissatisfaction, but this cannot be avoided. If the critics pass the ammunition, that is one of the occupational hazards.

These chapters have not been made up from other biographies of Lincoln. The intent has been to take the basic material out of which history must be shaped (much of it in manuscripts never published and hitherto unused for this purpose), to discard the irrelevant or unhistorical, and to show the result. In treating McClellan the hope has been to give the reader some basis for forming his own judgment of a commander whose appraisal has not yet been cleared of the violent feeling of the time. So with other matters: the Ann Rutledge evidence has been sifted, Mrs. Lincoln restudied, the Lincoln-Douglas debates reanalyzed, wartime politics investigated, emancipation stripped of its crust of misconception, and so on.

Popular ideas of Lincoln are in large part traceable to that picturesque but provocative individual, William H. Herndon. One should give him credit for tireless searching, and for that intellectual questing which was almost pathetically revealed in his correspondence with Theodore Parker, but the Lincoln he has given us needs reconsideration. For long years his collection was closed to scholars generally. Only recently has general access been given to his impressive but unsatisfactory body of manuscripts, so that the presentation to the public of a full appraisal of Herndon may at the moment be regarded as unfinished business. Mr. David Donald, completing doctoral work at the University of Illinois, is doing a competent life of Herndon, and the author, who assigned him the subject, has benefited by seeing his chapters thus far prepared. Mr. Donald has found that, along with qualities that make this partner-biographer well worthy of study, he is sometimes unreliable even about the facts of his own life.

To take Herndon at face value is no longer permissible; we can now see his actual material. Mere citations to the Herndon-Weik Collection are by no means enough; the stuff of this collection is uneven and needs sifting. Beveridge used these manuscripts at a time when previous users included only Herndon, Weik, and Lamon (or Lamon's ghost writer), but in going over the papers at length the author cannot give as full acceptance to Herndon's material as Beveridge did. A body of sources, however, may not be all of a piece. Some of Herndon's statements have greater validity than others. He was Lincoln's partner for many years; he tried in his way to give the world both Lincoln's greatness and the everyday man; to use Lord Charnwood's apt phrase, his was "the task of substituting for Lincoln's aureole the battered tall hat, with valuable papers stuck in its lining, which he had long contemplated with reverent irritation." One can doubt his accumulated masses of reminiscence and still give a measure of credence to descriptions which arose from close daily association.

Herndon has profited by his well known statement that he loved the truth. But, as a court examines the competence of a witness, one must go back of this assertion to ask whether a man who thought he could grasp truth by intuition, who wrote of his "mud instinct" and "dog sagacity," who claimed he could "see to the gizzard" of a question, could recognize and adequately set forth the truth. Herndon was a self-made psychoanalyst long before that somewhat modern art became widely known. He prided himself on a kind of clairvoyance and a knack for mind reading. Information which he acquired by assiduous effort had to undergo Herndonian processing. It is not so much a matter of blaming him for the common human frailty of inaccuracy; it is enough to perceive it and bracket it with the Herndon record. One can follow a middle course, neither rejecting him out of hand nor accepting him in full, but assessing his uneven product and using it for what it is worth. His down-to-earth frankness, his pioneer tang and flavor, may be appreciated while one keeps a wholesome distrust for his excesses of rhetoric and his psychoanalytical conjecture.

In taking a subject as broad as that of the present work it has been found necessary at every point to condense, to select, and to leave out a great deal that the author has collected. Practically every paragraph could be elaborated from the material assembled; the purpose has been to keep the main story before the reader. By its title the book is concerned with the presidency; chapters for the period prior to 1860 are to be regarded as background; no treatment of Lincoln's early life is attempted. Chronologically speaking—though chronology is not all—the present study goes no farther than the latter part of 1863, the time of the Gettysburg address. A large mass of Lincoln manuscripts in the Library of Congress is to be opened in 1947, and it is the author's intention to publish a companion work (with a different subtitle) to deal with further aspects of Lincoln the President. If certain matters of the period are omitted here, the plan for that later work may in part offer the explanation. Life in Lincoln's day, the Lincolns in the White House, problems of government, the manner and technique of the war leader, cabinet dealings, relations with an uncoöperative Congress, further attacks and intrigues, new international episodes, military developments, plans and counter-plans for reconstruction, the dark summer of 1864, the presidential election of that troubled year, Grant's long delay and final triumph, Lincoln's planning for peace, his thought for the soldiers, his method of addressing the public, his second inaugural, his part in the ending of the war, the magnanimity which gave him serenity in the final phase despite war weariness, the statesmanship with which he looked ahead—these and other large matters are reserved for the later work.

For the present purpose the Gettysburg address, marking a climax in Lincoln's thought of America's larger role, offers a convenient terminus. To recover the Gettysburg Lincoln, to catch up with him, to put him in his full mold, belongs to the agenda of our times. There is a challenge for today in the study of his career as a proof of the meaning and opportunity of democracy. There is need for a fuller understanding of his grasp of liberal thought, his interest in the common man, his sense of human values, his sympathy for labor, his rising above partisanship, his concept of the statesman's task in its relation to order in society, and to peace and democracy in the world.

J. G. R.

Urbana, Illinois
September 8, 1945

CONTENTS

VOLUME I

CHAPTER		PAGE
I	A Man's Outlook	1
II	Thus Stood Lincoln	26
III	The House on Eighth Street	51
IV	North and South	75
V	Lincoln and Douglas	104
VI	The Political Scene in 1860	129
VII	Destiny in a Wigwam	154
VIII	Campaign and Election of 1860	178
IX	The Vexed Question	207
X	President Elect	246
XI	Lincoln Takes Hold	273
XII	Sumter	311
XIII	Eighty Days	351
XIV	Democracy's Testing	380

LINCOLN THE PRESIDENT

SPRINGFIELD TO GETTYSBURG

VOLUME ONE

CHAPTER I

A MAN'S OUTLOOK

IN THE year of Our Lord 1860 the United States was at peace. In all that was sound and fundamental, in every instinct that was normal and sane, the people of America, and their genuine friends abroad, wanted that peace to endure. It is true that vicious forces were at work which would sweep beyond the point where reason could check them. An incredible and devastating war was to come; that war would become an absorbing preoccupation, greedily claiming energies that might have gone into natural pursuits; then, during and after the fighting those who survived would look back and discover in the "pre-war" age only elements of strife and seeds of sectional hate.

Yet to refer to the period as "pre-war" is only retrospection, however much it may be supported by massive historical studies that eternally point toward the Civil War as either the terminus or the point of departure of all discussion. Must an age be only ante- or post-? While a country is at peace are not the facts of peace worthy of note for their own sake?

I

Abraham Lincoln of Illinois thought that they were. He deplored strife and sought to dissociate himself from sectional hatred. Occupied with a considerable law practice, but recognized as an outstanding leader in Illinois and mentioned for the presidency, he made it his business in the period preceding his presidential nomination to emphasize the peacetime pursuits of his country and to recover for his own day some of the nation-building stimulus of the fathers. He was concerned with problems of slavery, and with such a handling of those problems as would allay strife, as he hoped; but this was not all. He turned his thoughts also to discoveries and inventions, to the "iron horse," to "hot-water power" harnessed to help mankind, to the "seventy or eighty thousand words" of the English language, to influences that tend to "bring us together" and "make us better acquainted," to the harvest-machine and the "steam plow," to the problem of fifty bushels of wheat to the acre.

He made observations on the size of farms, disliking mammoth ones. He gave thought to the farmer as a man, to the farmer's pride in his work, to the laborer's enjoyment of the fruit of his labor, to the relation of labor and capital. He disliked the "mud-sill" theory, "that whoever is once a hired laborer, is fatally fixed in that condition for life." He was concerned for the "prudent, penniless beginner," anxious that he should acquire a surplus and one day arrive at the point where he could own his own land and tools. It was not only untutored folk who must labor, he reflected; men with education must work. The country could not sustain them in idleness; the laborer should not be "a blind horse upon a tread-mill." These workings of the mind do not make sense in terms of sectional strife; nevertheless these were Lincoln's thoughts. He was like the majority of the people of the nation. He was thinking of peace.[1]

He had been about considerably, this Lincoln, more than is usually supposed. He knew Illinois, and chiefly the picturesque life of the eighth judicial circuit which he had traveled for over twenty years. He had journeyed rather widely in other states, from the eastern seaboard to Kansas, from New Hampshire [2] to New Orleans. Men of culture and training were his constant associates, but pioneers came closer to the springs of his origin. The areas of his birth (Kentucky), his boyhood (Indiana), and his rising career (Illinois) had been pioneer regions; he had moved west as pioneering itself moved west. He had pondered the history of his people. He knew the law, not from books only, but from life. He could draw a deed, collect a

[1] Up to this point Lincoln's statements are from his lecture on "Discoveries . . . [etc.]," given in 1858–60, and his address before the Wisconsin state agricultural society at Milwaukee, Sep. 30, 1859. *Complete Works of Abraham Lincoln,* ed. by John G. Nicolay and John Hay (12 vols.), V, 99 ff., 236 ff. (hereafter cited as *Works*). This set is far from complete and has textual inaccuracies. These, however, are of a minor and formal nature (relating to punctuation, capitalization, the spelling out of abbreviated words, etc.); the editing is not of a type to distort the meaning.

[2] Elwin L. Page, *Abraham Lincoln in New Hampshire.*

claim, argue an assumpsit; yet he could also advise a client to avoid litigation. He could put himself in his client's place. Law treatises and court reports, passing under the processes of his mind, had given him a respect for principles that must prevail because they are fundamental.[3]

He would tug at a problem and wrestle until he could make sense of it. Complicated though it was, he would not rest until he had mastered it. It is interesting to read what editors of his works call "fragments." In these bits of writing his concern was not mental gymnastics; it was clarification of some issue of his day, whether or not he was thinking of a particular speech or statement for publication. He would pose a question, then try to answer it, using processes of thought and speech to solve a thing, turn it around, see it whole, apply it to his times. In this manner as a boy, in early backwoods days, he had laid his own foundations in study. Self-education was his way; it had made him familiar with a few serviceable classics; what is more, it carried over into adult life. This was his liberal education.

His methods of thought and study had never proceeded in bookish fashion nor in the academic style. It was not sufficient that he know what a thing meant; it was not his to use unless it sounded right as he himself spoke it. When he could make it click in his own language, he felt that he had it; then he could impart it to others. Latin phrases or classical allusions, not uncommon in his day even on the frontier, did not appeal to him. They were like a frilled shirt, the kind of thing someone else might wear—Orville Browning or Ninian Edwards perhaps—but not himself. He did not use language to display his own learning, but to clinch a point. He had become adept at stump speaking, having learned to meet people by small groups or by shouting and jostling thousands and to divert and instruct them with ready anecdote and frontier oratory. His speeches had not only content; they had flavor.

He knew the ways of politicians, the manner in which things are arranged among leaders, the give and take of party maneuver. For politics he had a natural gift. He took to it avidly. As for ambition, the desire to rise and be influential, he had it in marked degree; at times it had become an almost pathetic craving. Yet he had met disappointment, and meeting it, had reasoned and tried to believe that

[3] For brief comment on Lincoln as a lawyer, see below, pp. 33–40.

it did not matter. Some of the accessories of ambition, such as self-conceit or low intrigue, he had somehow avoided. He could retaliate sharply, at times too sharply; yet he was learning, though perhaps slowly, to take a rebuff or feel an affront, but give no sign. He referred to himeslf as having come of "second families," [4] and spoke of his early life in terms of undistinguished poverty.

Mr. John L. Scripps of Chicago wrote to William H. Herndon of Lincoln's conscientiousness and sincerity in supplying data for what became the Scripps campaign biography of 1860. "The chief difficulty I had to encounter," wrote Scripps, "was to induce him to communicate the homely facts . . . of his early life. . . . 'Why Scripps' said he . . . 'it is a great piece of folly to attempt to make anything out of my early life. It can be all condensed into a simple sentence, and that sentence you will find in Gray's Elegy; "The short and simple annals of the poor." That's my life, and that's all you or any one else can make of it.' " [5]

His humility, however, did not end with self-depreciation, for he did not lack confidence; it was a quality of deferring to others, of working with men. It became more marked with him as the years passed. His character had defects and inadequacies; it had not reached its final phase. There were elements in the man yet undeveloped, indeed unsuspected.

II

Since the method and content of this volume requires that space be reserved for the crowded years of Lincoln's leadership, there is no room for the details of his early life. That is a considerable subject in itself; the theme of the present book is the presidency. Lincoln's ancestral heritage, his birth, boyhood, young manhood, lowly family, hardscrabble surroundings, limited schooling and persistent self-education, his father's shifting from one unimproved farm to another,

[4] "My parents were both born in Virginia, of undistinguished families—second families, perhaps I should say." Brief autobiography sent to Jesse W. Fell, December 20, 1859. Lincoln's words in transmitting this short record are significant and characteristic: "Herewith is a little sketch, as you requested. There is not much of it, for the reason, I suppose, that there is not much of me. If anything be made out of it, I wish it to be modest, and not to go beyond the material." *Works*, V, 286.

[5] J. L. Scripps to Herndon, Chicago, Illinois, June 24, 1865, Herndon-Weik MSS. See also Paul M. Angle, ed., *Herndon's Life of Lincoln*, 1–2.

must be left to the reader's knowledge obtained elsewhere. The same must be said for Lincoln in tiny New Salem: his adventures and misadventures there as storekeeper, postmaster, mill manager and surveyor; his prowess in frontier sports; his rapid progress in making friends; his familiarity with debt and financial failure; his slowly widening opportunities; his early recognition among pioneer neighbors in the drawing of legal papers; his service in the Black Hawk War in which he was made captain by the men of his company. These matters, vivid and important as they are, are not treated here; it is too much to ask that one book contain everything about Lincoln.

From England to Massachusetts, to Pennsylvania, to Virginia, to Kentucky, to Indiana, to Illinois—such was the course of this branch of Lincolns over the generations. Contributions of three states were of abiding significance: Kentucky and Indiana influences remained with Abraham Lincoln as Illinois became his chosen home. He could not in later years identify the precise place of his birth though he knew the approximate location. It remained for later investigation to mark the site—the farm of the sinking spring near Hodgen's mill not far from Elizabethtown. The little that is known of the mother in that log-cabin birth but emphasizes the utter obscurity and limitations of her brief life, which was one with that of the American pioneer woman. Of that other Kentucky home to which the Lincolns moved when Abraham was two years old, he had more vivid memories: a cabin "on Knob Creek, on the road from Bardstown, Kentucky, to Nashville, Tennessee, at a point three or three and a half miles south or southwest of Atherton's Ferry, on the Rolling Fork." [1] That knobby region, richer in wild beauty than in fertility, took its place in Lincoln's enduring impressions of little things in these earliest years: of pumpkin seeds planted on a hillslope and washed down by a dashing rain, of boys' adventures in and about the creek, of catching a fish and giving it to a passing soldier, of attending ABC schools kept by Riney and Hazel, of an old stone house—the Kirkpatrick place—where young people gathered for dances, of laboriously carrying water to the cabin and grist to the mill. It was here that the pithy informality of Lincoln's familiar conversation, with its wealth of anecdotes, began, but this did not exhaust Kentucky's contribution.

[1] Autobiography, *Works*, VI, 26. For the Lincolns' moving to the Knob Creek location in 1811, see Pratt, *Lincoln, 1809–1839*, 1.

Cultured Lexington, heart of the Blue Grass, center of gentlemanly living, being the birthplace of Mrs. Lincoln, was the scene of family visits by her husband. Lincoln kept up with Kentucky newspapers while in Illinois; indeed early Illinois itself was in considerable part a projection of Kentucky people and ideas into the West. The pioneers of New Salem were largely from Kentucky. All three of Lincoln's Springfield law partners were born in that state. His friend Joshua F. Speed was of Kentucky and his visits to Speed's Louisville home in 1841 was of more than ordinary personal importance. His developing political concepts followed the Clay pattern. The state of his childhood never ceased to hold a special place in his thought and feeling. Ties to Kentucky held strong and sure; they would later give the key to much of his presidential policy. Still later he was even to be suggested as one of the commonwealth's two sons to be honored in Statuary Hall in the Capitol at Washington.[2] Take it all in all, from his earliest breath to the public burdens of the fuller years, Kentucky was a part of Lincoln.[3]

III

It was in the woods and brush of southern Indiana that Lincoln spent fourteen basic years from the age of seven to his majority at twenty-one. Indiana too was part of him. If he had an appreciation of natural beauty, he did little to show it, but no visual impression of the lusty youth in the setting in which he moved would be complete without the picturesque features of the Indiana country: its thick-grown hills, its abundant game and fish, its wild fruit, its sassafras, pawpaw and dogwood, its heavier beech, maple, poplar and walnut, its tanagers and jays, its serene sky and friendly scene. Outwardly his life, in these teen-age years of sturdy growth, was one with that of his undistinguished father, Thomas Lincoln, and of that rugged individual and unforgettable country cousin, Dennis Hanks.[1] Inwardly there

[2] There were a number of suggestions that Lincoln and Jefferson Davis be chosen. The commission for the purpose chose Henry Clay and Ephraim McDowell. Frank L. McVey to author, Lexington, Ky., May 12, 1944.

[3] For a favorable account of Thomas and Nancy (Hanks) Lincoln, and for detailed study of Lincoln's birthplace and boyhood, with documentary support in court records, see Louis A. Warren, *Lincoln's Parentage and Childhood*. This book treats the Kentucky period.

[1] In the Herndon-Weik manuscripts one finds many pages of recollections touching

was something of Indiana that offered a stimulus to the poetic sense; there was a reaching out for the mastery of a few books, and there was trial of skill in tentative public speaking. Home ties, neighbors none too close, pioneering labors, early intellectual questing, were associated with the Indiana years. Much of all this was buoyant energy, though there was deep tragedy in the illness, death, and crude, remote burial of his pioneer mother.[2] Much of it also was raw pioneer life —packing through from Kentucky, rigging up a half faced camp in the brush, rearing a log cabin, squatting on land that was but slowly acquired by legal right, going to school "by littles" to Crawford, Sweeney, and Dorsey, spending long hours in that noble institution, Jones's village store at Gentryville, hearing an occasional preacher, never ceasing to wield the ax. Keeping soul and body together—an expression found in Lincoln's works as well as in the works of Dennis Hanks—was the pioneer's main preoccupation, but it is not to be forgotten that there was culture within the range of Lincoln's long legs and that the reading of well chosen classics was a basic factor in the determined self-education of the growing youth.

In this Indiana period the spell of the river, beckoning to unexplored worlds beyond the bend, was upon him. Floating on broad western currents all the way down to New Orleans by flatboat and traveling back by steamer, he found new experiences and gained wider contacts. Earning a few dollars by carrying passengers from the Indiana shore to passing steamers, the gawky youth was haled before the majestic presence of Squire Pate in the log house that served for home and court, charged with violating the laws of Kentucky by infringing upon ferrying rights. There was the dark threat of a heavy fine, but the squire settled the case of "Kentucky versus

---

Lincoln's life in the Indiana period by such pioneers as Mrs. Josiah Crawford, Nathaniel Grigsby, Charles Friend (a rather voluminous contributor), Dennis Friend Hanks (backwoodsy, amusing in spelling, unreliable on Hanks ancestry), Mrs. Allen Gentry (née Roby), and others by the names of Chapman, Romine, Wood, Turnham, Burba, Lamar, Pitcher, etc. Herndon also interviewed Mrs. Sarah Bush Johnston Lincoln, Abraham's stepmother. These recollections are the sources for much of what is known of Lincoln's Indiana life; unfortunately there is a lapse of forty or more years between the events and their recording. Herndon's account is based on this material, but the fullest history of the Indiana phase is in Beveridge, *Abraham Lincoln,* I, 38–99. Lincoln's autobiography, *Works,* VI, 24 ff., is, of course, indispensable.

[2] For an examination of milksickness, in which pioneer lore is skillfully combined with competent historical and medical investigation, see Philip D. Jordan, "The Death of Nancy Hanks Lincoln," *Ind. Mag. of Hist.,* XL, 103–110 (June 1944).

Abraham Lincoln" by enlightening interpretation of the statute and dismissal of the charge. It is the belief of W. H. Townsend that enduring impressions of the mystery and practical value of the law were thus engraved upon the mind of the eager youth.[3]

Thus passed these important Indiana years.[4] When Lincoln left the Hoosier state his physical stature had been reached; his thought was opening to national problems; his political maturity was far in the future, but he knew his mind as to the party of his choice. He was a Clay man in a Jacksonian family and a Democratic state. His politics came by independent reasoning, not by inheritance or inertia. He had known in Indiana a definite, not-to-be-repeated phase of western life. It was Indiana before the railroads. It had no dependence on factories though it needed local handcraftsmen, one of whom was Thomas Lincoln; its long journeys were by foot or horseback; its traffic by river craft, ox cart, or pioneer wagon; its farming resembled that of many centuries before; each community was a self-sufficing world. "Local self-dependence was well-nigh perfect. The town depended on the country and the country on the town, for nearly everything that was eaten or woven or otherwise consumed." [5] Men growing up in this setting learned much that was not in books. "Better still, each unlearned the prejudices, the bigotries, and the narrownesses in which he had been bred, and life in the West took on a . . . breadth of tolerance and sympathy, a generous humanity such as had never been known in any of the . . . provincial regions that furnished the materials of this composite population." [6] From now on Lincoln's character as a man and an American would include something of the Hoosier genius [7]—a mixture having its own distinct and friendly human ingredients, a product of migration and intermingling, a down-to-earth quality, a sense of humor, a self-dependence, yet a blending of customs, a western flavor of ideas and folkways.

---

[3] William H. Townsend, *Lincoln the Litigant*, 34–39.

[4] See "Indiana's Contribution to Abraham Lincoln," address by Louis A. Warren before Military Order of the Loyal Legion of the United States, Indianapolis, Sep. 28, 1944.

[5] George Cary Eggleston, *Recollections of a Varied Life*, 19.

[6] *Ibid.*, 27.

[7] *Ibid.*, 27. There were, of course, less admirable aspects of Indiana life and of the peopling of the West. "There is much in that story for Americans to be proud of, but there is also a seamy side to certain phases of the history of the Valley. . . . The splendid area . . . has been abused as well as used." William O. Lynch, in *Democracy in the Middle West, 1840–1940*, ed. by Jeannette P. Nichols and J. G. Randall, 39–40.

IV

In Lincoln's time Illinois was not all unbroken prairie, woods, wild life, and Indians.[1] He lived in the state from 1830 to 1861 and during that time the population of Illinois increased from 157,445 to 1,711,-951.[2] In 1860 Illinois was the fourth state in population in the Union, exceeded only by New York, Pennsylvania, and Ohio. Most of the states of the Union at that time had less than half the population of Illinois.[3] In no state in those three decades could one have better witnessed the stirrings of American growth from the breaking of virgin sod to the busy throb of great cities and modern industry. Nowhere else could one have had a better view of what all this meant in human migrations, surveyings, boom towns, fabulous increase of land values,[4] speculative fever, and the multifarious types of improvements and readjustments that a rising community exhibits.

Lincoln saw the world of civilized society starting from scratch and developing around him. He not only saw it; he was part of it. The man who was moved to lecture on discoveries and inventions, who thought of Young America moving on to material and moral conquests, had seen the burgeoning of a great society with his own eyes. In 1840 few towns of Illinois had more than two thousand people.[5] It is a curious fact that the largest Illinois settlement by far in the middle forties was the Mormon city of Nauvoo, beautifully situated on the broad Mississippi about a hundred miles northwest of Springfield. "Here, in the 1840's, when Chicago was a stripling village of less than 5,000, and Springfield . . . a muddy little town recently planted on the prairie, stood the largest city in Illinois, a community

---

[1] For an account of Illinois in this period, see T. C. Pease, *The Frontier State, 1818–1848*, and A. C. Cole, *The Era of the Civil War, 1848–1870* (*Centennial Hist. of Ill.*, vols. II, III). See also Florence Walton Taylor, "Culture in Illinois in Lincoln's Day," *Transactions*, Ill. State Hist. Soc., 1935, 125–137.

[2] In 1818, when Illinois entered the Union, its population was about 40,000, with only the far Southern portion settled. In its earlier decades the commonwealth had many of the features of a Southern state; in "Egypt" (southern Illinois) the people have always been unmistakably Southern in their manners and characteristics.

[3] By the census of 1860 only twelve states had more than half the Illinois population; twenty-one had less than half.

[4] Such was the "town lot" fever in Chicago that an acre near South Water Street had sold in 1830 for $1.55, while in 1834 lots in this area were selling for $3,500 each. Taylor, "Culture in Illinois," 130.

[5] Only four had over two thousand in 1840: Quincy, Chicago, Springfield, and Alton. The rise of Nauvoo to the stature of the largest city in Illinois came just after that.

of more than 20,000. Center of . . . Mormonism, Nauvoo possessed thousands of dwellings, and a great Temple into the construction of which had been poured a million dollars." [6]

Dickens might find an Illinois town crude with its hitching racks, its mud and slime, its music of pigs and frogs; [7] but Gustave Koerner, who lived in the region through which Dickens hastily passed, remembered an extraordinary social circle in historic Kaskaskia (the old capital) with its wealthy families, its "large and handsome Catholic seminary for ladies," and such gifted and forceful leaders as Nathaniel Pope, Pierre Menard, William Morrison, and Elias Kent Kane, "a descendant of a very well known family in New York, a relative of Chancellor Kent and of Judge Kane of Philadelphia and of the north-pole explorer, Elijah Kane." [8] Vandalia, capital in the days of Lincoln's earlier legislative service, had only eight hundred people, but in the season of the legislature it was a center of fashion and society. When Springfield became the capital,[9] it was no less gay with its "hops" and levees and its young ladies taking occasion to visit Springfield relatives during the legislative session, a custom by which Lincoln himself was not unaffected.

Adolescent Illinois had its quota of religious denominations, the Methodists, Baptists, and Presbyterians being specially active. It had its hopeful colleges.[10] Shurtleff College (later located at Alton) was organized in 1827; McKendree College was founded at Lebanon in 1828; Illinois College, a kind of New Haven in Illinois, began at Jacksonville in 1829; [11] Knox College at Galesburg was born in 1837 under the original name of Prairie College; Jubilee College was founded in a rural setting near Peoria two years later by the Right

---

[6] *Nauvoo Guide,* Federal Writers' Project of Illinois, Works Progress Administration (Chicago, 1939), 9.

[7] Charles Dickens, *American Notes for General Circulation* (1842), 67.

[8] Thomas J. McCormack, ed., *Memoirs of Gustave Koerner, 1809–1896,* I, 390–393. (The reference to the explorer, of course, is to Elisha Kent Kane of Pennsylvania.)

[9] The act making Springfield the capital was passed in 1837; the legislature first met there in December of 1839.

[10] In giving the dates when these colleges "began" (without writing a treatise on the subject) the author would caution the reader that beginning dates are not strictly comparable; there are distinctions between such words as established, founded, organized, chartered, and opened for first instruction. These distinctions are not elaborated above, and the purpose is not to deal with competitive claims among colleges. See Ernest G. Hildner, "Colleges and College Life in Illinois One Hundred Years Ago," *Papers in Illinois History,* 1942, 19–31.

[11] Charles H. Rammelkamp, *Illinois College: A Centennial History, 1829–1929,* 9–37.

Reverend Philander Chase, pioneer bishop of the Episcopal Church.[12] Rockford College began at Rockford in 1847. Other early colleges in the state were McDonough College at Macomb, Blackburn at Carlinville, Illinois Wesleyan at Bloomington, and Northwestern University at Evanston. The state had also its Bible societies, its theological seminaries, its public schools, inadequate to be sure, its state superintendent of public instruction (from 1854), its girls' seminaries, its laws for teachers' qualifications, its state medical society and medical colleges, and its ubiquitous press, for there was a surprising number of newspapers including not a few in the German language. The commonwealth was not lacking in its lyceums,[13] theaters, library associations,[14] dramatic reading societies, hippodromes, circuses, literary or musical festivals, and courses of public lectures. An example of its intellectual activity was a solemn discussion of "Comparative Capabilities of the Human Intellect in 'Different Sexes' " conducted at the "Owl Club" of Ottawa in 1850.[15] Nor was the state backward in its agricultural fairs, shooting matches, and balloon ascensions (as early as 1859).

In the view of William H. Herndon, Lincoln's unique partner-biographer, there was human excellence in Illinois in its primitive pioneer aspects. The settlers in the great West, thought Herndon, "were men of culture—so were the women—God bless 'em if culture includes sharp observation—quick & broad experience and a manly reason of or about men—commerce—laws—institutions—human nature and the world & its affairs generally." Herndon had "never seen such a people"; "for good horse sense . . . the old settlers [he thought] were . . . equals, if not . . . superiors" of people in Massachusetts.[16]

---

12 Lorene Martin, "Old Jubilee College and Its Founder, Bishop Chase," *Transactions*, Ill. State Hist. Soc., 1934, 121–152.

13 The Rockford *Register*, November 21, 1857, mentioned that the lyceum met at the court house to discuss the "license question" with ladies and gentlemen in attendance.

14 For these early cultural factors—libraries, lyceums, the "Chicago Polemical Society," the "Chicago Pythagorean Institute," and the like—see Gwladys Spencer, *The Chicago Public Library: Origins and Backgrounds*, esp. chap. i. What is said of the high average of Chicago's pioneers could be largely applied also to those areas of Illinois that Lincoln knew best.

15 Ottawa *Free Trader*, Feb. 9, 1850.

16 Herndon to Joseph H. Barrett, Springfield, Illinois, July 27, 1887, MS., Mass. Hist. Soc. Herndon was playing on the word *culture*. In the same letter he wrote: ". . . I said of us western people . . . that they had no culture . . . you state that that expression

Men with whom Lincoln grew up in Illinois were largely Southern by birth and antecedents. Among his Southern-born associates one may mention John Todd Stuart, Stephen T. Logan, William H. Herndon, Orville H. Browning, David Davis, Ward H. Lamon, Stephen A. Hurlbut, Archibald Williams, Ninian W. Edwards, Usher F. Linder, Richard Yates, John J. Hardin, William Butler, Albert T. Bledsoe, W. L. D. Ewing, Josiah Lamborn, Jesse B. Thomas, and Orlando B. Ficklin. The first settlers of central and southern Illinois, said Herndon, "came from the limestone regions of Virginia—Kentucky—Tennessee &c and were men of giant strength— . . . mentally strong. They were . . . individualists. They had no education and no culture but good nature helped them. The strong *alone* . . . could get here and the strong *alone* could survive . . . ." Identifying himself with these men, Herndon wrote: ". . . the struggle for life in the wilderness—& the South gave us . . . mental force & forest life makes us sad—and thoughtful. I think that by nature we were a great people. We were rude and rough—had no polish nor culture. Each man and woman was himself or herself. . . . Lincoln was Lincoln—Grant Grant—Douglas was Douglas. Had Lincoln been a man of high culture—polish—of literary taste . . . he may have been a good country lawyer—that's all." [17] Just what Herndon meant by this will be for the reader to judge: perhaps he had in mind a quality of understanding derived from experience of life, a practical wisdom, a distinct originality in contrast to the conventional or imitative conduct that comes from academic polish or bookish training. As to his emphasis upon crudeness, he had already spoken of the settlers as people of "culture," then a few sentences later had said they had "no . . . culture." It was a matter of finding words to express shades of meaning; the meaning itself was not obscure.

V

The politicians' world in Illinois in the day of Lincoln's earlier career has been drawn from life in the vivid pages of Governor Thomas

---

in your section [Massachusetts] means a college education &c and not the culture that comes of observation experience—and reason."

[17] Herndon to Truman H. Bartlett, Springfield, Ill., July 8, 1887, MS., Mass. Hist. Soc. For a comprehensive treatment of the people of early Illinois see T. C. Pease, *The Frontier State*, 1–32.

Ford. It was not an inspiring picture. Because of the want of true "issues" and the scramble for favor, as explained by Ford, an election became "one great fraud, in which honor, faith, and truth were . . . sacrificed, and politicians were debased below the . . . popular idea of that class of men." [1] Government might mean one thing to the people; its purpose in the minds of politicians was another matter. They had a "destiny to accomplish, not for the people, but for themselves." With the people caring little for matters of government, said Ford, the "politicians took advantage of this lethargic state of indifference . . . to advance their own projects, to get offices and special favors from the legislature, which were all they busied their heads about." [2] Politicians, he said, operated on the principle that "the people never blame any one for misleading them"; it was merely a matter of supporting or opposing measures because of their popularity or unpopularity at the time. A "public man," said the governor, "will scarcely ever be forgiven for being right when the people are wrong." That was why "so many" politicians were "ready to prostitute their better judgments to catch the popular breeze." [3] Whatever may have been the basis of parties in their early origin, Ford observed that "little big men, on both sides . . . feel the most thorough hatred for each other; their malice often supplying the place of principle and patriotism. They think they are devoted to a cause, when they only hate an opponent; and the more thoroughly they hate, the more . . . are they partisans." Party newspapers, he thought, promoted and perpetuated this unhealthy state of things.[4]

The convention system—i. e., the holding of conventions for party nominations—was an innovation in Illinois in the thirties which many defended because of its tendency to promote party concentration, but to Governor Ford it seemed "a most admirable contrivance to enable active leaders to govern without much responsibility to the people." [5] Digesting the arguments of the time, the governor said: ". . . it was urged, that the whole convention system was a fraud on the people; that it was a mere fungus growth engrafted upon the constitution; that conventions themselves were got up and packed by cunning, active, intriguing politicians, to suit the wishes of a few." [6] Referring to politicians' methods generally, Ford wrote: "The

---

[1] Thomas Ford, *History of Illinois*, 87. [2] *Ibid.*, 90. [3] *Ibid.*, 194. [4] *Ibid.*, 199. [5] *Ibid.*, 207. [6] *Ibid.*, 205.

State [party] leaders . . . give the word to the little cliques . . . in each county; these . . . convey it to the little big men in each neighborhood, and they do the talking to the rank-and-file of the people. In this way principles and men are put up and put down with amazing celerity. And gentle reader . . . this is government! and if there is in point of fact any other sort, its existence cannot be proved by me, and yet I have been governor of the State for four years." [7]

The unlovely situation thus reflected in Governor Ford's pages is a necessary backdrop for a treatment of Lincoln as a developing leader. Lincoln himself spoke bitterly of "the spirit of party" taking "the lead in the councils of the State," of a party going beyond all expectations to "assume to itself the entire control of legislation," even invading the "sanctuary of the Constitution," and entering "with its unhallowed and hideous form into the . . . judiciary system." At the time Lincoln the Whig, with other Whig colleagues, was denouncing what the opposite party had done in the Illinois legislature by enacting a measure through which they obtained control of the state judiciary. With rising indignation not unlike that of Governor Ford but from a different angle, Lincoln in a statement signed by himself and other Whigs continued:

> . . . measures were adopted by the dominant party to take possession of the State, to fill all public offices with party men, and make every measure . . . operate in furtherance of their party views. The merits of men and measures . . . became the subject of discussion in caucus, instead of the halls of legislation, and decisions there made by a minority . . . have been . . . carried into effect by . . . party discipline, without any regard whatever to the rights of the people or the interests of the State.
>
> . . . the party in power, . . . wholly disregarding the rights, wishes, and interests of the people, has, for the unholy purpose of providing places for its partizans and supplying them with large salaries, disorganized that [the judiciary] department of the government. . . . Men professing respect for public opinion . . . have avowed . . . that the change . . . was intended to produce . . . results favorable to their party and party friends. The immutable principles of justice are to make way for party interests, and the bonds of social order are to be rent in twain, in order that a desperate faction may be sustained at the expense of the people.

[7] *Ibid.*, 274–275.

. . . The declarations of the party leaders . . . prove . . . that the object has been not reform, but . . . the predominance of party.[8]

Simultaneously with this Whig circular, Lincoln and his Whig colleagues in the legislature placed on the record of the lower house a signed protest on this same subject of party abuse apropos of the judiciary bill. They declared in part: "To the majority of a Legislature whose idol is party supremacy, we have addressed our reasons in vain. Announced as a party measure for party purposes, it has been strengthened by the startling admission [of such purpose], and it only remains for us to present to the people of the country, the causes of our opposition, ..." [9] It is amusing to note that Nicolay and Hay, in their huge biography, refer solemnly to Lincoln's having "uttered the voice of the conscience of the party." [10]

It was, of course, with parties and politicians that Lincoln had to work. That in so doing he kept his record clear is an achievement whose full value is not perceived until the Ford portrayal of the political merry-go-round in Illinois is read and appreciated. It cannot be denied that Lincoln was a party man; he had to be if he wanted a political career. He worked by and through party organization; he engaged in party maneuvers; it was as party candidate that he obtained elective office. But it is also worth noting that he saw the evils of party politics and that the worst party excesses never had his approval. In coming days of presidential leadership he was to speak of parties as existing on a low plane. "In . . . time of national peril" he "would have preferred to meet . . . upon a level one step higher than any party platform, because . . . from such more elevated position we could do better battle for the country we all love than . . . from those lower ones where . . . we . . . expend . . . our ingenuity and strength in finding fault with and aiming blows at each other." [11]

---

[8] "Circular from Whig Committee, February [8?], 1841. Appeal to the People of the State of Illinois," *Works,* I, 160–166. This paper was signed by Lincoln as one of a committee of six Whig members of the legislature.

[9] Protest against judiciary bill, Feb. 26, 1841, House *Journal,* 1840–41, 539–545. A small part of this protest, which was signed by thirty-five members including Lincoln, is included in his *Works* edited by Nicolay and Hay (I, 166–167), but the "extract" which they give is incomplete and textually inaccurate, as shown by a comparison with the *Journal.* The above-quoted passage is not given by Nicolay and Hay.

[10] John G. Nicolay and John Hay, *Abraham Lincoln: A History* (10 vols.), I, 167. This huge biography by Lincoln's secretaries is hereafter cited as Nicolay and Hay, *Lincoln.*

[11] *Works,* VIII, 310 (June 12, 1863).

VI

In the pioneer legislature of Illinois Lincoln had his earliest experience of public service on more than a local stage. Elected in 1834 at a time when earning the bare necessaries of life was a major problem,[1] he served continuously through four terms till 1841. That he was the leading man of his party at Vandalia and later at Springfield, was signified by his service as Whig floor leader and by caucus support as speaker of the lower house; his party being in the minority, he was not elected to this office. Making his mark in a body controlled by opponents, he was a man of influence beyond the average of legislators. He phrased petitions for friends to present and drafted bills for others to introduce. This part of his service would have remained almost hidden but for the recent discovery in the Illinois archives of papers recognizable as of Lincoln's handwriting but not otherwise identifiable.[2] Out of legislative sessions he used his time well in the study of law. "When the legislature met, the law-books were dropped, but were taken up again at the end of the session." [3]

Lincoln's one term in Congress (1847–49) fell in the period of the Mexican War and just before the 1850 crisis between North and South. His election as representative in 1846 showed strength especially in two respects: he became the only Whig in Congress from Illinois, and his victory at the polls was won over the redoubtable pioneer preacher, Peter Cartwright. Taking his seat after all the battles of the Mexican War had been fought, Lincoln voted and spoke to the effect that the war had been unnecessarily begun by President Polk,[4] but he was always careful in later years to add that he had supported

---

[1] Autobiography, *Works*, VI, 32.

[2] Harry E. Pratt, "Lincoln's Petitions for Pardon," *Illinois Bar Jour.*, Feb., 1942; S. Ambrose Wetherbee, "Lincoln Collection: Illinois State Archives," *Illinois Libraries*, Feb., 1943, 114–125.

[3] Autobiography, *Works*, VI, 33.

[4] Lincoln voted for the Ashmun amendment to a resolution of thanks to General Taylor (January 3, 1848); the amendment declared that the war was "unnecessarily and unconstitutionally begun by the President" (*Cong. Globe*, 30 Cong., 1 sess., pt. 1, 95). On January 12, 1848 Lincoln made a speech supporting his own "spot resolutions." By a series of questions he plainly implied that the spot on which American blood was shed as indicated in Polk's war message of May 11, 1846, was an isolated area never acquired by the United States and that Polk's statement justifying the war was "the sheerest deception." *Works*, I, 318–320; 327–345.

supply bills and measures favorable to officers, soldiers, and their families.

On the slavery question, while in Congress, Lincoln voted for the Wilmot proviso to prohibit slavery in national territory to be acquired from Mexico, and he worked out a formula of conservative legislation for the abolition of slavery in the District of Columbia.[5] According to Lincoln's proposal children born of slave mothers after 1850 were to be "free," but during minority were to be dependent upon their mothers' owners for support and education, being meanwhile treated as apprentices to such owners. Slaves then held in the District were to remain slaves, but owners, if they wished, could emancipate them at any time, receiving "full value" from the treasurer of the United States. Lincoln was thus applying the process of gradual emancipation. The board for the fixing of compensation was to consist of none other than the President of the United States, the secretary of state, and the secretary of the treasury. Fugitive slaves from the outside, finding their way into the District, were to be arrested and returned to owners. Finally a vote of free white male citizens over twenty-one years of age was to be taken in the District, and the act was to go into force only if a majority favored it. Here Lincoln applied the principle of a popular referendum on a congressional statute.

Thus the man who was later to become the emancipator was making an early tentative effort toward liberation. In doing so his approach was vastly different from that of radical abolitionists. It is true that he was seeking to deal with the question only on a very limited scale and at a time when slavery was strongly entrenched in the United States. He could hardly have gone farther in the existing Congress, but the significant point is that he recognized the realities. The phrasing of the bill—which if passed would have made Lincoln somewhat famous for a legislative measure even if fame had given no greater rewards—revealed the character and point of view of Lincoln the statesman: his conservatism, his patience in letting a process work itself out over the years, his lack of antagonism toward the South, his regard for the rights of slaveholders, his attention to legal details, and his valuing of popular and democratic processes.

---

[5] *Works*, II, 96–100. Lincoln presented his plan for abolition in the District and gave notice of intention to introduce it as a bill, but in the strict parliamentary sense it appears that this was never done. Beveridge, I, 482 n.

Lincoln fulfilled his duty in Congress, did committee service, watched out for Illinois interests in such a matter as land grants, and on party affairs showed himself an ardent hard-working Whig and supporter of General Taylor, candidate for President in 1848. His speech in the House on July 27, 1848, filling thirty pages of his *Works,*[6] was an example of rollicking and badgering campaign oratory, more suitable for the western stump than for the halls of a legislative body. Pertaining to no legislative proposal, it was a purely party speech, viewing Cass with alarm and pointing with pride to Taylor; it was a rather unconvincing defense of the candidate against the accusation of having no declared principles. The speech represents an exuberant, likable, joke-cracking Lincoln; it gives a clue to what he must have been when he let himself go on the hustings; but it does not give us the man at his best. Lincoln did not rise to his full stature when speaking merely the party language. Much the same can be said as to what we know of his campaign speeches in 1848 in New England, at Worcester, New Bedford, Boston, Lowell, Dorchester, Taunton, Chelsea, Cambridge, and Boston again, these being mostly unrecorded except in briefest summary. One of his tasks in these speeches was to show why men of Free Soil tendencies ought not to vote for the Free Soil candidate, but for Taylor. In this same campaign he spoke also in Maryland and canvassed "quite fully" and successfully his own district in Illinois.[7]

Lincoln's congressional term had given him little distinction, and there may have been somewhat of a feeling of futility in his mind as he returned to Springfield to resume the practice of law "with greater earnestness than ever before," [8] as if political leadership were no longer his main preoccupation. This futility may have increased as the nation met and temporarily averted a great crisis in 1850 without his help, and as General Winfield Scott led a declining Whig party to defeat in the campaign of 1852. In that year, by Lincoln's own words, he "did less than in previous presidential canvasses" owing to "the hopelessness of the cause in Illinois.[9] Lincoln's political frustration can be rather definitely dated. It belonged to the period 1849 to 1854. He saw his former partner Stephen T. Logan go down to defeat as candidate for Congress to succeed him; this could have been interpreted as an adverse verdict on Lincoln's record in his

[6] II, 59–88. [7] Autobiography, *Works,* VI, 37. [8] *Ibid.* [9] *Ibid.*

own district, while the action of the national Whig party in nominating Scott could have been deemed a repudiation of President Fillmore. That a Whig administration was in power (1849–1853) was small consolation to Lincoln;[10] Illinois was of the opposite persuasion.

VII

If in seeking Lincoln's view of things one opens a window, that window may be the concept of Young America versus Old Fogy, for Lincoln himself used that approach. By Young America he did not mean militant expansionism nor war-making "manifest destiny."[1] Boastful patrioteering or flag-waving was not his thought. To know what his thought was, one may read his essay or lecture on "Discoveries, Inventions, and Improvements," delivered in and around Springfield on various occasions in 1858, 1859, and early 1860. It is a bit of Lincoln's writing that has not received the analysis or attention that it deserves.[2] In its flow of sentences it marks Lincoln as something of a stylist, but that is secondary. The main point is that in lecturing on discoveries and inventions he was thinking of enlightenment, of progress down the centuries, of the emancipation of the mind, of men rising from the "dark ages." He stood in wonder of human achievement, in admiration of "articulate sounds rattled off from the tongue," of "phonetic writing," of "representing . . . sounds by marks," and of printing, which he considered the "better half" of writing. He thought the process was not ended. In considering inventions, he considered even more the factor of inventiveness, the "destined work of Adam's race to develop . . . hidden treasures." Some of the mines had been overlooked. "There are more mines above the earth's surface than below it," he said. "All nature—the

---

10 Further humiliation came when Lincoln, seeking a crumb of patronage in the office of commissioner of the general land office, was passed over and Justin Butterfield, a Whig who had opposed Taylor, was chosen. Having made a real effort to obtain the appointment, and feeling that he had a claim upon the Taylor administration, Lincoln was deeply mortified. *Works*, II, 114–115 (Apr. 25, 1849).

1 The best possible evidence that Lincoln did not think of conquest or aggressive expansion as the fit expression of Young America is found in his attitude toward the Mexican War, above noted.

2 See below, p. 44, for the manner in which Lincoln's lecture was received. It appears in his *Works*, V, 99–113, under date of Feb. 22, 1859. Two versions of the lecture in manuscript are in the collection of Oliver R. Barrett.

whole world, material, moral, and intellectual—is a mine . . . ." Thus viewing Lincoln on the threshold of the presidency, one notes how strife and sectionalism was not his main concern. Contemplating the aspiration of his people, his mind was reaching out in terms of normal progress and peaceable endeavor.

It had not been otherwise at the beginning of his political career. Having read Lincoln's statements in the late 1850's, one can go back to the thirties, when his thought was in its formative stage, its expression being already definitely Lincolnian in epigrammatic force. In those days when Lincoln as a youth was living close to the frontier, he had given some of his best pronouncements. He pointed to the greatness of his country, which in his view was a matter of free institutions in a setting of law, order, and community will. Reverently he referred to the edifice which the Fathers had bequeathed and of which men of his generation were "legal inheritors." He spoke of "that fair fabric which for the last half century has been the fondest hope of the lovers of freedom throughout the world." He thought of what the nineteenth century of the Christian era meant in "the great journal of things happening under the sun." He found its meaning in a political "system . . . conducing more essentially to the ends of civil and religious liberty than any of which the history of former times tells us."

The Fathers had possessed the land. They had upreared the edifice. For his own generation the task, he thought, was to "transmit" the heritage "unprofaned . . . , undecayed . . . and untorn by usurpation." It was a solemn duty, not a thing to prate about, and on this theme young Lincoln uttered a stinging warning of "danger" and "ill omen." If destruction was to come to the fair democracy of America, he believed that "we must ourselves be its author and finisher." He was thinking of the rough and ready vigilantism of his day, of men setting themselves up as bigger than the government, of mob law, of lynching, of those who regard government as a bane and "make a jubilee of the suspension of its operations." It is an entirely correct interpretation to note that he was thinking of those arrogant, law-defying influences which a century later were to go by the ugly name of Fascism. His views on this point were unmistakably given. If one doubts it, let him read Lincoln's address before the Young Men's Lyceum of Springfield, January 27, 1838, as good a speech against

Fascism, or elements characteristic of Fascism, as was ever delivered.[3]

It would be by "suicide," he thought, if American destruction should come; by "disregard of law," by "wild and furious passions," by "savage mobs." Any supposition that by mob savagery he meant free men asserting their rights or aggrieved citizens seeking redress is belied by the context. That was not the problem he was discussing; those were not the elements causing the violence that distressed him. The days of the Revolution were over, he said. He was thinking of "dead men . . . dangling from . . . trees . . . in numbers almost sufficient to rival the native Spanish moss . . . of the forest." It was an ugly spectacle and he was not mincing words. He spoke of vicious men being "permitted to gather in bands of hundreds and thousands, and burn churches, ravage and rob provision-stores, throw printing-presses into rivers, shoot editors, and hang and burn . . . at pleasure and with impunity . . . ."

It is obvious that Lincoln in 1838 was giving a comment on his own time; if one thinks of the alleged purity of that early age it is a shock to realize the turbulent conditions that were causing so much concern to one who believed in democracy. It was Herndon's recollection that the occasion of this lyceum speech, whose "essence" was "obedience to and respect for law," was the "burning of a negro by a mob in St. Louis."[4] Lincoln, however, was dealing with a serious and widespread problem, not with one incident. Revolutionary agitation had degenerated into frontier vigilantism; this had further deteriorated into lawless violence. There had been bad men in Illinois—kidnappers, counterfeiters, horse thieves, desperadoes, and outlaws. Crime ranged widely; it was wholesale; law enforcement was local and ineffective. Courts being inadequate, a group known as "regulators," wishing to enforce order, had set up their extra-legal organization, with its irregular military force, conventions, trials, and executions in the name of the people. Development of this situation, however, had taken a downward trend till the result was a condition of private warfare—gang against gang—with the "regulators" pursu-

[3] *Works*, I, 35–50.

[4] Herndon to Weik, Springfield, Ill., Jan. 27, 1888, Herndon-Weik MSS. One thinks, of course, of the murder of Lovejoy at Alton in November, 1837. Though this particular incident is not specified, Lincoln's reference to throwing "printing presses into rivers" was an obvious allusion to the Lovejoy affair. For the dating of the Lyceum address, see below, p. 22. n. 6.

ing a course little better than the thieves. Finally the legislature and governor had to step in to tone up the courts and put down the regulators.[5]

Lincoln had his answer to this ill omen: ". . . let every man remember that to violate the law is to trample on the blood of his father, and to tear the charter of his own and his children's liberty." He continued: "Let reverence for the laws be breathed by every American mother to the lisping babe that prattles on her lap; let it be taught in schools, in seminaries, and in colleges; let it be written in primers, spelling-books, and in almanacs; let it be preached from the pulpit, proclaimed in legislative halls, and enforced in courts of justice. And, in short, let it become the political religion of the nation . . . ." Bad laws, he thought, should be repealed, but while on the books they should be "religiously observed." If there should be an unprovided case not covered by law, he would have people bear with it till "proper legal provisions be made . . . with the least possible delay."

The American experiment was successful, he proclaimed, but some man of ambition might rise to smash the edifice, some man to whom a seat in Congress or a presidential chair would not be enough. If such a person should spring up, some designing chief bigger than the law, someone of "the family of the lion, or the tribe of the eagle," the temple must be upheld by "pillars, hewn from the solid quarry of sober reason." "Reason, . . . unimpassioned reason—must furnish all the materials for our future support and defense." All this would have to be met by solidarity, not division. It would "require the people to be united with each other, attached to the government and laws, and generally intelligent . . . ."[6]

---

[5] Governor Thomas Ford, in his *History of Illinois* (written in the forties) 232 ff., dealt at length with the "mobocratic spirit" in Illinois, the very thing Lincoln was talking about. For criminal and terroristic gangs in Illinois see T. C. Pease, *The Frontier State, 1818–1848* (*Centennial Hist. of Ill.*, vol. II), 427–429. The matter is also well treated in "The Regulator Movement in Illinois," by Alice Brumbaugh, master's dissertation (ms.), Univ. of Ill., 1927.

[6] Lincoln's address before the Young Men's Lyceum of Springfield, Illinois, January 27, 1838. This address appears in Lincoln's *Works*, I, 35–50, edited by Nicolay and Hay with the incorrect dating January 27, 1837. That 1838 is the correct date is shown by a number of facts presented by Beveridge (I, 230 n.), and by the present author's examination of the files of the *Sangamo Journal*, the newspaper in which the address was announced on January 27, 1838, and printed on February 3 of that year. In Herndon's letter to Weik, January 27, 1888 (Herndon-Weik MSS.), 1838 is given as the date. Lincoln was not in Springfield but in attendance at the legislature at Vandalia on Jan. 27, 1837. Pratt, *Lincoln, 1809–1839*, 65.

For that broad intelligence he favored popular education, and this in the earliest of his collected addresses, the first item in his *Complete Works*. Education, he said at the age of twenty-three, was "the most important subject which we as a people can be engaged in." Its value would be that "every man . . . may duly appreciate the value of our free institutions." These were his sentiments far back in the days when as an ungainly New Salem youth he was stepping out for political office for the first time in his life. He was addressing his neighbors in Sangamon County as a candidate for the state legislature and in doing so he was apologizing for having been "more presuming than becomes me," but already he felt it "a privilege and a duty to take that stand which . . . might tend most to the advancement of justice." [7]

VIII

Among the nation's founders it is clear that Jefferson offered more of a cue for interpreting Lincoln than Hamilton. In a halting way Lincoln favored a protective tariff.[1] Somewhat more confidently he favored a national bank. He believed in those measures that emphasized the functions of the Federal government, especially in the matter of expenditures within the states for public works ("internal improvements"). These, it is true, were Hamiltonian, though it should not be overlooked that in 1843 Lincoln was careful to quote Jefferson in support of a Federal tariff for the promotion of domestic manufactures.[2] When, however, one has enumerated a few matters of this nature, the similarity to Hamilton ends. On fundamental issues Lincoln's unlikeness to Hamilton and his resemblance to Jefferson are evident. Even in the matter of federalism Lincoln was closer to Jefferson than to Hamilton. Hamilton would have reduced the states to subordinate divisions and would have set up a life president and life senators, with state governors appointed by the national government. Lincoln could not support any such extreme program. He could, however, agree largely with Jefferson without surrendering his national policies, for Jefferson, though a prophet of state rights,

[7] Address to the People of Sangamon County, Mar. 9, 1832, *Works*, I, 1–9.

[1] Reinhard H. Luthin, "Abraham Lincoln and the Tariff," *Amer. Hist. Rev.*, XLIX, 609–629 (July, 1944).

[2] *Works*, I, 244 (Mar. 4, 1843).

actually did important things—e. g., in the Northwest Ordinance, the Louisiana Purchase, the Lewis and Clark Expedition, and the giving of advice looking to the Monroe Doctrine—which mightily promoted the success and prestige of the Federal government. It was in the bedrock of his beliefs that Lincoln was like Jefferson. The Declaration of Independence was his platform, his confession of faith. In those deeply sincere passages in which he expressed worshipful reverence for the Fathers, there was a Jeffersonian accent that was unmistakable. He favored human rights above property interests, repudiated (as noted above) the mudsill theory, spoke up for the farmer and the laborer, and withal showed trust in the people, which Hamilton assuredly did not. He favored the extension of popular education, a policy as prominent in Jefferson's urging and achievement as it was noticeably absent in Hamilton's.[3]

Lincoln frequently mentioned Jefferson, turning to him as to a basic authority. In the index to his writings, letters, and speeches, as edited by Nicolay and Hay, there are nineteen references to Jefferson while there are only two to Hamilton. References to Jefferson were on fundamental and far reaching matters; of the two meager citations of Hamilton, one was the briefest allusion to his support of the United States Bank, while the other was a passing mention of the New York leader as anti-slavery, which could have been said equally, indeed more emphatically, of Jefferson.[4] Lincoln was shocked to note the repudiation by a Virginia clergyman of Jefferson's doctrine of human equality. The repudiation, he thought, sounded "strangely in republican America." "The like was not heard," he said, "in the fresher days of the republic." [5] He found it painful in later troubled days to note that adversaries had "adopted . . . declarations of independence in which, unlike the good old one, penned by Jefferson, they

---

[3] Hamilton wrote of manufacturers employing large numbers of children "of a tender age," showing no concern for the obvious fact that such employment would interfere with their education. *Works* [etc.], *of Alexander Hamilton*, ed. by J. C. Hamilton, III, 208.

[4] In these references, found in the index of the Nicolay-Hay edition of Lincoln's *Works* (vol. 12), only citations to Lincoln's statements are noted; one omits accompanying matter such as Henry Watterson's brief reference to Hamilton in an address on Lincoln in 1895 (*Works*, III, v). If to Nicolay and Hay, one adds Tracy's *Uncollected Letters* and Angle's *New Letters and Papers*, the picture is much the same. Tracy gives four additional references to Jefferson (123–129, 161), and one to Hamilton (in connection with his support of national credit). Angle gives three new Lincoln references to Jefferson (134–135, 223, 251), but none to Hamilton.

[5] *Works*, II, 173–174 (July 16, 1852).

omit the words 'all men are created equal.' "[6] In 1854, the year of his stepping out for larger leadership in public affairs, he referred with admiration to Jefferson as "the author of the Declaration of Independence . . . a chief actor in the Revolution; . . . who was, is, and perhaps will continue to be, the most distinguished politician of our history . . . ."[7]

---

[6] *Ibid.*, VI, 320 (July 4, 1861).

[7] *Ibid.*, II, 193 (Oct. 16, 1854). Lincoln was using the word "politician" here in the sense of a man concerned with political affairs.

CHAPTER II

THUS STOOD LINCOLN

I

LINCOLN once penned a description of himself. With a characteristic quirk and amusing brevity the lines of that self portrait were as follows: "If any personal description of me is thought desirable, it may be said I am, in height, six feet four inches, nearly; lean in flesh, weighing on an average one hundred and eighty pounds; dark complexion, with coarse black hair and gray eyes. No other marks or brands recollected." [1] His friend H. C. Whitney of the law circuit, wrote: "He was six feet and four inches in height, his arms and legs were disproportionately long, his feet and hands were abnormally large, he was awkward in his gait and actions. His skin was a dark, sallow color, his features were coarse:—his expression kind and amiable:—his eyes were indicative of deep reflection, and, in times of repose, of deep sorrow as well. His head was high, but not large: his forehead was broad at the base, but retreated, indicating marked perceptive qualities, but not great reflective ones: and in this phrenology is sadly at fault. He wore a hat measuring seven and one-eighth. His ears were large; his hair, coarse, black and bushy, which stood out all over his head, with no appearance of ever having been combed." [2]

It was common to speak disparagingly of Lincoln's appearance, whether one was referring to his face, his figure, or his clothes. One observer wrote: ". . . his phiz *is* truly awful." [3] To another it seemed: ". . . he is the *homeliest* . . . and the *awkwardest* man in the

[1] Lincoln to J. W. Fell, Springfield, Ill., Dec. 20, 1859, *Works*, V, 288–289.

[2] H. C. Whitney, *Life on the Circuit with Lincoln*, Angle ed., 55.

[3] Journal of William L. Gross of Mt. Sterling, Ill., Oct. 19, 1858, MS., Ill. State Hist. Lib., printed in H. E. Pratt, *Concerning Mr. Lincoln*, 18–20.

Sucker State." [4] Edwin M. Stanton's description in 1858 was: "A long, lank creature from Illinois, wearing a dirty linen duster for a coat, on the back of which the perspiration had splotched wide stains that resembled a map of the continent." [5] The adjective "raw-boned" came to mind in characterizing him; it was said that he "might have passed for an ordinary farmer, so far as appearances were concerned." [6] His habiliments were country styled and careless, his tall hat innocent of nap, his carpet-bag delapidated, his outer garment "a short circular blue cloak, which he got in Washington in 1849, and kept for ten years." [7]

It is not easy to make up a composite of differing descriptions, and one should not give sole attention to comments by such an unfriendly and supercilious person as Stanton. In attire the quality that seemed to stand out was negligence of fashion rather than slovenliness. H. C. Whitney records that, though his clothes and shoes needed brushing, Lincoln was "scrupulously clean and close shaven." [8] In years of growing prominence his dress improved. "When he first ran for the legislature he . . . wore a blue jeans coat, claw hammer style, short in . . . sleeves, and . . . tail . . . homespun linen trousers, a straw hat and 'stogy' boots." "He commenced to dress better in the spring of 1858, and when he was absent from home on political tours usually did so: after he became President he had a servant who kept him considerably 'slicked up': but he frequently had to reason Lincoln into fashionable attire, by telling him his appearance was 'official.' " [9]

In passages which only William H. Herndon could write (and which are buried in manuscript collections) one gets flashes of Lincoln as pictorial as those of the camera, portraits which convey a setting and a sense of motion and sound as well as visual impressions of the man's face. Herndon's words are repetitious; he piles them high; yet there is a photographic quality in his record; he describes something he has seen. He seldom speaks of Lincoln's face or form alone; physical descriptions in the Herndonian manner usually blend with recordings of the man's mind, moods, and character. Often he goes into long paragraphs of psychoanalysis: [10] the reader is spared these

[4] Statement of J. H. Burnham, May 19, 1860, *Journal,* Ill. State Hist. Soc., XXVIII, 96 (Apr., 1935).

[5] Quoted in Whitney, *Life on the Circuit,* Angle ed., 48.

[6] *Ibid.,* 53. [7] *Ibid.,* 55. [8] *Ibid.,* 69. [9] *Ibid.,* 55.

[10] For Herndon's irrepressible tendency toward psychoanalysis, see vol. II, appendix.

disquisitions, which are less significant than the pictorial passages. One of these, despite the repetition, is presented here as a kind of sample:

Thus stood, walked—felt—thought, willed—acted and looked Abraham Lincoln: he was not a pretty man . . . , nor was he an ugly one: he was a homely man, careless of his looks, plain looking and plain acting: he had no aristocratic pomp—display or dignity so called. . . . Lincoln had . . . that inner quality which distinguishes one person from another, as much as to say "I am myself and not you." . . . Lincoln was easy of approach up to a certain limit and very democratic: he appeared simple in his carriage general behavior and bearing: . . . his sadness—gloom and melancholy dripped from him as he walked along. . . . Mr. Lincoln was sad and . . . humorous by turns. . . .

Mr. Lincoln sometimes walked our streets cheerily, . . . perhaps joyously and then it was, on meeting a friend, he cried—How'dy, clasping one of his friends in both of his wide long big bony hands, giving his friend a good hearty soul welcome. On a winters morning he might be seen stalking and stilting it toward the market house, basket on his arm, his old grey shawl wrapped around his neck, his little Willie or Tad running along at his heels, asking a thousand little quick questions, which his father heard not . . . . When he thus met a friend on the road he said that something . . . put him in mind of a story which he heard in Indiana or Egypt or elsewhere and tell it he would and there was no alternative in his friend but to patiently stand and hear it

. . . . . .

. . . Mr. Lincoln's perceptions were slow, cold, precise and exact. Everything came to Lincoln . . . clean and clear cut, stript of all extraneous matter whatsoever. Everything came to him in its precise shape—gravity and color. . . . No lurking illusion—delusion—error, false in itself and clad for the moment in robes of splendor, woven by the imagination, ever passed unchallenged or undetected over the threshold of his mind, that divides vision from the relm [*sic*] and home of thought. Names to him were nothing and titles naught—assumtions always standing back abashed at his cold intellectual glare. . . . There was no . . . refraction there, in this man's brain: he was not impulsive fanciful or imaginative, but cold, calm, precise and exact: he threw his whole mental light around the object seen . . . . In his mental view he crushed the unreal, . . . the hollow and the sham: . . . he saw what no man could well dispute, but he failed to see what might be seen . . . by other men. . . . His own mind was his own and exclusive standard. . . .[11]

---

[11] Herndon ms. fragment, "Lincoln Individually," undated, Herndon-Weik MSS.

Herndon reached out for rugged adjectives as he described his partner. He "was a great big—angular—strong man—limbs large and bony: he was tall and of a peculiar type." He "grew up like the forest oak, tough—solid—knotty—gnarly, standing out . . . against the storm, . . . defying the lightning." Herndon added: ". . . his mind was tough—solid—knotty—gnarly, more or less like his body: he was . . . a tall and big boned man and his speech was tall—strong . . . & enduring. The convolutions of his brain were long: they did not snap off quickly like a short thick mans brain: . . . when those convolution[s] . . . threw off an idea it *was* an *idea,* . . . ." In attempting to explain this to one of his numerous correspondents, Herndon wrote: "Please see Lincoln's strong—terse—knotty—gnarly and compact words—driven together as by a sledge hammer . . . ." "No other man on the continent," declared Herndon, "could have stood what Lincoln did in Washington: he had a frame of *iron.*" [12]

One would not forget that face—the face of the Macomb ambrotype, the Volk life mask, the beardless Hesler profile. The bony structure, with strong planes and angles, gave the head a sculptural quality; hollows and creases showed ruggedness of character; the look of the eyes added a haunting sadness. The mouth, while heavy lipped and full of strength, was sensitive and expressive. If one takes a paper and conceals one side of the Macomb face at a time, there is an impression not easy to describe—not only the obvious fact of asymmetry which artists have noted, but different facets of the man's nature which that asymmetry suggests. No first glance would take in every aspect of this countenance. The Americanism of the man is revealed with an effect that is almost startling if one looks at the full standing form with scroll in hand, shown facing this page, and then tries to imagine that figure in court costume, with knee-breeches, close fitting stockings, and buckles. There was little of Europe here, as Lowell noted. The man's appearance was both unique and related to a well known American type, the type that might have been found among people close to the woods or mountains.

One factor of his appearance was not seen in photographs: the

[12] Herndon to Truman H. Bartlett, Greencastle, Ind., Aug. 7, 1887, MS., Mass. Hist. Soc. Again he wrote: ". . . his flesh was dark—wrinkled & folded: it looked dry & leathery—tough & everlasting: his eyes were small and grey—head small and forehead receding, ..." Herndon to Bartlett, June 24, 1887, *ibid.*

sparkle of the face in animation noted by those who described him from life, but too much a part of the face in action to be captured by the camera. "The moment Lincoln took his seat at the pho machine [wrote Herndon] & looked down the barrel of it he became sad—rather serious, as all business with him was serious, life included." [13] To Whitney it seemed: "His mobile face ranged . . . through a long gamut: it was rare that an artist could catch the expression, and Lincoln's face was of that kind that the expression was of greater consequence than the contour of the features." [14] When Lincoln was "moved by some great & good feeling—by some idea of Liberty or Justice or Right then [wrote Herndon] he seemed an inspired man." "It was just then that Lincoln's nature was beautiful and in complete harmony with the laws of the great Eternal. I have seen him in this inspired condition and thought that he was molded in the Spirits best mold." [15] Again Herndon wrote: ". . . he was odd—angular—homely but when those little gray eyes . . . were lighted up by the inward soul on fires of emotion, defending the liberty of man or proclaiming the truths of the Declaration of Independence . . . , then . . . all those apparently ugly or homely features sprang with organs of beuty [*sic*]—or sank . . . into the sea of . . . inspiration that on such occasions flooded up his manly face." [16] In somewhat the same sense Herndon wrote: "You will find the plains, mountains & outlines of Lincoln's head & face hard to catch: they are so subtle." [17] This aspect of singular attractiveness in Lincoln's countenance in moments of animation, something of the inner man shining through the weather-beaten countenance, was so clearly noted by various observers that it comes down to us with as much authenticity as the photographs themselves.

II

On the matter of Lincoln's popularity in Illinois the evidence is not all of a piece. "Lincoln was the favorite of everybody," wrote

---

[13] Herndon to Bartlett, Feb. 27, 1891, *ibid.* At another time Herndon wrote that he would "give a good many dollars for a no one pho [number one photograph] of Lincoln," but added: ". . . there is none, as it appears to me." Herndon to Joseph H. Barrett, July 27, 1887, *ibid.*

[14] Whitney, *Life on the Circuit,* 55.

[15] Herndon to Bartlett, June 24, 1887, MS., Mass. Hist. Soc.

[16] Herndon ms. fragment, "Lincoln Individually," undated, Herndon-Weik MSS.

[17] Herndon to Barrett, July 27, 1887, MS., Mass. Hist. Soc.

Herndon,[1] and the manner in which people crowded round to hear his droll stories was proverbial. In the New Salem area in his earlier years he was popular for local reasons: he had been a wrestling champion,[2] and had favored improvements desired by the people of the region.[3] On the other hand, speaking of the attitude of Springfield, Herndon wrote: "Mr Lincoln was not appreciated in this city, nor was he at all times the most popular man among us. The cause of his unpopularity, or rather want of popularity here, arose out of two grounds—1st He did his own thinking and 2nd he had the courage of his convictions, and boldly and fearlessly expressed them."[4]

This comment by Herndon is seemingly corroborated by cold figures. Though for four terms (1834–1841) he was of the Sangamon County delegation in the state legislature, and despite his influence in procuring the removal of the capital to Springfield, the people of that county had a habit, on larger matters, of voting either against Lincoln when he was a candidate or against men of Lincoln's choice.[5] The strength of the Democratic party in the Springfield area was of course a factor in producing this result, which is not conclusive as to Lincoln's popularity. That in the troubled years of agitation and war he obtained as high a vote as he did in a section where the Republican party was unpopular, is significant, as also the fact that he sometimes carried his city of Springfield though not carrying the county of Sangamon.

That Lincoln should have referred to his own popularity is a matter of interest. In his autobiography (1860), after mentioning his service in the Black Hawk War, he wrote: "Returning from the

---

1 Herndon to C. O. Poole, Jan. 5, 1886, Herndon-Weik MSS.

2 Among other sources, an account of Lincoln's wrestling match with Jack Armstrong, said to be on a bet by Offutt, Lincoln's employer, that "Abe could throw down . . . any man in the county," is found in a long statement by R. B. Rutledge to Herndon, attested Oct. 22, 1866, Herndon-Weik MSS.

3 Herndon to Lamon, Feb. 25, 1870, MS., Huntington Lib.

4 Statement by Herndon, copied in letter, Alfred A. North to Truman H. Bartlett, July 1, 1887, MS., Mass. Hist. Soc.

5 In 1856 Sangamon County showed large Democratic pluralities in the presidential and gubernatorial votes; in 1858 Springfield and Sangamon County gave majorities to candidates that favored Douglas over Lincoln; in 1860 Douglas carried Sangamon County for President; in 1862, when votes for a congressman involved the question of support for President Lincoln, "in both Springfield and Sangamon County the Democratic candidates were elected by sizable majorities"; in 1864, with Springfield almost tied (in Lincoln's favor) between Lincoln and McClellan, the county favored McClellan by a majority of several hundred. Angle, *"Here I Have Lived,"* 223, 234, 253, 274, 287.

campaign, and encouraged by his great popularity among his immediate neighbors, he . . . ran for the legislature, and was beaten [1832],—his own precinct, however, casting its votes 277 for and 7 against him—and that, too, while he was an avowed Clay man, . . . the precinct the autumn afterward giving a majority of 115 to General Jackson over Mr. Clay. This was the only time Abraham was ever beaten on a direct vote of the people."[6] When one recalls Lincoln's knack of exact statement together with his habit of understating his own achievements, this autobiographical comment gives us the best indication that his local popularity was both real and of importance to himself.

III

A sobriquet commonly has less value as biographical record than as an influence in shaping a man's superficial reputation. The idea that Lincoln was a kind of backwoods character is a misconception suggested in part by his sobriquet of "rail-splitter." It is true that Lincoln's origin was in a backwoods environment,[1] and it is interesting to note that his father's long life of over seventy years was lived almost entirely in remote backwoods settings, but Lincoln's early life had many windows into the larger world, and his rail splitting,[2] for which he neither apologized or bragged, was of much less significance than his cultural associations. Because of such factors as his marriage into an aristocratic Kentucky family and his first partnership (beginning in 1837) with the courtly and socially favored John Todd Stuart, his opponents as early as 1843 actually put him down as the candidate of pride, wealth, and family distinction.[3]

---

[6] *Works*, VI, 31–32.

[1] "It was a wild region [southern Indiana], with many bears and other wild animals still in the woods. There I grew up." Autobiographical sketch for Jesse W. Fell, Dec. 20, 1859, *Works*, V, 287.

[2] In recalling his use of the ax Lincoln wrote as follows in his autobiography: "Abraham, though very young, was large of his age, and had an ax put into his hands at once; and from that till within his twenty-third year [1831–32] he was almost constantly handling that most useful instrument . . . ." *Works*, VI, 26.

[3] "It would astonish . . . the older citizens to learn that I (a stranger, friendless, uneducated, penniless boy, working on a flatboat at ten dollars per month) have been put down here as the candidate of pride, wealth, and aristocratic family distinction. Yet

Nor is it adequate to refer to Lincoln as a country lawyer. In the forties and fifties he was one of the outstanding lawyers of Illinois at a time when Illinois was a populous and flourishing state, well supplied with able attorneys. Lincoln handled important cases and many of them, often practicing before the Illinois supreme court and in the Federal courts. He was admitted to practice before the Supreme Court of the United States and was counsel in Lewis *v.* Lewis [4] decided in 1849. This implied a considerable standing at the bar. Lincoln could even be referred to as a corporation lawyer, though far indeed from the type suggested by that term in its modern connotation; he successfully handled a highly important case for the Illinois Central Railroad, from which he collected a fee of five thousand dollars,[5] and was one of a group of lawyers retained by a combination of manufacturers who resisted the McCormick Harvester Company.

Yet the homespun quality pertaining to the country lawyer was not foreign to Lincoln. Most of his cases were prosaic enough and even boresome to review, but some were redolent of the country or picturesquely associated with common people, as his famous defense of Duff Armstrong or his recovery, on behalf of a widow of a Revolutionary soldier, of an excessive fee charged by a greedy pension agent. The Duff Armstrong case, memorable for the calendar incident and its association with the redoubtable Clary's Grove boys, gives no more concept of Lincoln the lawyer than many other cases which are unknown in the popular mind. Incidentally, the setting of this case has been distorted: though it occurred in 1858 it is usually thought of as belonging to a period more than twenty years earlier, a moving picture [6] having dramatized it in the younger setting.

Lincoln's prowess in the law has probably been overstated, yet there is ample evidence that his name as counsel carried prestige in a suit. Local attorneys would work up cases for Lincoln to argue when court days came round. In the case of Ward H. Lamon this extended to the forming of a partnership, the Danville attorney being proud

---

so . . . it was." Lincoln to "Martin M. Morris," Springfield, Ill., Mar. 26, 1843 (correct name Martin S. Morris), *Works,* I, 262. In referring to the Illinois legislature of 1838–39 Governor Ford dismissed many of the members with mere surnames, giving only the names of "prominent men" in full: "Abram Lincoln," at the age of thirty or less, was listed as one of the prominent men. Thomas Ford, *History of Illinois,* 194–195.

[4] 7 Howard 777. [5] Pratt, *Personal Finances,* 48 ff. [6] "Young Mr. Lincoln."

to advertise under the title "Lincoln & Lamon." [7] Little of Lincoln's practice was in criminal cases; the main substance of it was in civil suits. His proportionate share of criminal business was much less than the ratio which such cases bore to the total on the dockets of a typical court in his circuit. If it be asked how far he "won" his cases—though winning in the law is not such a clear-cut matter as is often supposed—it is Paul M. Angle's conclusion that he was much more successful in the higher courts than on the circuit; especially "in the Supreme Court of Illinois, both as to the extent of his business and the degree of success he enjoyed, Lincoln's record was outstanding." [8]

Though much of Lincoln's most important work was outside and apart from the famous eighth judicial circuit, it was inevitable that he should become bracketed with that circuit in popular memory. The practice of lawyers riding from one county seat to another was a picturesque feature of the times which Lincoln evidently enjoyed, for he "was the only lawyer who traveled over the entire circuit; he . . . made it a practice to attend every court, and to remain till the end." [9]

This circuit, which sprawled widely over central Illinois, is remembered for its combination of pioneer flavor with legal talent, but above all for the fact that Lincoln was a part of it. One passes over its agenda—crime, slander, riot, damages, promissory notes, divorce, the value of a saw mill, responsibility for loss of sheep by foot rot, or ownership of a litter of pigs. One remembers rather the off-duty aspects, the migratory life of the ponderous judge, David Davis, and his coterie of attorneys jogging over dirt roads,[10] sometimes stopping at farm houses, holding protracted night discussions of politics or

---

[7] Lamon later became marshal of the District of Columbia with duties close to the President. He had pronounced ideas including bitter opposition to abolitionists. His life of Abraham Lincoln published in 1872 was based on material bought from William H. Herndon. It was written not by Lamon but by a ghost writer, Chauncey F. Black, son of Jeremiah S. Black, member of Buchanan's cabinet. See Albert V. House, Jr., "The Trials of a Ghost-Writer of Lincoln Biography," *Journal*, Ill. State Hist. Soc., XXXI, 262–296 (1938).

[8] "Abraham Lincoln: Circuit Lawyer," Lincoln Centennial Assoc. *Papers*, 1928, 40.

[9] Whitney, *Life on the Circuit*, 62. For an account of the eighth circuit of central Illinois with its various reorganizations, see Benjamin P. Thomas, "The Eighth Judicial Circuit," *Bulletin No. 40*, Abr. Lincoln Assoc., Sep. 1935.

[10] "I saw him as he drove into town behind his own horse, which was an indifferent, raw-boned specimen, in his own blacksmith-made buggy—a most ordinary looking one" (Whitney, 53). It should of course be added that, in traveling the circuit, Lincoln used trains when they were available. Paul M. Angle, *Lincoln, 1854–1861* . . . , 126.

philosophy, sleeping "two in a bed, and eight in a room," [11] enlivening the taverns with hilarious excitement, conducting "office" consultations, according to the weather, under a tree or "on the sunny side of a court house," [12] holding "orgmathorial court" [13] with mock solemnity, and, not the least of it, meeting the people of country and town, to whom the semi-annual "court week" was a shining period of shopping, entertainment, and political agitation.

It was natural and inevitable that the traveling lawyers should correlate their court practice with speech making. At Bloomington in September 1856, for example, finding himself on a case before the McLean circuit court (Bishop v. Illinois Central Railroad Co.), Lincoln addressed a Republican gathering in Major's Hall. It was reported that he spoke with "great eloquence and power. He showed up the position of the Fillmore party in fine style . . . ." [14] Another example was when Lincoln, while in Urbana on court duty, addressed a meeting at the court house on October 20 of the same year.[15] Lincoln's travel arrangements were known in advance and in July 1856, when his arrival in Chicago on legal business was anticipated, it was hoped that his arrangements would "permit him to meet the universal wish of the people of Chicago" by addressing them on political issues. A few days later Lincoln was reported having addressed an open-air Republican meeting at Dearborn Park.[16] Color and excitement were thus added to circuit duties. The lawyers were there—sometimes a choice assemblage of them. So were the crowds. The people demanded speeches and the lawyers needed no coaxing to satisfy them.

IV

The serious study of Lincoln as a lawyer has been covered elsewhere.[1] The law was his livelihood; it was the absorbing object of his

---

11 Whitney, *Life on the Circuit,* 62. 12 *Ibid.*

13 In the *orgmathorial* court (it was a made-up word) the judge and his coterie, in proceedings said to be better than those of the Pickwick Club, amused and entertained themselves with great secrecy, dealt with breaches of decorum, and ranged at will over any topics they chose, including "metempsychosis" (*ibid.,* 67).

14 Bloomington *Pantagraph,* Sep. 17, 1856, quoted in Angle, *Lincoln, 1854–1861,* 141.

15 Angle, *Lincoln, 1854–1861,* 147. 16 *Ibid.,* 133.

1 Frederick Trevor Hill, *Lincoln The Lawyer;* John T. Richards, *Abraham Lincoln: The Lawyer-Statesman;* Albert A. Woldman, *Lawyer Lincoln;* Paul M. Angle, *One Hundred Years of Law;* Paul M. Angle, "Abraham Lincoln: Circuit Lawyer," in Lincoln Centennial Assoc. *Papers,* 1928, 19–41; Benjamin P. Thomas, "Lincoln's Earlier Practice

self-directed efforts as a young man arduously preparing for a career; it was his avenue of acquaintance; it was for long years his main interest. His practice embodied all phases of a lawyer's work, from jury eloquence to business documents, from office consultation to elaborate briefs and pleadings. One could write a considerable book to show the kaleidoscope of human problems, large and small, which passed before his eyes in his capacity as lawyer, and another book to exhibit, in Lincoln the lawyer, the essential qualities of Lincoln himself, his habits of thought and his character as a man. It was largely through the law that he acquired his knowledge of American institutions, of democratic traditions, of civil rights and duties.

It was also in the law that Lincoln exhibited one of his most characteristic traits, his knack of taking a complicated subject, going to the core of it, and coming through with a lucid statement of essentials. It was Herndon's observation that he was deficient in the knowledge of legal technicalities. He "knew nothing of the laws of evidence—of pleading or of practice, and did not care about them: he had a keen sense of justice and struck for that, throwing aside forms—methods and rules of all law. Lincoln look[d] for justice through forms, pure as a ray of light flashes through a fog bank."

Herndon thought he knew in what respects Lincoln excelled as a lawyer and in what respects he fell short: ". . . if Mr. Lincoln had his time and thought that he was right, and could get the case swung to the jury, freed from technicalities he was a good lawyer, but if he did not have his time—did not think that he was right, and could not get his case swung to the jury, . . . then he was a very weak brother. In the Circuit Courts of the United States he was a good lawyer, because the practice of the Courts was liberal—moved slowly—freed from technicalities and gave Lincoln his own time to arrange his ideas and his plans for attack or defence. . . . But it was in the Supreme Court of the State of Illinois that he was truly a great lawyer, & no where else." Herndon believed this to be true because in the state supreme court Lincoln had time to prepare; everything

---

in the Federal Courts, 1839–1854," Abr. Lincoln Assoc. *Bulletin* (June, 1935); Benjamin P. Thomas, "The Eighth Judicial Circuit," *ibid.* (Sep. 1935); Paul M. Angle, "Lincoln and the United States Supreme Court," *ibid.* (May, 1937); Paul M. Angle, "Lincoln and the United States Supreme Court: A Postscript," *ibid.* (June, 1937); Harry E. Pratt, "The Genesis of Lincoln the Lawyer," *ibid.* (Sep. 1939); John M. Zane, "Lincoln, the Constitutional Lawyer," Abr. Lincoln Assoc. *Papers*, 1932.

that went before the court, the record of the case and briefs of counsel, was put in writing in advance. Sureness of slow reasoning rather than nimbleness or resourcefulness in inventing legal pitfalls, seems to have been Lincoln's forte. In this respect Lincoln compared himself to an old jack-knife that opens more clumsily and cuts more slowly than a "woman's little knife," but could "do more execution." [2]

There is both autobiographical detail and keen human wisdom in a Lincoln fragment, dated 1850, in which he set down his advice to lawyers. First of all he stressed diligence, attention to correspondence, leaving nothing for tomorrow which could be done today. He pointed out the importance of examining the books, noting authorities, giving close attention to the examination of titles and the drafting of decrees. Emphasizing extemporaneous speaking as "the lawyer's avenue to the public," he nevertheless warned against the "fatal error" of too much speech making, especially if relied upon as a substitute for "the drudgery of the law." He continued:

> Discourage litigation. Persuade your neighbors to compromise whenever you can. Point out to them how the nominal winner is often a real loser—in fees, expenses, and waste of time. As a peace-maker the lawyer has a superior opportunity of being a good man. There will still be business enough.
>
> Never stir up litigation. A worse man can scarcely be found than one who does this. Who can be more nearly a fiend than he who habitually overhauls the register of deeds in search of defects in titles, whereon to stir up strife, and put money in his pocket? A moral tone ought to be infused into the profession which should drive such men out of it.
>
> . . . . . .
>
> There is a vague popular belief that lawyers are necessarily dishonest. I say vague, because when we consider to what extent confidence and honors are reposed in and conferred upon lawyers by the people, it appears improbable that their impression of dishonesty is very distinct . . . . Yet the impression is common, almost universal. Let no young man choosing the law . . . for a moment yield to the popular belief—resolve to be honest at all events; and if in your own judgment you cannot be an honest lawyer, resolve to be honest without being a lawyer. Choose some other occupation, rather than one in the choosing of which you do, in advance, consent to be a knave.[3]

---

[2] Herndon ms. fragment, "Lincoln as Lawyer, Politician & Statesman," undated (written in the 1880's), Herndon-Weik MSS.

[3] *Works*, II, 140–143.

Toward those traits in a lawyer that smacked of chicanery, sharp practice, or anti-social attitudes Lincoln was indignant. In this he had both a high conviction of the ethics of his profession and a deep sense of personal integrity. Though not setting himself up as a "knight-errant of the law," as Beveridge has pointed out, he had been known to withdraw from a case during trial after being convinced that justice was not on the side of his client.[4] It was not in him, said his friend Gillespie, to "attempt to bolster up a false position." "He would abandon his case first." [5]

That Lincoln could be slighted by fellow counsel in a case to the point of stinging humiliation and chagrin, and yet take the snub in generous good spirit was shown in the McCormick reaper trial. For this and other reasons the case has "a national significance far broader than the immediate issues involved." [6] The McCormick Harvester Company was suing an Illinois manufacturer named Manny, together with eastern firms, for infringement of patent rights. It was a Federal case, first set for trial in Chicago, then shifted to Cincinnati. Lincoln was retained as counsel for the defendants (McCormick's rivals); others employed on the same side were George Harding of Philadelphia, Edwin M. Stanton of Pittsburgh, and (for assistance in preparation) Peter H. Watson of Washington, later assistant secretary of war and president of the Erie Railroad. Lincoln was impressed with the importance of the case, and made elaborate preparation, only to find himself excluded from active participation in the trial. Evidence was not put in his hands in advance, and it was Harding and Stanton who presented the argument. There are various versions of what passed between defense counsel. Lincoln's associates may simply have been watching their client's interests in a trial where a member of the Illinois bar proved not so indispensable as was expected, and where only two attorneys were needed in argument. Others have seen in the incident, not without cause, evidence of the disdain which smart eastern lawyers felt toward the gawky, unpolished, ill-dressed, and un-

[4] The matter of Lincoln withdrawing from a case because of scruple is not emphasized by Beveridge, who associates his conduct with that of "most high-minded and honorable attorneys." The "dirty hands" incident (Lincoln leaving the court room during a trial and sending word to the judge that he had come to the tavern to clean his hands) is treated by Beveridge as non-typical; it is pointed out that as attorney Lincoln "did not try both sides." Beveridge, I, 546–547.

[5] Statement of Joseph Gillespie, Jan. 31, 1866, Herndon-Weik MSS.

[6] William T. Hutchinson, *Cyrus Hall McCormick: Seed-Time, 1809–1856*, 436.

prepossessing Lincoln—"that d—d long armed Ape"[7] as Stanton is said to have called him. Lincoln was deeply hurt and disappointed; yet he took the incident in good part. He yielded to superior talent, sat with rapt attention while the arguments were given, and accepted a lesson in the need for heavy study if he were to measure up to eastern lawyerly standards.[8] In appointing Stanton secretary of war in 1862 he rose magnanimously above personal resentment; as for Stanton, his manner toward his Chief was never to lose its overbearing tone.

Though careful to charge and collect what was due him,[9] Lincoln wanted no more. Not only would he not "consent to be a knave"; he would decline to accept unjustifiably high fees; if a case were questionable, he would refuse it. There was no unctuousness about such conduct; it was a matter of practicing what he preached. It is this that makes the more interesting those passages in which he extended advice. He had been through it himself; he warned that there was no royal road to success. In the midst of his campaign for the presidency he took the time to answer an inquirer who wanted to know "the best mode of obtaining a thorough knowledge of the law." He wrote:

> . . . The mode is very simple, though laborious and tedious. It is only to get the books and read and study them carefully. Begin with Blackstone's "Commentaries," and after reading it carefully through, say twice, take up Chitty's "Pleadings," Greenleaf's "Evidence," and Story's "Equity," etc., in succession. Work, work, work, is the main thing.[10]

---

[7] Herndon to Weik, Jan. 6, 1887, Herndon-Weik MSS.

[8] Information on the McCormick reaper case is found in Hutchinson, *McCormick (Seed-Time)*, 431–452 (fullest account of the business and legal aspects); Beveridge, I, 575–583 (a thorough analysis); Gilbert A. Tracy, ed., *Uncollected Letters*, 58–59, 61; W. M. Dickson, "Abraham Lincoln at Cincinnati," *Harper's*, LXIX, 62–66 (June, 1884); Harry E. Pratt, *Personal Finances of Abraham Lincoln*, 54–56. The side on which Lincoln was retained won the decision; his fee has been placed at $1,000 (Pratt, 56). Those versions of the episode that stem from Lincoln himself are remarkably free from resentment. For example, the account which Joseph Gillespie had from Lincoln's lips, while confirming that Lincoln had prepared carefully and expected to participate in conducting the suit, indicates also that Lincoln readily admitted greater mastery on the part of his younger associate. Gillespie to Herndon, Dec. 8, 1866, Herndon-Weik MSS. It has been said that it was Stanton's performance on this occasion that so impressed Lincoln that he made him secretary of war (statement of Ralph Emerson, based upon Lincoln's statement while President, Beveridge, I, 581).

[9] Lincoln made a comfortable income from the law, as was to be expected from a man of his prominence, ability, and industry. His earnings were adequate though moderate. He made a success of his chosen profession, but by no means did he grasp all the gains within his reach. Harry E. Pratt, *The Personal Finances of Abraham Lincoln*, 25–57.

[10] Letter to J. M. Brockman, Springfield, Sep. 25, 1860, *Works*, VI, 59. See also *ibid.*, XI, 114; *Ore. Hist. Soc. Quart.*, XXIII, 267 (1922).

On the basis of many years of partnership William H. Herndon made the following statement in which Lincoln the lawyer was blended with Lincoln the man:

. . . In 1843–4 [11] Mr Lincoln and I became partners in the law business in Springfield, but did business in all the surrounding counties. Our partnership was never legally dissolved till the night of his assassination. The good man the noble man, would take none of my fees made in the law business after his election to the Presidency. Mr Lincoln was a safe councilor, a good lawyer and an honest man in all the walks of life.

. . . Mr Lincoln was a cool, cautious, conservative, and long headed man. Mr Lincoln could be trusted by the people. They did trust him and they were never deceived. He was a pure man, a great man, and a patriot. In the practice of law he was simple honest, fair and broad minded. He was courteous to the bar, and to the court. He was open candid and square in his profession, never practicing on the sharp or low. Mr Lincoln met all questions fairly, squarely, . . . , making no concealments of his . . . intentions in any case. He took no snap judgments, nor used any tricks in his business . . . .

Mr Lincoln never deceived his brother in a law case. What he told you was the exact truth. . . . [12]

V

It is incorrect to regard Lincoln as versatile, or brilliantly accomplished in many fields. He was no Leonardo da Vinci, no universal genius; nor was he so variously gifted or widely read as, for instance, Thomas Jefferson,. His main interest was in politics, using that word both in its original and derived sense.[1] His studies focused on problems of government and of peaceful American development. It should of course be added that, over and above his main occupation as lawyer and political leader, Lincoln was an inventor, a surveyor, fond of geometry, something of a specialist in western river transportation (no mean subject), an athlete, a soldier (for a brief period,

[11] Surprisingly, Herndon was in error here as to the beginning of his partnership with Lincoln. The statement seems to imply that the year "1843–4" was the first year of their partnership; in Herndon's *Lincoln* (Angle ed., 210–211) the year 1843 is given. Though Lincoln writers have almost invariably followed Herndon on this point, the statement is incorrect. The Lincoln-Herndon partnership began late in 1844. Paul M. Angle, in Lincoln Centennial Assoc. *Papers*, 1927, 29–30.

[12] Statement by W. H. Herndon, Apr. 14, 1886, copied in letter, Alfred A. North to Truman H. Bartlett, July 1, 1887, MS., Mass. Hist. Soc.

[1] "Politics were his life . . . ." Herndon to C. O. Poole, Jan. 5, 1886, Herndon-Weik MSS.

including reënlistments, in the Black Hawk War, 1832), a lecturer (briefly),[2] a newspaper owner (again briefly),[3] and an orator. In the period before his career took shape he had been ferry boy, flatboatman, mill manager, small town clerk and merchant, day laborer at odd jobs, and postmaster. By his own statement he had "thought of learning the blacksmith trade." [4] He had been a part of his growing community wherever fortune had landed him, helping in community tasks while earning his livelihood. Later, in days of prominence, he referred to himself as a working man; [5] it was a satisfaction to him to identify himself with the ranks of labor. His range of activities, however, had not been so wide as to be remarkable. Farming was not his occupation at any time after he struck out for himself in 1831. Only on a limited scale, in New Salem days, was he ever a business man. He had neither a native nor a developed taste in art; country merrymaking was more to his liking than classical music; and, while growing up in picturesque regions, he showed little conscious appreciation of the beauties of nature.[6] Yet there was latent poetry in the man, there was fondness for Shakespeare, and there were times when he expressed himself in verse.

VI

As a speaker Lincoln ran the gamut from stumps in the woods through village platforms to juries, outdoor crowds, and cultured audiences. In the speaking to which he was accustomed there were no tables "to hit, beat and . . . bang"; the speaker's whole form was visible; he stood out "fully to public view." Lincoln did not like his speeches to smell of the study. In going over his debate with Douglas for publication he did not embellish, elaborate, or revise;

---

[2] See below, pp. 43–44.

[3] In collaboration with Theodore Canisius in 1859, Lincoln maintained ownership and control of the *Illinois Staats-Anzeiger*, published at Springfield, with a view to reaching German-American readers. Angle, *New Letters and Papers of Lincoln*, 204–205. Barton, *Life of Abraham Lincoln*, I, 416 ff.

[4] *Works*, VI, 32.

[5] "I am not ashamed to confess that . . . I was a hired laborer, mauling rails, at work on a flatboat—just what might happen to any poor man's son." Speech at New Haven, Conn., Mar. 6, 1860, *ibid.*, V, 361.

[6] "I do not think that New Salem scenery . . . had much to do with Lincoln: he had no sense of the beautiful in the *physical* world but had in the *moral* world." Herndon to Bartlett, Aug. 22, 1887, MS., Mass. Hist. Soc.

he "only corrected his speeches—made them talk as he had talked on the stump."[1]

. . . When he rose [wrote Herndon] to speak to the jury or to crowds of people he stood inclined forward—was awkward—angular—ungainly—odd . . . ; he was a diffident man, somewhat, and a sensative one, and both of these added to his oddity—awkwardness . . . as it seemed to me. Lincoln had confidence, full and complete confidence in himself, ... Lincoln's voice was, when he first began speaking, shrill—squeaking—piping—unpleasant: his general look—his form—his pose—the color of his flesh wrinkled and dry, his sensativeness & his momentary diffidence, everything seemed to be against him, but he soon recovered. I can see him now—in my mind distinct. On rising to address the jury or the crowd he . . . generally placed his hands behind him, the back part of his left hand resting in the palm of his right hand. As he proceeded and grew warmer he moved his hand to the front of his person, generally interlocking his fingers and running one thumb around the other. Sometimes his hands, for a short while, would hang by his side. In still growing warmer as he proceeded in his address he used his hands—especially and generally his right hand in his gestures: He used his head a great deal in speaking, throwing or jerking or moving it now here and now there—now in this position and now in that, in order to be more emphatic—to drive the idea home. Mr Lincoln never beat the air—never sawed space with his hands—never acted for stage effect—was cool—calm, earnest—sincere—truthful—fair—self possessed—not insulting—not dictatorial—was pleasing—good natured, had great strong naturalness of look, pose, and act—was clear in his ideas—simple in his words—strong, terse and demonstrative:[2] he spoke and acted to convince individuals and masses: he used . . . his right hand, sometimes shooting out that long bony forefinger of his to dot an idea or to enforce a thought, resting his thumb on his middle finger. Bear in mind that he did not gesticulate much and *yet* . . . every organ of his body was in motion and acted with ease—elegance and grace—so it all looked *to me*

As Mr Lincoln proceeded further . . . , if time—place—subject and occasion admitted of it, he . . . gradually warmed up—his shrill—squeaking—piping voice became harmonious, melodious—musical, . . . with face . . . aglow: his form dilated—swelled out and he rose up a splendid form, erect straight and dignified; he stood square on his feet with both legs up and down, toe even with toe— . . . he did not put one foot before an other: he kept his feet parallel and close to and not far from each other. When Mr. Lincoln rose up to speak, he rose slowly—steadily—firmly: he never moved much about on the stand or platform when speak-

[1] Herndon to Bartlett, July 11, 1887, MS., Mass. Hist. Soc.

[2] In the word "demonstrative" here, Herndon seems to have had in mind the quality of one who demonstrates, the habit being informative or explanatory as to one's meaning.

ing, touching no desk—table—railing: he ran his eyes slowly over the crowd, giving them time to be at ease and to completely recover himself, ... He frequently took hold with his left hand, his left thumb erect, of the left lapel of his coat, keeping his right hand free to gesture in order to . . . clinch an idea. In his greatest inspiration he held both of his hand [*sic*] out above his head at an angle of about fifty degrees—hands open or clinched according to his feelings and his ideas. If he was moved in some indignant and half mad moment against slavery or wrong . . . and seemed to want to tear it down—trample it beneath his feet and to eternally crush it, then he would extend his arms out, at about the above . . . angle with clinched big, bony, strong hands on them—. If he was defending the right—if he was defending liberty—eulogizing the Declaration of Independence, then he extended out his arms—palms of his hands upward somewhat at about the above degree—angle, as if appealing to some superior power for assistance and support; or that he might embrace the spirit of that which he so dearly loved. It was at such moments that he seemed inspired, fresh from the hands of his creator. Lincoln's gray eyes would flash fire when speaking against slavery or spoke volumes of hope and love when speaking of Liberty—justice and the progress of mankind—[3]

VII

In days when lyceums were a prominent feature of intellectual life Lincoln took briefly to the lecture platform, but most of the contemporary comments on this phase are disparaging or even devastatingly unfavorable. The lecture that Lincoln fixed up for the purpose was the one on "Discoveries, Inventions, and Improvements" which has already been noted;[1] he delivered it in Springfield and other Illinois towns in 1858, 1859, and 1860. One of his hearers at Pontiac, Illinois, in January 1860 observed that Lincoln was a "Big Gun" in the political world, but that the "people . . . were disappointed" in the performance.[2] In Bloomington, about a year before his nomination for the presidency, Lincoln actually refused to give a scheduled lecture because on arriving to do so he found too scant a crowd.[3]

---

[3] Herndon to Bartlett, July 19, 1887, MS., Mass. Hist. Soc.

[1] See above pp. 19–20.

[2] "Gus" to Mary P. Christian, Pontiac, Ill., Jan. 28, 1860 (MS. owned by Jewell F. Stevens of Chicago), in Harry E. Pratt, *Concerning Mr. Lincoln*, 21–22. Later in the letter the writer reveals himself as a great admirer of Stephen A. Douglas. "Gus" has been identified as Augustus W. Cowan; see *Abr. Lincoln Quart.*, III, 150 (Sep., 1944).

[3] Writing from Bloomington, Illinois, to his father on May 19, 1860, J. H. Burnham recalled that "one year ago" Lincoln had been advertised to lecture at Bloomington

Herndon's explanation of Lincoln's venturing into the lecture field was that he felt hurt by his "failure" as inventor[4] and eulogist[5] and by his frustrated attempt to pick up the German and Latin languages "by some short cut," but, thought Herndon, he "had none of the elements of a lecturer." These efforts, said Herndon, before "the elite and cultured" were "utter failure and very disappointing: they went the way of his Clay eulogy." Though the lecturer "thought so much of one of these efforts" that he presented a copy as a friendly remembrance, Herndon reported that "Lincoln's friends were deeply and thoroughly mortified at all of these efforts."[6] Yet in its main content and in the pithy phrasing of some of its passages, the lecture when read today carries real significance.[7]

VIII

Lincoln's character was treated at great length by Joseph Gillespie of Edwardsville, Illinois, whose association with the Illinois leader went back to the time (1840–41) when they were fellow members of the state legislature. From this portrait we gather that he was "genial but not very sociable," "ambitious but not very aspiring," skillful in story telling yet thinking his debate with Douglas "too grave & serious"

"on *Invention,* . . . admittance 25 cts." He added: "I paid a quarter and went early . . . . It was a beautiful evening, and the lecture had been well advertised but . . . only about 40 persons were present, and old Abe would not speak to such a small crowd, and they paid us back our quarters at the door." *Journal,* Ill. State Hist. Soc., XXVIII, 95–97 (April, 1935).

[4] In 1849, with his continuing interest in river navigation, Lincoln patented a device for "buoying vessels over shoals" by means of adjustable air chambers. The patent, no. 6469, was dated May 22, 1849. Lincoln's model can be seen at the National Museum (Smithsonian Institution) in Washington; for illustration, see Tarbell, I, facing p. 226. The inventor's detailed specification, with mechanical drawing, has been supplied to the author by the U. S. Patent Office.

[5] At Springfield on July 6, 1852, Lincoln delivered a eulogy on Henry Clay. See *Works,* II, 155–177, where the address is misdated July 16.

[6] Herndon memorandum entitled "Lincoln's Ambition . . . [etc.]," (on pension office letter head, some time in the eighties), pp. 15–16, Herndon-Weik MSS. At another time Herndon wrote of Lincoln's lecture: "it was a failure—utter failure." Herndon to Lamon, Mar. 6, 1870, p. 8, MS., Huntington Lib.

[7] This is no more than the observation of the present writer; disparagement of this "effort" by Lincoln has been the stock comment. The lecture was uneven. Rather prosy throughout, it combined well written passages with an occasional banal or mistakenly humorous remark—e. g., a reference to Adam and Eve sharing in "the getting up of the apron," as showing that "the very first invention was a joint operation." *Works,* V, 106. Despite its unfavorable reception the lecture has meaning to one who would study the trends of Lincoln's thought on the eve of his nomination to the presidency.

for such levity. "He did not seek company but when he was in it he was the most entertaining person I ever knew." In "the discussion of great questions," said Gillespie, Lincoln thought "nothing adventious [*sic*] should be lugged in as a make weight. That was contrary to his notions of *fairness.*" He was a man of comfortable means,[1] but did not reach out for easy gains in land speculation as did Judge Davis. His children "ran over him"; he was "powerless to resist their importunities." Gillespie had "seen him on several occasions display great heroism." He was sensitive where he thought he had fallen short, as when he "was pitted by the Whigs in 1840 to debate with Mr. Douglas." [2] Conscious of his failure and deeply distressed, he "begged to be permitted to try it again" and Gillespie had "never heard . . . such a triumphant vin[di]cation . . . ."

The importance of his homely origin in the molding of his outlook and in the shaping of his conversation is borne out by Gillespie's description. He was "never ashamed of the poverty and obscurity of his early life," was "master of . . . frontier life and woods craft," full of anecdote of "boyish days amongst his country playfellows," and had "the happiest faculty of turning . . . reminiscences to good account." "He never missed the nib of an anecdote. He always maintained . . . that the best stories originated with Country boys & in the rural districts. He had great faith in the strong sense of Country People and he gave them credit for greater inteligence [*sic*] than most men do. . . . Mr. Lincoln had more respect for & confidence in the masses than any statesman this Country has ever produced He told me in the spring of 1864 that the People were greatly ahead of the poloticians . . . . He prized the suggestions of . . . unsophistocated People more than what was called statecraft . . . ." Mr. Gillespie continued:

> . . . Mr. Lincoln could hardly be considered a genius, a poet, or an inventor but he had the qualities of a reformer He endeavored to bring back things to the old landmarks but he never would have attempted to

---

[1] Treated with a wealth of detail in *The Personal Finances of Abraham Lincoln,* by Harry E. Pratt.

[2] It is of interest to think of Lincoln as debating against Douglas at so early a period, though this phase has received little attention. As to pitting him against Douglas "in 1840" the reference is to the preliminary campaign for 1840. The Whig state central committee arranged two weeks of debates in November and December of 1839, in which Lincoln and Douglas were antagonists. Harry E. Pratt, *Lincoln, 1840–1846,* xii.

invent and compose new systems He had boldness enough when he found the building rocked and going to decay to restore it to its original design but not to contrive a new & distinct edifice He believed that the framers of our government expected slavery to die out and adapted the system to that end but that their views were being frustrated by adventitious circumstances by which we were surrounded . . . . He contended that we were more indebted to our government than it was to us and that we were not entitled to greater credit for our liberality of sentiment on political questions than others equally liberal who were born and raised under less favorable auspices. . . .

Tracing further the Gillespie Lincoln, if we may so call it (for Gillespie's accounts were full and circumstantial), we find a man "contemplative rather than speculative," "fond of astronomy . . . and mechanical science," anxious "to trace out the source and development of language," [3] touched with "a slight tinge of fatalism," "a believer in destiny," one who put trust "more in Divine power than in human instrumentality." He "had a remarkably inquiring mind . . . [which] roamed over the whole field of knowledge . . . with special interest [in] those which were of a practical character . . . [with] a solid and indisputable basis." Being "undemonstrative," his salient traits were not perceived at first acquaintance; hence he was "sometimes misunderstood." He "would rather disoblige a friend than do an act of injustice to a political opponent." His never failing anecdotes were both humorous and illustrative; the application was perfect, yet entertainment was also the motive. Clearness and simplicity of statement he "cultivated with . . . assiduity." Logic appealed to him more than ornament; his forte was "an immense stock of common sense." "Mr. Lincoln was a great common man," "the representative of the unsophisticated People." [4]

Perhaps a man is never great to his valet. Herndon had at times served almost as Lincoln's caddie [5] (though such a statement conveys no idea of Lincoln's generous and partnerlike attitude towards him); yet in the close-up view, if we can trust his later accounts, the younger

[3] In his lecture on discoveries and inventions (above pp. 19–20) Lincoln paid a good deal of attention to language as a human invention.

[4] Gillespie to Herndon, Dec. 8, 1866, Herndon-Weik MSS. Gillespie's letters to Herndon in this period are carefully written accounts. They constitute thoughtful monographs on Lincoln's character by one who knew him well, writing not long after his death.

[5] Referring to a debate which Lincoln had in 1844 with John Calhoun on the tariff, Herndon wrote "I heard this discussion—*'toated books'* & *'hunted* up *authorities'* for Lincoln, as I did in law." Herndon to Lamon, Mar. 6, 1870, p. 15. MS., Huntington Lib.

man saw always the soul and spirit of the older. Lincoln was Herndon's great enthusiasm. That he idolized and worshiped the man of "mystery" whom he "knew well," is beyond doubt. When writing on Lincoln he would burst into a tribute as if a spring of deep feeling were released. Emphasizing Lincoln's plainness and admitting his faults, he also repeatedly stressed what he thought his greatness. Whatever might have been Lincoln's changing aspects, Herndon saw him "through all situations, positions & conditions . . . one and the same—ever honest, & simple, & sincere . . . a primitive type of character . . . ." [6] He found him "incapable of falsehood—of base deception or of fraud"; [7] *"humble—tender—forbearing—liberal— . . . tolerant . . . ."* [8] "Lincoln," he said, "rose over so many disadvantages that he seems to me a hero . . . ." [9] "Mr. L's life is a sweet —clear—clean—manly noble life." [10] Lincoln was "a great man," [11] "truly a noble man." [12] Herndon considered him "Christ like" in his charity and liberality.[13]

IX

It would require deep understanding to depict Lincoln, thought Herndon. It could not be done with superficial strokes: "he was Lincoln and Lincoln alone, and none exactly like him." "Mr. Lincoln," he said, "thought too much and did too much for America and the world to be crammed into an epigram or shot off with a single rocket: he was too close to the touch of the divine everywhere and too near to the suggestions and whisperings of nature for such quick work, done with a flash." [1] He did not want Lincoln retouched by over-friendly art or too-refined portraiture. "Mr. Lincoln can stand unstaggeringly up beneath all *necessary* or other truths." [2]

---

[6] Herndon to Charles H. Hart, July 22, 1866, *ibid.*

[7] Herndon to Lamon, Mar. 6, 1870, p. 12, *ibid.*

[8] Though Herndon almost outdoes himself here in the piling up of adjectives, his choice of words is significant. Herndon to F. B. Carpenter, Dec. 11, 1866, Herndon-Weik MSS.

[9] Herndon to Lamon, Mar. 6, 1870, MS., Huntington Lib.

[10] Herndon to Hart, July 22, 1866, *ibid.*

[11] Herndon to Bartlett, June 24, 1887, MS., Mass. Hist. Soc.

[12] Herndon to Bartlett, July 8, 1887, *ibid.*

[13] Herndon to Hart, Dec. 28, 1866, MS., Huntington Lib.

[1] Herndon to C. O. Poole, Jan. 5, 1886, Herndon-Weik MSS.

[2] Herndon to Hart, Nov. 26, 1866, MS., Huntington Lib.

In Herndon's view his partner was always growing. "Lincoln," he said, "had not arrived, when he was assassinated, at the meredian of his intellectual power." [3] "Mr. Lincoln had not arrived at maturity in 1865 . . . ." [4] "He grandly rose up . . . and this is . . . why I say that Lincoln was not fully developed . . . he may have just entered the field of his . . . intellectual power . . . ." [5]

Such were his moods that he would sometimes pass by his friends unnoticed on the streets; to Herndon this did not matter, except that he "felt for him" in moments of suffering.[6] He was "sad and cheerful by turns—he was good natured generally, but it was terrible to see him mad"; [7] ". . . a gloomy man at one moment and a joyous man the next." [8] Herndon often repeated that he was unknown, "a big mysterious man," a puzzle to friends and neighbors, a "hidden man" who kept his secrets, a man of "deep prudences," a man to admire but "hard to get at." [9] Yet Lincoln's moods did not overwhelm or engulf him; they are rather to be regarded as among the elements blended in that composite which became his character. If he achieved serenity, he did not come by it easily. His philosophy, which gave steadiness to a sensitive, troubled nature, was chiefly a reliance on the working of elemental and eternal laws; his "patience sprang from his philosophy —his calm quiet waiting on the events of the times—his coolness . . . —his charity . . . and . . . want of malice." [10]

Viewed in retrospect the rise of Abraham Lincoln to influence and leadership was no inscrutable mystery. Given the conditions, the result was natural and logical. Politically, as will appear in later pages, the man was "available." He had distinctiveness—oddness perhaps, but without unfortunate eccentricities. He had no antagonisms, no attachment to special interests; yet he had character. He came from

---

[3] Herndon to Bartlett, June 24, 1887, MS., Mass. Hist. Soc.

[4] Herndon to Bartlett, Aug. 7, 1887, *ibid.*

[5] Herndon to "My Friend," (probably Truman H. Bartlett) Aug. 16, 1887, *ibid.*

[6] It is not feasible fully to present Herndon's analysis of Lincoln's sadness. In part the junior member of the firm attributed the man's suffering to domestic unhappiness, but, as this was somewhat of an obsession with Herndon, and as he confessed himself mystified, it is hard to know what degree of value to put upon this explanation as a matter of authentic biography. See below, chap. iii.

[7] Herndon to Bartlett, July 8, 1887, MS., Mass. Hist. Soc.

[8] Herndon to Bartlett, June 24, 1887, *ibid.*

[9] Quoted phrases are culled from manuscript letters written by Herndon: to Bartlett, Aug. 22, 1887; to Poole, Jan. 5, 1886; to Lamon, Mar. 6, 1870; to Hart, Dec. 28, 1866.

[10] Herndon to Weik, Feb. 25, 1887, Herndon-Weik MSS.

a large and "doubtful" state, from a broad section whose votes in 1860 were to be decisive of the outcome. He had a log-cabin origin, though this was less of an asset than has been usually supposed; he had also a peculiar reputation for honesty and a flair for appealing to what was fundamentally and basically American. If one takes a cue from Frederick Jackson Turner, Lincoln embodied the West when the West was the most characteristically American of the sections. From the great prairie environment [11] he had drawn his strength. In western campaigning he had developed aptness in assimilating the subject matter of politics and skill in the art of public appeal. His apprenticeship had been served, not chiefly in office (save as state legislator and briefly as congressman), but on the law circuit, the hustings, the political forum.

He was no stranger to the arts of rhetoric. No one could rightly call his speeches crude; on the contrary they sometimes rose to the height of literary mastery, though in familiar conversation and informal utterance he lapsed into colloquialisms. Not offending the scholar, his addresses seized the understanding of the man in the street. He had his own style, his special tang. In all his careful expression there was simplicity combined with distinction, an economy of competently chosen words, an easy flow of sentences, and a readiness in epigram which served well in the place of brilliant scintillation. Some of his statements have that unerring quality of hitting the target that stamps them as proverbs or aphorisms.

The tricks of the agitator or demagogue were foreign to Lincoln's nature. He avoided emotional harangues. This avoidance was total; his manner was not that of the rabble rouser, the passionate orator, the professional patrioteer. There was in Lincoln more of Euclid than of Demosthenes. He kept on a conservative keel, yet managed to infuse into his leadership enough stirring enthusiasm to rally the reformer and to make a campaign seem a crusade for a cause. Few leaders were less given to sentimentalism; few were more concerned with reason and mental testing. Though it cramped his soul to operate within the limitations of a party, and though as candidate he was to be everyone's game, he appreciated the meaning of statesmanship. He was

---

[11] Middle western intellectual life and culture are well treated in H. C. Hubbart, *The Older Middle West, 1840–1880;* see also *Democracy in the Middle West, 1840–1940,* ed. by Jeannette P. Nichols and J. G. Randall.

made of better stuff than that of politicians reaching out for the spoils of office. In later pages the devastating storm of sectional conflict usurps the theme, but no understanding of Lincoln in the days of his coming ordeal will be complete without envisaging the man he was and viewing his qualities against the quiet background of peace within which he had developed for fifty years.

CHAPTER III

THE HOUSE ON EIGHTH STREET

THE tangled story of Lincoln's courting of Mary Todd and the years of their married life are themes that call for more than common historical caution. In much of the writing concerning these matters regard for Lincoln often coexists with gross unfairness toward his wife. To do simple justice to that wife, and by honest inquiry to restore a kind of balance in the use of what evidence we have concerning this American home, is the plainest duty of a biographer.

I

Mary's story began amid genteel and well favored surroundings. Aristocratic background, ambition, conversational skill, and a vivid interest in politics, were attractively combined in the person of this Springfield belle.[1] Coming of a socially prominent and distinguished family of Lexington, Kentucky, she lived in the fine mansion of her brother-in-law, Ninian Wirt Edwards, son of Governor Ninian Edwards. That she and Lincoln should become acquainted was inevitable; it belonged to the natural course of events that she should know men of political prominence at the capital.[2] Douglas also was of

[1] On Mary Todd Lincoln one should read (in addition to the leading biographies of Lincoln) Katherine Helm, *The True Story of Mary, Wife of Lincoln;* W. A. Evans, *Mrs. Abraham Lincoln: A Study of Her Personality* . . . ; Gamaliel Bradford's well drawn portrait in *Wives;* William H. Townsend, *Lincoln and His Wife's Home Town;* and *Mary Lincoln: Wife and Widow,* by Carl Sandburg and Paul M. Angle. In the Sandburg-Angle volume one finds a sympathetic and readable account buttressed by numerous documents.

[2] "In our little coterie in Springfield, in the days of my girlhood, we had a society of gentlemen, who have since, been distinguished . . . in the political world. My great and glorious husband comes *first* . . . . Douglas, Trumbull, Baker, Hardin, Shields, such choice spirits, were the habitués, of our drawing room." Mary Todd Lincoln to Mrs. Gideon Welles, Dec. 6, 1865, Welles MSS.

her circle, though emphasis on his seeking her hand has probably been overdone.

Study of the Lincoln-Todd courtship is rendered difficult by inadequacy of contemporary evidence and by the unreliable nature of the account by Herndon. Herndon's amazing recital reads as follows:

> The time fixed for the marriage was the first day in January, 1841. Careful preparations for the happy occasion were made at the Edwards mansion. The house underwent the customary renovation; the furniture was properly arranged, the rooms neatly decorated, the supper prepared, and the guests invited. The latter assembled on the evening in question, and awaited in expectant pleasure the interesting ceremony of marriage. The bride, bedecked in veil and silken gown, and nervously toying with the flowers in her hair, sat in the adjoining room. Nothing was lacking but the groom. For some strange reason he had been delayed. An hour passed, and the guests as well as the bride were becoming restless. But they were all doomed to disappointment. Another hour passed; messengers were sent out over town, and each returning with the same report, it became apparent that Lincoln, the principal in this little drama, had purposely failed to appear! The bride, in grief, disappeared to her room; the wedding supper was left untouched; the guests quietly and wonderingly withdrew; the lights in the Edwards mansion were blown out, and darkness settled over all for the night. What the feelings of a lady as sensitive, passionate, and proud as Miss Todd were we can only imagine—no one can ever describe them. By daybreak, after persistent search, Lincoln's friends found him. Restless, gloomy, miserable, desperate, he seemed an object of pity. His friends, Speed among the number, fearing a tragic termination, watched him closely in their rooms day and night. "Knives and razors, and every instrument that could be used for self-destruction were removed from his reach." [3]

The necessary point of departure is to go to Herndon's source. In 1840–41 he was not yet associated with Lincoln in the practice of law, and was not of the Edwards circle. He makes no claim to have been present on the alleged occasion he glibly described, but got his material, or rather an inadequate cue, many years later from Mrs. Ninian W. Edwards, Mary Todd's sister, who seems to have made three statements on the subject in two interviews with Herndon and one with Weik. In her first statement her words as recorded in Herndon's handwriting were: "Lincoln & Mary were engaged—Every thing was ready & prepared for the marriage—even to the supper &c—. Mr. L. failed to meet his engagement—Cause insanity."

[3] *Herndon's Life of Lincoln,* Angle ed., 169–170.

A number of years later, Mrs. Edwards made a second statement to Herndon, which also is available only in his handwriting. This time she referred to "the match" being "broken off," but said nothing of a non-appearing bridegroom on a wedding occasion.[4] Her statement to Weik appears as follows in Weik's diary of December 20, 1883: "Called on N. W. Edwards and wife. Asked about marriage Mary Todd to Lincoln—Mrs. E. said arrangements for wedding made—even cakes baked but Lincoln failed to appear. At this point Mr. Edwards interrupted—cautioned wife she was talking to newspaper man—she declined to say more—had said Mary greatly mortified by Mr. Lincoln's strange conduct. Later were reunited—finally married." [5]

There is also a vague record by Weik of recollections in later life by James H. Matheny, who, as Weik said, was one of Lincoln's "two best men." In this passage, which is poorly constructed as a historical treatment, it may be Weik rather than Matheny who states that the "marriage was originally set for a day in the winter of 1840–41, probably New Year's Day," but that Lincoln "failed to materialize at the appointed time." [6]

Such is Herndon's statement and such his evidence. All of it comes through indirectly; none was even approximately contemporary. Many who must have known whether such an event had occurred seem not to have been sought out or questioned. Mrs. Edwards's account came no nearer to the picturing of an actual wedding party than the statement that "Every thing was ready & prepared for the marriage—even to the supper &c—," and the later statement (attributed to her by Weik) that "arrangements for wedding [were] made—even cakes baked but Lincoln failed to appear." Her story stops short of Herndon's narrative in that she makes no mention of invitations issued, of guests assembled, of the bride "bedecked," of her grief, of the untouched wedding supper, of messengers sent out over town, of the guests' wondering departure after hours of waiting. These details are made up; they are fictional embellishments supplied for the Herndon-Weik biography.

---

[4] Mrs. Edwards's first statement, undated, was made before 1872; it appears in the Lamon biography published in that year, Lamon having acquired Herndon's material. Her second statement is dated Sept. 27, 1887, and then apparently changed to July 27. Herndon-Weik MSS. These statements attributed to Mrs. Edwards have a greater vagueness as to date than is common in the Herndon papers.

[5] Jesse W. Weik, *The Real Lincoln: A Portrait*, 63.

[6] *Ibid.*, 59–60. (Weik gives the misspelling "Matheney.")

It is obvious that Herndon did not assemble all the material he might easily have found, nor did he rightly use the material he had. In his papers there is a record of a statement by Ninian W. Edwards commenting on Lincoln's courtship with Mary Todd and telling how Lincoln loved Matilda Edwards [7] (of which, however, the alleged lover gave no hint directly or indirectly!), how the engagement with Miss Todd was broken in consequence, and how Mary released Lincoln, who "went crazy as a *loon*." [8] In this statement, however, there was a significant omission; there was no mention, not even the faintest suggestion, of a wedding occasion and an absent groom. Herndon also had a statement by Lincoln's friend James H. Matheny representing Lincoln as being greatly distressed at being "driven into the marriage" with Miss Todd, but giving no hint of his absence at the time of a planned wedding, this in spite of the fact that Matheny was the man described by Weik as one of Lincoln's "two best men." [9]

II

With so much pen swinging on so thin a basis, no competent historian will accept as authentic the Herndon-Weik story of the wedding party and the defaulting groom. Weik's passage on his conversation with Matheny [1] is vague as to what Matheny actually said. Mrs. Edwards's testimony, aside from the fact that it only partially upholds Herndon's narrative,[2] is insufficient; it exists in a kind of vacuum; it stands unsupported in the complete absence of contemporary proof. Mr. Angle has pointed out that recollections of the matter involve flat contradictions of Herndon's statements, and that no marriage

---

[7] Cousin of Ninian W. Edwards; later married William Strong of Alton. The infatuation of Lincoln for Miss Edwards is without serious historical support; see Sandburg and Angle, *Mary Lincoln*, 335–336.

[8] Statement of Ninian W. Edwards, Sep. 22, 1865, from Lamon copy in Huntington Lib.

[9] Statement of James H. Matheny, May 3, 1866, *ibid.*

[1] *The Real Lincoln*, 59–60.

[2] All of Mrs. Edwards's statements are indirect. None are contemporary. The time elapsed between the alleged event and the record is about a quarter of a century. Of three statements which she is said to have made, only two—her first to Herndon and the one mentioned in Weik's diary (see above)—give even partial support to Herndon's narrative. Where her statements seem to offer limp support to Herndon they are uncorroborated by her husband and flatly denied by Mary's other sisters. Finally, on the whole subject of her testimony one must consider how a broken engagement or release could, after the passage of years, have become somewhat confused in her own mind, so that her reminiscence might clumsily have suggested a wedding default.

license was issued, "which would hardly have been the case had he [Lincoln] changed his mind at the last moment." [3]

Some might make light of the failure to take out a marriage license, or construe it as consistent with Lincoln's default. Yet the tale of that default, in conjunction with the known lack of a license, suggests a most excessive degree either of deception or of mental derangement. To suppose that a wedding was planned with Lincoln not fully intending to go through with it, to assume that that is why he took out no license, and to believe that he nevertheless permitted wedding plans to go forward to the assembling of guests on the appointed night as Herndon asserts, is to put a severe strain on the reader's credulity, a strain which becomes disbelief in the lack of substantiating evidence.

The fact that no license was issued, as shown by the records of Sangamon County,[4] does not in itself refute the wedding-default story, but it harmonizes with the complete absence of any known facts whatever as of 1840–41 tending to suggest that a wedding was arranged. This, however, is not all; the matter has importance in another sense, for it happens that in one of Herndon's effusive literary flourishes—a kind of rough draft for this portion of his biography—we have the following: "The time came on for Mr Lincoln & Miss Todd to be married. The license for their marriage was issued by the Clerk of the County Court. . . . The hour was set—the room where the ceremony of marriage was to be performed was . . . richly and gorgeously draped. . . . The cultured—the wealthy—the brilliant were there, merry and happy . . . . Parson Dresser had, as supposed the license in his hands— The brides maid and the groomsman were dressed and anxious to perform their part. . . . [etc.]" [5] The chief point of this whole business is that Herndon was drawing on his imagination, depending on no source for his details, yet supplying those details with fabricated minuteness. This particular mention of the issuing of the license was not given in his book; we are dealing here with an earlier draft; but so far as the wedding default

[3] *Herndon's Life of Lincoln,* Angle ed., xliv.

[4] In the old marriage records of Sangamon County, which the writer has consulted, the issuing of licenses and the solemnizing of marriages are duly entered. In the period of Lincoln's alleged wedding default there was no license issued to him; the only license to Lincoln was at the time of his marriage to Mary Todd, November 4, 1842.

[5] Herndon ms. fragment, "Lincoln & Mary Todd." Herndon-Weik MSS.

is concerned the passage was of a piece with his published biography; this detail was dropped, but others, equally the product of invention, were kept. Herndon, lawyer that he was, made this statement concerning a non-existent license "issued by the Clerk of the County Court," in precisely the same sense in which he invented other aspects of the alleged scene. The falsity of his statement as to the license is of significance in judging his credibility.

Persons close to the Edwardses and to Lincoln had no recollection to support Herndon's narrative. Mrs. Elizabeth J. Grimsley, cousin of Mary Lincoln, remembered only an interruption in the courtship due to Lincoln's depression; Mrs. John Todd Stuart had "never heard" of the alleged absent groom till Herndon brought out his book; Mrs. Joshua F. Speed likewise had "never heard" of it; Mrs. B. S. Edwards, sister-in-law of Ninian W. Edwards, declared it a "fabrication." Mary's surviving sisters emphatically denied it.[6] One of these sisters, Mrs. William Wallace of Springfield, née Frances Todd, said: ". . . he did not break off one wedding," adding that she "would have known of it" if such an incident had occurred.[7] One should note also the statement by Mary Todd's niece, Katherine Helm: ". . . Emilie Todd (Mrs. Ben Hardin Helm), Mary Todd's sister, who at this writing [1928] is living and possessed of all her faculties, declares Herndon's story to be absolutely false . . . ."[8]

Then there is the question of Lincoln's presence in the Illinois legislature in this unhappy period. Though his attendance during January 1841 has been referred to as showing "negligence,"[9] he was present at least for a time on nineteen of the twenty-six days when sessions were held that month. Such presence, including a number of votes, does not bear out the theory of "insanity." His record in these weeks falls short of his habitual punctuality, but his illness in this month would account for nearly all his absence, which has been greatly exaggerated and misrepresented. On the day known as "the fatal first of January, 1841," he was recorded present.[10] On this point again, we have an instance of the unreliability of Herndon; he stated

---

[6] Tarbell, *Life of Lincoln*, I, 176 ff.

[7] "Lincoln's Marriage: Newspaper Interview with Mrs. Frances Wallace, Springfield, Illinois, September 2, 1895" (privately printed pamphlet, 1917).

[8] Katherine Helm, *Mary, Wife of Lincoln*, 90. [9] Beveridge, I, 289.

[10] As to Lincoln's attendance the author has been assisted by an excellent memorandum supplied by Miss Margaret C. Norton, archives division, Illinois State Library.

that "Lincoln did not attend it [the legislature] for some weeks";[11] this is a flat misstatement.

An excellent basis for doubting that a wedding had been planned as Herndon states is that Mary Todd made no mention of it in a letter she wrote in mid-December of 1840 to her close friend Mercy Levering, later Mrs. James C. Conkling. In this letter Mary gave details of what went on in her own affairs and in the Edwards circle, mentioned Lincoln and Speed, chatted of matrimony in general, and gave reports of newly married friends in particular. She had not written to "Merce" for a considerable time and was giving news from "the hill," by which she meant the Edwards home.[12] Her letter is nicely phrased. It is spicy and refreshingly natural. Miss Todd had an air in such things.

III

From the man who has been called Lincoln's most intimate friend, Joshua Fry Speed,[1] we have another account of the troubled courtship which Herndon misused. Since history is a matter of evidence, and evidence a matter of statements by those who knew, the quality of Herndon's history at this point is best revealed by first giving the Speed statement and then noting how Herndon twisted it. We have Speed's statement in the Herndon-Weik manuscripts. It is undated; it is in Herndon's handwriting, not Speed's; it obviously belongs to the period after 1865 in which Herndon was collecting his material; it has all the appearance of being Herndon's record of an interview with Lincoln's friend; it is a hasty job, less legible than Herndon's usual hand; it is disjointed and hard to make out. It reads as follows:

In 1840 Lincoln went into the southern part [?] of the state as election canvasser debater speaker— Here first wrote his *Mary*—she darted after him—wrote him—Lincoln—seeing an other girl—& finding he did not love his wife [*sic*] wrote a letter saying he did not love her—.

[Here the manuscript has the following insertion] Speed saw the letter to "Mary" written by Mr Lincoln. Speed tried to persuade Lincoln to burn it up. Lincoln said— "Speed I always knew you were an obstinate man. If

---

11 Herndon ms. fragment, "Lincoln & Mary Todd," p. 17, undated, Herndon-Weik MSS.

12 Sandburg and Angle, *Mary Lincoln*, 174–178. This letter (the original), along with many other treasures, is in the collection of Oliver R. Barrett of Chicago.

1 Robert L. Kincaid, *Joshua Fry Speed: Lincoln's Most Intimate Friend.*

you won't deliver it I will get some one to do it. I shall not deliver it nor give it to you to be delivered: Words are forgotten—misunderstood— . . . but once put your words in writing and they stand as a living & eternal monument against you. If you think you have *will* & manhood enough to go and see her and speak to her what you say in that letter, you may do that. Lincoln did go and see her—did tell her &c—Speed said—Lincoln tell me what you said and did"—Lincoln told him—Speed said—The last thing is a bad lick, but it cannot now be helped—Lincoln kept his promises and did not go to see her for months—they got together somehow.

[Here the insertion ends; the statement continues:]—tell the conversation—between Lincoln & Speed—Went to see "Mary"—told her that he did not love her—she rose and said "the deceiver shall be deceived wo is me"; alluding to a young man she fooled—Lincoln drew he[r] down on his knee—kissed her—& parted—he going one way & she an other—Lincoln did love Miss Edwards—"Mary" saw it—told Lincoln the reason of his change of mind—heart & soul—released him—[At this point there is a marginal insertion which reads as follows:] Lincoln went crazy—had to remove razors from his room—take away all knives and other such dangerous things—&c—it was terrible—was during the special session of the Ills Legislature in 1840 [End of marginal insertion] Lincoln married her for honor—feeling his honor bound to her—[2]

Turning now from Herndon's basis (his own account of the Speed interview) to the Herndon-Weik biography, we find a result both subtly and palpably different from the record. The biography has it as follows:

. . . One evening Lincoln came into our store and called for his warm friend Speed. . . . Lincoln, drawing from his pocket a letter, asked Speed to read it. "The letter," relates Speed, "was addressed to Mary Todd, and in it he made a plain statement of his feelings, telling her that he had thought the matter over calmly and with great deliberation, and now felt that he did not love her sufficiently to warrant her in marrying him. This letter he desired me to deliver. Upon my declining to do so he threatened to intrust it to some other person's hand. I reminded him that the moment he placed the letter in Miss Todd's hand, she would have the advantage over him. 'Words are forgotten,' I said, 'misunderstood, unnoticed in a private conversation, but once put your words in writing and they stand a living and eternal monument against you.' Thereupon I threw the unfortunate letter in the fire. 'Now,' I continued, 'if you have the courage of manhood, go see Mary yourself; tell her, if you do not love her, the facts,

[2] For a reproduction of this statement from the Herndon-Weik collection (a print from a microfilm) the author is indebted to the division of manuscripts of the Library of Congress.

and that you will not marry her. Be careful not to say too much, and then leave at your earliest opportunity.' Thus admonished, he buttoned his coat, and with a rather determined look started out to perform the serious duty for which I had just given him explicit directions."

. . . Speed was satisfied, from the length of Lincoln's stay, that his directions had not been followed.

"Well, old fellow, did you do as I told you and as you promised?" were Speed's first words.

"Yes, I did," responded Lincoln, thoughtfully, "and when I told Mary I did not love her, she burst into tears and almost springing from her chair and wringing her hands as if in agony, said something about the deceiver being himself deceived." Then he stopped.

"What else did you say?" inquired Speed, drawing the facts from him.

"To tell you the truth Speed, it was too much for me. I found the tears trickling down my own cheeks. I caught her in my arms and kissed her."

"And that's how you broke the engagement," sneered Speed. "You not only acted the fool, but your conduct was tantamount to a renewal of the engagement, and in decency you cannot back down now."

"Well," drawled Lincoln, "if I am in again, so be it. It's done, and I shall abide by it." [3]

Immediately following this, Herndon gives the famous above-quoted narrative of the wedding party and the absent Lincoln.[4] The reader may compare the Speed statement with the account given in the Herndon biography. The Speed account presents a severed engagement, a painful scene in which Lincoln tried to break the troth only to find himself drawing Mary to him and kissing her, after which Mary, seeing his perplexity, "released" him. The biography, on the contrary, treats the incident not as a release but as a ratification of the engagement; only so could it have been used as setting for the story of the wedding default. The biography's comment that things "went on smoothly as before" is not justified by Speed's statement. Above all, Speed made no mention of Lincoln's wedding default. This is very significant; if such default had occurred Speed would certainly have known of it. He had a long correspondence with Lincoln on matters of the heart in this period, he was of the Edwards circle, and Lincoln made an extended visit to his home (Louisville, Kentucky) in 1841.[5]

Mrs. Edwards also referred to Mary's release of Lincoln. Her words

[3] Herndon's *Life of Lincoln,* Angle ed., 168–169.

[4] Above, p. 52.

[5] Having lived some years in Springfield, where he kept a store, Speed moved to Louisville in 1841. Beveridge, I, 317.

come to us thus: "The world had it that Mr L backed out and this placed Mary in a peculiar situation & to set herself right and to free Mr Lincoln's mind she wrote a letter to Mr L stating that she would release him from his engagements. . . . Mrs L told Mr L that though she had released him . . . yet she . . . would hold the question an open one—that is that she had not changed her mind, but felt as always." [6] The date and sequence of this release as mentioned by Mrs. Edwards are a bit vague, so that a Herndonian might ask: Could not the release have been given after Lincoln had failed to appear at the wedding? This would sound better if there were any proof that such default ever occurred. In the absence of proof such a query suggests a debater begging the question; it implies assent to the thing which remains to be proved. Among other factors, Mary's lack of resentment, for which there is supporting evidence, is difficult to reconcile with the absent-groom story. The fancy touches which Herndon gratuitously added must be borne in mind in any discussion of the subject.

What, then, did happen in this troubled courtship? Taking all the evidence we have and sifting it carefully, one is led to the picture of a severed engagement—not a troth rudely broken, but an episode in which Lincoln's painful struggle with doubt and Mary's reluctant yet unresentful release were the main factors. The incomplete history of the case does not hold together without that release. Lincoln's deep and shattering depression, which may have approached the stage of collapse and prostration, is evident in his own letters of the period. Writing to John Todd Stuart, January 23, 1841, he referred to himself as "the most miserable man living," [7] and in his letter to Speed on March 27, 1842, he used the expression "the fatal 1st of January, 1841," [8] which evidently referred to an acute crisis in the disturbed courtship.[9]

A letter which Lincoln wrote on January 20, 1841, to John Todd Stuart concerning Dr. Anson G. Henry, his physician, also bears upon the matter. Lincoln said: "I have within the last few days, been making

[6] Mrs. Edwards's first statement to Herndon, undated, Herndon-Weik MSS.

[7] *Works*, I, 159. [8] *Ibid.*, I, 214.

[9] In "The Fatal First of January, 1841," by Mary Leighton Miles, *Journal*, Ill. State Hist. Soc., XX, 13–48 (1927), emphasis is placed on the lack of evidence concerning a wedding party, the absence of proof that invitations were issued, and the like. Attention is given to Lincoln's doings and writings in the period as belying the charge of insanity, and to the inaccuracies of various biographies concerning Lincoln's visit to the Speed home in 1841.

a most discreditable exhibition of myself in the way of hypochondriasm[?] . . . ." He considered Henry "necessary" to his "existence," and sought Stuart's influence to have the physician appointed postmaster at Springfield; otherwise he would leave the city. Stuart was at that time congressman and Lincoln's law partner. Lincoln added that his heart was "very much set" upon this appointment; he concluded as follows: "Pardon me for not writing more, I have not sufficient composure to write a long letter." [10] All the evidence is that Lincoln's condition was that of severe mental distress with accompanying effects upon his health, that the interrupted courtship was the cause of it, and that he was making a conscious and deliberate effort toward restoration of normal life.

IV

The renewal of the engagement in 1842 was assisted by Mary's friend, Mrs. Simeon Francis, wife of a prominent Springfield editor, the reconciliation [1] being related to Lincoln's generously taking the blame for a partisan newspaper skit which Mary and her friend Julia Jayne had perpetrated at the expense of a prominent Democratic politician, James Shields.[2] Writing to Mrs. Gideon Welles in the year of Lincoln's death, Mary Todd Lincoln recalled the Lincoln-Shields incident, in which a duel was arranged and its consummation narrowly averted, and gave interesting details concerning her relation to Lincoln prior to their marriage. ". . . I committed his [Shields's]

---

[10] Harry E. Pratt, "Dr. Anson G. Henry, Lincoln's Physician and Friend," *Lincoln Herald,* XLV, nos. 3 and 4 (1943). This letter of January 20, 1841, is not in the Nicolay-Hay edition of the *Complete Works.* See Angle, *New Letters and Papers,* 8–9.

[1] According to Mrs. Edwards, "Doctr [Anson G.] Henry who admired and loved Mr. Lincoln had much to do in getting Mary and Lincoln together again." Second statement of Mrs. Edwards, Sep. 27 [corrected as July 27], 1887, Herndon-Weik MSS.

[2] In these pages the near-duel between Lincoln and Shields, and the "Rebecca" letters related thereto, are not treated. For an analysis see Roy P. Basler, "The Authorship of the 'Rebecca' Letters," *Abr. Lincoln Quart.,* II, 80–90 (June, 1942). The letters, which appeared in the *Sangamo Journal* in 1842, were abusive of Democrats in general and James Shields in particular. (A curious type of duel was arranged on Shields's challenge and Lincoln's acceptance, but by amicable arrangement it was averted.) It is Basler's conclusion that Lincoln did not write the first and third letters, but did write the second, in which Shields was subjected to "ridicule and contumely" (*ibid.,* 81). He concludes also that "Lincoln . . . had been responsible for the publication of the fourth, written by Mary Todd and Julia Jayne, and hence when Shields demanded to know the author . . . , Lincoln's name was properly given" (*ibid.,* 89). Basler's critical investigation is a check upon the account given by Beveridge (I, 337 ff.).

follies, to rhyme," she wrote, "and very silly verses they were, . . . offensive to the Genl." With her customary surplus of commas Mary proceeded: "A gentleman friend, carried them off, and . . . one day, I saw them, strangely enough, in the daily papers. Genl Shields called upon the Editor, and demanded the author. The Editor, requested *a day,* to reflect upon it. The latter called upon Mr Lincoln, to whom he knew I was engaged & explained to him, that he was certain, that I was the Author. Mr. L. then replied, Say to Shields, that 'I am responsible.['] Mr. L. thought no more of it, when about two weeks afterwards, . . . Shields . . . demanded satisfaction . . . ." There is here a reference to the planned duel and the reconciliation of the men. Mary added: "The occasion, was so silly, that my husband, was always so ashamed of it, that . . . we . . . agreed—never to speak of it . . . . This occurred, six months, before we were married . . . . We were engaged & greatly attached to each other—Two years before we were married." [3] When the wedding came it was a quiet affair in the Edwards home. The date was November 4, 1842. It was a ring-and-book ceremony conducted by the Episcopal minister, Charles Dresser. On the ring which Lincoln gave to Mary were inscribed the words: "Love is eternal."

V

Mr. and Mrs. Abraham Lincoln started their married life at the Globe Tavern in Springfield where room and board could be had for four dollars a week. Later they lived for a time in a modest cottage; in 1844 they acquired their residence on Eighth Street. It was a comfortable and dignified house, unpretentious but not lacking in architectural taste. In 1856 it was enlarged by the addition of an upper story.[1]

The humble setting at the outset of their wedded life contrasted strongly with the spacious living to which Mary Todd had been accustomed. The contrast was similar to that between their early environments. Where she had memories of being driven to Madame Mentelle's fashionable school by a liveried coachman in the Todd carriage,[2] his recollections were of lonely trips through a pioneer's

[3] Mary Todd Lincoln to Mrs. Gideon Welles, Dec. 6, 1865, Welles MSS.

[1] Pratt, *Personal Finances,* 87–88.

[2] W. H. Townsend, *Lincoln and his Wife's Home Town,* 61, 63.

woods to fetch water to the cabin. Beauty of clothes and furnishings, parties and entertainments, pride of family and social prominence, were the things that mattered to her; to the young man of backwoods origin these things were never to matter much or penetrate deeply into his consciousness.

"She is the very creature of excitement . . . and never enjoys herself more than when in society and surrounded by a company of merry friends" wrote a member [3] of the social group of Springfield in which Mary Todd had had a lively part. Her early letters bear out this description; they are full of vivid interest in people and affairs, with frequent italics to show her intensity of feeling. They are lightened with playful humor as when she refers to the two children of a widower suitor of hers as "his two *sweet little objections.*" [4] The slow-tongued young lawyer, by Mrs. Edwards's statement, hung upon her sparkling conversation as if fascinated.[5]

Mary Lincoln had the virtues of her defects. Along with outbursts of temper and emotion there was enthusiasm for undertaking and achievement, interest in dress and fashion, contagious zest for the color of life. Her qualities were complementary to those of her husband. She was to be a stimulus to him, even if at times that stimulus was somewhat of an irritant. His friends unanimously testify to his sadness, his periods of absent thought when he saw nothing around him. To his reflective mind she added vivacity; to his indifferent abstraction she brought a wholesome preoccupation with the affairs of daily living. Dependence on each other was reciprocal; she needed his reasoned statements, his seeing both sides of a question where she saw only one—her own, his tolerance and patience; these needs were to grow as her congenital lack of self-control increased.

They had their congenialities. Both loved politics with absorbing interest; both were politically ambitious. His advancement was their mutual aim in life. Each had a sense of literary style. Emilie Todd Helm tells of Mary reading and reviewing books for her husband and of his great respect for her judgment.[6] Both loved theatrical entertainment and never missed anything of the kind if they could help

[3] Sandburg and Angle, *Mary Lincoln,* 172–173.
[4] *Ibid.,* 183.
[5] First statement of Mrs. Ninian Edwards, undated, Herndon-Weik MSS.
[6] Helm, *Mary, Wife of Lincoln,* 108.

it.[7] Both idolized their children. These things became welding influences.

In its Springfield phase the life of these contrasting personalities lasted more than eighteen years. In ten years Mary Lincoln bore four sons: Robert Todd Lincoln on August 1, 1843; Edward Baker Lincoln on March 10, 1846; William Wallace Lincoln on December 21, 1850; Thomas ("Tad") Lincoln on April 4, 1853. When elected to the presidency Lincoln had three sons, Edward having died in 1850.[8]

Lincoln's doings have become more a matter of record than Mary's. For her, life was a strenuous round of childbearing, tending babies, feeding and clothing a household, sewing, struggling with servants, watching constantly to keep a suitable establishment, carrying on alone when her husband was away on the circuit—in short enduring the strains of any wife and mother. Lincoln, too, when in town, was busy with home tasks; a neighbor recalled that "he kept his own horse—fed & curried it—fed and milked his own cow: he sawed his own wood generally when at home." [9]

These years saw some triumphs for Lincoln, some disappointments. Major episodes were his election to Congress in 1846, his defeat for the senate in 1855 and 1858, and the supreme climax of his nomination for the presidency and election to that office. The house on Eighth Street mirrored these events. It witnessed family reunions on the occasions of the master's return from circuit travel. The furniture —ornate iron stove, cut-glass prisms of the candlesticks on the mantel, lady's chair designed with due allowance for hoop skirts, heavy lace curtains, whatnot, hassocks, sofa, mirror, oval-framed pictures—each of these objects, satisfyingly Victorian and suitable, as *Leslie's* said, to "a gentleman in comfortable circumstances," had for the Lincolns its personal history and its family association.

VI

The question of the happiness or unhappiness of the Lincolns has been as controversial as the matter of the defaulting bridegroom.

[7] *Ibid.*, 119.

[8] Willie died in the White House February 20, 1862; Tad died in Chicago on July 15, 1871; Robert alone lived to manhood. After a prominent career in public office and business, followed by many years of retirement, he died on July 26, 1926, without surviving male issue; Lincoln's name was not perpetuated in offspring.

[9] Statement of James Gourley, undated, Herndon-Weik MSS.

Herndon fixed the popular conception of this marriage as a tragically unhappy one, and of Mary Lincoln as an intolerable shrew. His descriptions of her stormy tongue and temper, her lack of self control, and her violence when in a rage are familiar not only in his own pages, but in countless authors who have followed him. The story which he tells of Lincoln's asking a man, who had been abused by Mrs. Lincoln, if he could not endure for a few minutes what he, Lincoln, had endured for fifteen years, alone would fix the whole concept of a miserable marriage in the reader's mind.[1] In the uninhibited language of the Herndon manuscripts this story has much more detail and vividness than in the biography, and one can better judge the nature of the evidence. According to this account, Lincoln was reclining on the counter in "Edwards' store" telling one of his best stories, when the man—his name was Tiger—called him outside, told him of Mrs. Lincoln's abuse punctuated with blows of her broom, and demanded that her husband do something about it; Lincoln then sadly asked the above question.[2] There is no evidence that Herndon was present on the occasion, but such a tale would quickly go the rounds among men who lingered in the store, then went home and told their wives.

Other incidents from the manuscripts may be mentioned briefly. A passerby and a neighbor witnessed Lincoln one day being pursued in his own backyard by "a little low squatty woman with a butcher knife in her hand." Noticing that other people were approaching, Lincoln unceremoniously carried his infuriated wife back into the house, rising to the occasion in action and language! Such is the story. Herndon claims not to have witnessed this incident of home life; he had it second-hand from a neighbor of the Lincolns named Whitehurst, whose account is given only through Herndon's memory; though he dated the occurrence about 1857, same period as the Tiger story, he wrote his version in 1886.[3]

Again in 1857 (this must have been a bad year) Mary is alleged to have asked her abstracted husband three times to mend the fire; then, wrote Herndon, she "blazed away at Lincoln with a stick of stove wood"; when he appeared next day his nose was "fixed up with court

---

1 *Herndon's Life of Lincoln*, Angle ed., 347–348.
2 Herndon to Weik, Jan., 1887, Herndon-Weik MSS.
3 Herndon to Weik, Jan. 23, 1886, *ibid.*

plaster." This tale came from a servant girl; Herndon added: ". . . it is more probable that it is true than untrue. I believe it: it went around among the members of the bar as true." [4]

There is no doubt that Mary Lincoln had an ungovernable temper. That she suffered in later life from temporary insanity is a matter of court record, but that was after life had dealt crushing and devastating blows. Dr. W. A. Evans, whose account is based on historical material medically interpreted, finds in her no breakdown of intellect, but rather a kind of excess, amounting at times to abnormality, in emotional reactions.[5] Dr. Evans's account is by no means entirely unfavorable; he gives her "first suspiciously false note" as of January 1861 in the matter of purchases in New York.[6] Mrs. Lincoln's physician, Thomas W. Dresser, son of the minister who married the Lincolns, also referred to her abnormality as belonging chiefly to the tragically clouded period of her later life. He wrote: "She was bright and sparkling in conversation . . . . Her face was animated and pleasing; and to me she was always an interesting woman; and while the whole world was finding fault with her . . . , it was clear to me that the trouble was a cerebral disease." [7]

Mrs. Lincoln's personality must be reconstructed from incomplete sources, with constant allowance for unfriendly testimony. Even so, much of that record, to say the least, is creditable. Scattered incidents of bad temper, indirectly transmitted and interpreted by a roughhewn mind disposed toward an unfavorable judgment, do not constitute the whole story of the Lincoln marriage. Things that made for content and affectionate adjustment rarely found their way into the record, especially as gathered by Herndon. Friends did not set pen to paper in order to report the normal, everyday incidents of this home. It is remembered that she was quick tempered, caustic, and tactless of speech; touchy, proud, and willful. It is too often forgotten that she was endowed with natural kindness, that she bore herself with gaiety and grace, that there was sparkle in her face and speech, that she rose to the standards of a gentlewoman, that rearing and education fitted her for cultured society, and that she brought a full measure of affection and devotion to the countless unrecorded duties of wife and mother.

---

[4] *Ibid.*

[5] W. A. Evans, *Mrs. Abraham Lincoln: A Study of her Personality* . . . [etc.].

[6] *Ibid.*, 158. [7] Thomas W. Dresser to Weik, Jan. 3, 1889, Herndon-Weik MSS.

In a lengthy account of Mrs. Lincoln angrily dismissing her servant, Sarah, Herndon said, after telling of the hiring of Sarah, "Everything went on well for sometime, Mrs L bragging on her Sarah all the while to her neighbors & visitors." [8] Evidently there were intervals of tranquillity in the household. To Weik, his literary collaborator, he wrote: "Lincoln, you know, was not a social man, and hence those little *incidents* in his office and around his hearth which you want so much are hard to gather and to get, for they are few and far between." [9] It is well to observe that "few and far between," to note that these stories were usually second hand, and to question how much Herndon knew at first hand about that hearth. He said, "This woman was to me a terror," [10] "She was a tigress," [11] and again "She hates me yet *I can* and *will do* her justice." [12] Writing freely to Weik he filled pages with comments of which the following is an example: "This domestic *hell* of Lincoln's life is not all on one side"; [13] ". . . sometimes he would rise and Cut up the very devil for a while—make thing[s] more lively and 'get.' " [14]

To "do . . . justice" is not always the same as being just; to love the truth, which Herndon did in his way, is not synonymous with knowing and understanding it. Herndon's testimony is refracted by his own emotions and mentality. He disliked and feared Mary Lincoln, perhaps the more because of his love for her husband, whom he represented as the victim of her temper. With his frontier, earthy type of mind, he "was firmly convinced that truth could be got at by intuition, and he never doubted his own clairvoyant capacity." [15]

To go further and explain in full the mutual dislike between Herndon and Mrs. Lincoln, and to give the documents, would require too much space. Her background was aristocratic, his quite the opposite. In attitudes, tastes, and standards they were miles apart. As a radical abolitionist and as a man whose drinking habits led to occasional sprees, he was not likely to be regarded by her as the most suitable partner for her husband. One can point to at least one friendly incident. When Herndon, in the earlier stages of assembling

---

8 Herndon to Weik, Jan., 1887, *ibid.*
9 Herndon to Weik, Feb. 24, 1887, *ibid.*
10 Herndon to Weik, Jan. 9, 1886, *ibid.*
11 Herndon to Weik, Jan. 8, 1886, *ibid.*
12 Herndon to Charles H. Hart, Nov. 26, 1866, MS., Huntington Lib.
13 Herndon to Weik, Jan. 9, 1886, Herndon-Weik MSS.
14 Herndon to Weik, Jan. 8, 1886, *ibid.*
15 *Herndon's Life of Lincoln,* Angle ed., editor's preface, xxxviii.

material for his biography, sought Mrs. Lincoln's help, she took the trouble in the period of her crushing bereavement to write him a gracious and cordial letter, promising an interview, referring to her husband's "truly affectionate regard" for his partner, and adding that those who idolized him were "very precious" to her and hers.[16] By January of 1874, however, there had been a definite break between them, brought on by Herndon's lecture on Lincoln's religion, in December of 1873, in which he quoted her in a manner which she resented. She indignantly and flatly denied statements which Herndon attributed to her; Herndon published a spirited refutation of her denial; from then on their relation was that of open warfare.[17] In interpreting Herndon's above quoted statements—calling her a "tigress" and noting how she hated him—it is not easy for the historian to know how much of this feeling harked back to the days when the Lincolns lived in Springfield and how much stemmed from the open break of 1873–74, but since this complete break occurred many years prior to the publication of Herndon's famous book, one must remember that when as a biographer he dealt with Lincoln's wife, Herndon was writing of a woman toward whom he had been for a number of years definitely unfriendly.[18]

The statement of James Gourley, Lincoln's back-door neighbor for many years, as preserved in manuscript by Herndon, sums up the situation in the Lincoln household: "Lincoln & his wife got along tolerably well, unless Mrs L got the devil in her: Lincoln . . . would pick up one of his children & walked off—would laugh at her—pay no earthly attention to her when in that wild furious condition." His further comment is a bit of testimony that any

[16] In his biography (Angle ed., 412) Herndon prints this letter with some editing. He omits a sentence in which Mrs. Lincoln asked the meaning of a tactless passage which Herndon wrote in a letter to Robert Lincoln, saying that he wanted to "do justice" to Mrs. Lincoln "so that the world will understand things better." The letter is in the Herndon-Weik collection, being dated at Chicago, August 28, but without the year; the Herndon biography gives it as 1866, but a study of the evidence makes 1865 seem perhaps more likely. See *Illinois State Journal*, Jan. 15, 1874, p. 3, c. 3.

[17] Herndon's lecture appeared in the *Illinois State Register*, December 13, 1873. As stated in the Springfield *Illinois State Journal* of December 19, 1873, p. 1, c. 1, Mrs. Lincoln denied the statement Herndon attributed to her and also denied having had the conversation with him. The same paper of January 15, 1874, p. 3, cc. 3–4, contained a wordy rejoinder by Herndon in which he referred to the "spasmodic madness of her denial."

[18] In this matter the author has been aided by Mr. David H. Donald, graduate assistant at the University of Illinois.

human being might be content to hear: "Mrs & Mr Lincoln were good neighbors." [19]

Mary's sisters, Mrs. Frances Wallace, who lived in Springfield, and Mrs. Emilie Todd Helm, who had ample association with the Lincolns on family visits, both made statements after the Herndon life had been published. Their reaction to Herndon's use of backdoor gossip can easily be understood. Mrs. Wallace said: "I don't see why people should say Mr. Lincoln's home life was not happy, for I certainly never saw a thing there that would make me think either of them was unhappy. He was devoted to his home, and Mrs. Lincoln thought everything of him. She almost worshiped him. . . . Why, she was devoted to him and to her children. And he was certainly all to her that any husband could have been." [20]

"They understood each other thoroughly," wrote Mrs. Helm, "and Mr. Lincoln looked beyond the impulsive words and manner, and knew that his wife was devoted to him and to his interests. They lived in a quiet, unostentatious manner. She was very fond of reading, and interested herself greatly in her husband's political views and aspirations. She was fond of home, and made nearly all her own and her children's clothes. She was a cheerful woman, a delightful conversationalist, and well-informed on all the subjects of the day. The present writer saw Mr. and Mrs. Lincoln together for some part of every day for six months at one time, but saw nothing of the unhappiness which is so often referred to." [21]

This testimony has been simmered over the gentle fire of family affection and loyalty, and the historian would prefer it raw, so to speak, but it is logical to use the evidence of those who were closest to the Lincoln family life.

In *Mary, Wife of Lincoln,* by Katherine Helm, Mrs. Helm's daughter, Mrs. Lincoln appears as a devoted wife who was proud of her husband, watched carefully over his health, saw that he was warmly or suitably dressed, had faith in him, and opposed her gay moods to his dark ones.

Life-like pictures flash out from Mrs. Helm's account as quoted by

---

19 Statement of James Gourley, undated, Herndon-Weik MSS.

20 Pamphlet newspaper interview with Mrs. Frances Wallace, September 2, 1895, privately printed, 1917.

21 Emily [Emilie] Todd Helm, "Mary Todd Lincoln," *McClure's Magazine,* XI, 479 (Sep., 1898).

her daughter: Mary calling Mr. Lincoln back to wrap his throat in a muffler, patting his arm with a little air of coquetry, wearing her new dress of "white silk with blue brocaded flowers scattered over it." In the latter incident, Mr. Lincoln had come home from his office to find her dressed in this creation of her own fashioning, and had been reminded he also must change his clothes to go to the Edwards's supper party. With a smile, he said, "Fine feathers enough on you to make fine birds of both of us," and added, "Those posies on your dress are the color of your eyes." Mary said to her sister "You see, Emilie, I am training my husband to see color. I do not think he knew pink from blue when I married him." [22]

VII

Both Herndon and Mrs. Helm agree that the Lincolns idolized their children and spoiled them. Herndon gives several accounts of Lincoln's bringing one or more of the boys to the office on a Sunday morning while Mrs. Lincoln was at church. They pulled the books out of the shelves, scattered legal papers, spilled ink, smashed pens, and generally tore up the office. Herndon wrote: "I have felt many & many a time that I wanted to wring their little necks and yet out of respect for Lincoln I kept my mouth shut. Lincoln did not notice what his children was doing or had done." [1]

The junior partner returns to the subject in another letter; again he "wanted to wring the necks of these brats and pitch them out of the windows." [2] One wonders if Herndon went to the office on Sunday mornings to salvage what he could from the wreckage. Perhaps his silent endurance can be explained by this statement: "He [Lincoln] worshipped his children and *what* they worshipped[;] he loved what they loved and hated what they hated . . . ." [3]

It was Herndon who preserved the familiar picture of Lincoln hauling his babies in a little wagon up and down the pavement in front of his house. A child would fall out, and lie squalling while the abstracted father pulled the wagon on, unaware of what was happening.[4]

"It was the habit—custom of Mrs Lincoln [wrote Herndon] when

---

[22] Helm, *Mary, Wife of Lincoln*, 109.

[1] Herndon to Weik, Nov. 19, 1885. Herndon-Weik MSS.

[2] Herndon to Weik, Jan. 8, 1886, *ibid.*

[3] Herndon to Weik, Feb. 18, 1887, *ibid.*

[4] Herndon to Weik, Nov. 19, 1885, *ibid.*

any big man or woman visited her house to dress up and trot out Bob—Willie or Tad and get them to monkey around—talk—dance —speek—quote poetry &c &c. Then she would become enthusiastic & eloquent over the children much to the annoyance of the visitor . . . ." [5] Herndon adds that Lincoln would make some remark about the children being "rareripes" but quickly states that he was proud of his children and blind to their faults.[6]

All the basic fulfillment of parenthood was in this marriage. Looking back, Mrs. Lincoln could write in later years, in one of her tender and loving letters to her daughter-in-law, that most mothers "consider that in the outset in life—a nice home—loving husband and precious child are the happiest stages of life." [7] In another letter of affectionate reminiscence she expressed indignation at the suggestion that she had ever whipped a child. "In the first place," she wrote, "*they* never required it. A gentle, loving word, was all sufficient with them . . . ." [8]

Old accounts of stores in Springfield bring the house on Eighth Street into near focus. They show Mrs. Lincoln busy with her needle; they suggest old-fashioned thoroughness in home dosing; they bring to mind in dry record the things that were worn, eaten, and used in this residence. Among the Lincoln purchases one reads of "5 yds. Drilling," "13½ yds. Muslin," "16 lbs. Batting," "10½ yds. French Chintz per Lady," "16 yds. Plaid Silk," "36 yds. Buff Linen," "Castor Oil," "Calomel," "Box Pills," "Bottle Vermifuge," "Syrup Ipecac," "1 pair Boys Boots by A. Lincoln," "1 pair Boys Boots per Lady," "2 doz. Whalebones," large purchases of wall paper, "1 pair White Gloves per Robert," "2 pair Heavy Drawers," "6 doz. Pearl Buttons," "1 paper Horse Powder," "8 lb. Turkey @ .10," "4 doz. Eggs @ .10," "6 Doz. Eggs @ 8⅓," "1 Hooped Skirt per Lady," "2 Barlow Knives," "10 cords of Wood," and numerous entries of such items as candles, thread, sugar, coffee, blacking, buttons, and matches.[9]

Hospitality in the Lincoln home was somewhat limited by circumstances, but O. H. Browning records on February 5, 1857, that he had attended a "large & pleasant party at Lincolns" that night.[10] Writing to her sister Emilie on the sixteenth of the same month, Mrs.

---

[5] Herndon to Weik, Jan. 8, 1886, *ibid.*

[6] *Ibid.*

[7] Sandburg and Angle, *Mary Lincoln*, 299.

[8] *Ibid.*, 231.

[9] Pratt, *Personal Finances*, 145 ff.

[10] Browning, *Diary*, I, 274.

Lincoln tells of giving a party, presumably the one Browning mentions, to which five hundred people had been invited, though, owing to a rain and the counter attraction of a bridal party in Jacksonville, only three hundred came.[11] Mrs. Lincoln's pride and satisfaction in this party are evident in her letter. Isaac N. Arnold spoke in nostalgic reminiscence of the dinners and evening parties at the Lincoln home, the excellence of Mrs. Lincoln's table, the "cordial and hearty Western welcome" of "both host and hostess," "her genial manners," and his "wit and humor, anecdote, and unrivalled conversation." [12]

VIII

A direct source for the relationship between Abraham and Mary Lincoln is found in a series of four letters which they wrote each other in the spring and summer of 1848 while he was in Washington in Congress and she was visiting the Todd family in Lexington. Not written for publication, they are the unstudied messages between a husband and wife who had been married for more than five years; to examine them is to let the couple themselves come back and testify as to their marriage.[1]

In the first of these missives he tells her that when she was with him he thought she hindered him somewhat from attending to business, but since she left and he had nothing but business it had grown "exceedingly tasteless" to him. He adds "I hate to stay in this old room by myself." He shares her delight over Eddie's treasured baby words, and tells of shopping for little plaid stockings for his young son. Mrs. Lincoln's inability to get along with people is hinted when he says "All the house—or rather, all with whom you were on decided good terms—send their love to you— The others say nothing—" The following paragraph was written by an affectionate and considerate husband: "And you are entirely free from headache? That is good—good —considering it is the first spring you have been free from it since

---

11 Sandburg and Angle, *Mary Lincoln*, 198–199.

12 Isaac N. Arnold, "Reminiscences of the Illinois-Bar Forty Years Ago . . . ," read before "The Bar Association of Illinois," Springfield, Jan. 7, 1881 (in miscellany pub. by Fergus Printing Co., Chicago), 137–138. This testimony, of course, must be taken with the reservation that applies to all sentimental reminiscence.

1 The four letters are in Sandburg and Angle, *Mary Lincoln*, 186–194. Originals are in the collection of Oliver R. Barrett. For Lincoln's letter of April 16, 1848, see illustration accompanying this chapter.

we were acquainted— I am afraid you will get so well, and fat, and young, as to be wanting to marry again— Tell Louisa I want her to watch you a little for me— Get weighed and write me how much you weigh—" Daily happenings that she would be interested in complete the letter. He asks what Bobby and Eddie thought of "the little letters father sent them," and adds "Don't let the blessed fellows forget father—" He signs it "Most affectionately."

Her letter written two or more weeks later deals with family news and events with much tender detail about the children. There are hints of coquetry in her lines as there is indulgent fondness in his. She expresses her longing for him: "How much, I wish instead of writing, we were together this evening, I feel very sad away from you." She reassures him: "Do not fear the children, have forgotten you, I was only jesting. Even E- eyes brighten at the mention of your name."

His next letter hints at Mrs. Lincoln's shortcomings and reveals his own wish for their reunion: "The leading matter in your letter is your wish to return to this side of the Mountains. Will you be a *good girl* in all things, if I consent? Then come along, and that as *soon* as possible. Having got the idea in my head, I shall be impatient till I see you."

These are the normal letters of a husband and wife who were adjusted, loved each other, and had common aims and interests. He does not hesitate to remind her of the results of her lack of self-control—that was nothing new to either one—but in his light way of touching on such things he suggests his adjustment to them.

All in all, the house on Eighth Street sheltered a typical American family where father and mother were united by love of their children, common interests, ties of affection, and the pattern of daily family life. To the extent that her tempestuousness was abnormal, the marriage was rendered difficult, but the husband had accustomed himself to this imperfection as husbands—and wives—have been adjusting themselves to imperfections from the beginning. In the larger picture each gave to the other full fidelity and devotion. Mrs. Lincoln, writing to a friend in later life, could say, "It was always, music in my ears, both before & after our marriage, when my husband, told me that I was the only one, he had ever thought of, or cared for." [2]

[2] Mary Todd Lincoln to Mrs. Gideon Welles, Dec. 6, 1865, Welles MSS.

In the first year of her bitter widowhood, referring to the last three weeks of Lincoln's life, she wrote: "Down the Potomac, he was almost boyish in his mirth & reminded me, of his original nature, what I had always remembered of him, in our own home—free from care, surrounded by those he loved so well & by *whom*, he was so idolized." [3]

It was the destiny of the Lincolns to live the latest years of their married life in the pitiless ordeal of war, personal sorrow, and fiercely ungenerous publicity. In an unfriendly White House these cruel forces were to beat upon an ailing woman in her forties whose lack of emotional balance unfitted her for the strain; in different manner they bore upon a harried President whose deepening sadness was a matter of general comment.[4] It was well for them that their earlier years had not been without their meed of daily happiness.

Something of all that those years of married life had meant and a consciousness that a certain phase of life had closed, might well have been in Lincoln's mind when he came to speak the moving words of his farewell to Springfield on February 11, 1861. He referred to events of deep personal meaning, the birth of his children and the loss of little Eddie. His words suggest that other domestic joys and griefs were in the unexpressed mental picture of those years. His utterance seemed tinged with premonitory homesickness for something past which, in retrospect, he found good.[5]

---

[3] Sandburg and Angle, *Mary Lincoln*, 242.

[4] The life of the Lincolns in Washington will be treated in a later companion work.

[5] In the present chapter on the Lincolns it has not been deemed necessary to include any account of Lincoln and Mary Owens, or Lincoln and Ann Rutledge. For a critical study of the Ann Rutledge story, and for some reference to Mary Owens, see vol. II, appendix.

CHAPTER IV

NORTH AND SOUTH

THAT America, devoted to peace and busy with the affairs of a growing nation, should have become a snarling arena of internal conflict, however voluminously explained, is a matter whose "causes" seem unconvincing. It happened; otherwise it would seem incredible. Psychological and social forces that engendered conflict, untoward incidents that aggravated it, have often been presented. They have become tiresome. In any recital of such forces it is important to remember that, by a different selection of subject matter, exactly the same period could be represented as one of progress, peaceable endeavor, hope-filled activity, and daily living. It is a question of trying to see a period as it was with all its crowded factors, instead of reading back from a later day and seeing only elements of discord. The ugly fate that showed itself in the sixties has caused the fifties to be read in terms of sectionalism and strife. It was as if the saner activities of the nation, the main purpose and essence of its life, had gone for nothing.

The menace of sectional bickering was not wholly grasped until its forces had passed the point where sanity and reason could check them. Its patterns were distortions. Its types of thought and propaganda were negations of essential truth. It is only fairly recently that some of its abnormal intensities have been duly exposed.[1] America was many things: "The Greater New England, The Ohio Valley, The Old Northwest, The Blue Grass regions, The Lower South, The Southwest, and The Prairies." Though the regions were many, there were, as Avery Craven has pointed out, four principal ones: "The North-

[1] These factors of strife are marshaled, interpreted, and effectively presented in *The Coming of the Civil War*, by Avery Craven (1942).

east, The Old South, The Northwest, and The Southwest." [2] Steady advance to subdue the wilderness, to master and occupy the vast national domain, had "meant modifications in economic life." In their pioneering, in going back to "first processes," [3] in facing compelling tasks of social order in new environments, the men of expanding America had not merely copied the old. The inland North was not a replica of New England; Texas was not another South Carolina.

Yet patterns of actual life were overlooked. A nation of many diverse areas and groups was oversimplified into a concept of two sections. Then a further trick was played: the two sections were pictured as hopelessly antagonistic. It was not merely North *and* South; it was North *against* South. Southerners might have cultural and financial dealings with the North and with Europe through the North. Men of Boston might be unaware that Virginians and Georgians should be deemed enemies or human opposites. No matter: let politicians and agitators work on them with pamphlets, tracts, and campaign speeches, let the stock phrases of sectionalism be repeated often enough, and there would come a wretched day when, "to the astonishment of the actors themselves," an explosion would be set off by an incident or occasion that was not validly disruptive but "comparatively trifling." [4]

Influences making for peace were of the quieter sort. They were not a matter of blare and noise. They attracted insufficient attention. Alarms tending toward war, on the other hand, were loud and vociferous. Their appeal was not to reason. Their menace was in a kind of emotional unbalance. Their language was that of name calling, shibboleths, epithets, tirades. Such mental currents bore within themselves the power to upset normal life and to precipitate a major conflict that no majority in any section would have deliberately willed. One of the most colossal of misconceptions is the theory that fundamental motives produce war. The glaring and obvious fact is the artificiality of war-making agitation.

I

It was not for any solid validity in itself that sectional antagonism became ominous. In a whipped-up crisis it is not enough to offset

[2] *Ibid.*, 5. [3] *Ibid.* [4] *Ibid.*, 3.

fanaticism with an equal amount of reason; somehow fanaticism seems to go farther. The decades prior to 1860 were years of notable achievement in western expansion, railroad development, growth of a brilliant merchant marine, education, science, discovery, invention, industrial advance, prairie agriculture, business organization, humanitarianism, literature, and intellectual life. The "cosmopolitan metropolis" that rose out of the Chicago mud on the shore of Lake Michigan and "gradually lifted itself by its own boot straps" [1] was an American fact. So was the series of Goodyear rubber patents, and the ambitious department store of A. T. Stewart of New York's Broadway. So also the Astor Library, the benefactions of George Peabody, the iron establishments of Pennsylvania, the oil drillings, the Morse telegraph, the Western Union Telegraph Company, the Cooper Institute, the *Atlantic Monthly*, the Saturday Club of New England's elite,[2] the western stage coach, the elevator, the balloon, the tireless struggles of Cyrus Field that would one day produce an Atlantic cable, the forward surge of steamer traffic on the Mississippi and the Great Lakes, the superb Yankee clipper, the new contact with the far orient, the spectacular era that was opening in California, the undaunted captains of the Gloucester fisheries, the many hopeful young colleges, the amazing quantity and energy of American newspapers, the Southern agricultural reforms, the rise of teeming commonwealths in newer parts of the South, the network of canals, the unceasing public works, and the masses of newly arrived immigrants.[3] All of this, and vastly more, was America. It somehow does not fit into the picture of an irrepressible conflict.

One could add that sectionalism was an American fact, but in this overworked field it is essential to avoid distortions. It has not yet been satisfactorily demonstrated that sectional tensions were greater than the possible elasticity of the Union; available resources of the Union were not put into full play while factors of sectional strife

---

[1] A. C. Cole, *The Irrepressible Conflict*, 21–22.

[2] Edward Waldo Emerson, *The Early Years of the Saturday Club, 1855–1870*.

[3] Anyone can conjure up his own picture of prewar America. To encompass the vast scene is impossible, yet some effort to see it whole is needful to correct sectional distortion. If in the above enumeration such things as the Goodyear patent and the Morse telegraph originated a considerable time before the war, they were part of the technical advance which one associates with that era, however backward it may seem by present standards. For comprehensive glimpses see Cole, *Irrepressible Conflict*, chaps. 1 and 2; Carl Sandburg, *Abraham Lincoln: The War Years*, I, 8 ff.

were greatly overplayed. Differences between North and South—e. g., industrial interests in one region and agricultural in another—were by no means inconsistent with a diversified and well rounded nation. Large Southern areas truly did not want to leave the Union. Particular grievances, when calmly considered, by no means amounted to serious injury of one section by another. Matters related to slavery offered no such injury, nor did the ante-bellum tariff, which existed by reason of Southern votes. Fear of future Republican action in the restriction of international trade did cause Southern apprehension, but it cannot be shown historically that the Union was broken for this reason. If sectionalism was a factor, so was integration. The very genius of the American federal system is multiplicity within unity. Southerners who ardently supported the Union would constitute a long and distinguished roster. Cohesive interests on these shores had as much valid popular basis as those tendencies that worked for division, subdivision, and Balkanization. If the question is raised whether the South was rightly entitled to its own type of integration, the answer is that in fact the movement for disunion was not promoted on an all-Southern level; coöperationists who wanted so grave a problem to be handled in that way were successfully opposed by the South-Carolina type of precipitate, uncoöperative, separate-state secession.

If one turns from sectional strife to regional values, there indeed is a subject worthy of study. The distinctive flavor of Southern culture was a priceless contribution to American civilization, if only the emphasis could have been centered on constructive contribution instead of upon truculent or ingrowing sectionalism. Statesmen who saw this were the ones who had a service to give. There was no need to blame the South for local attachment; such a sentiment was not only pardonable but wholesome. With all its variety and diversity the South was one in regional consciousness and cultural patterns. It had its plantation economy, its musical speech, its sense of orderly society, its emphasis upon human worth above riches, its chivalric honor, its habits and patterns of ancestral pride, hospitality, and *noblesse oblige*. The supreme beauty of Natchez mansions, the urbanity of Charleston, the unique flavor of Royal Street in New Orleans, were unrivaled elsewhere. The South, in its vocabulary, local settings and ways of life, rose above the commonplace and added richly to the American heritage. In popular literature, Northern audiences came long ago to accept this. In the longer run, in song and story, it is the South that has won the decision at Appomattox.

II

In studying the "prewar" years it is easier to note provocative episodes than to untangle conflicting threads of interest and causation. A sharp mid-century crisis had resulted from the Mexican War with its vast acquisition of new territory, and in 1850 it took all the statesmanship of such men as Henry Clay, Stephen A. Douglas, and Daniel Webster to prevent a break. Robert Barnwell Rhett of South Carolina favored disunion then, but the convention of Southern delegates which convened at Nashville, though not representing all the South, offered a forum by which opinions were aired and consequences weighed. The advantages of secession were faced and studied cooperatively in contrast to its evils and in the light of concessions at Washington. In the outcome, secessionists did not carry the South. Never, in fact, was secession to carry "the South" in any all-over popular vote or general conference.

After voluminous debate there evolved the Compromise of 1850: this was a series of enactments by Congress intended to allay, perchance to end, disruptive sectional strife. California came into the Union free; new territories (Utah and New Mexico) were organized without national statutory prohibition of slavery; ultimate slave or free status was to be determined by incoming states "as their constitution . . . [might] prescribe"; boundaries were adjusted between Texas and New Mexico; the slave trade (not slavery) was prohibited in the District of Columbia; and Federal processes for the recovery of fugitive slaves were made so drastic, one-sided, and destructive of civil rights (if Negroes had rights) that the law of 1850 was hard to square with the Constitution, or with elemental justice. Both sections had yielded something in this solution, which had not pleased anti-slavery elements. To speak of what each "side" gained or lost, however, was misleading. It was a stupid fallacy to conceive that all the vast teeming interests of "the North" were bound up with one segment of the compromise, and those of "the South" with the other.

Despite the 1850 settlement, balance remained uneasy, and when in 1854 it became necessary to devise a form of territorial organization for the "Platte country"—the areas of Kansas, Nebraska, and the Dakotas—old phrases and shibboleths were tiresomely repeated and the nation was again stretched on the sectional rack with all the old tensions and a few more. With his leadership among Northern Democrats and his specialization in western problems, Senator Stephen A. Douglas pushed through the Kansas-Nebraska act which applied, as in the compromise measures of 1850, "the principle of non-intervention by Congress with slavery in the States and Territories." It was specifically stated that the intent of the act was "not to legislate slavery into any Territory or State, nor to exclude it therefrom." While they were territories, the people were, by this act, "perfectly free to . . . regulate their domestic institutions in their own way, subject . . . to the Constitution of the United States." When ready to become states, the territories were to be received into the Union with or without slavery, depending upon the provisions of their constitutions. The time-honored principle of local self-government was thus to control both the territorial phase and that of statehood.

The main purpose of Douglas's bill had not been to deal with the slavery question at all. It is strange how many historical readers have missed the patent fact that the law was framed for the broad regions designated as Kansas and Nebraska. In these areas slavery and the prospect of future slavery were of negligible importance. The reason for the bill was that people were moving into those regions. They needed a government. In the accepted American sense, when new lands were opened up in the West, that necessarily meant a territorial organization, a regime under national sovereignty and under congressional regulation, yet with representative government for its own affairs.

Many interests, including Douglas's own Chicago constituents and those who were promoting a transcontinental railroad, were urging that a territorial government be provided. Such a system in that area was long overdue and could not be endlessly deferred. That in reality was the problem, but by a perverse fate any territorial legislation in the fifties, though prompted by familiar American pioneer needs, would have to go far out of its rightful setting and take account of what was emotionally called "the issue of slavery." This did not follow because of any reason pertaining to the region itself, nor was it true that an over-all code covering every phase of domestic institutions had to be included in a law for the creation of a territory. Horse stealing, for example, was not mentioned when such a law was passed in Congress, yet the territorial government could deal with horse stealing and a hundred other matters not specified in the act of territorial organization. In 1854, however, slavery in the territories was a topic on which every politician had to make a speech, and that in spite of the fact that both major parties—the Whigs and the Democrats—had agreed to the pacifying legislation of 1850. Mental patterns were obscuring realities. In the noise and clamor of the day an unhampered examination of territorial needs for their own sake had become impossible.

Douglas had not created the slavery issue. He was never a sectional agitator. He was a responsible national leader with a task to perform, a member of the Senate charged with devising a program by which westerners could live under an American type of government. He had to come through with a bill, the kind of bill that would stand some chance of being enacted in the year 1854 by the particular members who then sat in Congress. By leaving the matter of slavery for the people of the territories to determine as they wished, he went as far in avoiding the emotionally disturbing aspects of the slavery question as it seemed possible to go. Even now it is difficult to see how any more reasonable bill could then have passed Senate and House and have been signed by the President, Franklin Pierce. Antislavery people, for instance, had no better chance in 1854 than that offered by the Douglas bill; it was in fact a very good chance.[1]

If the people of a territory wanted to, reasoned Douglas, they could keep slavery out. (That was before the Dred Scott decision by the Supreme Court, but even that decision was not to shake Douglas from his position in favor of local self-government for the territories.) If they had a Kansas need or a Nebraska use for slavery—a hundred-to-one chance—they could establish it by approved constitutional processes. It was not that they should have what Douglas should dictate, but what they should choose. It was "popular sovereignty." Douglas believed in it. It was the only formula that seemed to him possible or practicable at the time. It was utterly unjust to accuse Douglas of

---

[1] On Douglas and the Kansas-Nebraska bill, see George Fort Milton, *The Eve of Conflict: Stephen A. Douglas and the Needless War*, 96–154; Frank H. Hodder, "The Railroad Background of the Kansas-Nebraska Act," *Miss. Vall. Hist. Rev.*, XII, 3–22 (1925).

consigning a naturally free community to the demon of slavery. A few years later, when a constitutional trick for Kansas was devised which would have fixed slavery upon a people wishing its abolition, no one opposed that trick more strenuously, nor with more hazard in political prestige, than Douglas.

III

As it turned out, all the old troubles were stirred up after the passage of Douglas's bill. It is probable that they would have been equally stirred up by any alternative law on the subject. If sectional reactions were stimulated by a law intended to subordinate the slavery question and hold it in proper proportion, how much more would such reactions have been stirred by a law to fasten slavery upon the territories, or to impose abolition. The latter might have been partially possible in 1820, though even then the matter was arbitrarily settled by latitude, not principle; but the Missouri Compromise, however consonant with the earlier concept of national housekeeping, was in 1854 beyond the sphere of practical politics. Times had changed. Many who were later to become good-and-true Republicans had refused to support the free-soil principle in the presidential election of 1848.

Times changed again, and men who had wanted slavery agitation muted in 1848, together with those who never wanted it muted, proceeded to use such agitation for a new party formed in 1854. The Republican party, whose story will not be attempted here, rose from early mass meetings (as at Jackson, Michigan, and Ripon, Wisonsin), spread rapidly in local movements, held its first national convention in 1854, and entered its first presidential campaign in 1856.[1] It evolved

---

[1] See William Starr Myers, *The Republican Party, a History* (1928); Francis Curtis, *The Republican Party . . . 1854–1904* (1904); Ruhl J. Bartlett, *John C. Frémont and the Republican Party* (Ohio State University *Studies*, Contributions in Hist. and Pol. Science, XIII); Andrew W. Crandall, *The Early History of the Republican Party, 1854–1856* (1930). Various attempts have been made to give a date and a locality for the "birth" of the party, but to speak in this sense of preliminary movements, local meetings, conventions, and the like, is misleading. Sherman W. Wakefield (*How Lincoln Became President*, 51, 69), refers to the meetings at Ripon, Wisconsin, Jackson, Michigan, and Springfield, Illinois, all in 1854, as occasions from which no permanent results followed. In the matter of unbroken continuity, he considers that what is known as the national Republican party "was born in Bloomington, Illinois, on May 29, 1856." Beveridge (II, 356) points out that on February 22, 1856 "the new party was organized on a national basis"

by a coalescence of various elements differing among themselves, including Democrats, Whigs, Free-Soilers, and Knownothings. Their original point of union was the "Wilmot proviso" doctrine that slavery must be excluded from national territory. In its founding there was enthusiasm, idealism, and withal the enlisting of thousands of men of high principle. Some, however, went into the new movement for lack of any other place to go in a day when old party patterns were dissolving. To promote a cause was the purpose of some; to have a party to belong to, was the motive of others; to make the party an end in itself and a vehicle for obtaining office was to become the interest of politicians.

The Republican party came upon the scene in an age of storm and stress. Kansas, intended as a normal American pioneer region, became so much a center of artificial agitation that Kansans were not allowed to live their own lives. "Bleeding Kansas" became a slogan. It suited distant outsiders to make it bleed. The real story of Kansas as a place to which people went to make homes has been obscured amid a welter of abolition agitation, artificially stimulated settlement, border-ruffian brawls, bogus legislatures, fraudulent constitutional devices, furious debates remote from Kansas itself, proslavery truculence, party conflict, and *opera bouffe* "wars." Kansas has been called a "state of mind." With equal truth it could be said that things un-Kansan constituted the national state of mind under which the birth-pangs of Kansas were endured. Had the territory been let alone, as was its sister Nebraska, a different story would have been told. The manner in which Kansas was used, abused, distorted, "investigated," and propagandized for partisan purposes is hard to realize. That a generation which could not settle Kansas without all this hysteria would soon find itself drawn into a maelstrom of civil war, is one of the few plausible things of the period.

While Kansas was thus playing, not its true part as a pioneer community, but a forced role as sectional troublemaker, many unsavory ingredients were being added to the witches' brew. Men were taking sides. A party that was entirely sectional was vigorously launched. Fire eaters, North and South—the Northern variety being as deadly

at Pittsburgh. In *Proceedings of the First Three Republican National Conventions*, 3–13, the formation of "the Republican Association of Washington," D. C. by a small group on June 19, 1855, is mentioned as the earliest organization of record, but the Pittsburgh meeting of February 1856 is treated as the national beginning.

as the Southern—were demonstrating how a small minority could become a great menace. Disturbance was engendered by men of honest intent. Humanitarian endeavor was taking a tack which involved abuse of the whole South, misrepresentation of slavery, and emphasis upon the slaveholder's brutality as if that were the typical Southern quality. To Southerners the word "Yankee" was becoming both a word of scorn and a label for all Northerners.

A new phraseology was coming into the language. Men spoke of "Beecher's Bibles," "doughfaces," "Black Republicans," "slaveocrats," "slave breeding," "a Southern platform," "a covenant with death [the Constitution]," "the Northern Democracy," "the Southern Democracy," "squatter sovereignty," "lawful property," "bogus delegates," "Northern men of Southern sentiments," [2] and of the day "when the Senate and the House shall swarm with Sumners and Lovejoys." [3] Words of hate, epithets that made it unrespectable to do otherwise than despise a whole class, or party, or area, phrases that burned and rankled (they cannot all be repeated here)—such was the jargon, not of most Americans perhaps, but of enough to create those mental images that rest on repetition and familiarity rather than on real content or rational thought. Such made-up images too often control the governance of men.

There was the tendency to associate slaveholding interests with expansion beyond the border. This would then be assailed both as a menacing wave of foreign conquest and as a program of slavery extension. Fuel for such assaults was supplied by adventuresome filibustering schemes, abortive though they were, in Cuba, Mexico's lower California, and Nicaraugua. Since these were not unlike earlier Texan episodes that entailed serious sectional troubles, men could not help asking themselves where it would all lead. Slavery in the world view was regarded as an anachronism, an abuse, a practice inharmonious with modern civilization; yet American ships were illicitly engaging in an international slave trade which was contrary to American law and in conflict with Britain's efforts to suppress the traffic by international coöperation. In such matters the United States had to speak internationally as a slave power, or as a nation that

[2] Said opprobriously of such men as Franklin Pierce of New Hampshire and James Buchanan of Pennsylvania as if it were a base thing for a Northern man to work with Southern fellows.

[3] D. L. Dumond, ed., *Southern Editorials on Secession*, 155.

recognized slavery, when other nations were treating it as an abomination and trying to stamp it out.

Sneers against the South as shiftless and unenlightened produced indignant reaction. Tempers of statesmen were on edge. They had been so for years. In December 1849 there had been bedlam in Congress when R. K. Meade of Virginia called William Duer of New York "a liar, sir." A duel was with difficulty averted, and, to quote the record, "Indescribable confusion followed—threats, violent gesticulations, calls to order, and demands for adjournment were mingled together." [4] The sergeant at arms raised high his mace, which people had thought a mere ornament or symbol, and somehow business was resumed without a knock-down fight, but a dangerous point had been reached if men could not debate, organize, and legislate without personal explosions. What would now be called pulp melodrama—*Uncle Tom's Cabin,* published (in book form) in 1852—became a sensation, reaching a sale of 300,000 copies the first year. Though its author, Harriet Beecher Stowe, had been able to see good in Southerners, the book functioned as an antislavery tract and a slogan of pious conflict.

Westerners were demanding liberal homestead legislation, which men of the South were resisting. A plan for establishing colleges to teach agriculture and the mechanical arts with Federal land-grant aid, originating in Illinois, met also the obstacle of Southern opposition. Economic rivalries between North and South were aired and fanned in the pages of *DeBow's Review*—an influential Southern publication—and in the proceedings of Southern commercial conventions. Northern and Southern groups were contending for control of a future transcontinental railway. Immigrants crowding in from Europe made for Northern destinations by the hundreds of thousands in the fifties; they were tending to produce in portions of the North a human type quite different from the native-grounded population of the South.

Questions pertaining to slavery, however, were the focal points of trouble and dissension. Paradoxically the matter of slavery was both enlarged and constricted. It was enlarged in agitation as if the very essence of all Southern life depended on the peculiar institution, and as if the slightest breath of criticism directed against human

[4] *Cong. Globe,* 31 Cong., 1 sess., 27; Craven, *The Coming of the Civil War,* 247.

bondage involved an attack upon vital Southern rights. At the same time, as will appear in later pages, the specific disputes that caused political wrangling did not touch large questions of slavery at all, being rather concerned with minor selected aspects such as western territorial status and recovery of fugitives. The broad question whether the fifteen slave states should keep their slaves was beyond controversy as a problem of American government within the Constitution; virtually no one in responsible political life was assailing this right. What should be done about an almost non-existent slave population in the West, or about a small trickle of runaway bondsmen, was magnified into an issue altogether out of scale with its importance.[5]

Pamphlets and books gave to slavery the aura of political, philosophical, social, economic, and religious sanction. Science, humanity, and fundamental instinct were marshaled in support of an institution which in fact was crumbling and declining in the presence of nineteenth century tendencies. In a made-up volume called *The Pro-Slavery Argument* these discussions became to many Southerners a kind of bible, to be set alongside the book entitled *Cotton Is King,* by David Christy, published in 1855. Scant hearing was given to realistic Southerners who saw the inadequacies of slavery and favored a more frank discussion of its merits and defects. The more Southern "institutions" were attacked, the more ardently were they defended. Arguments buttressing slavery were identified with basic Southern loyalty. Their hold in the press and in political discussion was dominant. Dissenting opinions were regarded as unorthodox and palpably false.

IV

No such widespread hearing or support was given in the North to antislavery screeds and tracts. Prewar abolitionist movements in the Northern states could claim among their followers only a tiny minority. Such leaders as Garrison and Lovejoy found in the North not only lack of support but scorn and persecution, and, in Lovejoy's case, fatal attack. That abolitionism existed at all was the serious thing;

[5] For the problem of fugitive slaves, see below, pp. 238–240. If there were slaveholders for whom the problem of the runaway may have been serious, this was especially true in the upper South or on the border, but in these sections secession *per se* (fundamental discontent with the Union) had small support.

it was exaggerated and advertised in the South out of all relation to its nationwide significance. As for William Lloyd Garrison, it could not be said that any sizable movement centered in this lone agitator. He offended the churches; he was mobbed in Boston; he lacked the support even of antislavery elements in New England; still less was he the guiding spirit of any antislavery crusade in the country. He was a free-lance journalist, tireless for the cause to which he devoted a burning and sincere loyalty, but utterly lacking in widespread influence.

Non-Garrisonian antislavery influences were already progressing toward national organization, and it was a fortuitous rather than a significant matter when Garrison, returning on a wave of reflected glory from England in 1833, prematurely organized at Philadelphia the American Anti-Slavery Society of which not himself, but Arthur Tappan, became the first president. In that year his *Liberator* had fewer than four hundred white subscribers. Never did its full subscription list exceed three thousand. As Gilbert H. Barnes has written, Garrison "had no qualifications for leadership. His one office in the society, secretary of foreign correspondence, was soon resigned; and so long as the national organization held together he was never asked to fill another. He was so little a leader that even in the New England Anti-Slavery Society his journal was endured as its official organ for but a brief, unhappy period." [1]

By 1839 the American Anti-Slavery Society was dwindling; in 1840 the national organization as it had existed in the thirties under the Tappans and other such leaders came to an end; it was felt by earnest antislavery men that decentralization was better and that a general society served no useful purpose. It was at this point that Garrison, deciding to capture the society as his own affair, packed its convention with his friends, carrying a boatload of citizens of Lynn, Massachusetts, to New York "at nominal cost, on the understanding that they would cast their votes at Garrison's direction" and using similar methods elsewhere.[2] It was this assembly of "delegates" that gave him the presidency of a now nominal organization from which the better element, such as the Tappans, had withdrawn.

Not Garrison's Northern supporters, but his Southern enemies, made him famous.[3] It was only at a distance that he was erroneously

[1] *The Antislavery Impulse*, 57–58. [2] *Ibid.*, 169. [3] *Ibid.*, 50.

supposed to embody a significant movement. His name cast "a vague and indefinite odium" over the abolition cause which "hampered its growth from the beginning."[4]

Those who did have influence with the small minority groups that conducted abolitionist movements were quite dissociated from Garrison. They included Arthur and Lewis Tappan of New York City, wealthy merchants, opponents of Garrison, philanthropists in many causes, pioneer organizers and financial supporters of the national society; Cassius M. Clay, whose neighbors of Lexington, Kentucky, expelled his *True American* from their cultured city; C. G. Finney, evangelist extraordinary, guiding spirit of the Oneida Community, and early leader of Oberlin College; Angelina and Sarah Grimké; and Angelina's husband, Theodore Dwight Weld, fellow worker in Finney's "holy band." It was Weld who became the chief promoter of abolitionism as an organized crusade. With burning zeal strangely combined with anonymity he marshaled speakers for popular meetings, conducted a lobby at Washington, and produced those pamphlets and tracts which purported to present slavery to the people, but in reality gave only selected instances of inhuman atrocity. If abolitionism is ground for canonization, Weld deserves sainthood more than Garrison.

The impact of the slavery issue upon American churches deserves a word. Long before war broke, secession had taken place among the Baptists and Methodists. In the Methodist church there was nothing resembling a violent attack of Northerners against Southern brethren; indeed there was an effort to smooth things over and to keep the family together. In 1844, however, the national governing body of the church, the general conference, mildly requested a Georgia bishop to desist from exercising episcopal duties while remaining a slaveholder; as a result, Southerners formed the Methodist Episcopal Church South and separation was complete. A Southern Baptist Convention was created in the same year with a similar motive.

It would be a serious mistake, however, to think of abolitionists as having captured the Northern churches. They fell very far short of doing that. While there was considerable antislavery sentiment among Northern Methodists, Baptists, and Quakers, as there might well be in an age of general humanitarian striving, such sentiment was not

[4] Barnes and Dumond, eds., *Weld-Grimké Letters*, I, viii.

always militant, and in general there existed in the ranks of organized religion in the North a considerable, perhaps a prevailing, attitude of abhorrence toward abolitionists as trouble makers, revolutionaries, and dangerous radicals. In the Presbyterian church in Northern states there was divided counsel, many of the socially influential of that sect being either proslavery or averse to agitation. Among Congregationalists there were a few bold abolitionists, but there were also "ardent defenders of the institution." [5] Such men as Finney and Weld, who burned with antislavery zeal, were very much like interlopers in the ecclesiastical field. They were evangelists, not church leaders. They went about exhorting; they made trouble within the churches in their drive for converts; they cared not if their preachings created dissension; they were not concerned with normal church activity; they were frowned upon by such a Congregational stalwart as Lyman Beecher.

In the South the power and prestige of organized religion was so completely enlisted in the cause of slavery that opposite church voices were negligible. Some of the most effective and emphatic writings in defense of slavery were penned by Southern ecclesiastics. This was in no sense surprising. It was but natural that Southern church leaders should be cut to the same pattern as Southerners generally; it was understandable that their guidance and interpretation should conform to the social order of which they and their flocks were a part. A Theodore Parker could contend for abolition in Boston in dissociation from other ministers who denounced him for his free thinking and iconoclasm; he could do this with no thought of being typical of the church. This was not easy even for Parker, whose friends organized a special church which became a social and religious forum; in the South such departure from orthodox and prevalent thought would have led to the most embarrassing and devastating consequences.[6]

Sentiment against slavery in this "ante-bellum" period was not all of a piece. There was a wide range of variation among men who

---

[5] Adelaide A. Lyons, "Religious Defense of Slavery in the North," *Historical Papers*, Trinity College Hist. Soc., Vol. 13, Durham, N. C., 1919, p. 8.

[6] For religion and slavery, with references, see Randall, *Civil War and Reconstruction*, 105–107; G. H. Barnes, *The Antislavery Impulse*, 64–78 (concerning the "rebels" [abolitionist students] at Lane Seminary); *Weld-Grimké Letters*, ed. by G. H. Barnes and D. L. Dumond; H. S. Commager, *Theodore Parker*.

deplored human bondage. Those who assumed to themselves a function of criminal violence and self-immolation to destroy slavery by murdering slaveholders were negligible. John Brown was not the prophet of anything that could be called a movement. Passing over Brown, one could begin the classification of antislavery men with William Lloyd Garrison as representing the extreme. His activity was that of agitator, not of responsible leader. He made no concessions, admitted no difficulties in the path of emancipation, and scorned any recognition of Southern feelings and interests. He and those who stood with him—Wendell Phillips, Thomas Wentworth Higginson, Gerrit Smith, Theodore Parker, and the like—were a small group; they were without serious political influence. It was a ticklish thing for anyone in political life in the North to be stamped with the abolitionist die. Less extreme was such a reformer as Horace Mann. He was vigorously antislavery, yet his quality was not that of a firebrand and the antislavery cause was not his main specialty. To bracket him with Garrison would be a mistake. Such a man as Joshua R. Giddings was a courageous and tireless advocate of antislavery causes in Congress, but his support was small, his cause was unpopular, and on one occasion, after presenting antislavery resolutions in the House of Representatives, he was "censured by his angry Whig colleagues, who refused him the right even to speak in his own defense.[7] Few indeed went so far as Giddings in futile congressional proceedings. James G. Birney was strong in the faith, but his emphasis was more upon free soil than upon the doings of the Anti-Slavery Society, from which he resigned in 1841. Running as the Liberty party's candidate for President in two elections, he polled only seven thousand votes in 1840, and while his support increased to sixty-five thousand votes in 1844, it constituted less than one-fortieth of the total.[8]

There were still other degrees and shades among those who did

[7] Barnes, *The Antislavery Impulse,* 187–188. On being censured, Giddings resigned, was reëlected by his Western Reserve constituency in Northern Ohio, resumed his antislavery attacks in the House, and escaped further formal censure, being from then on merely endured, but without appreciable influence. See also Robert P. Ludlum, "Joshua R. Giddings, Radical," *Miss. Vall. Hist. Rev.,* XXIII, 49–60 (1936).

[8] Birney "believed slavery to be directly contrary to the fundamental principles upon which the nation was founded; and that Congress not only had the power, but should use it, to abolish slavery in the states," but he emphasized that this end was to be gained by constitutional methods, for he believed that "slavery was not only sinful . . . but incompatible with the Constitution." Dwight L. Dumond, ed., *Letters of James Gillespie Birney, 1831–1857,* I, xix, xxii.

not favor slavery. Charles Francis Adams went for free soil policies, not for abolitionist excess. The same was true of Salmon P. Chase. More moderate than Chase was Lincoln, who did not even support the Free-Soil candidate in 1848. Lincoln was a Whig of democratic impulses whose fundamental antislavery views were held within bounds and were not always carried over into the field of political measures. There were things regarded as proslavery—such as the fugitive-slave law—which Lincoln stood ready to tolerate because they were part of the existing system, and because in matters of practical government Lincoln did not think that a man ought to indulge all his moral or theoretical preferences.[9] In the mild group with Lincoln stood Orville H. Browning of Illinois. Kentucky-born, courtly and old-fashioned, conservative in all things, Browning was nevertheless antislavery in thought; he became a Republican, though he did not remain so for long. He was a man of considerable influence; he reached senatorial and cabinet rank in the North; yet in no valid sense was he ever anti-Southern. These are selected examples, but it is only in taking examples of living human beings of the time that correct concepts can be formed. The Yankee world was made up of many elements, but among its varied millions, haters of the South were far from typical. When degrees and groups are noted, Lincoln's place is found to be many miles away from that of radicals and firebrands.

V

Two violent events in May of 1856, both relating to slavery, were like a firebell in the night: the Potawatomie massacre in Kansas and the Sumner-Brooks affair in the United States Senate. At the time of corn planting in Kansas—they actually did plant corn there—Old John Brown of Osawatomie, a fugitive criminal and bloodthirsty fanatic, stepped out at night with several of his sons to do as foul a deed as the annals of that turbulent territory record. At a time when murders in Kansas had been few despite near-clashes of armed groups claiming militia or "posse" status, a party led by John Brown, Sr., attacked the homes of proslavery families on Potawatomie Creek and killed five men: William Sherman, Allen Wilkinson, and three men

[9] *Works*, X, 65 (April 4, 1864). For Lincoln's disinclination to disturb slavery in the states, see below, p. 297; vol. II, 127

of the name of Doyle. For this crime the perpetrators were never properly prosecuted, though proslavery men took prompt revenge in what was called the "battle of Osawatomie" in which one of the Brown sons, Frederick, was killed.[1] Other events in Kansas loom large in the narrative of those times. Such were the so-called Wakarusa War and the sack of Lawrence: the "war" was a bloodless mustering of motley groups in and around Lawrence; the proslavery raid upon that town, though an outrage, amounted to little more than the destruction of various buildings, chiefly the free-state hotel. If the doings of John Brown had not occurred, violence upon human life would have been far less serious.

Kansas was peculiar. It was not viewed for what it was, but for what outside agitators pictured it to be. The concept of Kansas as a community of people "over head and ears—not in fighting—but in farming," to quote a contemporary newspaper, was "not . . . permitted to find lodgment in the public mind." [2] If stories of violence were played down by newspapers, it was when the perpetrators were their own party associates. The Republican press minimized the provocative deeds of such as Brown and James H. Lane, while always keeping up a high state of agitation in Kansan matters, giving particularly lurid accounts of proslavery "border ruffians." On the other hand, proslavery newspapers appealed for more Southern immigrants, denounced Lane, issued calls to arms, and did their part in fomenting what came to be called "civil war" within the territory. Squatter sovereignty became a turbulent thing not so much because of genuine conflicts of local interests, but because a minority of trouble makers, aided by outside agitators, made turbulence rather than reasonable pacification their business. In spite of all this, pacification went farther than one would realize when reading only partisan chronicles.

Occurring simultaneously with the Kansan trouble, the Sumner-Brooks affair produced a sensation throughout the nation. The senator from Massachusetts, in a speech on the floor of the Senate, May 19–20, 1856, had assailed slaveowners, denounced South Carolina, and indulged in personal abuse of an absent South Carolinian senator,

---

[1] Conditions in Kansas are elaborately treated and fully documented in James C. Malin, *John Brown and the Legend of Fifty-Six*, published in 1942. This rigidly critical book belongs in a category of its own; it is the first major study of John Brown by one who is primarily a historian.

[2] Malin, 109.

Andrew P. Butler. The speech had "abounded in such . . . terms as harlot, mistress, rape, pirate, tyrant, falsifier, assassin, thug, swindler, and criminal." [3] Coming at a time when sectional tension was bad enough in all conscience, this verbal assault was not offhand. It was a deliberate and studied insult to Butler. It was not typical of the North, and little harm would have come from ignoring it (supposing that were possible); but to the mind of Preston Brooks of South Carolina, relative of Butler and member of the House of Representatives, such a gross personal insult could not go unpunished. Confronting Sumner with all the self-control he could muster, Brooks stated that it was his duty to punish him. Then, wielding his cane, he rapped the senator with repeated blows upon the head, leaving the statesman "bloody and insensible." [4]

If, in studying this incident, one wishes an insight into Southern nuances and implications, he will find them developed by Charles S. Sydnor.[5] In the courtly Southerner's unwritten code of conduct personal matters were vital, but they were to be handled out of court. It was a man's own business to defend his honor or that of his family; to expect lawyers, judges, and juries to regulate an affair of honor was not the gentleman's way. Sumner being no gentleman in Brooks's view, the occasion did not call for a duel, but it did call for chastisement. Combat according to the *code duello* was not appropriate: a cowhide whip or other weapon of dishonor might have been chosen; a cane served as well, and the significance of its use would not be missed by Carolinian friends.

That was one side of the question; the other side was seen in the angry emotion of Sumner's friends who found a new theme for denunciation of Southern "brutality." The senator became a hero and the incident not only assisted the Republican party, but intensified all those elements of discord on both sides which moderates were pathetically hoping to repress.

VI

Such were some of the factors at work in the troubled fifties. There has been no effort to review them in detail. To do so would require

[3] Charles S. Sydnor, "The Southerner and the Laws," *Jour. of So. Hist.*, VI, 22 (Feb., 1940).

[4] *Ibid.*

[5] *Ibid.*, 3–23.

volumes. Lincoln knew of them as he studied documents, perused the newspapers, and read the controversial literature of the time. At times he seemed a passive observer. He was one of many. Moderate ideas, of the sort which he entertained, seemed unfortunately dormant, however deeply significant they might be. Lincoln was slow. In the early formation of the Republican party he was not out in front.[1] Something was happening to the country; people were using a new terminology; yet Lincoln still clung to the old. The Whig party had meant much to him. It hurt him that this historic party of the nation, a party of North and South which had never hoped to elect a President except with Southern support, was crumbling and passing into oblivion. In an elaborate speech on questions of the day at Peoria on October 16, 1854, a speech which occupies over seventy pages in his *Works,* he did not even mention the Republican party whose initial organization was by that time well launched.[2] Nor in this speech did he use the awkward early name for that party, which was "anti-Nebraska." With a disturbed glance at the changing times and a wistful desire for old alignments, Lincoln wrote as late as August 1855 to Joshua F. Speed:

> You enquire where I now stand— That is a disputed point— I think I am a whig; but others say there are no whigs, and that I am an abolitionist— When I was at Washington I voted for the Wilmot Proviso [for prohibition of slavery in national territory] as good as forty times, and I never heard of any one attempting to unwhig me for that— I now do no more than oppose the *extension* of slavery—
>
> I am not a Know-Nothing— That is certain— . . . As a nation, we began by declaring that *'all men are created equal—'* We now practically read it 'all men are created equal, *except negroes'* When the Know-Nothings get control, it will read 'all men are created equal, except negroes, *and foreigners, and Catholics.'* When it comes to this I shall prefer emigrating to some country where they make no pretense of loving liberty . . . ."[3]

Where did Lincoln stand? He did not favor those influences that were making for disruption. He was willing to rest upon the Com-

[1] When an effort was made in October 1854 to create at Springfield a Republican organization for Illinois, Lincoln neither joined nor encouraged the attempt. "A Republican State Central Committee was appointed, which included Abraham Lincoln, but he took no part in the convention [at Springfield] and refused to serve on the Committee." Wakefield, *How Lincoln Became President,* 50.

[2] *Works,* II, 190–262. For further comment on this speech, see below, p. 105.

[3] *Ibid.,* II, 286–287. (Though Nicolay and Hay's alterations, of punctuation etc., are unimportant, the text is given above as Lincoln wrote it.)

promise of 1850 with its concessions to the South. He was willing to let South Carolina continue to have the same number of representatives in Congress as Maine, though Maine had more than twice the number of white people.[4] He would go for Union-saving, but only when he believed that the means employed would actually save the Union.[5] Reorientation in the challenging fifties was difficult for him. He did not like being unwhigged. All this stirring of new factors sent him back to the contemplation of fundamentals. In this he was not overawed by phrases or labels. "Stand," he said, "with anybody that stands right. Stand with him while he is right, and part with him when he goes wrong. Stand with the Abolitionist in restoring the Missouri Compromise, and stand against him when he attempts to repeal the fugitive-slave law. In the latter case you stand with the Southern disunionist. What of that? You are still right. In both cases you are right. In both cases you expose the dangerous extremes. In both you stand on middle ground, and hold the ship level and steady. In both you are national, and nothing less than national. This is the good old Whig ground. To desert such ground because of any company, is to be less than a Whig—less than a man—less than an American." [6]

New party alignments being essential for all who had thought they were Whigs, and for others as well, Lincoln made his party affiliation definite, though still avoiding the name Republican, in the earlier months of 1856. The traditional account, accepted by a long line of Lincoln writers, is that Herndon maneuvered Lincoln into the party by a kind of trick, signing his partner's name to a published call for a meeting of Sangamon County men to choose delegates for the state convention to be held in Bloomington. There are, however, excellent reasons for doubting the Herndon version, especially insofar as it implies that Lincoln was not managing his own party alignment in this formative period.

On February 22, 1856, a group of Illinois editors of the "anti-Nebraska" persuasion gathered at Decatur.[7] Several interesting points

[4] *Ibid.*, II, 233–234. [5] *Ibid.*, II, 236. [6] *Ibid.*, II, 243.

[7] As to Lincoln's importance in these party beginnings in Illinois, we have a clue in a letter from Paul Selby (young Jacksonville editor who promoted the Decatur meeting of editors) to Richard Yates, dated at Springfield, February 14, 1856. Selby wrote: "I have had an interview with Mr. Lincoln to-day, ... He tells me he thinks he will try and have some business at Decatur at the time of the Convention. Can't you do the same. I think we all agree as to what is to be done . . . ." A postscript suggests concern that party strategy be not patterned in terms of "too much *ultraism*." Yates MSS.

about this gathering should be noted: it marked the "real beginning of the Republican party in Illinois";[8] it was definitely preliminary to the state convention held at Bloomington in May; it summoned the clans for that very gathering; its business was party organization; it created a state central committee which included Herndon; and, significantly, all this was done with Lincoln present and in attendance, he being the one non-editor.[9] It is hard to believe that Herndon would have had the appointment to the central committee without Lincoln's consent. It was Herndon's business to organize the new movement in his own area, chiefly Sangamon County, and he was acting in this recognized capacity when on May 10 he issued a call for a convention of Sangamon County men. The county gathering met on May 24; the Bloomington state convention was to come on May 29. Such was the relation of Lincoln and Herndon that if the junior partner took action committing the senior partner, the latter probably knew and approved of it.

Herndon's garrulous correspondence in this period—e. g., with Theodore Parker and Lyman Trumbull—gives no contemporary corroboration of the later biography version so far as it implied that Lincoln was drawn into the new party by Herndon's bold stroke and by an unexpected use of his name. Lincoln was capable of speaking for himself; he was careful to make a correction if someone pledged him without authority; he had already participated in the Decatur convention of February; he had been concerned in planning the earlier movements of which both the local Sangamon gathering and the Bloomington convention were the logical results. Herndon may indeed have signed for his partner, but this was because of Lincoln's absence from Springfield; he probably knew Lincoln's wishes in the matter. Herndon himself stated that Lincoln promptly ratified the decision once the call was issued. In any case, on so important a matter as joining a party, Lincoln's motives and plans were

---

[8] Angle, *Lincoln, 1854–1861*, 112.

[9] At the time of the convention Lincoln gave a happily phrased after-dinner speech at the Cassell House in Decatur. Being toasted as the next candidate for the United States Senate, he opened with a story about a man being held up by a robber and giving his note for the money. "Mr. Lincoln then proceeded to address the assemblage for some half hour, in his usual masterly manner, frequently interrupted by the cheers of his hearers." *Illinois State Chronicle* (Decatur), Feb. 28, 1856, p. 1. cc. 6–7.

under his own hat.[10] He did not share all the opinions of those who were pushing the new party; he looked longingly back to Whig days before the new organization was launched; he particularly wished that the party should take a "conservative" (not strongly abolitionist) turn; this very concern, however, was because it was to be his party; from February 1856 it was from the inside that his influence was exerted.

Having become thus committed to the new party, Lincoln took a leading part in this Bloomington convention.[11] Staying at the mansion of the wealthy Judge David Davis (who was later to promote Lincoln's nomination as Republican candidate for President, and still later to withdraw from the party), Lincoln loomed as a leading figure among a small group of influential men whose prestige and conservatism were counted on to make the gathering "as respectable as possible." [12] Without the initial support of such men the new party could hardly have got very far in Illinois in 1856. The problem involved was revealed by Lincoln's concern lest the southern part of the state should be unrepresented—it turned out that a few delegates did appear from that area—and also by the attitude of John Todd Stuart, prominent Whig and first partner of Lincoln, who carefully avoided adherence to the new party.

Conservatives gave the party not only respectability; they supplied its platform, which was written by Orville H. Browning.[13] Hailing the "principles . . . of Washington, Jefferson and their great and good compatriots of the revolution" [14]—this ought to please everyone—the party declaration announced opposition to the existing administration, denounced the effort to force slavery upon Kansas, and favored

---

10 For Herndon's version, see *Herndon's Life of Lincoln* (Angle ed.), 311–312. On this matter the author has been greatly assisted by a well-documented memorandum prepared by David H. Donald, graduate assistant at the University of Illinois, who is preparing a book on Herndon. Newspapers and manuscripts of the period were closely examined by Mr. Donald.

11 This was known as "A State Convention of the Anti-Nebraska party of Illinois." The name "Republican" was avoided, being a term of reproach used by opponents, preceded by the word "Black." Soon after this, however, the term "Republican" was adopted in Illinois. Wakefield, *How Lincoln Became President*, 58–60, 68.

12 George T. Brown, editor of the Quincy *Whig*, to Lyman Trumbull, May 12, 1856, Trumbull MSS.

13 Browning, *Diary*, I, 237.

14 These platitudinous verbalisms of the Republican state platform, written by Browning, are quoted in Beveridge, II, 370.

congressional prohibition of slavery in national territory. On one point the balancing act in the convention was truly amazing. Browning, according to his own statement, prepared "a resolution intended to reconcile both Know nothings and German's to act with us." [15] Finding discordant elements present and taking upon himself the framing of resolutions to harmonize them, he had procured a room, brought leading men of differing opinions together, and, after difficulty, obtained consent to his resolutions. Next day the resolutions he prepared, having been accepted in committee, were "unanimously adopted without change." [16] When one remembers how offensive to Germans and other foreign-born elements were the openly declared views of the Knownothings, this bit of reconciliation deserves a high place in the history of political straddling. At about this time Browning wrote: "We wish, if possible, to keep the party in this state under the control of moderate men, and conservative influences, and if we do so the future destiny of the state is in our own hands—victory will inevitably crown our exertions. On the contrary if rash and ultra counsels prevail all is lost." [17]

With conservatism so prominent in its making, but with feeling on slavery and sectionalism reaching a peak in that sensational month of May 1856, the occasion required something a bit unique in the matter of oratory. In addressing an eminently moderate convention, someone was needed who could make a vigorous and fighting speech. This need was notably supplied by Lincoln, who addressed this party gathering in which "all shades" of opinion had been neatly reconciled and brought it to its feet with cheers for his fervid eloquence. Beveridge has extravagantly called it "the greatest piece of oratory he ever produced." Then he added: ". . . Lincoln had to say things which, for the very same reason that he then spoke them extemporaneously, he never would put on paper for publication thereafter." [18]

This was the alleged "Lost Speech" concerning which a famous legend has arisen. Newspaper reporters, the story goes, were so thrilled by Lincoln's oratory that they gave up trying to take notes, Medill being in a kind of hypnotic trance.[19] But young H. C. Whitney, associate of Lincoln on the law circuit, was in attendance. He kept a

---

[15] Browning, *Diary*, I, 237. [16] *Ibid.*, I, 238.
[17] Browning to Trumbull, May 19, 1856, Trumbull MSS. [18] Beveridge, II, 372.
[19] Statement of Joseph Medill, quoted in Tarbell, *Life of Abraham Lincoln*, I, 295.

cool head, made notes, and many years later, when the lost speech had become famous, he published in *McClure's Magazine* for September 1896 what purported to be a verbatim report of Lincoln's words. Miss Tarbell accepted the Whitney reconstruction of the speech, incorporating copious extracts in her biography; Joseph Medill of the Chicago *Tribune* endorsed its accuracy; Beveridge gave emphasis to the Whitney version and quoted it at length.

By the canons of strict historical criticism, however, the Whitney report stands discredited. As Paul M. Angle has pointed out, Whitney's notes were sketchy. The speech is not included in Whitney's *Life on the Circuit with Lincoln* published in 1892, which is strange if Whitney had kept notes of the text; the report lacks Lincoln's "logical precision"; some who heard it later declared that it "bore no relation" to what Lincoln had said; and finally, a contemporary report of the speech in the Alton *Courier* of June 5, 1856, shows "too great a divergence in content to be easily reconciled." [20]

Considered as oratory, the speech was truly remarkable in its effect upon the immediate audience. Yet it remains lost; [21] its content can only be conjectured; its presentation by Whitney in an alleged verbatim report of an address which lasted an hour and a half, is unjustified; its inclusion in Lincoln's works edited by A. B. Lapsley is an editorial error. The fame of the speech, of course, remains. Herndon said that on this occasion his partner was "seven feet" tall.[22]

Following the state convention at Bloomington the Republicans held a ratification meeting at Springfield, in which Lincoln naturally took part. It was a most curious affair according to Herndon's account. Though all the usual efforts had been made to draw a crowd, the courthouse being the place of assemblage, only three persons appeared, said Herndon, one man in addition to Lincoln and himself. Lincoln writers have usually followed Herndon in treating this incident, but his statement, despite his presence on the occasion, is in error. The *Illinois State Journal* (Republican) reported a large meeting, while the *Illinois State Register,* whose Democratic editor was ready at all times to belittle Republicans, admitted two hundred.[23] At this meeting (June 10), according to the *Journal,* "Lincoln took the stand

[20] Whitney, *Life on the Circuit with Lincoln,* Angle edition, intro., 24–25.
[21] Wakefield, *How Lincoln Became President,* 65.
[22] Herndon (Angle ed.), 313.
[23] See Paul M. Angle's editorial comment in *ibid.,* 315 n.

and pronounced the most logical and finished argument against the evils to be apprehended from the continued aggressions of the slave power, that it has ever been our good fortune to listen to." [24]

VII

In 1856 the Democrats nominated a man whose availability consisted in his having been outside of the country for a number of years. Douglas and Pierce being too close to the tempest of conflict to qualify as candidates, the choice fell upon James Buchanan of Pennsylvania. His career had been that of Federalist, Jacksonian senator, secretary of state under Polk, and diplomat in the capitals of Russia and Britain. His concepts and attitudes were those of Christian piety, orderly government, the rule of law, abhorrence of abolitionist agitation, alarm at the divisive tendencies of Republican policies, and a troubled sense of crisis as the tornado of discord was sweeping over the land. John C. Breckinridge of Kentucky was chosen for Vice President.

The American (Knownothing) party, promoting its prejudice against what were deemed non-American racial groups, nominated ex-President Millard Fillmore for President, and Andrew Jackson Donelson for Vice President.

As if to emphasize its obsoleteness and unimportance, the Whig party—or a pitiful remnant of it—met in Baltimore and went through the motions of a national convention. Instead of offering any candidate of their own in an age when most Whigs had gone into American or Republican ranks (though some preferred the Democratic party) they merely endorsed the candidates of the Knownothings. In the words of Edward Bates, who presided over its demise, this once powerful party "committed suicide, in 1856, and thereby left the nation without a *bodyguard*." [1]

In an era when Republicans were emphasizing Bleeding Kansas, other parties revealed a marked unwillingness to touch the sensitive question of slavery. The Whigs announced no principles but deplored the danger of sectionalism. Spokesmen of the American party made the enlightening statement that on the subject of slavery they stood "upon the principles . . . of the Constitution . . . , yielding noth-

[24] *Illinois State Journal*, June 11, 1856.

[1] Howard K. Beale, ed., *The Diary of Edward Bates* (*Annual Report*, Amer. Hist. Assoc., 1930), 390.

ing more and claiming nothing less." [2] The Democrats resisted all attempts at renewing the agitation concerning slavery and took their stand on "non-interference by Congress with slavery in state and territory, or in the District of Columbia." [3] The Republicans condemned slavery along with polygamy as twin relics of barbarism, and demanded that slavery be excluded from national territory.[4]

This declaration by the Republicans was a part of the platform adopted by their national convention of 1856 at Philadelphia. For presidential candidate the convention chose a man whose name was later to be associated with inefficiency, vindictive radicalism, and anti-Lincoln excess—John C. Frémont, "Pathfinder" and romantic hero. His surname bore, like an exotic flourish, the French accent mark. His merits for high civil office were largely negative; it was felt that he would not offend many people; it would have been difficult for his supporters to demonstrate that he possessed qualities requisite for a responsible leader and chief magistrate of the nation in the difficult fifties. More solid leaders, however, such as Seward, were not pushed forward with vigor; prospects for Republican success at the polls were not bright; it has been remarked that the party selected "a candidate whose defeat in November would not harm the party's future." [5]

For Vice President the Republicans presented William L. Dayton of New Jersey. His only serious rival was Abraham Lincoln, who received 110 votes for Vice President on informal ballot.[6] Orville

---

[2] This solemn statement was issued by the national council of the American party which met at Philadelphia on February 18, 1856. Bancroft, *Seward,* I, 417. The party convention which met at Philadelphia, February 22–25, 1856, did not adopt this resolution, noncommittal as it was, nor did it mention slavery. McKee, *National Conventions,* 101–102.

[3] McKee, *National Conventions,* 92. The quoted words were printed in full capitals.

[4] *Ibid.,* 98.

[5] Milton, *Eve of Conflict,* 230.

[6] H. C. Whitney tells of Lincoln, while attending court in Urbana (June 20, 1856), hearing a report of his receiving 110 votes for the vice-presidential nomination and passing it off with the remark that he thought it was "the other *great man* of the same name from Mass." This account, with additional details, appears in a MS. statement by Whitney, of which a copy was made for Ward H. Lamon. On the margin of the copy appears the comment: "This is not true L." Why Lamon doubted the statement is not known. (The Lamon MS. copy is in the Huntington Library.) Hertz (*Hidden Lincoln,* 390) gives the erroneous reading: "This is not true. H.", incorrectly implying that Herndon doubted the account. Soon after the time this news would have been received Lincoln is known to have been in Urbana, and it is quite possible that he was there as Whitney relates. Whitney, *Life on the Circuit,* Angle ed., 95–96; William B. Archer, in *Journal,* Ill. State Hist. Soc., XII, 273–275 (1919); *Bulletin No. 51,* Abr. Lincoln Assoc., March 1938, 3–5.

H. Browning of Illinois remarked laconically in his diary: "Heard to day of the nomination of Freemont by the Republican Convention at Philadelphia for President. He was not my first choice, but I am content. Would have preferred McLean . . . ." [7]

Lincoln had also preferred McLean (not a very exciting leader), yet he took an active part in the canvass of 1856, making over fifty speeches.[8] Fragments only of these speeches appear in his collected works. The campaign of that year is for the most part an unrecovered chapter in his life. At Galena he spoke vigorously for preservation of the Union, insisting that "All this talk about the dissolving of the Union is humbug." [9] At Kalamazoo [10] he stressed the preservation of a civilization in which "every man can make himself." [11] This type of civilization he considered doubtful of survival if the spread of slavery was not halted. And, as elsewhere, he strongly urged that the election of a Northern President should not be regarded as cause for disunion. He considered it "shameful" that so much was said of dissolution of the Union if Frémont and Dayton were elected.[12] As to Frémont being an "abolitionist," Lincoln answered "no such thing"; he added that he knew "of no word in the language that has been used so much as that one, 'abolitionist,' having no definition." [13]

When election came in November 1856 the popular vote stood: Buchanan 1,838,169; Frémont 1,341,264; Fillmore 874,534. Buchanan received 174 electoral votes Frémont 114, Fillmore 8. Fillmore had only the vote of Maryland; Buchanan carried the rest of the South and border, and in addition the states of Pennsylvania, California, Illinois, Indiana, and New Jersey; all the other commonwealths—including New York and constituting a startling number from the Southern viewpoint—went for the new Republican party. In commenting on the election Lincoln pointed out that voters for Buchanan were "in a minority of the whole people by about four hundred thousand votes" and that Buchanan's opponents were "divided between

---

[7] Browning, *Diary*, I, 241–242. [8] *Works*, VI, 38. [9] *Works*, II, 295 (Aug. 1, 1856).

[10] It is odd that one should speak of "the lost speech" of Lincoln. There are many lost speeches. After long remaining unknown, the speech at Kalamazoo on August 27, 1856, an ambitious extemporaneous effort before a huge crowd, was discovered a few years ago in the files of the Detroit *Daily Advertiser*. For the text of the speech stenographically reported, together with an account of its discovery and the circumstances of its delivery, see Thomas I. Starr, ed., *Lincoln's Kalamazoo Address against Extending Slavery*.

[11] *Ibid.*, 39. [12] *Ibid.*, 40–41. [13] *Ibid.*, 43.

Frémont and Fillmore." He hoped that factions then divided would "let bygones be bygones" and "come together for the future" on the basis of the "central idea" of the "equality of men." [14]

To the sectional disturbances of this overwrought decade the Supreme Court in 1857 made its own contribution. There had arisen the case of Dred Scott, a Missouri slave whose vicissitudes had carried him from slavery into territory made free by law of Congress, and back into slavery. Confused litigation in Missouri was followed by a misleading and fictitious transfer of ownership. Finally, via a Federal court in Missouri, the case found its tedious way into the Supreme Court of the United States.[15] From the impressive bench of that high tribunal nine justices gave nine opinions. Cutting through reams of legal verbosity the historian notes two main points, or doctrines, in the opinion as issued by Chief Justice Roger B. Taney. (1) A Negro, he held, can have no status as a citizen of the United States. (2) Congress has no constitutional power to exclude slavery from national territory; it has only "the power coupled with the duty of . . . protecting the owner in his rights." This meant that the law by which Congress had excluded slavery in the territories north of latitude 36° 30′ (the Missouri compromise of 1820), together with similar laws, was unconstitutional and void. Antislavery circles resounded with denunciations of Taney, of the opinion, and of the Court. Far from clarifying a point which many considered settled in the opposite sense, the decision intensified the unfortunate controversy. The Republicans, elated by the large popular support they had received in the election of 1856, were pleased to have an issue on which Douglas would be painfully embarrassed, and to which many good voters would honestly rally.

---

[14] *Works*, II, 308–312 (Dec. 10, 1856).

[15] Randall, *Civil War and Reconstruction*, 148–156.

CHAPTER V

LINCOLN AND DOUGLAS

I

THE year 1854 in Lincoln's life had marked a renewal of political activity.[1] After the close of his uneventful term in Congress in 1849 there had been a period of recession and passivity in which it appeared that Abraham Lincoln's story was to be that of a fameless Illinois lawyer, but in 1854 the Kansas-Nebraska question was changing the face of parties and offering a challenge to new leadership. It was plain that Lincoln's great opponent would be Douglas, with whom he had debated as long ago as the 1830's unless, as some feared and others hoped, Douglas would go over to the Republicans and become their leader.

In October 1854 the State Fair was in progress at Springfield, and the "gathering, devoted primarily to the interests of the farmer, became a rendezvous for state politicians," causing resentment as members of the Agricultural Society saw political leaders distracting the people's attention from their "Annual Jubilee and School of Life." [2]

[1] In 1854 Lincoln had been elected to the Illinois legislature but resigned his seat. His partner has stated that this was done because of his ambition to be chosen United States senator by that same legislature. Herndon (Angle ed.), 301. His senatorial ambition was real and intense, but when, after heavy strength in the initial balloting, his friends began to turn to Trumbull, Lincoln advised his "remaining friends" to support Trumbull, who was elected on the tenth ballot (February 8, 1855). This was not mere generosity to Trumbull. Lincoln had made a determined effort to obtain the senatorship and had promoted this effort to the point where all hope had ceased. Had he been chosen then, the famous senatorial canvass with Douglas in 1858 would not have occurred, and Lincoln's chance for the presidency might never have risen higher than Trumbull's. In a letter to E. B. Washburne, February 9, 1855 (*Works*, II, 274–277), Lincoln gave an account of the "agony" over the senatorship, from which one cannot but conclude that he wanted the office keenly. Other letters point to the same conclusion.

[2] Edwin Earle Sparks, ed., *The Lincoln-Douglas Debates of 1858* (Ill. Hist. Coll., III), 10–11.

This tendency of politicians to invade other than political domains was both a sign of the times and an American trait. It was a field day for political agitation, and both Lincoln and Douglas spoke at length before audiences in the hall of the House of Representatives.[3] Two weeks later at Peoria they met again, each making an extended address. Repeating the Springfield speech [4] of October 4, Lincoln was in his best campaigning form as he urged his countrymen to purify the republican robe, to wash it white, to readopt the Declaration of Independence, to turn slavery "back upon its existing legal rights," to save the Union, and in doing so to "make and to keep it forever worthy of the saving." This he urged in terms of "Fellow-countrymen, Americans, South as well as North," joining in "the great and good work." [5]

Between those October debates of 1854 and the great debate of 1858 Lincoln had continued his political activity, though busy with law practice, had been drawn somewhat tardily into the Republican party, had, as noted above, received 110 votes as vice-presidential nominee in 1856, and in that year had spoken many times for Frémont, whom he disliked.[6] Then on June 16, 1858, the Republican state convention at Springfield gave him its highest honor next to endorsement for the presidency by nominating him for United States senator. Having been the leading Whig of Illinois while yet in his thirties, he was now its leading Republican.

On the occasion of this nomination Lincoln delivered a carefully prepared speech which was not only to become one of his most famous; it was also to require frequent explanation and interpretation. "If we could first know *where* we are," he said, "and *whither* we are

---

[3] Douglas spoke on October 3. Next day Lincoln answered him, speaking for more than three hours. Douglas immediately followed with a rejoinder. At this point radical abolitionists, calling themselves "Republicans" (a word Lincoln was avoiding), arranged a meeting to form a Republican organization for Illinois. Lincoln deliberately avoided attending this meeting. Herndon (Angle ed.), 299; *Works*, III, 224.

[4] That this famous "Peoria speech" was a repetition of the Springfield speech of twelve days before has been pointed out by Beveridge (II, 268). Not to be outdone in city pride, Sherman D. Wakefield goes farther (*How Lincoln Became President*, 42–49, 165–173) and argues that the same speech was given still earlier, at Bloomington on September 12, 1854. He makes his case convincingly in parallel columns. See also Angle, *New Letters and Papers*, 133–137; E. E. East, "A Newly Discovered Speech of Lincoln," *Jour.*, Ill. State Hist. Soc., XXVIII, 65–77 (April, 1935).

[5] *Works*, II, 247–248 (Oct. 16, 1854).

[6] ". . . Frémont's strongest characteristics were those which Lincoln did not like or trust . . . ." Beveridge, II, 395.

tending, we could then . . . better judge *what* to do, and *how* to do it." Then he proceeded:

> We are now far into the *fifth* year, since a policy was initiated, with the *avowed* object . . . of putting an end to slavery agitation,
>
> Under . . . that policy, that agitation has not only, *not ceased,* but has *constantly augmented.*
>
> In *my* opinion, it *will* not cease, until a *crisis* shall have been reached, and passed—
>
> "A house divided against itself cannot stand."
>
> I believe this government cannot endure; permanently half *slave* and half *free.*
>
> I do not expect the Union to be *dissolved*—I dot [*sic*] expect the house to *fall*—but I *do* expect it will cease to be divided.
>
> It will become *all* one thing, or *all* the other.
>
> Either the *opponents* of slavery, will arrest the further spread of it, and place it where the public mind shall rest in the belief that it is in course of ultimate extinction; or its *advocates* will puch [*sic*] it forward, till it shall become alike lawful in *all* the States, *old* as well as *new—North* as well as *South.*[7]

The speech was an attack upon Douglas's "popular sovereignty," a doctrine which Lincoln proceeded to assail by history, ridicule, homely illustration, and rhetorical question. Citing the Kansas-Nebraska bill of Stephen Douglas, the Dred Scott decision of Roger Taney, and the endorsement of that decision by Franklin Pierce and James Buchanan (outgoing and incoming Presidents), he asserted that all the pieces fitted together in terms of a one-sided proslavery application of popular sovereignty till, as he said, "Under the Dred Scott decision 'squatter sovereignty' squatted out of existence, tumbled down like temporary scaffolding . . . —helped to carry an election, and then was kicked to the winds." [8]

Timbers had been turned out at different times by different workmen—Stephen, Franklin, Roger, and James; then behold, "we see these timbers joined together . . . , all the tenons and mortises exactly fitting, . . . in such a case we find it impossible not to believe that Stephen and Franklin and Roger and James all understood one another from the beginning . . . ." [9]

---

[7] *Illinois State Journal,* June 18, 1858. Because of Lincoln's reading of the proof, the *Journal's* version, with its italics, paragraphing, and somewhat eccentric punctuation, may be accepted as the best text; it reveals that Lincoln was weighing his words.

[8] *Works,* III, 6–7. [9] *Ibid.,* III, 10.

Warming to his argument, Lincoln denounced what he called Douglas's "care not" policy regarding slavery, declared that slavery was being extended by putting "this and that together," observed that "another nice little niche" remained to be filled by a decision of the Supreme Court denying a state the power to exclude slavery, thus making slavery "alike lawful in all the States," and predicted the day when the people would "awake to the reality . . . that the Supreme Court has made Illinois a slave State," unless what he called the "present political dynasty" should be overthrown.[10] Then he took care to destroy the argument that Republicans should turn to Douglas as their leader, conceding that Douglas was "a great man," but adding, in a rather ill chosen phrase, that " 'a living dog is better than a dead lion.' "[11] He ended with the plea that if the Republicans should stand firm when their enemy was faltering, they would surely have the victory.

Unless biography is to be treated solely as fulsome eulogy, it becomes a duty to analyze this speech. Analyzing it, one finds in the first place that Lincoln had done the thing which fans a leader's fame without clarifying his position—that is, he had coined a quotable but debatable phrase. From now on, people might know next to nothing in true substance about Lincoln, yet know that he had used the words "house divided" and "half slave, half free." The difficulty about this was that Lincoln was in reality a conservative[12] when considered in contrast to those who were urging "radical" changes as to slavery; yet his slogan-like phrase was of the kind that an abolitionist, and a radical one at that, might have used. From 1858 Lincoln was in the position of Seward who was also a non-radical but whose phrases —"higher law" and "irrepressible conflict"—were so indissolubly as-

[10] *Ibid.*, III, 12.

[11] *Ibid.*, III, 13.

[12] Basically Lincoln was a liberal; this becomes clear when one considers his attitude on matters of human dignity, civil liberty, justice, and fundamental problems of government. It has already been pointed out how Lincoln's thought went along with Jefferson's. On practical questions of dealing with slavery, however, Lincoln was the opposite of "radical" in a day when that word was coming to be applied to a policy of extreme measures toward the South—a policy which was radical only in the sense of being drastic and oppressive. Since the politicians who came to be called "radicals" were in truth reactionaries, as became evident in reconstruction days in economic as well as political matters, Lincoln's opposition to the radicals should be counted for liberalism. One cannot treat Lincoln at all in this period without recognizing two things which could only superficially be considered contradictory: his fundamental liberalism, and his marked preference for non-drastic measures in the realm of slavery and sectional adjustment.

sociated with his name that he could be superficially misrepresented as a radical. Lincoln's friends had urged him to omit this house-divided part of his speech, but Lincoln, in a moment of reliance on his own judgment of public policy—a reliance that was to reappear on occasion as President—concluded that his speech was the right doctrine and decided to stick to it.[13]

From the standpoint of correct representation of what was happening at the time, the speech was susceptible of criticism in at least two respects: (1) It implied a conspiracy or understanding between Douglas, Taney, Pierce, and Buchanan which (in the sense of a deliberate plot or agreement among these men) was quite fanciful and non-existent. (2) It assailed Douglas and his popular sovereignty as if in Douglas's mind the policy had never been intended otherwise than as promoting the proslavery cause in the territories. The battle royal that Douglas was waging with the Buchanan administration on that very point, with Douglas holding out against the Lecompton constitution in Kansas, ought to have been sufficient refutation of such a charge. Yet Lincoln had so phrased the case, with his homely illustration of the workmen and the timbers, that the accusation sounded most convincing.

The speech involved a certain shaping of interpretations for the speaker's purpose in a situation where another speaker could quite honestly have given an opposite interpretation. Lincoln was representing Douglas's break with Buchanan as if it amounted to nothing. One can hardly read the history of those times without realizing that it amounted to a great deal, and that Lincoln was denying to Douglas credit for resisting the very acts against Kansas which Lincoln himself was assailing.

There were yet other points open to question in this house-divided speech. Just what did Lincoln mean when he said that the Union would become all one or all the other? What Lincoln was in fact trying to do in this whole period was to put the damper on sectional conflict. Over and again that position was clearly stated. Yet people who knew nothing of that, or chose to ignore it, would quote this phrase and picture Lincoln as a man who would either insist on uniformity as to slavery or else divide the country—a man who would perhaps assent to disunion as many abolitionists were quite willing

[13] Herndon (Angle ed.), 326; Sparks, 23–24.

to do. Lincoln did not mean it that way. He thought of a peacefully continuing Union, as his very words in the whole passage implied; in this continuing Union he seemed to envisage a future day when uniformity as to slavery would exist, but he was not demanding disunion while it should not exist. Yet it was not the whole speech, nor even the connected passage, that was quoted; rather, it was only those few challenging words that kept recurring when Lincoln was mentioned. The fact that Lincoln was no firebrand and that he did not intend disunion nor any attack upon legitimate Southern rights, would be overlooked, especially by his opponents who would make it appear that he would oppose any type of Union-saving compromise.

At the time the speech went well. It added to Lincoln's fame, caused him to be in wide demand, and served as an opening salvo in the coming party contest in Illinois. It gave Lincoln's party an issue not only against Democrats generally but against Douglas at a time when otherwise men were thinking of the close similarity of Douglas to those Democrats who, like Trumbull, were now shifting to the new Republican party and being received with ready endorsement. One thing Lincoln could not endure was to have it thought that Douglas was Republican timber. Lincoln was concerned not only with promoting his party but with exerting large leadership within the party.

II

The coming legislature of Illinois would have the constitutional function of choosing a senator of the United States, and the extralegal obligation (or practical necessity) of restricting its choice to the two recognized party candidates. It looked like a close matter, and Lincoln was pushing hard. He was determined to follow on Douglas's trail, address audiences in the same places, and give a resounding reply to every one of his opponent's pronouncements. He was preparing carefully, assembling material, keeping a political notebook, writing letters, courting his friends in and out of the state, and watching the matter of alignment with the right groups. He would have pursued Douglas in any case had there been no special series of seven formal "joint debates." When Douglas's speaking engagements were announced, and when the Democratic senator was shifting emphasis away from Lincoln by assailing Trumbull, Lincoln seized the initiative, using Norman B. Judd of Chicago as intermediary, and formally challenged Douglas "to divide time, and address the same audiences the present canvass." [1] In a personal interview at Bement, Illinois, the agreement between the two senatorial candidates was duly sealed, and from then on the joint debates were the subject of main interest in the prairie state.

Considering that there were only seven such joint debates, the sizable state of Illinois was pretty well canvassed. The selection of places went by congressional districts, the Chicago area having already been the scene of a lively encounter between the candidates (July 9–10, 1858, at the Tremont House). The first two debates were in northern Illinois, at Ottawa on August 21 and Freeport August 27. Far down in "Egypt" the third debate was held at the picturesque Southern-like town of Jonesboro on September 15. The midway point was reached at Charleston in eastern Illinois on September 18. This was near the Thomas Lincoln home, in a region "prolific in Republicans." [2] Then in October the contest would draw to its close with debates at Galesburg on the seventh, at Quincy on the thirteenth, and lastly at Alton on the fifteenth. Election day, a time of excitement and some disorder, was to come on Tuesday, November 2.

People of the time thought of it as a "momentous" encounter.[3] Writing of the canvass while it proceeded, men noted that it was something new,[4] that both men were material from which Presidents might be made,[5] and that Illinois was "the battleground of the year." [6] A vigorous, some said "desperate," fight was expected.

Stump speaking was a powerful magnet in the Middle West, and huge crowds poured out. It is amusing to read the estimates of these crowds, varying according to partisan claims of the papers in which

---

[1] *Works*, III, 189 (July 24, 1858).

[2] New York *Evening Post*, Sep. 21, 1858, reprinted in Sparks, 319.

[3] The word "momentous" as well as "desperate" was used by the Cincinnati *Commercial*, July 6, 1858. On July 13 the New York *Evening Post* declared: "Illinois is just now the theatre of the most momentous political contest, whether we consider the eminence of the contestants or the consequences which may result . . . , that has occured in this country in any state canvass since the defeat of Silas Wright [of New York] for Governor in 1846." These comments are quoted in Sparks, 31, 49. Perhaps the writer in the *Post* did not realize how soon men would scratch their heads in doubt as to why the Silas Wright campaign was so momentous, or even as to who Silas Wright was.

[4] The New York *Herald* (July 27, 1858) referred to the canvass as "somewhat of an anomaly." Sparks, 46.

[5] Sparks, 49.

[6] *Ibid.*, 43.

they appeared. A Chicago crowd amounted to thirty thousand by one account, twelve thousand by another.[7] An open-air crowd at Charleston, drawn from adjacent counties in a strictly rural district, was estimated at from "twelve to fifteen thousand." [8] The canvass was more than a contest; it was a spectacle and a show, replete with all the devices and claptrap of rough-and-ready campaigning. It was clamorous and colorful, with bands, bells, artillery salvos, fluttering banners, fireworks, torchlight processions, placards, rockets, floats, decorations, shouts and cheers, boys hired for the congenial task of making a racket, and at Charleston a gayly bedecked wagon carrying thirty-two "pretty and intelligent ladies" representing the thirty-two states in the Union.[9] It was noted with pride that a Lincoln procession from Mattoon to Charleston was headed by the "Bowling Green Band" from Terre Haute.[10]

Speeches were long, but attention was good despite the difficulties of open-air acoustics and the discomfort of crowding masses. Rivalry was keen. Each side was eager to have the largest flag, the longest parade, the best and loudest music. The debates were stenographically —or, as they said, "phonographically"—reported, but each journalist colored his descriptions by his obvious preference for Douglas or for Lincoln. The wordy discourses were not all reason and light. There was twitting and banter, maneuvering for party advantage, and the shaping of appeals for local effect. Emphasis was upon the position that each party and each champion took on the "vexed question" of slavery in the territories. Lincoln made more effort to confine the discussion there than Douglas, who sought to broaden the controversy to cover the disruptive issue of social and political equality between the races and to associate Lincoln and the Republicans with all the stigmas that attached to abolitionists, whose popularity in large parts of Illinois was at zero level. Douglas was effective in ridiculing Lincoln's party, scoring its lack of a consistent name: up north they were Republicans or Abolitionists; at Springfield they avoided the name Republican, but referred to their meeting as "a Convention of all men opposed to the Democratic party"; in lower Egypt they advertised a "meeting of the Free Democracy" whereat Trumbull would speak. "Did you ever hear," said Douglas, "of this new party, called the 'Free Democracy'?" "What object have these Black Republicans in changing their name in

[7] *Ibid.*, 39. [8] *Ibid.*, 312. [9] *Ibid.*, 324. [10] *Ibid.*, 267.

every county? . . . They have one name in the north, another in the center, and another in the south." [11]

In pointing to his long record in public life, Douglas made no apology. He defended his popular sovereignty—local self-determination—as right in principle and wise in practice. To his mind it was the only practical and typically American solution. He was in fact having trouble with the doctrine, as his article next year in *Harper's Monthly* [12] was to show, but there is no reason to doubt his sincerity in urging that he intended his doctrine to be understood and applied in good faith, and that he had never known "the Democratic party to violate any one of its principles, out of . . . expediency, that it did not pay the debt with sorrow." "There is no safety or success for our party," he said, "unless we always do right . . . ." [13] He conceived of the task and destiny of the Democratic party in terms of Union. The party must unite and stand together, he said, resisting men who thought only of sections. He reminded his hearers that both major parties, Whigs and Democrats, had united for Union in 1850 and had joined "in establishing the Compromise . . . and restoring tranquillity and good feeling." [14] Showing how Clay had worked for compromise in the mid-century crisis and how Lincoln had worked to throw Clay overboard, he declared: "Lincoln is the man, in connection with Seward, Chase, Giddings, and other Abolitionists, who got up that strife that I helped Clay to put down." [15]

He added that for himself, he stood in 1858 where he had stood in 1850, 1854, and 1856. Prior to 1854, said Douglas, the two leading parties were both national. "An Old Line Whig could proclaim his principles in Louisiana and Massachusetts alike." [16] But times had changed. Lincoln and his party had "set themselves up as wiser than . . . men who made this Government, which . . . [had] flourished for seventy years under . . . popular sovereignty . . . ." [17] On the practical question as to how slavery could be excluded from a territory if the people so desired, being pinned down on this point by Lincoln's famous question at Freeport, Douglas "emphatically" answered that it could be done by "local police regulations." Sensing at once that his

[11] *Ibid.*, 299.

[12] "The Dividing Line between Federal and Local Authority: Popular Sovereignty in the Territories," *Harper's Monthly*, XIX, 519–537 (Sep., 1859).

[13] Sparks, 458. [14] *Ibid.*, 461. [15] *Ibid.*, 491. [16] *Ibid.*, 86. [17] *Ibid.*, 98.

assertion conflicted with the Dred Scott decision, he added that the people of a territory would have "the right . . . to make a Slave Territory or a Free Territory . . . under the Nebraska bill" despite the attitude of the Supreme Court on the "abstract question." [18] If it be said that this involved a certain disregard of the Olympian finality and sanctity of the Court, an equal objection to the Court's infallibility was evident on Lincoln's side, such objection being counted a virtue. Douglas rode hard on Lincoln's house-divided declaration, declared that the "Black Republican" party had been abolitionized, and sought to make it appear that Lincoln and his partisans favored Negro equality.

On two points Douglas spoke with particular scorn and bitterness. (1) He resented the use of the ax against him by the Buchanan administration because he refused to allow his popular sovereignty to be distorted into a proslavery maneuver as at Lecompton. (2) He was equally indignant at the alliance of Illinois Republicans with Buchanan Democrats, both groups assailing him for agreeing with Lincoln in the Lecompton matter.[19] "A Democratic Administration," he said, "deems it consistent . . . to wield its power in this State in behalf of the Republican Abolition candidates in every county . . . ." [20] At another time he said: "What do you Republicans think of a political organization that will try to make an unholy combination with its professed foes to beat a man merely because he has done right? . . . You know that the axe . . . is suspended over every man in office in Illinois, and the terror of proscription is threatened every Democrat by the present Administration, unless he supports the Republican ticket . . . ." [21]

For each state its own laws, for each territory its own popular decision, was Douglas's principle. For the country, union and tolerance, defeat of the one party he deemed purely sectional, return to early principles. He would have each state allow or disallow slavery as it should choose; [22] he also thought that each state should choose whether to give or deny the vote to Negroes.[23] In the peroration of his first speech opening the joint debates, he grew eloquent on the

---

[18] *Ibid.*, 161–162.

[19] Phillip G. Auchampaugh, "The Buchanan-Douglas Feud," *Journal*, Ill. State Hist. Soc., XXV, 5–48 (1932).

[20] Sparks, 460. [21] *Ibid.*, 337.

[22] This was also Lincoln's principle. [23] Sparks, 97.

theme of a nation that had grown great, had crossed the Alleghenies, and had turned "the prairie into a garden" on the principles of the "fathers" who "intended that our institutions should differ," knowing "that the North and the South . . . [had] different climates, productions, and interests." What he opposed was "trying to array all the Northern States in one body against the South, to excite a sectional war between the Free States and the Slave States, in order that the one or the other may be driven to the wall." [24]

III

The amenities of debate were honored. There was some horseplay, but for the most part the etiquette though perhaps not altogether the purest ethics of forensic discussion was preserved. Verbal assaults were sharp and crushing, but unseemly personalities were usually avoided, and one witnessed the spectacle, as Douglas said, of a "large mass of people" made up of "various . . . parties" giving "kind and respectful attention" not only to friends, but to those with whom they disagreed.[1] At Springfield in July 1858, according to the New York *Herald,* whenever either Lincoln or Douglas referred to the other, it was "in the kindest, most courteous and dignified manner." [2] There was taunting, chafing, and derision; yet it stopped short of offensive insult. Douglas held Lincoln up as a man who had kept a "grocery" [3]—i. e., who sold liquor—which Lincoln denied,[4] who had made a kind of bargain to dissolve both the Democratic and Whig parties in order to erect an abolitionist party under the name Republican,[5] who proclaimed abolition doctrines,[6] and who "had to be carried from the platform" at Ottawa because of embarrassment at Douglas's questions.[7] When Lincoln stated that he would be sorry to have to vote on the admission of another slave state, Douglas said: "I trust the people of Illinois will not put him in a position [as senator] which he would be so sorry to occupy." [8]

Lincoln's manner toward Douglas was usually respectful and free

---

[24] *Ibid.*, 97–98.

[1] Sparks, 159.

[2] Sparks, 46–47.

[3] *Ibid.*, 91.

[4] *Ibid.*, 102.

[5] *Ibid.*, 88.

[6] *Ibid.*, 93.

[7] Lincoln had been borne off in the manner of a hero; Douglas admitted that he was merely playful in making it appear that he "had to be carried" because of embarrassment. *Ibid.*, 248, 250.

[8] *Ibid.*, 251.

from personal ill-feeling. Sometimes his banter took the form of ironic compliment, as when he blandly commended his opponent for "gradually improving" [9]—i. e., becoming more severe against the Buchanan administration. For this Lincoln claimed credit, flattering himself that Douglas had taken his advice. Lincoln, as he himself said, had used no "vulgarity or blackguardism." [10] Some months after the debates he was careful to point out that he felt "no unkindness . . . toward Judge Douglas." [11] As for Douglas, his attitude was indicated by a Cincinnati newspaper in which it was noted that while he was "able and bold," his relations with Lincoln were "friendly." [12]

In argument Lincoln drove in his strokes wherever he sensed a weakness in Douglas's position or an embarrassment because of matters for which, if all the truth were told, Douglas was not to blame. He severely scored Douglas's indifference as to slavery and riddled his popular sovereignty creed as either proslavery or unjustifiably noncommittal on a moral issue. He twitted Douglas for his inconsistency in once favoring the Missouri compromise and later opposing it.[13] On the Dred Scott decision Lincoln's position in debate was a bit like having it both ways: the decision was riddled, yet Douglas was rapped for taking a position not in accord with it. Asserting that in former years there had never been a man who said that the Declaration of Independence did not include Negroes in the term "all men," Lincoln said that Taney was the first man who said it and next to him was Douglas.[14]

He did not permit Douglas and his party to go unscathed with an assertion that the Dred Scott decision was merely a negative or hands-off declaration. He drove hard on the point that the decision was an affirmation of Federal power to protect slavery, and that, if Douglas's party was sustained in the elections, the result would be a

---

[9] *Ibid.*, 466. Feeling was in fact tense, but usually it was kept under control. Reports of the Ottawa debate, however, suggest that Lincoln lost his temper, making angry interruptions during Douglas's rejoinder (*ibid.*, 118).

[10] *Ibid.*, 182.

[11] *Works*, V, 116 (Mar. 1, 1859).

[12] Cincinnati *Commercial*, July 12, 1858, quoted in Sparks, 42. This was during the senatorial canvass, though prior to the formal joint debates. At Ottawa Douglas was careful to say that he meant "nothing personally disrespectful or unkind" to his opponent (*ibid.*, 91).

[13] Sparks, 466. Henry Clay, with whom Lincoln agreed in the early phases of his career, as well as other Whig leaders, could have been twitted for the same inconsistency.

[14] *Ibid.*, 470.

"new Dred Scott decision, deciding against the right of the people of the States to exclude slavery." [15] The Taney type of constitutional reasoning, argued Lincoln, would legalize slavery in all the states, in the sense that the right of property in slaves, according to that decision, was affirmed in the Constitution.[16]

In this phase of his argument there were two respects in which an opponent could have said with some reason that Lincoln was vulnerable. (1) He was using the familiar device of denouncing a thing because it *might* possibly lead to a predicted result, as in an earlier day opponents had denounced the Federal Constitution and argued against its ratification on the ground that the ten-mile-square Federal district *might* become a terrible arsenal of tyranny. Governmental power of whatever sort must be reasonably used; the chance that a power *might* be abused—e. g., the power of taxation or of raising an army—does not mean that government must never be trusted, under popular controls, to exercise the power. On this point Lincoln was carrying the Dred Scott decision beyond its setting. While he remained within that setting, he had better justification for assailing the decision. In strict logic, perhaps, he ought to have been content to denounce the decision for what it was, rather than to predict an imaginary new decision.

(2) It was by tendencies quite the opposite of those for which Douglas stood that a fundamental constitutional alteration was introduced in 1868 by which civil and property rights in the states were made subordinate to and controllable by the Federal Constitution. This was done not by a new Supreme Court decision, but by a constitutional amendment, the fourteenth. When Lincoln spoke in 1858, his declaration that the Taney property doctrine of 1857 *might* some day lead to a Federal imposition of slavery upon all the states, was something of a non-sequitur. Few constitutional lawyers would contend that the domain of the fifth amendment included the vastly broader field of the fourteenth. That a future Supreme Court would ever rule that the Federal government could impose slavery upon unwilling states was extremely unlikely. Such a doctrine would have been opposed where Northern states prohibited slavery and in the South because of state-rights principles. In such matters one must make allowance for campaign technique, in which Lincoln was skill-

[15] *Ibid.*, 359.

[16] *Ibid.*, 358 (Oct. 7, 1858, at Galesburg).

ful, without concluding that his every argument was unanswerable.

Not allowing Douglas an interpretation that would preserve his favorite doctrine, Lincoln showed popular sovereignty to be inconsistent with the Supreme Court's decision. Here he was on firmer ground. Douglas, of course, could not be blamed for the inconsistency. He believed in a doctrine which the Court had pretty well demolished. He was in a dilemma; it was not of his making, but it gave him no end of embarrassment. Lincoln was not the man to let him off or avoid making him squirm; this particular inconsistency was one of Lincoln's most telling points. The great difference was that it cost Lincoln nothing, and gained him much, to denounce the Court, since the winning of Southern support was not a prime object of the Republican party. Douglas had to consider all parts of the country. It would be fatal for him to offend the South. Rights all around, thought Douglas, were protected by what he called popular sovereignty. It injured no one.

Lincoln too had his embarrassment which Douglas did not hesitate to exploit. It was the stigma of abolitionism. He repudiated it with spirit, asserting at Alton that Douglas was trying to place him "in an extremely Abolition attitude" before an audience which had "strong sympathies southward." [17] On various occasions Lincoln explained his house-divided declaration. He went so far as to say (in the month before the first joint debate) that in his half-slave-half-free speech he did not say he "was in favor of anything"; he was making "a prediction only—it may have been a foolish one, perhaps." [18]

Was Lincoln regretting his famous slogan? Only to the extent that it was being used to make him appear as an abolitionist or a promoter of strife and war. In explaining it he brought out what he insisted was the "real issue" [19] of the whole contest: that slavery was wrong, that peace and harmony in the country prior to 1854 had been based on the belief that it was "in course of ultimate extinction," [20] that these were the sentiments of the fathers, and that he intended only to resist the "farther spread" of the institution, and to "place it where the founders . . . originally placed it." [21] This sentiment he repeated, with renewed declarations against slavery as a wrong, many times.

---

17 Sparks, 468.

18 *Works*, III, 31–32 (July 10, 1858).

19 Sparks, 482.

20 *Works*, III, 32 (July 10, 1858).

21 *Ibid.*, III, 34 (July 10, 1858).

He did not hedge on his house-divided declaration in the sense in which he said it should be interpreted, but he did resent Douglas's effort to make it appear that he was stirring up sectional strife. He agreed that diversity of institutions according to state choice was desirable; "instead of being a thing to 'divide the house' . . . [he said] they tend to sustain it." [22] But he insisted that the territories—future homes of free men—be kept free, not only for the native born but for "Hans, and Baptiste, and Patrick, and all other men from all the world." [23] Reducing the matter to the simplest terms, he said: "The real issue in this controversy . . . is the sentiment . . . of one class that looks upon the institution of slavery as a wrong, and of another class that does not look upon it as a wrong." His party, he said, looked upon it "as being a moral, social, and political wrong." [24]

IV

Lincoln's electioneering in 1858 was not confined to the formal joint debates. Indeed, if one thinks of what was doing in Illinois in the summer and fall of 1858 rather than of particular things singled out for historical emphasis, the famous seven debates were a minor fraction of the whole story. The period of July to October 1858 was a time of intense activity. He traveled almost constantly. Cheering crowds met him, escorted him through the streets, greeted him with banners and brass bands, and everywhere insisted on hearing him speak. He did not disappoint them. Besides the seven formal debates he spoke in this period at Clinton, Beardstown, Havana, Bath, Peoria, Henry, Augusta, Amboy, Carlinville, Bloomington, Edwardsville, Greenville, Danville, Urbana, Pekin, Oquawka, Monmouth, Lincoln, Mount Sterling, Carthage, La Harpe, Macomb, Petersburg, and many other places. At the last-named town, so close to the familiar New Salem haunts, Lincoln's address before "a large and enthusiastic assembly" was referred to as his sixty-second speech of the 1858 campaign.[1] During all this time, in addition to the joint debates and numerous

---

[22] Sparks, 478. [23] *Ibid.*, 481. [24] *Ibid.*, 482.

[1] *Menard Index*, Nov. 4, 1858. After referring to Lincoln's clear logic, his alignment with the doctrines of the Fathers, and his dissipation of misrepresentations and slanders, the *Index* added: "As a whole, we have seldom heard a political speech so perfect in all the essentials of candor, force & completeness." (The date of the Petersburg speech was October 29.) See also Henry Villard, *Memoirs*, I, 96.

minor speeches, he conferred with party workers, struggled with his correspondence, took a hand in the party affairs of this or that district, arranged to have thousands of his speeches printed (not omitting German-language copies), and managed to attend several local Republican conventions as at Tremont on August 30.

The adventures of Lincoln in this senatorial campaign included dining with Douglas, riding a river packet to be met at the wharf by cheering adherents, witnessing a balloon ascension, attending barbecues, celebrating with German Turners and parading firemen, sitting at Macomb for the famous ambrotype, being carried on the shoulders of admirers, meeting men of his company in the Black Hawk War who greeted him on the platform of one of the towns, and recalling at the same town (Bath) that as a surveyor he had staked it out of a "wooded wilderness." At one place he rode in a conestoga wagon drawn by six white horses. A "constant stream of old friends" met him at Hillsboro. At Sullivan his supporters interrupted Douglas and a "brawl" was "narrowly averted." The weather was cruelly hot, and at Winchester it was remarked that "His horses were white with sweat and he and his friends were black with dust." Crowds were huge; much of the speaking was in the open air; and a typical speech would last for two hours. Add these labors to the weary journeyings and one can believe that there was truth in the opposition report that he looked "jaded."

This vigorous popular campaigning meant a strenuous effort for Lincoln, but it was an American show, an exciting recreation for many thousands, a series of reunions with friends, and a genuine demonstration of Lincoln's popularity in Illinois. His arduous trips, his readiness to meet everyone, the homely incidents of his wide ranging itinerary—all the informal and spontaneous aspects of his electioneering—meant as much as his many long hours of speaking. People expected all this. They seldom thought of sparing him. To Lincoln it all came naturally; this was one of the sources of his strength. Few political leaders have known the people by way of wide travel and close personal association as did Lincoln.[2] Some would make it appear that in 1858 Lincoln was after bigger stakes, that he was in reality

[2] Incidents here briefly sketched are treated in Angle, *Lincoln, 1854–1861*, especially pp. 235–253. Angle's pages give detailed references to sources and, of course, Lincoln's correspondence is largely found in his collected writings. (Other sources have been consulted by the writer.) Quoted phrases are from Angle.

campaigning for the presidency. For this supposition there seems to be no adequate basis so far as Lincoln's 1858 intentions were concerned. Nevertheless, the many popular incidents and associations of the canvass against Douglas, as well as the content of his speeches in that campaign with the publicity they received in the nation, were a significant part of his road to larger leadership.

On election day (November 2, 1858) Douglas was "triumphantly sustained" by the "invincible Democracy of Illinois." [3] Yet the *Illinois State Journal* pointed out that a fair apportionment of legislative seats according to population would have given Lincoln's friends forty-one members in the lower house and fourteen in the upper (majorities), as compared with the actual result, by which in the lower house the membership was forty to thirty-five in Douglas's favor, while in the upper house Lincoln had only eleven senators, the Douglas and Buchanan elements having fourteen.[4] It was claimed that Lincoln's friends who were elected, though a minority in the legislature, represented a larger population than Douglas's friends. On the other hand it was asserted by Lincoln's opponents that the apportionment was the same under which a legislature had been elected which chose Trumbull, a party associate of Lincoln, for the Senate, and that Governor Bissell, a Republican, had vetoed a new apportionment bill in the session of 1856–57.[5]

Lincoln felt his defeat keenly, but looked to the future, promised to "fight in the ranks," pledged support for Trumbull's reëlection, urged that the "fight must go on," and declared that the "cause of civil liberty must not be surrendered at the end of one or even one hundred defeats." [6] He took comfort in the thought that the "popular vote of the state" was with him. The "plain old Democracy" was on his side; the "silk-stocking Whiggery," the "nice exclusive sort," was against him.[7] He was glad he had made the race. It gave him "a hearing

---

[3] Quincy *Herald*, Nov. 4, 1858. See illustration in Sparks, facing p. 534.

[4] The actual choice of senator was made by joint ballot of the Illinois General Assembly on January 5, 1859, Douglas receiving 54 votes and Lincoln 46. *Journal of the House of Representatives* Jan. 5, 1859, p. 32; *Senate Journal*, p. 30. In certain accounts (Beveridge, II, 695–696; Wakefield, 93) it is erroneously stated that on this occasion Lincoln received only 41 votes.

[5] Sparks, 535. Bissell at first approved the bill, then recalled it, expunged his approval, and vetoed it. His action came so late in the session that there was no chance for the Democrats to pass it over his veto.

[6] *Works*, V, 94 (Nov. 19, 1858).

[7] *Ibid.*, V, 95 (Nov. 19, 1858).

on the great and durable question of the age." Even though he should "now sink out of view, and . . . be forgotten," he had "made some marks . . . for the cause of civil liberty." [8]

V

It is surprising how little attention has been given to the actual content of the debates. The canvass had been conducted in dead earnest, yet it has always been easier to relate its picturesque features than to analyze its substance. It was symptomatic of the times that the debaters were not concerned with a representative coverage of national questions, but almost entirely with slavery, and with only a limited and comparatively unimportant aspect of that subject. Public attention is seldom devoted to a balanced and fully rounded estimate of public problems. It takes some selected issue and concentrates on that. So do political parties, with the added factor that parties make it appear that they are more opposite than they really are, that their points of difference on an incomplete statement of issues are the only things the people need to contemplate, and that party voting is the infallible method of accomplishing large results. One may distinguish between a discussion that strives always for a solution of governmental problems and a "canvass" in which the participants engage in sparring for popular effect and party advantage. In the main the joint debates between Lincoln and Douglas belong in the latter category.

Swinging up and down and back and forth across Illinois, making the welkin ring and setting the prairies on fire, Lincoln and Douglas debated—what? That is the surprising thing. With all the problems that might have been put before the people as proper matter for their consideration in choosing a senator—choice of government servants, immigration, the tariff, international policy, promotion of education, westward extension of railroads, the opening of new lands for homesteads, protection against greedy exploitation of those lands (a problem to which Congress gave insufficient attention), encouragement to settlers, and the bettering of agriculture, not to mention such social problems as guarding against economic depression, improving the condition of factory workers, and alleviating those agrarian grievances

[8] *Ibid.*

that were to plague the coming decades—with such issues facing the country, these two candidates for the Senate talked as if there were only one issue. Thus instead of a representative coverage of the problems of mid-century America, the debaters gave virtually all their attention to slavery in the territories. More specifically, they were concentrating on the question whether Federal prohibition of slavery in western territories, having been dropped after full discussion in 1850, should be revived as if it were the only means of dealing with the highly improbable chance that human bondage would ever take root in such a place as Kansas, Nebraska, or New Mexico. It is indeed a surprising thing to suppose that the negligible amount of human bondage in Kansas,[1] or the alleged inability of the people of that nascent state to decide the matter for themselves, constituted the only American question of sufficient importance to occupy nearly all the attention of senatorial candidates in one of the most famous forensic episodes of the century. Remembering that slavery in the large was not the subject of the debates, it may be said that if the highly unlikely inflow of slavery into Kansas was the main topic of national concern, the American people were more fortunate than they knew.

It was not that any frontal attack upon slavery in the states was involved. Lincoln was far from being an abolitionist, and nothing was more obvious in the controlling counsels of Lincoln's party in that period than the avoidance of any "ultra"—i. e., strongly abolitionist—tone. The "peculiar institution" was not being assailed by the Republican party in the commonwealths where it existed. Nor was it a case of one side demanding full civil and social equality for the Negro while the other side opposed such equality. Big and fundamental things about slavery and the Negro were not on the agenda of national parties. Each speaker could swell or mute the discussion on those fundamentals as he saw fit, and they were usually muted so far as commitments or constructive proposals were concerned. Despite all this, the intensity of the discussion baffled description. The people of Illinois were being worked up in party feeling by a discussion which contributed little to the practical solution even of such a matter as slaves in Kansas.

The debate was a spectacle, a drama, an exhibition, almost a sporting event. In addition it was a serious matter, but its dramatic quality

[1] For the tiny amount of slavery in Kansas see below, pp. 240–241.

could not be ignored, and that quality would perhaps have been lost if the speakers had not used the language of controversy. In other words, the Lincoln-Douglas canvass was not an effort to work out a formula of agreement. Had such an effort been made, it would have been found that these two leaders had much in common. On the broad problem of racial relations they did not fundamentally differ. Lincoln was not proposing any marked change in the depressed status of the Negro. "I am not . . . in favor of . . . the social and political equality of the white and black races," he declared.[2] Again he said: ". . . I am not in favor of negro citizenship." [3] It is not easy to put Lincoln's actual position in a word, for it did not fit any pat formula, certainly not that of the abolitionist. He cited Clay as showing that equality was abstract; you could not apply it.[4] The idea that he favored Negro suffrage or equality, he said, was a misrepresentation.[5] It was "untrue," a "fabrication." [6] As if to leave no doubt on that point he said: ". . . I did not at any time say I was in favor of negro suffrage; . . . I declared against it." [7]

This was not the whole of Lincoln's position on Negro rights. He denounced the principle that "all men" did not include the Negro.[8] He qualified his statements carefully. While holding that there was a "physical difference" which would "forever forbid the two races living together on terms of social and political equality," and while favoring the "superior position assigned to the white race," he did not believe that "the negro should be denied everything." [9] He did not favor "a tendency to dehumanize the negro, to take away from him the right of ever striving to be a man." [10] Matters of racial equality, intermarriage and the like, he dismissed as "false issues." [11] The equality he was interested in was not a matter of color or size but of inalienable rights.[12] He believed the Southern people entitled to a fugitive slave law. As to slavery in the states, not only did he recognize a lack of Federal power to overthrow it; he also disclaimed any "inclination" to "disturb" it.[13] He was not insisting that Missouri should emancipate its slaves. No such thing. Such a thought was a "perversion" of his meaning. His concern was for new societies, not old states.[14]

---

2 Sparks, 267. 3 *Ibid.*, 303. 4 *Ibid.*, 471. 5 *Works*, V, 141 (Sep. 16, 1859).
6 Sparks, 468. 7 *Works*, V, 145 (Sep. 16, 1859). 8 Sparks, 472–473. 9 *Ibid.*, 268.
10 Sparks, 473. 11 *Ibid.*, 482. 12 *Ibid.*, 469. 13 *Works*, IV, 328–329.
14 Sparks, 473.

As to slavery in Kansas, Lincoln wanted Kansas free by congressional prohibition; Douglas favored a program that would inevitably have made Kansas free both as a territory by popular sovereignty and as a state by constitutional processes. The attitude of the two men toward the Kansas policy of Buchanan was virtually identical, though on this point the Republicans were unwilling to give Douglas credit for agreeing with them—this in spite of the fact that some Republicans, but not Lincoln, even spoke of Douglas as a suitable leader for their own party.

Lincoln and Douglas were also alike in deploring sectionalism. Douglas wanted always to subordinate any issue that would split the people North and South. For that very reason he did not want to agitate the slavery question. Lincoln equally deplored disruptive tendencies, but he attributed the disunity to the discarding of the old concept that slavery was to remain of limited extent.

Statements flung about in the debates did not define the issue as a choice between a position taken by Lincoln and an opposite position taken by Douglas. This became evident when, early in the canvass, each candidate sought to impale his opponent upon spikes of formal interrogation. At Freeport Lincoln answered seven questions put to him by Douglas. In the first five his position differed not at all from his rival's. His answer to the seventh was noncommittal. Only on the sixth (prohibition of slavery in all the national territories) was there a difference between the two men.[15] Yet even on that point the difference was not vital in its practical effect upon the results. That is to say, in the territories that existed or might later be organized, Lincoln's demand of congressional prohibition for slavery would produce freedom, but so also would Douglas's principle of popular sovereignty honestly applied.

Conversely, Douglas's answers to Lincoln's questions at Freeport

[15] By negative answers to the first five questions Lincoln asserted that he (1) did not favor unconditional repeal of the fugitive slave act, (2) did not oppose the admission of any more slave states, (3) did not oppose the admission of a new state with such a constitution as the people might make, (4) did not "stand to-day pledged" to abolition in the District of Columbia, and (5) did not insist upon prohibition of the domestic slave trade. His principal difference with Douglas consisted of his belief (6) "in the *right* and *duty* of Congress to prohibit slavery in all the United States Territories." On the question whether he would oppose acquiring new territory without prior prohibition of slavery, (7) he answered that he "would or would not" oppose such acquisition according to his judgment as to whether it would aggravate the slavery question. Sparks, 149–150.

showed him taking either a free-state position or a non-committal attitude on those points on which Lincoln was also non-committal. Douglas's answers were as follows: (1) He would consider Kansas entitled to admission as a free state before reaching a set figure of population which Lincoln mentioned. (2) By police regulations he considered that slavery might be kept out of a territory. This was the famous question which has caused the others (on both sides) to be unjustly dwarfed. (3) Asked whether he would favor a decree of the Supreme Court that states could not exclude slavery, Douglas showed himself "amazed" at the question and clinched the matter in the free-state sense by saying that such a declaration "would be an act of moral treason that no man on the bench could ever descend to." (4) In the possible future acquisition of any new territories he would leave the people thereof free to make it slave or nonslave as they should prefer.[16]

VI

As to forensics the canvass can hardly be said to have exhibited the purest technique. In a genuine procedure of debate each speaker would have taken a position opposite to his opponent's, stuck to the question, shaped the argument as a progressive unfolding of the main issues, noted what was said by the opposite speaker, and, since the senatorship was at stake, would have shown the people how, on matters likely to come before the Senate, he would have taken a stand contrary to that of his rival. For the debate to have had significance the contestants would also have been expected to enter upon the practical and substantial results of their contrary positions.

Instead of that in the case of Lincoln and Douglas, the two men *seemed to differ* while actually agreeing on many points, dragged red herrings over the trail, indulged in misrepresentations, hurled taunts, introduced extraneous matter, repeated the same statements from place to place with little regard by one debater for what the other had said, and seemed often more interested in casting reproach upon party opponents than in clarifying the issues. After laboring through the voluminous speeches, which few people ever do, any serious student of the subject should turn to the proceedings in Congress early in

[16] *Ibid.*, 159–165.

1861. If Lincoln had been elected senator, and if in that period he had voted as did the great majority of Republicans in Congress on bills organizing the territories of Colorado, Nevada, and Dakota, he would actually have been taking the Douglas position, for these territories were organized by Republican votes without prohibition of slavery. Or, if he had demanded prohibition of slavery in these territorial bills, thus seeking to enact into law what he had demanded in the debates, his position, as compared with men of his party in Congress, would have been very lonely indeed. This seems to suggest that, as events turned out, and as concerned the Republican party in a broader analysis, the "issue" of abolition in the territories was a talking point rather than a matter for governmental action, a campaign appeal rather than a guide for legislation.

The subject is bound up with the startling crisis of 1860–61 and will be dealt with later in that connection; [1] for the present purpose it is significant to note that Douglas was able, with pardonable self-justification but also with generous comments on the patriotism of his opponents, to show in 1861 that Lincoln's party had abandoned its basic principle—the principle which constituted the only point of difference in the debates of 1858 when the contestants were pinned down to specific governmental proposals as shown in the seven interrogatories above noted.

As to red herrings and such, there was little to choose between the contestants. Both were guilty. Douglas rang the changes on "Black Republicans," on Missouri abolishing slavery and sending a "hundred thousand emancipated slaves into Illinois, to become citizens and voters," on turning "this beautiful State into a free negro colony," [2] on Lincoln's fancied collusion with Trumbull, on his alleged lack of patriotism with reference to the Mexican War, and on his changeable doctrines, "jet-black" in the north, "a decent mulatto" in the center, and "almost white" in Egypt.[3] Lincoln countered with taunts as to Douglas's alleged support of a hypothetical future Supreme Court decision that would make slavery national, with accusations as to a conspiracy between Stephen, Roger, *et al.*, and with charges of "fraud, . . . absolute forgery" traceable to Charles H. Lanphier, editor of the *Illinois State Register,* T. L. Harris, member of Congress, and Douglas.[4]

---

[1] See below, pp. 229–231. [2] Sparks, 95. [3] *Ibid.*, 300. [4] *Ibid.*, 355.

It cannot be said that the debates as such, in any clarification of issues, loomed large in the solution of the "vexed question" with which the nation was bedeviled. By 1858 it was evident that slavery in Kansas had no chance. Indeed the decisive step on this matter was taken in the free-state sense on August 2, 1858, before the joint debates began. After that, as Professor W. O. Lynch has shown, "there was no remaining Federal territory where the conditions were so favorable to slavery." [5] The fight against the Lecompton proslavery constitution was won not by reason of any debate between Lincoln and Douglas, but by the logical workings of natural causes and by a specific contest in which, with "the aid of Republicans, he [Douglas] won the Lecompton fight." [6] In 1861 Kansas was admitted as a free state, but this was just as much in accordance with Douglas's principles as with Lincoln's. In no sense did it occur by any overruling of Douglas. It came about while Federal law concerning slavery in the territories remained *the same as in 1854*. Douglas "won" the debate, as they say; yet the free-state objective was not only successful in Kansas before war broke; it was successful with Douglas's free consent [7] and outspoken leadership. On the whole, any attempt to add luster to Lincoln's fame by belittling Douglas or by exaggerating the seriousness of differences between the two men, would be a perversion of history. In the sequel, when the severe national crisis came, Douglas "defended the Inaugural address of Mr. Lincoln against the assault of opposition senators," [8] and stood firmly with Lincoln in upholding the union.

On their merits, said Beveridge, the debates "deserve little notice." [9] The same general conclusion has been reached by George Fort Milton, who has written as follows: "Judged as debates, they do not measure up to their reputation. On neither side did the dialectic compare with that in the debates between Webster, Hayne and Calhoun." [10] Historically, aside from their content and merit, there were two main results of the debates, both of which were revealed in 1860: (1) Douglas's position at Freeport in answer to Lincoln's second question, gave Southern extremists a handle by which to produce a fateful schism

---

[5] *Dic. of Amer. Hist.*, IV, 309. [6] *Ibid.*

[7] When in 1861 Kansas was admitted free while at the same time western territories were organized without prohibition of slavery, Douglas was in agreement with Republican congressional action in all the significant particulars.

[8] Blaine, *Twenty Years of Congress*, I, 287–288. [9] Beveridge, II, 635.

[10] *Dic. of Amer. Hist.*, III, 278.

in the Democratic party. This Southern result followed not from any difference between Douglas and Lincoln but from what might be called the free-state aspect of Douglas's declaration. Douglas suffered, not from any dodge nor from Lincoln's adroitness in pinning him down to an embarrassing position, but rather by his own forthright courage in expounding an interpretation of popular sovereignty which would favor freedom where people wished it. (2) The debates so advertised Lincoln that he became a figure of national importance; without them his becoming the Republican presidential candidate in 1860 would have been far less likely. Lincoln achieved this result while taking an attitude on specific proposals that was antislavery only in the mildest and most cautious sense. He managed somehow to obtain both radical and moderate support. Dissociating himself from abolitionists without quite repelling them, he made a telling appeal to moderates of the North. With the help of circumstances, and by a kind of irony, he made Douglas pay dearly for a position which offended the South only as far as it favored freedom, which Lincoln also favored.

CHAPTER VI

THE POLITICAL SCENE IN 1860

I

AFTER the debates with Douglas it was remarked that Lincoln, like Byron, awoke and found himself famous. His office holding had been slight, his public career meager; yet he was now a political personage. Numerous invitations to speak had to be declined.[1] He had reached a point where every word he said had to be carefully weighed for its effect both upon his own fortunes and upon those of his party. His correspondence with well known leaders of the Republican party showed how his counsel was being sought in other states than his own. Typical examples were his exchanges of letters in 1859 with Schuyler Colfax and Henry J. Raymond. To each of these it was as if he had said: do nothing that will rock the Republican boat. The prospects of the party were now an important concern, and for this reason he warned Colfax that local Republican groups ought to make no declaration that could not safely be generalized as the position of the whole party. We should "look beyond our noses," said Lincoln, and "say nothing on points where it is probable we shall disagree." [2] Colfax's reply recognized the expediency, if also the difficulty, of this advice for a party made up of "men of all shades . . . of opinion." [3]

[1] Lincoln's speeches in 1859 cannot be fully noted, but special mention must be made of his address before the Wisconsin State Agricultural Society at Milwaukee, September 30, 1859 (*Works*, V, 236–256). It was a non-political address, and for that reason it is all the more interesting, as it shows his attention to agricultural matters, his attitude toward labor and the common man, and his broad philosophy of life. For an excellent account of Lincoln in Milwaukee see George William Bruce, ed., *History of Milwaukee City and County*, chap. xiv. Comments of Milwaukee papers which handled the speech do not suggest that Lincoln was then generally considered as a candidate for the presidency.

[2] *Works*, V, 132 (July 6, 1859).

[3] Nicolay and Hay, *Lincoln*, II, 180.

In these matters Lincoln was definitely conservative. He still looked back to Jefferson as the source of right principles, the more so as he accused Jefferson's party of defection from the standard of their founder, but for his own party and his own time he wanted no radicalism, no abolitionist excess, no striking of the wrong note. "The chief and real purpose of the Republican party," he said in one of his 1859 speeches, "is eminently conservative." [4] His was not, however, the reactionary type of conservatism. His praise of Jefferson, written in declining an invitation to attend a Jefferson's birthday celebration in Boston, was a reaffirmation of liberal faith in matters of fundamental right,[5] and on one subject concerning which many politicians were timid, he spoke out boldly—the matter of prejudice against foreigners. It may be counted as one of the main evidences of Lincoln's liberal mind that in an era of what was called "Americanism"—an age rife with laws, movements, propaganda, and pressure politics directed against Catholics and immigrants from Europe—Lincoln stood out as one of the none-too-numerous leaders of his party who labored for tolerance among races.

Asked whether he favored the constitutional amendment recently adopted by Massachusetts to curb aliens and delay their acquisition of political rights,[6] he answered clearly that he was opposed to it. To Theodore Canisius, German-American publisher at Springfield, he wrote: "Understanding the spirit of our institutions to aim at the elevation of men, I am opposed to whatever tends to degrade them. I have some little notoriety for commiserating the oppressed negro; and I should be strangely inconsistent if I could favor . . . curtailing the . . . rights of white men, even though born in different lands, and speaking different languages from myself." [7] In May 1859 Lincoln purchased control of the German newspaper which Canisius was publishing, the *Illinois Staats-Anzeiger*. By the contract the types, etc., were to "belong to Abraham Lincoln"; Canisius was to have full use of them, and if he conducted the paper according to agreement "until after the Presidential election of 1860" the "said press, types

---

[4] *Works*, V, 147–148 (Sep. 16, 1859). [5] *Ibid.*, V, 124–127 (April 6, 1859).

[6] This constitutional provision, adopted by the voters of Massachusetts in 1859, was known as the "two year" amendment. It provided that no naturalized citizen of the United States could exercise the voting or office-holding right in Massachusetts until after a period of two years.

[7] *Works*, V, 130 (May 17, 1859).

&c" were to become Canisius's property. It was stipulated in the bond, however, that "said paper, in political sentiment, [was] not to depart from the . . . Republican platforms," nor "to print . . . any thing . . . designed to injure the Republican party." [8] It is clear that Lincoln was courting the German vote. This, however, was a matter of principle; he was not courting the nativist or intolerantly nationalist vote. He had the courage to repudiate those with whom he could not work because of principle. His policy was not that of the trimmer-politician who accepts all kinds of support, however diverse, and endeavors to repel no one.

In prominent speeches in 1859 at Columbus, Ohio, and Cincinnati, Lincoln carried forward the same type of political campaign as in the 1858 debate with Douglas. Indeed, these Ohio speeches were also a debate with Douglas who had previously spoken in the same cities.[9] The emphasis of these speeches was that in yielding to Douglas's popular sovereignty one yielded everything to the slave interests. Considering the savage fight waged against Douglas by Southern ultras, this might seem like strange doctrine. Over and over Lincoln stressed that to his own mind and to the Republican party slavery was wrong and should be checked in its further spread, while Douglas's view that it was neither right nor wrong, but a matter of indifference, would have the practical effect of making the institution national. On this point Lincoln wanted his party to stand foursquare. He took painful note of Republican embarrassment when its members in Congress failed to live up to this high principle. It hurt him sadly, for example, to reflect what the Republicans had recently done in the House of Representatives concerning what was known as the Crittenden-Montgomery bill. This was a measure providing that the proslavery Lecompton constitution be put to a vote in Kansas and that the state should be admitted as a slave commonwealth if the constitution were adopted. All the Republicans in Congress, said Lincoln, voted for the bill, whereupon Douglas claimed that they were "committed to his 'gur-reat pur-rinciple.' " For this, Republicans were accused of abandoning their own principles and were "embarrassed" in "trying to explain" that this was not so.[10]

---

[8] Angle, *New Letters and Papers*, 204–205.

[9] *Works*, V, 145, 190 (Sep. 16–17, 1859). Frank E. Stevens, *Life of Stephen A. Douglas* (*Journal*, Ill. State Hist. Soc., XVI, 1924), 607; Milton, *Eve of Conflict*, 399.

[10] *Works*, V, 278 (Dec. 1–5, 1859).

II

In this troubled year 1859 there were two factors which augmented, or reflected, the intensity of sectional feeling—the dissemination of a book by Hinton R. Helper, and the startling sensation created by John Brown's mad and criminal raid into Virginia. Helper was a North Carolinian writer of the non-planter class. Severely scoring the aristocracy of slaveholders and analyzing their potent influence, he presented with searing rhetoric the blighting effect of slavery upon the South itself. His book, *The Impending Crisis of the South: How to Meet It,* had been originally published in 1857; in 1859–60 it became a national sensation. A sum of money was subscribed for its extensive publication, and in 1860 it was widely disseminated in condensed form as a Republican campaign document. Endorsement of the book by leading men had been part of the drive for its use and politicians who had given this endorsement were made to suffer for it. An example was the supercautious John Sherman of Ohio, whose offhand endorsement of Helper, an uncharacteristic act accompanied by no conviction as to the merits of the book which he later confessed he had not read, served to prevent his election as speaker of the House of Representatives in 1859.[1] The fact that Lincoln had not given his endorsement to the book did not necessarily make him more conservative than certain men who had, but it enabled him to avoid the predicament of Sherman.

Having escaped punishment for his foul Kansas crime of '56, the abolitionist fanatic John Brown had concocted a scheme of bloody revolution against slaveholders, and for the furtherance of his violent enterprise had obtained the support of such men as Gerrit Smith of New York and Theodore Parker, S. G. Howe, T. W. Higginson, G. L. Stearns, and Franklin B. Sanborn of Massachusetts. These were high

[1] The New York *Tribune* assumed a special sponsorship of the Helper book, promoted its wide distribution, and solicited subscriptions for the purpose from Republicans in precisely the same spirit in which one would seek contributions to a party campaign. Many prominent Republicans did subscribe—including Schuyler Colfax, Anson Burlingame, Owen Lovejoy, Galusha Grow, Joshua R. Giddings, Justin S. Morrill, William Kellogg, E. B. Washburne, John Covode, F. P. Blair, Jr., John Jay, Lewis Tappan, Samuel May, and John Sherman—but not Lincoln. New York *Weekly Tribune,* Mar. 26, 1859. Seward, having endorsed Helper at an earlier time, found the subject so embarrassing that his endorsement was deleted in the edition of January 1860; see Luthin, *The First Lincoln Campaign,* 32.

minded men; they meant well; they were humanitarian reformers; Parker stood at the front among Boston ministers. Their willingness to sponsor or encourage Brown is hard to understand. The most serious misunderstanding would be to represent it as typically Bostonian or representative of the Bay State. When one remembers the powerful opposition encountered by abolitionists in Boston even in such a matter as rescuing a fugitive slave, one realizes that substance, influence, and government support in Massachusetts assuredly did not belong with Parker, Higginson, Stearns, and Sanborn in their encouragement of Brown. Much of the Brown legend, as has been shown by Professor James C. Malin,[2] is posthumous. As it has come down to us, the pro-Brown myth is a retrospective stereotype which grew up after Brown's execution and which is as far removed from historical truth, concerning Kansas and otherwise, as it is from sober rational thought.

The John Brown raid occurred in October 1859. From the Maryland side of the Potomac opposite Harpers Ferry, Virginia, on the night of October 16, the Brown party, approximately a score of desperate men including three of Brown's sons and led by the old man himself, assaulted the United States arsenal at Harpers Ferry. It was a forlorn and crack-brained affair and was easily suppressed by United States marines under Col. R. E. Lee with the assistance of Virginia militia. It embodied no serious movement in the North or anywhere else.[3] It was Brown's irrational idea, futile even for his wild purpose, and not even linked in its actual execution with the fantastic intention to form somewhere in the Virginia mountains a base for organizing and arming free blacks.

For this crime John Brown was executed at Charles Town, Virginia, on December 2, 1859. He had been tried in a local civil court at this small county seat; the indictment against him had listed three offenses, each of which carried the death penalty: traitorously making war and rebellion against Virginia, inciting slaves to insurrection, and murder.[4] In terms of popular passion, whipped-up hate, and intolerant social

[2] James C. Malin, *John Brown and the Legend of Fifty-Six.*

[3] Lee made light of the Brown affair. "It influenced his views of pending political questions not at all . . . ." He considered the plot an "attempt of a fanatic or madman" and let it go at that. "If he felt depression at the . . . appearance of . . . anti-Southern spirit in the North, he doubtless reflected that there were also extremists in his own section." Freeman, *Lee,* I, 403.

[4] John D. Lawson, ed., *American State Trials,* VI, 723 ff.; Villard, *John Brown,* 488.

psychology, the John Brown raid had an effect wholly out of balance with its intrinsic importance. The South was aroused, and odium for the crime was attached to the Republicans as if Brown's terrorist methods were the deliberate policy of their party. The affair was misrepresented by extremists as typical of "the North," this effect being heightened by a few radical abolitionists who joined in fatuous praise of Brown; thus on both sides the more extreme attitudes tended to overshadow the saner view of the nation's best minds. In genuine meaning the John Brown incident signified very little; it should have been passed off, as Lee thought; even as a disaster it was minor as compared with ocean wrecks in the same year; yet irrationally and as unfair sectional propaganda it was made into an ominous tragedy.

III

When all was said it was realized that Lincoln did not have much of a record in public life and that few men had any concept of his life story. Jesse W. Fell of Bloomington, Illinois, thinking at an early date of Lincoln as presidential timber, was not troubled by the lack of a record. "What the Republican party wants [he thought], to insure success in 1860, is a man of popular origin, of acknowledged ability, committed against slavery aggressions, who has no record to defend and no radicalism . . . to repel votes . . . ." [1] Fell did think, however, that more should be known of Lincoln's personal history, so at his request Lincoln prepared a very brief autobiography, submitting it to Fell on December 20, 1859, with the comment: "There is not much of it, for the reason, I suppose, that there is not much of me." [2] Fell took Lincoln's tiny self-sketch, made some additions, and sent them to Joseph J. Lewis of Westchester, Pennsylvania. Thus there appeared in the *Chester County Times,* Westchester, Pennsylvania, February 11, 1860, what W. E. Barton has called the first published life of Abraham Lincoln.[3] Lincoln's modest account covered less than six hundred words; the Westchester enlargement was more than six

[1] Wakefield, *How Lincoln Became President,* 96–97.

[2] *Works,* V, 286 (Dec. 29, 1859).

[3] W. E. Barton, "The Lincoln of the Biographers," *Transactions,* Ill. State Hist. Soc. 1929, 81. (At this point in the *Transactions* the Westchester article is printed in full.) See also Paul M. Angle, "Lincoln: Self-Biographer," *Abr. Lincoln Quart.,* I, 144–160 (Sep., 1940). Mr. Angle calls attention to Lincoln's tiny account of himself for the Dictionary of Congress compiled in 1858; it comprised but four printed lines.

times as long. Some of the statements were definitely pointed toward a Pennsylvania constituency, as for example the passage recommending Lincoln as "a consistent and earnest tariff man." In his sketch Lincoln had not mentioned the tariff. Lewis stated, contrary to fact, that "Mr. Lincoln was among the first to join in the formation of the Republican party." [4] In referring to the Lincoln-Douglas debates the Lewis article showed marked prejudice against Douglas, even berating him for supporting majority rule. The article had all the earmarks of a campaign biography, though belonging to the period of the prenomination canvass. It had a wide circulation "not only in Pennsylvania but in Illinois and throughout the country." The Chicago press reproduced it "almost entire, in response to the inquiry, then become general, 'Who is Abraham Lincoln?' " [5]

IV

As a continuance of his campaign of political speech making, but in a larger arena, Lincoln traveled to New York in February 1860 where, at the Cooper Institute, on the evening of the 27th he delivered one of his most significant speeches. There had been an earlier effort to have him speak in lyceum fashion at Plymouth Church, Brooklyn; after further consultation the place was shifted to New York, the purpose was changed to that of politics, and sponsorship of the address was assumed by the "Young Men's Central Republican Union of New York City," an organization which included such youths as William Cullen Bryant, aged sixty-five, and Horace Greeley, aged forty-nine. At the Cooper Institute Lincoln spoke as the contender against Douglas (the rising Democratic presidential possibility), and, in the immediate scene, as challenger against Seward. With Bryant presiding and Greeley present it was clearly an anti-Seward sponsorship under which he appeared. Greeley's *Tribune* gave special emphasis to the speech. It was almost as if it were the *Tribune's* party.[1]

---

[4] "The Lincoln of the Biographers," Barton, 83–84.

[5] Statement of Fell as quoted in Wakefield, 100. As noted earlier, Lincoln by this time had become measurably famous, but that did not mean familiarity with his career. The frequent question—Who is Abraham Lincoln?—exactly expressed both the growing interest in the man and the meagerness of knowledge concerning him.

[1] On February 27, 1860, the *Daily Tribune* (p. 4) urged one and all to come and hear Lincoln at the Cooper Institute that night, bringing non-Republican friends, and added: "It is not probable that Mr. Lincoln will be heard again in our City this year if

Lincoln's theme was a formulation of the principles on which the Republican party should face the electorate in 1860; but instead of attempting a full coverage of issues he spoke only of the slavery question. Federal slavery restriction, he urged, was consistent with the doctrines of the fathers. All that Republicans asked was to leave slavery where the fathers left it, as an evil to be tolerated but not extended.

His party, he urged, was not sectional. It would do no wrong to the South; it would deny the South no essential right. It was conservative, not revolutionary. It would stick to ways that were old and tried. It was the South, he said, that wanted a change, wishing to reject the old policy, though disagreeing among themselves as to any substitute. The John Brown raid, he insisted, was not of Republican instigation, nor was it traceable to Republican activity. Accusations to that effect were a slander. "Republican doctrines and declarations," he said, "are accompanied with a continual protest against any interference whatever with your slaves, or with you about your slaves. Surely, this does not encourage them to revolt." [2] The power of emancipation, Lincoln clearly recognized, was not in the Federal government. As for the "judgment and . . . feeling against slavery in this nation," [3] that was a thing that could not be destroyed; it was therefore better to keep it in the peaceful channel of the ballot box; to do otherwise would hardly lessen the number of John Browns. The threat that Southerners would not abide the election of a Republican President, that they would break up the Union in that event, blaming the crime upon the Republicans, he compared to the case of a highwayman terrorizing his victim.

In such passages there was indignation and biting sarcasm in Lincoln's speech. In its main emphasis, however, it was conciliatory toward the South. He advised his party associates to yield to Southerners wherever possible, to "do nothing through passion and ill temper," to try to determine what their demands involved, and make every effort to "satisfy them." [4] "Wrong as we think slavery is," he

---

ever. Let us improve the present opportunity." (The *Tribune* had been urging Douglas for Republican standard bearer. As nomination time approached, Greeley favored Bates.) On February 28 the *Tribune* printed the speech in full, giving it five full columns.

[2] *Works*, V, 315–316 (Feb. 27, 1860). [3] *Ibid.*, V, 319. [4] *Ibid.*, V, 323–324.

urged, "we can yet afford to let it alone where it is . . . ."[5] He concluded: "Neither let us be slandered from our duty by false accusations against us, nor frightened from it by menaces of destruction to the government, nor of dungeons to ourselves. Let us have faith that right makes might, and in that faith let us to the end dare to do our duty as we understand it."[6]

Other speeches by Lincoln in this general period were in the same vein. Though not mere repetition, they struck the same note, emphasizing that slavery was wrong, but hoping for a cure, together with an abatement of factional strife and controversy. Besides the speeches mentioned in Ohio in 1859 he had spoken in that year at various places in Illinois, Wisconsin, Iowa, and Kansas. Now in February-March 1860 he made a New England tour, speaking in Providence, Concord, Manchester, Dover, Exeter (where his son Robert was a student), Hartford, New Haven, Meriden, Woonsocket, Norwich, and Bridgeport.[7] He arrived home in Springfield on March 14.

He was not merely a passive candidate, but was concerning himself actively with matters preliminary to the Republican national convention. Viewing his own chances for the presidential nomination at this stage, he reasoned that he was not the first choice of a great many, and that wise strategy was to give no offense, looking for second-choice support (for the presidency) if and when first choices should fail.[8] That he was now eager for the prize, which he considered not hopeless, is shown by his offering to furnish one hundred dollars to a Kansas supporter, expecting him to serve as delegate.[9]

V

The making of high policy by an aggregation of politician-delegates backed by ill-defined constituencies, uncertain as to credentials,

[5] *Ibid.*, V, 327.

[6] *Ibid.*, V, 327–328.

[7] P. C. Eggleston, *Lincoln in New England.*

[8] *Works*, VI, 7–8 (Mar. 24, 1860).

[9] In a letter to Mark W. Delahay, March 16, 1860, Lincoln made the offer of one hundred dollars to cover Delahay's trip to Chicago as Republican delegate. That Lincoln did not consider this unethical is shown by his statement to Delahay that he could not "enter the ring on the money basis," and that "in the main, the use of money is wrong," but that "for certain objects in a political contest, the use of some is both right and indispensable." Delahay was not a delegate, and the Kansas delegation was instructed for Seward; yet Lincoln advised his friend to come to Chicago anyhow, adding that he would keep his word about the expense money. *Works*, VI, 5–6. Pratt, *Personal Finances*, 106–107.

swayed by demagogues, pulled apart by factional caucuses, diverted from any unified course by clamoring minorities, deadlocked and stymied for desperate weeks, and finally breaking up into warring fragments—such was the story of the various Democratic conventions of 1860. The one man who seemed best able to lead the party to success if it remained united, and who on the same assumption seemed most likely to avert disunion if elected, was Stephen A. Douglas. When the Democrats themselves failed to unite for Douglas, failing also to unite on any common program or leader, it was almost as if they themselves had decreed disunion.

It was Congress and the President who were regularly authorized to legislate and govern; yet, by process none too regular, affairs had been turned over to the maneuverings and intrigues of parties, which had no constitutional existence. Parties controlled and exercised great public functions, yet they were so subject to manipulation that they served in a most unsatisfactory manner as public instruments.

It is not feasible to review the manner in which parties had fastened themselves upon the government. It is sufficient to note that, practically, there was no other available device by which the people were able to determine the most vital of their political affairs in the election of President and Congress. Not only was there no method by which the people could go ahead without parties to enact their will; neither was there much likelihood that they could compel a national party to perform adequately for the nation the task which its hands had seized. A convention was unpredictable, and in a time of artificial excitement the exertion of calm, reasoned, public opinion upon a convention was well nigh hopeless.

For the background of this party warfare among the Democrats one must read such a book as Laura A. White's study of R. B. Rhett, aggressive disunionist of South Carolina; for the intrigues of 1860 one may turn to George Fort Milton's *Eve of Conflict.* Rhett and his *Mercury* of Charleston worked for secession by a deliberate calculation of the cumulative measures, step by step, which were designed to produce that result. Rightly he has been called the "father of secession." Steps in the South toward preservation of the Union were countered by him with a boldness of purpose that was artfully combined with strategic skill. Working along the same line as Rhett was William L. Yancey of Alabama. Against the judgment of conservative

Southerners (numerous, distinguished, and as "Southern" as one could wish) Yancey, Rhett, and their colleagues built up among vigorous elements in the lower South a savage antagonism against Douglas for his popular sovereignty doctrine—the doctrine which, oddly enough, Lincoln characterized as yielding everything to the slave interests. It became evident, not only that Douglas was no spokesman for slave interests in any aggressive sense, but that a kind of secession against Douglas was the implacable purpose of a determined Southern element. If this element, failing to rule, should ruin the Democratic party, they were already prepared to take the next step—secession and the formation of a separate nation of the South. Some of their followers might not look that far ahead (as it turned out, it was just ahead); yet by being drawn into the earlier stages of the movement, they contributed to its main consequence.

The details being too elaborate and tiresome to repeat, it will be appropriate here to summarize what happened in Democratic councils. This may be done in terms of the five gatherings in April and June of 1860 which took the form of Democratic conventions, or meetings of Democratic convention delegates.

(1) When in April the national convention of the party, after canvasses in the states, met at Charleston, a long and bitter struggle ensued in which the Yanceyites seized upon the issue of slavery in the territories as a platform matter on which they staged a revolt, or bolt, from the convention. A majority of the convention favored a platform declaration that would reaffirm the Cincinnati platform of 1856 —i. e., non-intervention by Congress in the territories, with adherence to the Compromise of 1850; to this they added that on the whole question they would willingly abide by the decision of the Supreme Court of the United States. The Yanceyites, however, insisted on a platform declaration affirming the positive duty of Congress actually to establish and protect slavery in the territories. This would have meant that, even if the people of a territory were overwhelmingly opposed to slavery, Congress must forcibly maintain it in their midst and against their will. It would have been regarded by Douglas men as a slave code imposed upon territories. Douglas could not have well agreed to this doctrine; it would have been a repudiation of his whole position and a betrayal of both Northern and Southern supporters. By agreeing to abide by the action of the Supreme Court, however,

Douglas and his followers made as much of a concession as was decently possible; in this manner they even left the door open to the Yancey doctrine if the Court should endorse it.[1] Unwilling to accept compromise or consent to majority rule, Yancey headed a movement of bolters. With his Alabama delegation he left the convention hall; in this secession he was joined by certain other delegates of the lower South. By this defiant act the signal for disunion in the party of Jefferson, Calhoun, Benton, and Jackson, had been flashed.

There was now deadlock, Douglas men having a majority but not the two-thirds necessary to nominate. After protracted and anxious sessions they decided to adjourn, to meet in Baltimore in June. Meanwhile the appeal was made for the appointment of new delegates in those states where "vacancies" existed.

(2) Meeting in another hall in Charleston, and calling themselves the "Constitutional Democratic convention," the Yancey seceders decided to hold their own type of extreme Southern convention at Richmond in June. In this action the strings were not entirely pulled by Southerners. The maneuvers of Benjamin F. Butler of Massachusetts, the attitude of Caleb Cushing,[2] also of the Bay State, and the activities of the "Buchanan Ultras" with their plentiful use of Federal patronage to knife Douglas, served to strengthen the Southern extremists.

(3) The main adjourned convention met again in June in Baltimore. Here a curious thing happened. After revolting against the convention and withdrawing to form their own organization, the Yancey group, some of them, turned up at Baltimore and demanded that they be taken back into the fold. (This they did with no change of heart in

---

[1] If it be thought that the Court had already endorsed the Yancey doctrine, it should be remembered that the subject was not viewed in the same light even by Democrats. Douglas held the people of a territory to be empowered to prohibit slavery by unfriendly legislation despite the Dred Scott decision; on the other hand, the high court seemed by many to be in line with the extreme proslavery, or Yanceyite, view. When Douglas men at Charleston made the concession as to abiding by a future decision of the Court, they implied that if the Court should unequivocally uphold the Yancey view they would agree to it; but, at a time when both lawyers and laymen were puzzled by the Court's ponderous verbiage, they also implied that a further word from the Court would be needful.

[2] Caleb Cushing of Massachusetts, affiliated with the Buchanan wing of Northern Democrats, presided over the regular Democratic convention at Charleston and the main Democratic convention at Baltimore; in both these capacities he persistently gave rulings in the anti-Douglas sense. After the break at Baltimore he also presided over the convention of Southern bolters.

the matter of national or party unity; they were as determined as ever to insist upon the Yancey view as to slavery; nor were they ready to compromise with Northern delegates on this overemphasized point.) In the interval between April and June, however, a reaction against Yancey had developed, at least partially, in some of the lower Southern states, and organizations in these states, noting the Yancey revolt and obeying the injunction to fill vacancies, had sent delegates to Baltimore who were prepared to coöperate with the main convention. In Louisiana, for instance, there was a severe contest between Slidell, who was carrying his anti-Douglas attitude to the point of breaking up the Democratic party, and Pierre Soulé, who appeared at Baltimore as leader of a newly chosen Democratic delegation of Louisiana moderates. These moderates, supported by the *True Delta* of New Orleans, expressed the Union-saving sentiment of Louisiana, claiming that Slidell's seceders and bolters did not truly represent the state. There being similar cleavages in other states, one could see in this Louisiana situation an epitome of the angry struggle within the Democratic party in the South.

The pressure upon this Baltimore convention was so tremendous and its proceedings so difficult that at one point Douglas authorized the withdrawal of his name if that should become necessary to promote harmony. When votes in the convention went contrary to the Southern ultra faction, though some of the seceders (as from Mississippi, Texas, and Georgia) were readmitted to the roll, there occurred another bolt of Southern opponents of Douglas, animated by Yancey leadership but led this time by Russell of Virginia. Thus both at Charleston and at Baltimore the quarrels between pro-Douglas and anti-Douglas men had resulted in a bolt of the latter. In this phase there were intrastate quarrels, some of the delegates refusing to join this bolting movement. Having struggled with the problem of its membership, the Baltimore convention proceeded to the nomination of President and Vice President, choosing Stephen A. Douglas of Illinois and Benjamin Fitzpatrick of Alabama. On Fitzpatrick's declination, the Democratic national committee later chose Herschel V. Johnson, Georgia unionist, as Douglas's running mate.

(4) Up to this point, though numerical order is not the purpose, mention has been made of three convention meetings among the Democrats—the main convention at Charleston, the seceders at

Charleston, and the adjourned (reconstituted) convention at Baltimore. Another now occurred at Baltimore, whither Yancey had traveled with a considerable group of followers, instead of confining themselves to the Richmond gathering which the bolters themselves had promoted. By an amazing reach of authority, this Yancey group at Baltimore assumed the function of their own Richmond meeting as well as that of the main national convention. Adopting the Yancey platform, they nominated John C. Breckinridge of Kentucky for President of the United States and Joseph Lane of Oregon for Vice President. This Baltimore group was presided over by Caleb Cushing; one of its most prominent members was Benjamin F. Butler of Massachusetts. The country was now witnessing the spectacle of bogus party devices, easy to concoct, but difficult for the people to use as instruments in the management of public affairs. Yancey delivered a long speech to this Baltimore convention in the midst of which large numbers left the hall.

(5) The seceders had gathered at Richmond on June 11 [3] according to schedule, but had marked time while proceedings were in progress at Baltimore. Having waited, they found that they had virtually nothing to do. As if they constituted the Democratic party of the whole nation, they now made their nominations for President and Vice President of the United States; but since Yancey's group had already performed this function at Baltimore, the Richmond convention merely ratified the nominations of Breckinridge and Lane.

Douglas would now have to wage a campaign not only against Republicans, and against the Bell-Everett group (organized in May), but also against recent party associates whose enmity toward him was ugly and bitter. Had he been chosen President in such an atmosphere,

[3] If one wanted to spin out this analysis, he could speak of two conventions—or rather two convention sessions—at Richmond. The first met on June 11 and adjourned without transacting any significant business on June 12, most of the delegates (though not those of South Carolina) going to Baltimore. Reassembling at Richmond, with a very limited membership present, on June 21, the convention did nothing till June 26 when the Baltimore proceedings were over and a greater number of Southern delegates were in attendance. Then in a very brief and perfunctory session they ratified the nominations of Breckinridge and Lane. The numbering of these party gatherings is meant above only as a handy device. Since the Richmond convention marked time awaiting developments in the anti-Douglas convention at Baltimore, the latter has been called the fourth in these pages; the Richmond convention, which was the last of the Democratic conventions to act, has been called the fifth. Some might number them differently where conventions were running simultaneously, but numerical order is of little significance.

one can only wonder what the result would have been. It has already been noted that Douglas's ability to hold the country together was conditioned upon unity within his party. Would he as President have had the same type of secession to deal with that Lincoln had? Lincoln and Douglas had never in fact been so far apart as party exigencies had made them seem, and on the matter of the Union they thought alike. Soon the time would come when they would stand squarely together as they faced the sectional crisis.

VI

In early May, in between the Democratic gathering at Charleston and the Republican convention at Chicago, there met at Baltimore a group of conservatives whose main characteristic was "disgust at political trickery" [1] combined with deep patriotic concern for the endangered Union. If any body of men ever felt that they had a vitally important task to perform in other than partisan terms, it was these men; if any group saw clearly the coming effect of disruptive tendencies in 1860 and, seeing, hoped and endeavored to do something about it before it was too late, it was they. The tendency of most writers has been to speak lightly of them, while admitting their eminent respectability. The most vivid description of their convention, in an old church in the Maryland metropolis, is by the ubiquitous Murat Halstead who packed as much sarcasm into his account of their proceedings as his racy journalism could muster. Halstead wrote of the gathering as that of dignified venerables. On the fringes of the crowd, however, he found "plugs" and "Yahoos on a spree," while at a high spot in the proceedings he wrote of "Bedlam broken loose." [2]

These men carried forward the Whig and "American" tradition. Some of their proposed candidates were Crittenden of Kentucky, Houston of Texas, Bell of Tennessee, Everett of Massachusetts, and Botts of Virginia. Among those who figured in their convention were Washington Hunt of New York, W. G. Brownlow and Andrew Jackson Donelson of Tennessee, R. W. Thompson of Indiana, Alexander H. H. Stuart and Waitman T. Willey of Virginia, John Scott Harrison of Ohio, William L. Sharkey of Mississippi, Leverett Saltonstall of

---

1 Halstead, *Caucuses of 1860*, 112. 2 *Ibid.*, 110, 116.

Massachusetts, Leslie Combs of Kentucky, and John M. Morehead of North Carolina.

In a facetious speech as chairman Washington Hunt announced that he had prepared three platforms: one for the Democrats, "one for the 'irrepressible conflict' gentlemen," and one for "this Convention." For the "harmonious Democracy" he suggested two declarations: "one in favor of excluding slavery from the Territories . . . , and the other in favor of forcing it into them . . . ; both to be adopted unanimously . . . ."[3] For "the 'irrepressible conflict' philanthropists about to assemble at Chicago" he proposed the Connecticut blue laws amended to permit kissing one's wife on Sunday and burning "old witches." For his own convention he proposed: ". . . the Constitution . . . as it is, and the Union under it now and forever." That is "all we need," he said; if he were making a creed for Christians he would take "the Bible as it is, leaving all to construe it."[4]

In tune with the Hunt keynote the Constitutional Union convention adopted a refreshingly brief platform. Following a preamble in which "platforms . . . by . . . partisan conventions" were held to be misleading and disruptive, the sole resolution of the convention called for "no political principle other than the Constitution of the country, the union of the states, and the enforcement of the laws."[5]

Though on the first ballot Bell's vote did not greatly exceed that of Houston, he became on the second ballot the nominee of the convention, with the distinguished Everett as candidate for Vice President. With a Southerner and a slaveholder for standard bearer the appeal of the Constitutional Union party was chiefly to the upper South and border, to non-Republican areas in which Lincoln was impossible while both Douglas and Breckinridge were largely distrusted as being too factional.

This Bell group was to become an important anti-Douglas force, both in the process of party nomination and in the election. Feeling that they would have trouble carrying their own states for Douglas against a Southerner, those Democrats of the South who were not disposed toward a moderate course found additional reason, after Bell's nomination, to reject Douglas as standard bearer. According to James G. Blaine, they felt that it "would be poor recompense . . .

---

[3] *Ibid.*, 108. [4] *Ibid.*

[5] Emerson D. Fite, *The Presidential Campaign of 1860*, 242–243.

to recover certain Northern States from the Republicans, if . . . an equal number of Southern States should be carried by Bell, and the destiny of the South be committed to a conservative party, which would abandon threats and cultivate harmony." [6] Later, when it came to the election, the really formidable opponent of Breckinridge in states of the South was not to be Douglas, but Bell. In that Douglas was a man of greater national leadership than Bell while his policy was moderation and sectional harmony, the followers of the Tennessean, by opposing Douglas, played into the hands of the ultras and helped to defeat their own cause of peace and union.

VII

In the prenomination situation in the Republican party there were five prominent contenders for chief place, and a somewhat indeterminate number of minor ones. The leading five were Seward of New York, Cameron of Pennsylvania, Chase of Ohio, Bates of Missouri, and Lincoln of Illinois. With all eyes on Chicago where the nominating convention of the party was to be held in mid-May, the hopeful candidates and their scheming managers marshaled their forces with the energy, maneuvering, and intrigue that is characteristic of preconvention politics. In this preliminary phase the man who stood out most conspicuously was Seward. His partisans took his coming success at Chicago for granted. He could point to a long record of public service as governor and senator, having been well known as a Whig during practically the whole lifetime of that party. Somewhat tardily, but in time, he had shifted to the new Republican party (this was in 1855); in 1860 it would not have been an overstatement to describe him as that party's most distinguished leader. It was a Republican necessity to "carry" New York with its heavy electoral strength, and those who knew were convinced that no one could do that better than Seward. In addition, he had in Thurlow Weed the shrewdest and most experienced of managers.[1] It was like a partnership—Seward, Weed and Company—and the sheer weight of party technique, clien-

[6] Blaine, *Twenty Years of Congress*, I, 163–164. Blaine adds: "Bell's nomination had, therefore, proved the final argument against the acceptance of Douglas by the Southern Democracy."

[1] For Weed's complex personality, his tendency to put the politician's interest first, his increasing big-business affiliation, and like matters, see Glyndon G. Van Deusen, "Thurlow Weed: A Character Study," *Amer. Hist. Rev.*, XLIX, 427–440 (Apr., 1944).

tele, and organization wielded by such a firm would have been hard to match.

Weed is an outstanding example of the type of American politician that operates in the field of party strategy, seeking not public office, but rather the patronage, power, spoils, and Warwick-like influence that comes of steering a party through the unseen intricacies of committee, caucus, and preliminary canvass, and down through the more visible processes of popular appeal and election. After election the processes again become somewhat invisible, being concerned with the rewards and perquisites of office. In all such matters Weed was regarded as a past master. The familiar term given to such a man is boss; Weed was Republican boss in New York, and he aspired to the same mysterious eminence for the nation. It was characteristic of his methods and of the time that he had his newspaper; for decades the famous Albany *Evening Journal* served as his medium, being usually more concerned with merchants and industrialists than with the common people, its interests in the latter being a matter of harvesting their votes.

These were elements of Seward's strength, but he had points of weakness. In 1850, when elder statesmen—Webster, Clay, Calhoun—were debating the great compromise, he had given his eleventh of March speech in which he opposed measures to appease the slave interests; on this occasion he had referred to "a higher law than the Constitution." In this same speech he had said: "The Constitution regulates our stewardship; the Constitution devotes the domain to union, to justice, to defence, to welfare, and to liberty." [2] This was entering the treacherous field of phrase-making; the better the phrase, the more tricky its effect in terms of practical politics.

Again, at Rochester on October 25, 1858, he had said: "Shall I tell you what this collision means? They who think that it is . . . the work of . . . fanatical agitators, and therefore ephemeral, mistake the case altogether. It is an irrepressible conflict between opposing and enduring forces, and it means that the United States must . . . become either entirely a slave-holding nation or entirely a free-labor nation." [3] Such phrases, with their judgment-day suggestion and their abolitionist flavor, did not suit the Republican party in its 1860 mood. There was an irony in it all, for in truth Seward in 1860 was the

[2] Bancroft, *Seward*, I, 247.

[3] *Ibid.*, I, 458–459.

opposite of radical. Weed was never the man to break a lance for abstract moral principles; both Weed and Seward had chosen the part of caution and moderation; between the sections they wanted nothing of irrepressible conflict; they wanted conciliation. It does not make sense that Seward should have suffered for these phrases or that he should have been represented as a stirrer of sectional trouble. His 1860 note was sounded on February 29 of that year in the United States Senate, and it was very far indeed from irrepressible conflict. For the time at hand and for the view ahead he believed that the Republican party must think little of metaphysical speculation and must hold itself within "the necessity of being practical in its care of the national health and life." Calling attention to the dominant strength of the Republican party in the North, and to the long standing attitude of Northern forbearance toward the South, he repudiated the charge that the party was sectional. In this he was not altogether convincing, but at least it could be said that in his view the party ought not to be sectional at the moment when it was about to enter upon the responsibility of office and of government. Instead of conflict, Seward urged a mutuality between North and South by which each might continue to cherish its own institutions, remembering that "All the world discusses all systems." With every thought of allaying sectional strife, he emphasized fraternity between all parts of the country and sought to make it appear that trouble was only imaginary. "There is not one disunionist . . . among us all," he declared. "We are . . . unconscious of any process of dissolution going on among us or around us." [4]

In addition to his undeserved and misleading reputation as a radical, Seward was otherwise vulnerable. His connection with Weed, useful as it was, savored too much of machine rule to suit progressive spirits. The very thoroughness and frankness of Weed's bossism produced dissension in New York. The name of Weed connoted tricky politics. In 1859–60 he had headed "a scheme to furnish, through the New York legislature, charters for city railroads, whose grantees were in turn to supply several hundred thousand dollars for the Republican campaign of 1860, in which Seward was expected to be the party candidate." [5] As a result of such methods there had arisen an influential anti-Seward faction of the Republican party in New York, headed by the

[4] *Ibid.*, I, 513–515.

[5] *Ibid.*, I, 524.

powerful Greeley, and graced by the adherence of the highminded W. C. Bryant. This lively faction stood squarely athwart the former governor's path.

In Pennsylvania Simon Cameron was not alone a Seward or a Weed; he was something like a combination of the two. He was both boss and candidate. After long years of service (if it could be called that) in the Democratic party, in which he had managed to antagonize many of its chief leaders, he had turned a full somersault, and the year 1860 found him in the United States Senate as a Republican. He was now over sixty, had amassed a fortune, had practiced on the profitable borderline of politics and business, had become an industrial magnate, and had managed to bring within his experienced grasp the complex range of party management. Regard for ideals or principles was less a factor with him than the use of his adopted party as a tool of large manufacturing interests. To get support in Pennsylvania, which had cast its vote for Buchanan in 1856 but which seemed a promising Republican state in 1860, meant appeasing Cameron; that in turn required support of a protective tariff. Such a tariff, for example, would coddle the iron business in which Cameron was personally interested. Nor were his other interests, such as banking and railroading, unlikely to color his political thought.

Cameron's men would come to Chicago with bargaining power. They would have to be reckoned with. Pennsylvania could not be ignored. The main prize, however, was not so likely to be within his reach. His name was associated with undertakings that did not imply the highest code of honor; his forte was party intrigue; few if any would think of calling him a statesman. That he had been a Democrat was not so serious as the obvious fact that mere expediency had caused him to shift his allegiance. Opposition to slavery had little if anything to do with this shift. He had traded on the confused party situation in Pennsylvania in the fifties. In this he had accepted Knownothing support and was therefore distrusted by the Germans. When in early summer, 1858, the New York *Herald* published a numerous list of Republican candidates (Bissell and Grow being included, but Lincoln omitted), Cameron was designated as "Democratic Know Nothing Republican Conservative." [6] Early in 1860 an effort to promote a

[6] New York *Herald*, June 28, 1858, p. 4, c. 3. The *Herald's* flair for picturesque journalism was illustrated in the labels attached to the various candidates. Some of

"Cameron and Lincoln" club (for Cameron as President with Lincoln as Vice President) made little progress; assuredly if it had achieved its object, the result would have been highly uncongenial to Lincoln. Within his own state Cameron had to contend with the determined opposition of the McClure-Curtin faction of the Republican party. This was one of the bitterest feuds of partisan history; it "continued as long as they [Cameron and Curtin] were in active political life." [7]

Salmon P. Chase of Ohio, puritan in politics, had done noble service in the antislavery cause, his activities in this capacity having been more pronounced than Lincoln's. After laboring in the Liberty party in 1840 and 1844, and in the Free Soil party in 1848, and after noting the futility of these third-party efforts, he had changed his strategy and had sought manfully to capture the Democratic party for the cause of antislavery, or to be more exact, the cause of slavery limitation. Failing in that, he had shifted, as inevitably he had to shift, to the Republican party, and as its leader had been elected governor of Ohio in 1855. In the course of his career he had incurred the opposition of old line Whigs, old line Democrats, and also Republicans of certain groups, as for example those who had little antislavery zeal and those who opposed nativism, for he had been embarrassed by the unsought support of Ohio Knownothings. Having been a free trader, he had shifted his economic position for political reasons and had come over to the cause of protection. In a letter to a member of the Ohio legislature, October 25, 1859, he had referred to international free trade as a policy which could not be realized and had indicated squarely that he would support legislation "to protect American industry." [8] His background was not Whig, nor would regular Democrats have called it Democratic. Entering the Republican party, he brought it little strength in terms of influential following. Moreover, he had little more than the prospect of complimentary support from Ohio. The faction of Benjamin F. Wade opposed him bitterly,[9] and

---

them were: "Anti-Know Nothing Democratic Free Soil and Free Trade Republican" (Frémont); "Know Nothing 'Free Wool' Republican" (Banks); "Other Republicans of the Kansas Tribe" (Chase, Hale, Wilson, Trumbull, Bissell, Grow). Douglas was bracketed with "Anti-Lecompton Anti Administration Democrats."

[7] A. K. McClure, *Abraham Lincoln and Men of War Times,* 149.

[8] Chase to Senator Stanley of the Ohio legislature, Columbus, October 25, 1859, Chicago *Press & Tribune,* Jan. 25, 1860, p. 3, c. 4.

[9] Wade was without appreciable strength. Greeley wrote as follows: ". . . I am not so sure about Wade. He is a good soul; but he has made some *awful* speeches—worse

he was to be denied full Ohio support even on the first ballot. Yet there was an upstanding quality in Chase. Toward this competitor Lincoln asked especially that "no ungenerous thing" be done. Chase, said Lincoln, "gave us his sympathy in 1858 when scarcely any other distinguished man did." [10]

Edward Bates, bearded patriarch of Missouri, was regarded as one of the outstanding Republican contenders; in 1860 he was sixty-seven years of age. In his unspectacular career a mild antislavery attitude had been superimposed upon a Southern planter tradition, but this attitude was held in bounds by an eminently respectable Whig conservatism. Bates's strength lay in the solidity of this conservatism and in the hope that his following in the border states and perhaps farther south might serve to avert secession if he should be elected. The movement to promote his candidacy was supposed to be of national proportions, being sustained by the impressive support of Horace Greeley as well as of the Blair clan. Being anti-Seward, yet finding no favorite son in New York to pit against Seward, being also something of a specialist on the great West, Greeley found no difficulty in going as far west as Missouri for his candidate. "My candidate for President in 1860 is Edward Bates of Missouri," he wrote in February of that year. He added: "As he is an old time Whig, and supported Fillmore . . . in 1856, I do not see how the Americans of that year can refuse to take him; and I, as a pretty advanced Republican, can risk a man who quietly, years ago, emancipated and provided for his own slaves." [11]

On the other hand, Bates's supposed or reputed favoring of nativist tendencies offended the Germans who were strong in the Middle West; he was a bit too much of a relic to suit the stirring times; his almost pathetic attachment to the Whigs seemed like harking back to a lost cause; and his practical chances were seriously reduced when Norman Judd, member of the Republican national committee, induced that committee to select Chicago as the place of meeting instead of Bates's home city, St. Louis.

---

than the 'irrepressible conflict.'" Greeley to Colfax, May 7, 1860, Greeley-Colfax MSS., New York Pub. Lib. For a characterization of Wade, see vol. II, 209–210.

[10] *Works*, VI, 8 (Mar. 24, 1860).

[11] Greeley to Hector Orr, Feb. 11, 1860, Greeley MSS., New York Pub. Lib.

VIII

In this brief survey of what we may call the big five, another glance at Lincoln, considered nominationwise, is desirable. When the convention met in Chicago, Lincoln's working support in Illinois had been fully implemented. The state Republican convention meeting at Decatur on May 9–10, 1860, had instructed its delegation for Lincoln for President.[1] In political parlance this marked him as more than a "favorite son," for many a favorite son has had little more than home-state support on early and indecisive ballots. Missouri Republicans were to put forth a considerable effort for Bates and New York men for Seward; but if one considers the others, Illinois was back of Lincoln to an extent that was not true of Pennsylvania toward Cameron or of Ohio toward Chase. Illinois men, with strategic concentration on control of the convention itself, worked for Lincoln. They labored not merely to give him initial support, but to make him President. They did this because of personal enthusiasm, or out of the zeal of conviction, or, as in the case of Browning, by reason of what was expected of them under the circumstances; but the point is, they did it. It is true that the degree of Illinois unanimity for Lincoln in the pre-convention phase is hard to estimate and has perhaps at times been exaggerated. Many of Trumbull's correspondents seemed to favor him—at least they wrote him so—and one may wonder what would have happened if Trumbull had made a determined fight for Illinois presidential support, which he did not do, favoring Judge McLean. Whatever may have been the previous possibilities of conflict or rivalry within Republicans of the state, support for Lincoln was strong and solid in the active and effective sense—i. e., in the work actually done from the opening of the convention and carrying through to the final ballot.

Lincoln had the conservatism which certain other candidates did

---

[1] Lincoln was present at this convention which is chiefly remembered for a backwoodsy incident. His country cousin, John Hanks, with a fellow pioneer, carried in two rails with a placard which said that they had been split by Lincoln; following this, amid rousing cheers, Lincoln spoke briefly, indicating that he had split rails in Macon County, of which Decatur was county seat, though not claiming that these particular rails were his. Angle, *Lincoln, 1854–1861*, 332. For further particulars on this homely incident, which "set a keynote for the campaign," see Helen Nicolay, in *Abr. Lincoln Quart.*, I, 129 (Sep., 1940).

not have, at least in reputation; to this he added an element not too common among conservatives—the vitalizing talent of arousing enthusiasm. Middle-of-the-road men could support him, but so also could ardent zealots. There were some, of course, who were all out for Lincoln. A correspondent of Lyman Trumbull wrote: "Of those *now* prominently before the people as Candidates for the Presidency, I think Lincoln is by far the strongest man for the race." [2] Others wrote in the same vein to Trumbull. "I believe we could elect either Seward or Chace [*sic*], but with Lincoln our success would be *much more certain* . . ." [3] " 'Old Abe,' " wrote another, "is the man for this region beyond a doubt, We can carry Illinois with him easy." [4] The very difficulty and uncertainty of Republican unity, not to mention the wish to win converts outside the fold, gave added logic to the Lincoln cause. Lincoln's chances were also enhanced by the feeling that a western man was needed in 1860; yet it should be such a western man as would find support in the East.[5] It was, therefore, of importance that Lincoln had made his appearance at the Cooper Institute at a significant moment in the prenomination canvass, that he had gone from there to various places in New England, and that in doing so he had made a favorable impression. In all these political situations there was an element of luck and chance. One of the chances to guard against was that the Lincoln movement would be sidetracked into the vice-presidency. Preferring Bates or Dayton as President, Greeley thought well of Lincoln for Vice President, though disliking the idea of two Whigs.[6] The idea of Lincoln for second place on the ticket was also put forth by an editor in Danville, Illinois. Carrying the name of Chase for President at his masthead, he wrote: "For Vice President the name of Hon. A. Lincoln . . . I have found to meet the hearty approbation of the leading Republicans of this County." [7]

Another chance to guard against was that the cause of compromise and harmony might overreach itself and go to such a limit as to choose

---

[2] S. York to Trumbull, Paris, Ill., April 20, 1860, Trumbull MSS.

[3] C. D. Hay to Trumbull, Newton, Ill., March 11, 1860, *ibid.*,

[4] J. R. Bulion to Trumbull, Marshall, Ill., April 9, 1860, *ibid.*

[5] "The 'Cinti Gazette' thinks the Republican candidate for Prest will be a western man." Lewis Dyer to Trumbull, Duquoin, Ill., Jan. 3, 1860, *ibid.* "My . . . opinion is that we must have a western, well known good & true Republican & from a free State . . . ." G. O. Pond to Trumbull, Griggsville, Ill., Dec. 28, 1859, *ibid.*

[6] Greeley to Colfax, Feb. 3, 1860. Greeley-Colfax MSS., New York Pub. Lib.

[7] G. Price Smith to S. P. Chase, Danville, Ill., Dec. 16, 1859, Trumbull MSS.

Judge McLean.[8] Joseph Medill of the Chicago *Tribune,* for example, feeling some doubt as to the nomination of Seward or Bates or Lincoln, thought it not unlikely that McLean would emerge as "the compromise candidate to harmonize . . . all segments of the opposition." [9]

Putting Lincoln's cards together, he had conservatism combined with zeal; he was a westerner not unacceptable to the East; his pre-Republican background had been Whig, which was an advantage for the presidential nomination, while a Democratic background might serve for the vice-presidency; he could enlist the Germans; he had prominence as a second choice; he stood forth as a challenger of Douglas; he was regarded as having thrown into the background those questions (except indeed that of the union) which divided the North and the South; [10] he was free from drawbacks, such as those which plagued Chase and Bates; he had the immense local advantage of the Chicago setting; he had the friendship of certain men even though they were pledged to Seward; [11] finally, he had the skillful support of political strategists working tirelessly for him at the tumultuous front of political action.

---

[8] McLean's frequent candidacy for the presidency though a member of the United States Supreme Court, and his support by some in 1860 though he was then seventy-five years old, are treated in Weisenburger, *The Life of John McLean: A Politician on the United States Supreme Court.*

[9] J. Medill to Trumbull, Chicago, April 16, 1860, Trumbull MSS.

[10] A. L. Kohlmeier in *Transactions,* Ill. State Hist. Soc., 1923, 161.

[11] In Kansas, for example, the delegates were for Seward but regarded Lincoln "as a highly acceptable and available candidate." T. Ewing, Jr., to A. Lincoln, Leavenworth, Kansas, May 6, 1860, T. Ewing MSS.

CHAPTER VII

DESTINY IN A WIGWAM

I

IN THE "vast tabernacle" [1] or "wigwam" erected for the purpose, the national convention of the Republican party assembled in Chicago for a three-day session, May 16–18, 1860. The off-duty activities of the delegates were convivial to say the least, perhaps in some cases disreputable; the make-up of the convention was ill defined; the assembly was disorderly; floor proceedings were hard to control. It was complained that delegates passed their tickets of admission over the railings and through the windows to friends not entitled to seats. So many spectators or guests were mixed in with the accredited delegations that the chairman had to ask each delegation to "purge itself." [2] There was an immense and restless crowd inside the hall, while outside the building surging thousands had to be entertained in the manner of stump speaking by orators selected from the convention.

It is an amazing exercise to read in cold print the proceedings of that gathering. There was haste, impatience, rudeness, uncertainty or inattention as to parliamentary situations, and a tendency of some to cry down a speaker they did not like. There were laughs and hisses, cheers and yawps, and moments that came close to the farcical. At one point the chair (George Ashmun of Massachusetts) was asked to inform the convention what motion was before it.[3] At another it was feared that the delegates would transact their business and pass their resolutions before they were "organized." [4] Far along in the third session (on the morning of the second day), when a vote by roll of

[1] *Proceedings of the First Three Republican National Conventions* . . . , pub. by Charles W. Johnson, Minneapolis, Minn. (1893). (Cited below as Johnson, *Proceedings*.) 91.

[2] *Ibid.*, 107, 146. [3] *Ibid.*, 92. [4] *Ibid.*, 93.

the states was called for, the chair knew of no rule by which that could be arrived at.[5] At the outset the convention got all tangled up because an invitation to an excursion on the lake seemed about to steal the show. After the acceptance of the invitation, followed immediately by the discovery of practical difficulties, a delegate from Missouri hoped that they would not "stultify" themselves by rescinding their acceptance.[6] So difficult did the momentous problem of the excursion seem, with the announcement that the Board of Trade had its fleet all ready for the purpose (though this would have interfered with the afternoon or evening session of the first day), that the convention's business seemed threatened with serious interruption. When at this stage a Rhode Islander suggested that "we are here on important business," the reporter recorded that there was so much confusion that the speaker's words could not be heard.[7] The matter was disposed of by deferring the excursion till after the convention was concluded. In this the delegates declined the gracious suggestion of the Board of Trade that their sessions could just as well be held on the decks of the ships. Another farcical touch occurred when a travel-weary delegate from California objected to the early hour for the next morning session; [8] still another when the convention, about to consider a night session on the first day, was informed that the hall was engaged that night for a Zouave drill.[9]

In the matter of fundamental organization two problems had to be threshed out by the convention—the question of admitting certain doubtful delegations, and that of determining what should constitute the majority necessary to nominate. Most doubtful of all was the admission of a bogus delegation from Texas,[10] but there was difficulty also as to groups offering themselves from Virginia, Kentucky, and Maryland, in which states it was charged that genuine Republican organizations did not exist. This topic brought heated and angry discussion, in which on the one hand it was feared that men might come in from the Southern states to demoralize the party,[11] while on the other hand it was answered that men from farther south had

---

[5] *Ibid.*, 123. [6] *Ibid.*, 97. [7] *Ibid.*, 100. [8] *Ibid.*, 106. [9] *Ibid.*, 96.

[10] Presenting themselves as the Texas delegation, six men were admitted to membership and their votes counted on various matters, including the nomination for President. Four of them supported Seward (these having been recruited in Michigan), while two supported Bates. *Ibid.*, 149; Reinhard H. Luthin, *First Lincoln Campaign*, 137.

[11] Johnson, *Proceedings*, 112.

been the ones who had really suffered for the cause.

When Wilmot of Pennsylvania contended that the convention was no mere mass gathering but a body of representatives with home constituencies, and that they "never had a Republican party in Maryland," Armour of Maryland dramatically insisted that having been mobbed and burned in effigy because of freedom, he had "dared more than he [Wilmot] has ever dared." "We are unpurchased, and unpurchaseable," he said. "And we tell Pennsylvania to put that in her pipe and smoke it." [12] As it turned out, these doubtful delegations (Texas, Virginia, Maryland, and Kentucky) were admitted; when it came to voting Virginia cast more ballots than Illinois.[13]

Related to the difficult matter of authorized delegates was the question whether a majority to nominate should be construed as a majority of the whole number of delegates when all states were represented, or merely a majority of delegates present. The rules committee favored the first-mentioned principle, but amid parliamentary confusion the majority-present rule, solidly favored by New York's seventy, was adopted.[14] When Mr. Goodrich of Minnesota wanted to say a word while this vote was being taken, there were hisses and cries of "Sit down." When the president said "Gentlemen do not forget yourselves. You must keep order," there were further cries of "Sit down," and renewed hisses.[15]

Though there were many confused moments in the convention, the ugliest snarl was over the resolutions, otherwise known as the platform. On the afternoon of the second day (Thursday) the platform was taken up and there was great applause for the tariff and homestead clauses. At this point Joshua Giddings of Ohio rose to speak, while Cartter of Ohio arrogantly and impatiently insisted on the previous question—that is, shutting off discussion. At this there was "Great confusion, and cries of 'Giddings' by the audience." [16]

---

[12] *Ibid.*, 113. [13] *Ibid.*, 149. Virginia cast twenty-three votes, Illinois twenty-two.
[14] *Ibid.*, 129. [15] *Ibid.*, 130.

[16] It is difficult to convey an idea of the snarl over Giddings's amendment. When the "previous question" was demanded, not only had copies of the resolutions not been distributed; no motion had even been put. It was supposed that the question was on acceptance of the platform in full, as read, but this was an assumption rather than a parliamentary fact. Immediately after the platform had been read, without even waiting for a motion that it be adopted, Cartter had moved to shut off all discussion. The matter is further complicated by the fact that in the official proceedings the platform, inserted at this point, is given not in the form in which it then stood, but as later amended and finally adopted. *Ibid.*, 130–135. Just before this (*ibid.*, 124 ff.)

There was now a full sized parliamentary tangle. Up to then the delegates had not seen copies of the printed resolutions, yet Cartter wanted them jammed through without debate. Further confusion was then "caused by the anxiety of the delegates and the crowd . . . to obtain copies of the platform, which . . . was being distributed." [17] Cartter used every parliamentary trick he could think of to prevent discussion, even questioning the vote after he had been voted down. The proceedings in dry print show a marked contrast between his rude bluntness and Giddings's courteous efforts to be heard. Amid great applause the previous question was voted down the second time, upon which Giddings grew eloquent on self-evident truths of the Declaration of Independence. He wanted the fundamental principles of human equality included in the platform; "when you leave out this truth you leave out the party," he said. He would amend the resolutions to this effect. Cartter referred sneeringly to "this amendment and the gas expended upon it." [18] Giddings's amendment to reaffirm the Declaration of Independence was submitted and voted down. "The old man quickly rose," wrote Murat Halstead, "and made his way slowly toward the door. A dozen delegates begged him not to go. But he considered everything lost, even honor. . . . The 'twin relics' [19] were not in the new creed. And now the Declaration of Independence had been voted down! He must go." [20]

The matter could not be dropped so easily, however, and the convention had to hear an eloquent appeal from Curtis of New York. Moving an amendment which was essentially the same as that of Giddings, he asked the convention "whether they are prepared to go . . . before the country as voting down the words of the Declaration of Independence." [21] The chair had ruled that Curtis's amendment, being equivalent to Giddings's, was out of order; after further explanation, and after a member stood ready to take an appeal to the floor,

---

there had been a sizable conflict as to the rules governing the membership of the convention, and the sense in which a majority vote should be construed.

[17] *Ibid.*, 134.

[18] *Ibid.*, 136.

[19] Polygamy and slavery, denounced as the "twin relics of barbarism" in the Republican platform of 1856. *Ibid.*, 43.

[20] Halstead, *Caucuses of 1860* . . . , 136. In this vivid book Halstead reported all the party conventions of 1860. It is far more colorful than the Johnson publication. For Giddings's lasting indignation concerning this Chicago episode, see vol. II, 209–210.

[21] Johnson, *Proceedings*, 141.

the chair changed his decision and the amendment was declared in order.[22] It was put to a vote and adopted; so the Declaration became a part of the Republican platform by a kind of general reference, though without any application in terms of racial equality. The voting down of Giddings, however, the gesture of dramatic departure on the part of that antislavery stalwart,[23] who felt that the party was deserting its whole cause, and a number of impatient remarks by various members who were irked because the Declaration was brought into the picture at all, were parts of this Chicago record.

II

Next morning, the third day (Friday), "Rev. M. Green, of Chicago" offered thanks that Providence had permitted the delegates to proceed "with such harmony and mutual respect," and, amid renewed admonitions from the chair that order be preserved and as much silence maintained "as possible," the convention got down to the business of nomination. To this end there had already been feverish and sleepless activity behind the scenes. A kind of grim, unremitting series of attacks upon the state delegations, together with caucuses within those delegations, had been occupying the real attention of the delegates. To this had been added pressure by paid shouters, and a self-constituted but influential mass "conference" of Germans at the Deutsches Haus.

It has been noted that there were five prominent candidates for the nomination, but by the time the convention actually proceeded to the balloting for candidates, the practical problem had been fairly well reduced to a choice between Seward and Lincoln. Seward's strength was found in certain "safe" states (New York, Maine, Michigan, Wisconsin, Minnesota, California, Massachusetts); his doubtful-state support had begun to slip. In the matter of convention strategy, these safe states, being taken for granted, were not the targets of the most concentrated attack. Courting their votes was not the main problem. One could write them off for Seward and the result would still remain open. Let Seward be stopped somewhere in the balloting, and the

[22] *Ibid.*

[23] Instead of a complete departure, Giddings seems to have lingered somewhere in the rear; when the Curtis amendment was carried he returned to his seat in the Ohio delegation. Baringer, *Lincoln's Rise to Power*, 262.

candidate who was best able to recruit support from states considered doubtful would come through with the prize. The word "doubtful" in this immediate connotation is applied to states whose delegations at Chicago were considered open or negotiable rather than irrevocably committed. It was also true that these same states were doubtful in another sense; they were likely to show a close contest between the major parties at election time.

Though not neglecting any delegates open to persuasion, Lincoln managers devoted particular attention to three important states—Indiana, Pennsylvania, and New Jersey. Fortunately for Seward's opponents, there was an interlocking of the situation as between the Indiana and the Pennsylvania delegations because of teamwork between followers of Andrew G. Curtin of Pennsylvania and Henry S. Lane of Indiana. Both the Curtin men and the Lane men were vigorously opposed to Seward; this was a fact of importance for Lincoln. Curtin felt that he did not wish to go before the people of Pennsylvania as candidate for governor if Seward were to be the Republican candidate for President.[1] By this he meant that a man with a more conservative reputation than Seward was needed. Since Lane, seeking election as governor of Indiana,[2] felt exactly the same way, being equally unwilling to have his fortunes tied with Seward on the Indiana stage, Curtin and Lane worked gladly together at Chicago, which signified that they worked against Seward.

They might have worked for Bates; thus it came about that in the more advanced maneuvers the problem of the Lincoln men, assuming that Seward could be stopped, was to stop Bates. Could this be done, the rest was easy. In each of the doubtful state delegations—especially those of Indiana, Pennsylvania, and New Jersey—the anti-Seward movement could be trusted to take care of itself, despite the lavish offering of money, with all of Weed's generalship, and with a thousand Seward marchers behind a blaring Seward band. It was not so necessary for Lincoln men to stop Seward; other forces in the convention were doing that. If, therefore, the Illinois group could put a damper on the Bates movement, the tricks were theirs. Let it be noted here that Seward, Lincoln, and Bates were the only men with a measurable

[1] Luthin, *First Lincoln Campaign,* 154.

[2] After being elected governor in 1860, with Oliver P. Morton as lieutenant governor, Lane immediately allowed himself to be elected United States senator, resigning the governorship which thus fell to Morton. All this was by previous understanding.

prospect of support beyond their own states. Outside of Pennsylvania Cameron sentiment was slight; outside of Ohio sentiment concerning Chase was for the most part colorless or definitely antagonistic.

This aspect of the situation—the importance that Lincoln men placed upon checking Bates—is well revealed in the record of Gustave Koerner, upstanding German-American of Belleville, Illinois. Knowing that the Indiana and Pennsylvania delegations were meeting jointly at the courthouse in Chicago on the important night of May 17 (the second day of the convention), Bates men "appeared . . . in force" at this meeting at which Frank Blair and others carried the ball for the Missouri statesman. Koerner and Orville H. Browning turned up at this Pennsylvania-Indiana caucus, and after the Bates guns had been fired they took the floor for Lincoln. Koerner argued that Bates could not even carry Missouri and that German-Americans could not honestly support this man "who in 1856 had presided over a Whig . . . Convention at Baltimore, which nominated Fillmore and Donelson, after they had been nominated by the Know Nothings." [3] Browning urged support for Lincoln on the basis of his strength among former Whigs, with a special eye to Whigs of Pennsylvania and Indiana. He also emphasized Lincoln's opposition to nativism and concluded with an "eloquent eulogy on Lincoln, which electrified the meeting." [4] That these men had done their work well was attested by Koerner's statement that a secret session was held after which it was learned that Indiana would go at once for Lincoln, while Pennsylvania would do so as a second choice.[5]

This Browning performance is the more remarkable when one remembers that in fact Browning's opinion of Lincoln's merits was never very high, and that his preference for President in 1860 was for Bates. Lincoln strategy did not work entirely through men who supported him as a matter of spontaneous conviction. One of the

[3] Koerner, *Memoirs*, II, 88.

[4] *Ibid.*, II, 89. It is amazing to turn from this account of Browning electrifying the Indiana and Pennsylvania delegations to his own colorless treatment in his diary. There is a leaf missing at the point where he might have mentioned this meeting. Then, with a change of handwriting, he put in a passage stating that Bates was his first choice, "but under instructions our whole delegation voted for Mr Lincoln." Having thus hinted that his support of Lincoln was reluctant or unwilling, he followed with a statement of the reasons which "influenced" him "to support Mr Bates," who "would probably have been nominated if the struggle had been prolonged." Browning, *Diary*, I, 407–408.

[5] Koerner, II, 89.

secrets of Lincoln's success was the manner in which men like Browning, not originally nor primarily for Lincoln, were enlisted in the drive to promote his nomination.

III

In the problem of why Lincoln was selected one must not omit the German-Americans, whose contribution to the Republican nomination has been elaborately studied and well treated by Professor F. I. Herriott.[1] The story narrows down about as follows: If Lincoln was to ride to victory, it would be largely because of the elimination of Seward and Bates, as already noted. Politically the Germans were a power in the land; many of them, some would say most of them, were a power in the Republican party. They were generally antislavery, but the issue of antislavery, as realized even by Greeley's New York *Tribune,* was not the factor to be greatly stressed by the Republican party in 1860. By overstressing that issue they would incur the danger of losing support in such states as Indiana, Pennsylvania, and New Jersey. Moreover, antislavery votes needed no coaxing; it could be confidently predicted that they would be predominantly Republican. Let the party misfire on other questions, however, and the issue might hang in doubt. Every vote-getting factor had to be weighed, particularly any factor that might involve the support of a specific mass of voters. One may leave aside for a moment the question whether the foreign-born vote was going to decide the election; in the nomination process the wooing of the foreign-born, notably the Germans, could in no case be ignored.

Remembering all this, three factors in 1860 should now be noted: (1) the indignant opposition of German-Americans to Knownothingism in general and the two-year amendment in particular; (2) the association of Bates's name, whether justly or not, with anti-foreign prejudice; (3) the complete satisfaction of the Germans toward the attitude of Lincoln, as shown in his Canisius letter and otherwise, as to friendliness toward men of foreign origin.[2] German-Americans

---

[1] F. I. Herriott, "The Conference in the Deutsches Haus, Chicago, May 14–15, 1860," *Transactions,* Ill. State Hist. Soc., 1928, 101–191.

[2] Among the slightly known Lincoln documents is a letter he wrote to a committee of Chicago Germans in 1858. Finding himself unable to accept their invitation to a July 4 celebration, he gave them a sentiment: "*Our German Fellow-Citizens:*—Ever true

would willingly have supported Seward, but they had to consider the possibility of Seward's defeat for the nomination, and in that case it looked in the earlier phases of the race as if Edward Bates of Missouri might be the man, since he was favored by the Blairs, by Greeley, by influential elements in Indiana, and by statements in certain newspapers—e. g., the Springfield (Massachusetts) *Republican,* which doubted the extent of Seward's support and predicted that non-Seward or anti-Seward elements would go for Bates.[3] Support Seward, was the program of the Germans; but by all possible means be ready to stop Bates in case Seward fails to make the grade. This became the more important as signs grew that Seward was slipping, that he was deemed "too radical," that his name was associated, unfairly of course, with the criminal violence of the John Brown raid, and that potent elements were working against him. Chase, Frémont, or McLean might possibly have satisfied the Germans, but none of these compared to Lincoln in all-round availability.[4]

In such a setting and background there had assembled at the Deutsches Haus in Chicago a conference of German-Americans, May 14–15, 1860. It was the work of ardent idealists; it had been prepared carefully in advance; it bore the determined quality of organized discontent; it assembled in response to a ringing "Call"; its membership was open to delegates from organized German Republican clubs in any city or state in the union. The strongest delegations were from Illinois, Wisconsin, Iowa, Missouri, Ohio, Michigan, and New York; in addition other states—e. g., Massachusetts, Connecticut, and Kansas—were represented.

The men of this convention made up a notable roster. Practically all had been born in Germany or Austria. Not many were from Prussia, or if so they had left for good and sufficient reason. Typical ones hailed from Saxony, Bavaria, Baden, or Frankfort-on-Main. The

---

to *Liberty,* the *Union,* and the *Constitution*—true to Liberty, not selfishly, but upon *principle*—not for special *classes* of men, but for *all* men . . . ." Lincoln to A. C. Hesing and others, Springfield, June 30, 1858, Chicago *Daily Press & Tribune,* July 7, 1858, p. 1, c. 4. Some would call this catering to the German vote. That Lincoln deliberately had votes in mind when he made such appeals is true and it would be idle to deny it, yet in issuing such a sentiment in a day when some were appealing for votes in the opposite (i. e., anti-foreign) sense, Lincoln did so in genuine conviction.

[3] Herriott, "Deutsches Haus," 114.

[4] Gustave Koerner to Lyman Trumbull, March 15, 1860, Trumbull MSS.

liberal spirit of the "Forty Eighters" was prominent among the delegates. The most distinguished member was Carl Schurz from Wisconsin. Others of importance, to pick out a few, were Reinhard Solger of Massachusetts, Johannes Gambs and Frederick Kapp from New York; Frederick Muench from Missouri; Frederick Hassaurek from Ohio; Hermann Kiefer from Michigan; Theodor Hielscher from Indiana (in attendance though not an accredited delegate); Bernhard Domschke and Carl Roeser of Wisconsin; and, from Illinois, a group that included notably, as participants in the discussion, Gustave Koerner of Belleville, George Schneider of Chicago, Jens Peter Stibolt of Peoria, and Frederick Hecker of St. Clair County near Belleville. Hecker has been described as "in many respects, the most interesting and picturesque character in the Conference." [5] His career included studies at Heidelberg, service in the parliament of Baden, agitation for "intense republicanism," daring participation in the revolutionary underground, membership in the Frankfort Parliament (hopefully devoted to the unification of Germany on liberal and democratic lines), flight to Switzerland, emigration to the United States, spirited ovations at New York and elsewhere as he moved across the country, success in cattle raising, and early activity as worker and speaker in the Republican party.

In a series of five brief but significant resolutions the assembled Germans put themselves squarely on record. They adhered to the Republican principles of 1856 "in a sense most hostile to slavery," strongly favored a homestead act, and urged immediate admission of Kansas without slavery. More especially they demanded full rights for all citizens regardless of descent, denounced the Massachusetts two-year admendment, and pledged support for any aspirant for the presidency who had "never . . . been identified with the spirit of the Massachusetts Amendment." [6] This resolution, or threat, "effectually ruined the chances of . . . Bates and Banks." [7] If, therefore, Seward failed of nomination, it would be unwise for the Republican convention to hazard German-American resentment by naming Bates. On the other hand, because of Lincoln's liberal and well known record toward the foreign born, his selection would not only be acceptable but would add real strength. In the narrowing list of available men this was a most significant factor.

[5] Herriott, "Deutsches Haus," 182. [6] *Ibid.*, 189. [7] *Ibid.*, 190.

IV

A trick of fate in the balloting for the presidential candidate—or a casual incident in the proceedings—deserves passing notice. At the end of the second day (Thursday), just following the unanimous adoption of the platform, the whole assembly was swept into "a transport of enthusiasm," with tremendous shouts and cheers, fluttering handkerchiefs and waving hats.[1] It was regarded as a Seward wave, and at this moment of high feeling a motion was made to proceed at once to the balloting for President, but it was then announced "that the tally-sheets had not been prepared, and that it would subject the clerks to great inconvenience to proceed to a ballot at that time." [2] Such is one report. According to another report the chair announced that the papers were "prepared," though "not yet at hand," and would be ready "in a few minutes." [3] This was one of those little things that belong to the essential story of that convention. There now came a motion to adjourn on which the unrecorded vote was light and uncertain, after which the chairman announced that the motion prevailed and the convention stood adjourned till the next day.

Seward men were displeased; they did not desire further canvassing that night nor did they wish delay. This does not mean, however, that they were disheartened. They still "abounded in confidence." [4] It is unprovable that Seward "would have been" nominated if the balloting had been taken at the fag end of the second day, but the incident of the tally-sheets is illustrative of a certain factor that one notes in the proceedings of this gathering. It was the factor of undeliberative, unpredictable, sometimes almost accidental, action. The next business at this point had been the presidential nomination; the tally-sheets were not ready; the motion to adjourn was given; the chair said that it prevailed; adjournment occurred, and that was that.

Anyone familiar with the informal or behind-the-scenes history of that convention knows that what was done Thursday night, which was considerable even after midnight, was not in Seward's favor. As Halstead tells it, he "saw Henry S. Lane at one o'clock, pale and haggard, with cane under his arm, walking as if for a wager, from

[1] Johnson, *Proceedings*, 142; Halstead, *Caucuses of 1860*, 139–140. Halstead wrote: "A herd of buffaloes or lions could not have made a more tremendous roaring."

[2] Halstead, *Caucuses*, 141. [3] Johnson, *Proceedings*, 143. [4] Halstead, *Caucuses*, 143.

one caucus-room to another, at the Tremont House." [5] Lincoln supporters were greatly assisted by workers whose strong motive for Republican success was combined with a distrust of Seward's vote-getting appeal. Seward men were not idle, of course, and the phrase went round that "Seward's friends 'would *spend oceans of money.*' " [6] But the New Yorker's non-availability was stressed and it was reported "that the Republican candidates for Governor in Indiana, Illinois and Pennsylvania would resign, if Seward were nominated." [7] Though it may have been only a rumor concocted and circulated for its obvious purpose, such talk is the stuff of which delegate decisions are made.

V

On the morning of the convention's third day, the delegates being asked to refrain from demonstration (!), it was announced that the next business was the selection of a candidate for President of the United States. Before this could be entered upon, however, there was discussion even at this stage concerning the proper voting strength of Maryland, and there were complaints that unauthorized outsiders were occupying the seats of members. With everyone "impatient to begin the work," there now followed the naming of candidates to be voted on for the nomination. Evarts nominated Seward and the applause was "enthusiastic," but "When Mr. Judd named Lincoln, the response was prodigious, rising and raging far beyond the Seward shriek." [1]

What followed was something that required rather the talents of a hog caller than those of party delegates. It was a tournament of noise, a colossal contest of yelling between the followers of Lincoln and Seward. Lincoln's nomination had inspired the Seward men to another prodigious effort which caused Murat Halstead to bethink himself of the lines:

> "As all the fiends from heaven that fell
> Had pealed the banner cry of hell."

The effect [continued Halstead] was startling.

Hundreds of persons stopped their ears in pain. The shouting was absolutely frantic, shrill and wild. No Camanches, no panthers ever struck

[5] *Ibid.*, 142. [6] Ibid., 143. [7] *Ibid.* [1] *Ibid.*, 144.

a higher note, or gave screams with more infernal intensity. Looking from the stage over the vast amphitheatre, nothing was to be seen below but thousands of hats—a black, mighty swarm of hats—flying with the velocity of hornets over a mass of human heads, most of the mouths of which were open. Above, all around the galleries, hats and handkerchiefs were flying in the tempest together. The wonder of the thing was, that the Seward outside pressure should, so far from New York, be so powerful.

Now the Lincoln men had to try it again, and as Mr. Delano of Ohio, on behalf "of a portion of the delegation of that State," seconded the nomination of Lincoln, the uproar was beyond description. Imagine all the hogs ever slaughtered in Cincinnati giving their death squeals together, a score of big steam whistles going (steam at 160 lbs. per inch), and you conceive something of the same nature. I thought the Seward yell could not be surpassed; but the Lincoln boys were clearly ahead, and feeling their victory, as there was a lull in the storm, took deep breaths all round, and gave a concentrated shriek that was positively awful, and accompanied it with stamping that made every plank and pillar in the building quiver.[2]

There now came the tense moment of balloting for President. With the full support of New York, Michigan, Wisconsin, and California, and with considerable strength elsewhere, Seward came through on the first ballot with 173½ votes, easily the highest number; yet it was not a majority. Even at this early stage Lincoln was not only second; he stood far above any of Seward's other rivals. It was Lincoln 102, Cameron 50½ (of which 47½ came from Pennsylvania), Bates 48, Chase 49, Dayton 14, and McLean 12, with a negligible scattering of votes for Wade, John M. Read (of Pennsylvania), Collamer, Sumner, and Frémont. It was obvious now that the threat to Seward's success was formidable. The votes for three men—Lincoln, Cameron, and Bates—would be enough to outnumber Seward. Add those of Chase, and Lincoln would have more than the 233 necessary to a choice.

Under these circumstances the convention proceeded to the second ballot. The air was electric with impatience, taut nerves, and a kind of high strung ferocity.[3] The feature of the second ballot was the upswing for Lincoln. He picked up two votes from New Hampshire; then he gained the whole of Vermont's ten votes which had previously been cast for Collamer. Here was a significant turn of affairs; complimentary ballots cast at the outset for a minor favorite son were now

[2] *Ibid.*, 145.

[3] "The partisans of the various candidates were strung up to such a pitch of excitement as to render them incapable of patience, and the cries of 'Call the roll' were fairly hissed through their teeth." *Ibid.*, 147.

shifted to the support of an outstanding contender. At this the "New Yorkers started as if an Orsini bomb had exploded." [4] Then came the sensational action of Pennsylvania. Having given 47½ votes for Cameron on the first ballot to four for Lincoln, the state delegation on the second ballot gave one to Cameron and 48 for Lincoln. "Weed sickened as he perceived 'the change in the vote of Pennsylvania, startling the vast auditorium like a clap of thunder.' " [5]

In all Lincoln gained 79 votes on this second ballot. The tally now stood: Seward, 184½; Lincoln, 181; Bates, 35; Chase, 42½; Cameron, only 2; all others, 20 votes. There was "Great confusion while the ballot was being counted." [6]

With the third ballot the convention moved uproariously to its climax. As the roll of states was called, a "hundred pencils" [7] kept informal tally with attention riveted on the rising Lincoln vote. When Lincoln had come within a vote and one-half of the necessary majority, with a sense of fate and crisis stirring throughout the wigwam, Cartter of Ohio rose to announce "the change of four votes . . . from Mr. Chase to Mr. Lincoln." [8] "The deed was done," wrote Halstead. "There was a moment's silence. The nerves of the thousands, which through the hours of suspense had been subjected to terrible tension, relaxed, and as deep breaths of relief were taken, there was a noise in the wigwam like the rush of a great wind, in the van of a storm—and in another breath, the storm was there. There were thousands cheering with the energy of insanity." [9]

Having loosed the flood by his announcement of the change of four votes, Cartter now announced that Ohio's vote was unanimous for Lincoln. Thereupon one state after another announced that its entire delegation was for Lincoln, many of the states indicating a correction of their votes. "While these votes were being given," wrote Halstead, "the applause continued, and a photograph of Abe Lincoln which had hung in one of the side rooms was brought in, and held up before the surging and screaming masses." [10] When the third ballot was completed, it was announced that Lincoln had 364 of the 466 votes.[11]

---

[4] *Ibid.*, 147.

[5] Reinhard H. Luthin, in *Pa. Mag. of Hist. and Biog.*, Jan., 1943, 71, quoting T. W. Barnes, *Memoir of Thurlow Weed*, 264. Luthin adds: "Pennsylvania's action did more than any single thing to tip the scales in favor of Lincoln."

[6] Halstead, 147.

[7] *Ibid.*, 149.

[8] *Ibid.*

[9] *Ibid.*

[10] *Ibid.*, 150.

[11] Johnson, *Proceedings*, 155.

In an eloquent speech Evarts of New York moved that the nomination be made unanimous, but in the excitement of speeches on the motion, and amid the parliamentary irregularity which characterized the whole convention, it is impossible to find any evidence that the motion was ever put and carried. Reading the prosaic account by Charles W. Johnson, whose record was the official report of the party, one can only conclude that the motion was somehow lost in the proceedings; [12] in the vivid account by Halstead, however, it is stated, but with no parliamentary detail as to the passing of any particular motion, that "the nomination was made unanimous" after "a rather dull speech from Mr. Browning of Illinois." [13]

Balloting for Vice President was an unexciting anticlimax. If the "multitude" in the wigwam could have had its way, according to Halstead, Cassius M. Clay would have been nominated by acclamation; as it was he received 101½ votes on the first ballot to 194 for Hannibal Hamlin of Maine. On the next ballot, second thoughts taking effect, it was realized that Hamlin was geographically distant from Lincoln, that he was a friend of Seward, and that he had been once a Democrat. This ballot showed 357 for Hamlin, 86 for Clay, and 13 for John Hickman of Pennsylvania. More than half of the Clay vote came from the Virginia and Kentucky delegations. Lincoln's running mate, whom he had never met, had served as congressman, senator, and governor; he was dignified, handsome, and mildly popular; he was conservative while being sufficiently antislavery; he had done much to break down the Democratic party in his state; [14] taking it all together, in 1860 he filled a recognized party need.

VI

There were numerous factors that contributed to Lincoln's nomination, and not the least of them was the strategy of his managers. Judd had seen that united action by a few states—New Jersey, Indiana, Illinois, and Pennsylvania—would probably control the convention

[12] Johnson reports Evarts's speech with his motion for unanimity; several pages later, some speeches having intervened, he quotes Evarts as saying that his motion "has not yet been put"; he follows immediately with a speech by Browning (not particularly directed to the motion); then notes that the convention "then adjourned." On reassembling, it proceeded at once to the nomination of Vice President. *Ibid.*, 155, 159–160.

[13] Halstead, 151.

[14] Blaine, *Twenty Years of Congress*, I, 170.

and had worked for "a quiet combination" of these delegates.[1] The strategy was not to work for "delegates distinctly Lincoln," [2] for Illinois managers did not have their eye primarily on the first ballot. Rather they counted on Lincoln receiving enough second-choice votes on some later ballot to insure his success. There had been no movement of any significant force in the convention that could be called anti-Lincoln. This was one of the advantages of the fact that the Illinois leader, while enjoying prominence among the contenders, did not stand at the top in the pre-convention canvass. Leadership in the front ranks is a thing for which one may sometimes pay a high penalty in the American political scene.

The labors of David Davis were arduous and fruitful. Though in February Davis thought it likely that Bates or Seward would be chosen, he did probably more than any other man to crystallize the non-Seward elements behind Lincoln. "To Judge Davis," wrote Jesse W. Fell, "more than to any other man, . . . is the American people indebted for . . . the nomination . . . of Abraham Lincoln." [3] His work from headquarters at the Tremont House reached into every delegation whose vote was subject to persuasion. By midnight caucuses, ubiquitous pressure, and unauthorized bargains that were later to embarrass Lincoln, Davis skillfully promoted those behind-the-scenes maneuvers which usually do not find their way conspicuously into print but which have so telling an effect on the politician-like motives of party delegates.

In at least two instances the bargaining had gone to the point of proffering posts in Lincoln's cabinet. For the support of Indiana a promise was made for the appointment of Caleb B. Smith; for Pennsylvania a like promise was made "to place Simon Cameron at the President's council table." [4] "Make no contracts that will bind me," had been Lincoln's words,[5] but in playing for such high stakes this advice was disregarded. Lincoln did not like these maneuvers in his behalf.

---

[1] Judd to Trumbull, Chicago, April 2, 1860, Trumbull MSS. [2] *Ibid.*

[3] Letter of Jesse W. Fell, quoted in Chicago *Tribune*, June 27, 1886, p. 11, c. 2.

[4] Harry E. Pratt, "David Davis, 1815–1886," *Transactions*, Ill. State Hist. Soc., 1930, 167.

[5] Herndon relates that Lincoln penciled these words on the margin of a newspaper which was brought into the room where Davis and other managers were gathered in Chicago. Nevertheless, according to Herndon, deals were made on the theory that Lincoln was far from Chicago and could not appreciate the situation. *Herndon's Life of Lincoln*, Angle ed., 373–374. See also Baringer, *Lincoln's Rise to Power*, 214, 239.

Knowing his own caution in this respect, he would have liked to believe that the nomination had come to him unencumbered by conditions or pledges of favors to individuals or leaders. "It is . . . grateful to my feelings," he wrote, "that the responsible position assigned to me comes without conditions, save only such honorable ones as are fairly implied." [6] In some accounts it is made to appear that bargains did not exist and that Lincoln approached his task with a clean slate.[7] Yet Lincoln himself has been quoted as saying: "They have gambled me all around, bought and sold me a hundred times. I cannot begin to fill the pledges made in my name." [8] It is also true that Lincoln's own letters show how eager he was to win Indiana support at Chicago and how important was the influence exerted by David Davis and Jesse Dubois to that end.[9] All told, Lincoln was affected by commitments made by others. More than that, he was deeply embarrassed. The full effect of these convention maneuvers was to be regretfully felt by the new leader in his days as President Elect in connection with Cameron's forced entry into the cabinet.

Availability, or "a presumption of availability," [10] was the secret of the choice at Chicago. To the Seward men it was a grievous blow. They had been vociferously confident; they had in fact assumed success as a matter of course. With his customary economy of phrase Browning wrote that the New York delegation was "mortified and disappointed." [11] It was not only that the nomination of Lincoln struck the New Yorkers as a rude shock; it was also true that Seward, growing more conservative every day, was becoming the spearhead of a group that was constantly to be opposed to Republican radicals. In this dislike of radicalism, of course, Seward resembled Lincoln. James G. Blaine considered that the "great achievement at Chicago was the nomination of Mr. Lincoln without offending the supporters of Seward," [12] yet the tension in the Republican party was not between Lincoln and Seward. Beginning at the very outset of Lincoln's troubled

---

[6] Lincoln to Giddings, May 21, 1860, *Works*, VI, 13–14.

[7] T. W. Barnes, *Memoir of Thurlow Weed*, 330; Chicago *Press & Tribune*, May 19, 1860, p. 1, c. 1.

[8] O. J. Hollister, Life of Colfax, 147 n., quoted in Pratt, "David Davis, 1815–1886," 167.

[9] Tracy, *Uncollected Letters*, 145, 146–147. See also Baringer, *Lincoln's Rise to Power*, 215; White, *Trumbull*, 142.

[10] Halstead, 153.

[11] Browning, *Diary*, I, 408.

[12] Blaine, *Twenty Years of Congress*, I, 169.

administration, and from that time steadily forward, the Republican party, unified in appearance, was a thing of factions and severe internal pressures.

VII

In the making of the Republican platform the candidate had had no part. The convention's resolutions are best read in the light of the maneuverings and differences within the convention. In part the platform was a succession of noble phrases; in part it was a catch-all for a variety of vote-getting clauses; in part it was an appeal to special interests though the wording always pointed grandly to the general welfare; in part it was an indictment of the "present Democratic administration"; in general it identified the Republican party with all that was right in the nation and all that was fundamental in American institutions.

As already noted, the convention's action was unsatisfactory to staunch old Joshua Giddings in its hesitant and timid manner of dealing with the Declaration of Independence. In the wording finally adopted the platform declared "That the maintenance of the principles promulgated in the Declaration of Independence and embodied in the Federal Constitution, 'That all men are created equal; that they are endowed by their Creator with certain inalienable rights; that among these are life, liberty and the pursuit of happiness; that to secure these rights, governments are instituted among men, deriving their just powers from the consent of the governed' is essential to the preservation of our Republican institutions; and that the Federal Constitution, the Rights of the States, and the Union of the States must and shall be preserved." [1]

Certain principles of the Declaration, however, had not been "embodied" in the Constitution, and the Chicago resolutions did not, by any special mention of the Negro in the clause concerning the Declaration, unequivocally interpret human equality as covering that race even in the matter of political, much less social or economic, rights. Indeed it was only as an afterthought, after the ugly snarl in the convention which deeply offended Giddings, that the Declaration was recognized at all. As to slavery in general, the platform did not

[1] Johnson, *Proceedings*, 131.

characterize the institution as a moral wrong;[2] in that sense the party did not go so far as in 1856. Rather, the resolutions pointed emphatically to state rights—"especially the right of each state to order . . . its own domestic institutions according to its own judgment exclusively." This was contrary to the abolitionist demand that slavery, being wrong, must be abolished in the states where it existed. As to slavery in the territories—the over-agitated issue so importantly associated with the foundation of the Republican party—the platform denied as "heresy" the dogma that the Constitution carried slavery into the territories, declared that their normal condition was freedom, and denied the authority either of Congress or of a territorial legislature "to give legal existence to slavery in any territory of the United States."

The 1860 platform did not include the 1856 phrase that it was "the right and the imperative duty of Congress to prohibit" slavery (and polygamy) in the territories. The statement that neither Congress nor a territorial legislature could "give legal existence to slavery" was not so positive and unequivocal as the out-and-out statement that Congress was under the "imperative duty" to prohibit the institution. It could have been argued that the demand for such prohibition was implied in other clauses—i. e., the one denouncing the "new dogma" that the Constitution of itself carried slavery into the territories, and the clause declaring it "our duty" to uphold the constitutional guarantee against deprivation of life, liberty, or property —but since the explicit call for congressional prohibition had been made in the platform of 1856, its omission in 1860 was worthy of notice. The tendency of the party to recede from its 1856 position, stating that position less clearly and emphatically, is unmistakable in the record.

In a succession of miscellaneous "planks" the platform extolled the union, censured the opposite party for extravagance and subserviency to "a sectional interest," branded as a crime the reopening of the African slave trade, denounced popular sovereignty, proposed

---

[2] It is stated by Nicolay and Hay that in 1860 "the Republican party . . . held that slavery was a moral wrong . . . ." *Works*, VI, 12 n. If this refers to the official resolutions of the party it is an error; the platform of 1860 contained no denunciation of slavery itself on moral grounds, though it did denounce the reopening of the African slave trade. With this denunciation most Southerners, indeed Americans generally, agreed.

the immediate admission of Kansas under a free constitution, and commended a tariff policy that was ambiguously presented, but was supposed to favor protection. In addition it was declared that the Republican party favored a 'free homestead policy," opposed restrictions upon foreign immigrants, and, while urging "rigid economy," proposed Federal expenditures for "river and harbor improvements of a national character" and for a railroad to the Pacific Ocean.

VIII

Lincoln was fond of playing "fives" (handball) and it was the recollection of one of his neighbors—James Gourley—that he played the game on the day before his nomination, and "probably he played some on the morning—early." [1] That he was playing "a game of ball" when the dispatch was handed to him announcing his nomination has been emphatically denied by T. W. S. Kidd, court crier in Springfield.[2] The detail is unimportant except that in the personal feeling toward Lincoln one looks always for the close-up view and the personal touch. According to Kidd, he had been at the telegraph office awaiting dispatches, enduring the suspense until the balloting began at Chicago. Then he stepped into a store and was standing there when yell after yell was heard and a messenger ran to him with the news. People gathered quickly around him in great numbers, but, wanting to get out of the crowd, he remarked: "Well, there is a little woman who will be interested in this news . . . ," and started for home. Herndon, however, pictures him in a large arm chair in the office of the *Illinois State Journal* when the news came; he records also the remark about telling the little woman the news.[3]

In attempting to study Lincoln at close range, especially at climactic points in his life, one is impressed both with the importance given to small details by neighbors and the frequency with which recollections are fragmentary or contradictory. In addition to Gourley and Kidd there were various others who told of this exciting day in Springfield. We have the narrative of Clinton L. Conkling who explained that while the convention was in progress Lincoln remained in Spring-

[1] Interview with James Gourley recorded by Herndon (undated), Herndon-Weik MSS.
[2] *Journal*, Ill. State Hist. Soc., XV, 507–509 (Apr., 1922).
[3] "The news of his nomination found Lincoln at Springfield in the office of the *Journal*." Herndon (Angle ed.), 374.

field, going to his law office as usual, watching telegrams, and joining "in a game of hand ball, . . . favorite pastime of the professional men of the town." According to this account, Lincoln came into James C. Conkling's law office on the morning of May 18 (the day of the nomination), stretched himself on a settee, and chatted with James C., who had been in Chicago and had returned to Springfield. After Lincoln had left the office, according to this version, Clinton L. Conkling, having learned the big news, met him "on the west side of the Square" and was the first to tell him of his nomination, after which the nominee was surrounded by excited crowds.[4]

Gourley's reminiscence suggests the opposite of elation: "he was agitated—turned pale—troubled." Directly after the nomination, said Gourley, he went home from the *Journal* office.[5] If he hoped to retire to his own thoughts he was unsuccessful; at his house he was soon joined by friends in considerable number.

Next day, while the town of Springfield thrilled with demonstrations, music, fireworks, and festivity, the parlor in the house on Eighth Street became the scene of a restrained and solemn ceremony as the committee from the Chicago convention formally notified Lincoln of his nomination as President. Gustave Koerner, in describing the scene, mentioned that Lincoln "looked much moved, and rather sad, . . . feeling the heavy responsibility thrown upon him."[6] Carl Schurz, member of the committee, wrote:

---

[4] Clinton L. Conkling, "How Mr. Lincoln Received the News of His First Nomination," *Transactions*, Ill. State Hist. Soc., 1909, 63–66. In this article there are citations of further sources (66 n.), and photographic reproductions of "five original telegrams received by Mr. Lincoln on the day he was nominated." Weik (*Real Lincoln*, 263–267) repeats this Conkling account and adds details from other sources—e. g., as to Lincoln playing "fives."

[5] Gourley MS. interview, above quoted. Lincoln could have been told the news before the telegrams were given to him. He moved about that morning, and, as shown above, accounts differ as to just where he was when various phases of "getting the news" occurred. If one could piece together a complete narrative, which seems impossible now, the reminiscences, rightly interpreted, might be found to be supplementary rather than entirely contradictory. As to the handball detail there is really no contradiction between Gourley and Kidd.

[6] Koerner, II, 94. Koerner tells of Mrs. Lincoln's frustrated efforts in the matter of liquid hospitality. W. H. Townsend (*Lincoln and Liquor*, 100 ff.) adds further details, indicating that ice water was served at the Lincolns', whereas at the hotel (the Chenery House) the committee had everything except ice water. Townsend gives a photographic reproduction of a confidential letter of Lincoln to J. Mason Haight, June 11, 1860. "Having kept house sixteen years [wrote Lincoln], and having never held the 'cup' to the lips of my friends there, my judgment was that I should not, in my new position, change my habit in this respect."

Mr. Lincoln received us in the parlor of his modest frame house . . . . There the Republican candidate for the Presidency stood, tall and ungainly in his black suit of . . . new but ill-fitting clothes, his long tawny neck emerging gauntly from his turn-down collar, his melancholy eyes sunken deep in his haggard face. Most of the . . . committee had never seen him before, and gazed at him with surprised curiosity. He . . . did not present the appearance of a statesman . . . . Standing up with folded hands, he quietly . . . listened to the dignified . . . speech . . . by Mr. Ashmun, the president of the Convention, and then he responded with a few appropriate . . . and well-shaped sentences . . . . Then followed some informal talk . . . in which the hearty simplicity of Lincoln's nature shone out, and . . . the committee took its leave.[7]

Lincoln's response had been modest and brief, yet not colorless: he almost wished the "high honor" had fallen to another; he tendered "profoundest thanks"; he expressed himself as "painfully sensible of the great responsibility." By a literal reading it could almost be inferred that Lincoln was leaving open the question of his acceptance. He promised to read the platform and later to respond in writing "without . . . unnecessary . . . delay." [8]

This he did formally, again very briefly, on May 23, accepting the nomination, endorsing the platform, imploring Divine assistance, hailing the Constitution, and striking the note of "perpetual union, harmony, and prosperity." [9]

From among the millions of American citizens, delegates of a leading party had chosen one man. Upon him was now focused the hopes of party success, and beyond that the dread responsibility of chief magistracy. No longer for him the bustling county seat, the long rides on the circuit, the stir and challenge of western law practice. Abraham Lincoln was now candidate for President. He sat for his portrait to the photographer Alexander Hesler of Chicago. The camera caught him in perfect pose and expression; the Hesler profile is the finest of the Lincoln pictures. Without the beard, it has the sculptural ruggedness of the remarkable life mask by Leonard Volk. Lincoln now wrote out the basis for his campaign biography, producing an autobiography which was all fact and no flourish; yet for its priceless glimpses of

---

[7] *Reminiscences of Carl Schurz,* II, 187–188.

[8] *Works,* VI, 12–13 (May 19, 1860). This statement, giving thanks for the honor but promising a later response, did not include an acceptance of the nomination. Acceptance came four days later.

[9] *Ibid.,* VI, 14–15.

early life, its accuracy, and its unstudied revelations of character, it remains, now as in 1860, an indispensable source for any Lincoln biographer.

Soon the campaign "lives" appeared—the first trickles of a vast torrent of Lincolniana. With almost incredible promptness these books fell from the press.[10] Though priority in this field has been disputed, the "Wigwam Edition," published by Rudd and Carleton of New York, has been judged by a careful writer, Ernest J. Wessen, as the "first campaign life of Lincoln." Published on June 2, 1860, it was offered in paper wrappers at the price of twenty-five cents. The candidate's first name was spelled "Abram." No author's name appeared. The book was at once popular; 12,000 copies were sold within a week. Two days later came another paper-bound work by a journalist and popular writer, David V. G. Bartlett—price, twenty-five cents. Third place has been assigned to an anonymously written book brought out by Thayer and Eldridge of Boston and known to collectors by the publisher's name. It seems to have appeared about June 7, though "registered for copyright" on May 28, ten days after Lincoln's unforeseeable nomination. On June 11 there appeared a tiny 32mo volume edited and published by Reuben Vose of New York. Only a few pages were devoted to Lincoln's life; the rest consisted of Republican platforms (1856 and 1860), Lincoln's Cooper Union speech, and miscellaneous campaign material. The public was invited to apply to the publisher for other political publications, including, curiously enough, "5000 copies of the *Conservative,*" which "contains the names of five hundred of the richest men in New-York." Other biographies followed in quick succession. With no effort to enumerate them all, nor to specify dates or order of appearance, mention may be made of a longer work by Thayer and Eldridge called the "Wide-awake Edition," a book by Joseph H. Barrett published at Cincinnati, a life by James Q. Howard, published by the Columbus firm that had first published the Lincoln-Douglas debates, and a joint biography of Lincoln and Hamlin, hastily written by W. D. Howells with the use of material assembled by this same Howard. In our own day the Abraham Lincoln Association has handsomely reproduced a

[10] William E. Barton, in *Transactions,* Ill. State Hist. Soc., 1929, 87 ff. On this same subject one should not neglect Ernest J. Wessen, "Campaign Lives of Abraham Lincoln, 1860," *Papers in Ill. Hist.,* 1937, 188–220. See also Jay Monaghan, *Lincoln Bibliography, 1839–1939.* Wessen's account is more authoritative than Barton's.

special copy of this Howells biography in which a number of errors are corrected by penciled annotations in Lincoln's own hand.

Among the more substantial campaign biographies of 1860 was that by John L. Scripps, for whom Lincoln wrote the autobiography above mentioned. The Scripps book was closer to Lincoln and more truly a biography than any other of the campaign books. Yet none of the 1860 lives were particularly notable: they relied on "shears and pastebrush," [11] they bore the quality of padding, hasty writing, and party propaganda. It would have been better if the people had been given the superb Hesler profile along with Lincoln's autobiography undiluted and unadorned.[12]

---

11 Barton, as cited in preceding note, 70.

12 For fuller treatment of the subject matter of this chapter the reader is referred to the following important works: William Baringer, *Lincoln's Rise to Power* (1937); Reinhard H. Luthin, *The First Lincoln Campaign* (1944).

CHAPTER VIII

CAMPAIGN AND ELECTION OF 1860

I

FROM May to November, 1860, Lincoln must have seemed inaccessible to the country at large. The campaigning, all of it, was done by others while the Republican candidate remained quietly at Springfield. He had a flood of callers and his correspondence was heavy, yet his collected works contain only a moderate amount of writing for the period of the campaign. He made virtually no speeches, certainly none that could be called political declarations.[1] This avoidance of oratory, as also of talk and writing, was deliberate and was rationalized on the ground that "writing for the public" would "do no good." People, he thought, would not be persuaded, "though one rose from the dead." [2] When Trumbull delivered to Lincoln an invitation to speak in Detroit, the candidate declined, thinking it "would be departing from a line of policy he had adopted & which friends have commended." [3]

In his unadvertised manner Lincoln kept in touch with party strategy, noting the maneuvers of the three-fold opposition, showing concern as to the result in Maine, advising as to a speaking tour by Cassius M. Clay in Illinois, writing on politics to the past master politician, Weed, showing caution not to expose quarrels among friends in his party, discounting suggestions of intent to do him

[1] In his brief remarks at his home in Springfield on August 8, 1860, he was merely seeing the assemblage and being seen by them. Even such an appearance was rare. For the speech, if it could be called that, see *Works*, VI, 49–50, where it is given with the incorrect date of August 14. For an account of this Republican rally, see W. E. Baringer, in *Transactions*, Ill. State Hist. Soc., 1932, 253 ff.

[2] *Ibid.*, VI, 63–64 (Oct. 23, 1860).

[3] Lyman Trumbull to Zachariah Chandler, Springfield, Ill., Sep., 3, 1860. Chandler MSS.

violence, and taking care to deny campaign falsehoods.[4] With characteristic modesty he referred to the honor conferred upon him as "a tribute . . . to no man as a man" but as applicable to any "representative of the truth." [5]

In the excess of politics that swept the nation in this summer and fall, Republicans were exuberant and irrepressible. Their candidate's name inspired enthusiasm. Lincoln was a man that people could shout for, this being an early phase of his leadership. There was nothing tame or half-hearted about the canvass, nothing of the apathy that Lincoln himself had shown toward Scott. The American flair for political organization was impressively demonstrated, and with organization there went pageantry, merrymaking, feasting, shouting, singing, marching, and all those emotional outlets which have so large a part, yet make so little sense, in the political circus.

Things were not left to chance. There was a network of regular Republican committees, local, state, and national. Managers saw to it that Republican clubs were organized, not only down to the county, but to the township or precinct.[6] Long before the convention, plans had been laid for each county in Illinois to have its "guarantor" and "treasurer" for the party "assessment," [7] this phase being kept behind the scenes with the minimum of publicity. Correspondence was elaborately organized, with "corresponding secretaries" in the localities and voters' lists prepared for the mailing out of documents. These informal and unofficial lists were referred to as the *"registration of voters."* [8]

Marching groups or companies known as "Wide Awakes," with the importance of volunteer firemen and the exuberance of lodge brothers on parade, were formed throughout the North for pro-Lincoln campaigning. They functioned as party clubs, ready at all times with mottoes, torches, special uniforms, and exploding fireworks to demonstrate for the Union, for Lincoln, for free homesteads, free

---

[4] *Works*, VI, 44–55, *passim*.

[5] *Ibid.*, VI, 49–50 (Aug. 14, 1860).

[6] W. E. Baringer, "Campaign Technique in Illinois—1860," *Transactions*, Ill. State Hist. Soc., 1932, 203–281, esp. p. 248.

[7] The chairman and treasurer of the Illinois state central committee wrote as follows to Jesse W. Fell: "We need not tell you, that . . . we must have money. . . . In conclusion, we beg of you a prompt attention to the above, making, however, as little stir, and giving the matter as little publicity as may be compatible with the accomplishment of the objects designed." Quoted in *ibid.*, 205.

[8] *Ibid.*, 248.

labor, the Constitution, Plymouth Rock, Liberty throughout the world, American industry, river and harbor improvements, and, as catch-all for all this and more, the Republican party. Their music, pageantry, and army-like drill, being designed for spectacular show and sensational appeal, were unanswerable: it was theirs to shout, not argue; it was theirs also, at election time, to get out the vote. Some of the paraders, with the superiority of men on horseback, went by the name "Lincoln Rangers." In the wigwam-symbol the Republicans had their badge; in the *Railsplitter,* printed at Chicago, they had their special campaign sheet. Everywhere, as a matter of course, they had their newspapers. There were barbecues, rallies, processions, long wagon trips with farmers camping by the wayside, visits by delegations, and at Springfield a mammoth assemblage with a dozen speakers and several speaking stands. Led by carefully drilled glee clubs, people sang their party campaign songs, most of which have fortunately been forgotten. Their naïve rhythm and loud bluster usually had a pioneer flavor; the most famous of them, "Old Abe Lincoln came out of the wilderness," sang itself to the irresistible tune of "The Old Gray Mare." Another, belittling "Dug" as a plow "hoss" and rhyming him with "plug," was shouted to the melody of Stephen Foster's "Du da, du da day." [9]

II

If one turns from noise and show to the more serious aspects of the popular campaign, he finds a disturbing situation. The complex features of this momentous contest—the factions within historic parties (such as "Danites" [1] against Douglasites), the four contending parties of the troubled year 1860, the multiplicity of candidates, the talk of fusion across party lines, the simultaneous contests for presidential, congressional, gubernatorial, state executive, state legislative, and local tickets, the admixture of economic interests with moral questions, the contradictions among men supporting the same ticket —caused bewilderment whenever the campaign was thought of as an

[9] *Ibid.*, 261, 264.

[1] "The derisive term, 'Danite,' seems to have been taken from a despised Mormon group, and applied to the few Federal office-holders and pro-Southern Democrats who opposed Douglas in the elections of 1858 and 1860 in Illinois." H. P. James, *Lincoln's Own State in the Election of 1860* (abstract of doctoral thesis, Univ. of Ill., 1943), 7.

election instead of a spectacle or circus. The constant resort to misrepresentation, charges and counter charges, smirching and counter smirching, the ominous sectional flare-up, the ugly rumors of armed resistance in case of Lincoln's election,[2] the realization of thoughtful men that violent forces were lurking behind the politicians' façade —all such factors made it seem that in 1860 politics was running amuck and that the recklessness and irresponsible fury characteristic of American campaigns might this time lead to disaster.

As people listened to political speeches or read party newspapers, they either made allowances for unreason and fantastic exaggeration or else they believed, in words attributed to an English observer at an earlier and less violent time, that, judging by American journals, "the different candidates for the presidency were the greatest rascals in America." [3] If they swallowed the statements of the politicians and the editors, they believed that the nation's institutions were being destroyed, that submission to the vilest domination would be their lot unless a particular candidate were elected, that a perpetual war of races was about to be let loose, that corruption unspeakable was abroad, and that the fireside, the family, the Constitution, and society itself were about to be utterly subverted.

Speakers were numerous and distinguished. Traveling by the more active campaigners called for Marathon-like endurance. Hardly anything else in American life produced the Barnum-like thrill and excitement of party canvasses. Showmanship and popular entertainment were larger factors than most leaders would have admitted. The buffoonery of Artemus Ward was enlisted for Lincoln; other soapbox sages supported their chosen candidates; the raising of flagpoles and the stringing of banners were given as much attention as logic and solemn discussion.

There were appeals to party regularity—to the motive of voting first, last, and always for a party all the way down the line; yet there was also the plea that a party shift was indicated, that the issues of the time transcended partisanship, that old parties were crumbling with new ones developing, and that the inertia of established voting habits

---

[2] A writer unknown to Lincoln wrote him that army officers at Fort Kearny had determined in case of Republican success "to take themselves, and the arms at that point, South, for the purpose of resistance to the government." *Works,* VI, 65 (Oct. 26, 1860).

[3] Quoted in Fite, *Presidential Campaign of 1860,* 219.

must be shaken off. Such appeals, however, were themselves partisan; what was asked for was not nonpartisanship, which had no outlet and no focus, but a change in party allegiance.

Breckinridge's campaign was mediocre, noncommittal, and comparatively inactive so far as the candidate himself was concerned. He had the support of powerful elements both North and South—of President Buchanan, of the emphatic New York *Herald,* and of Yancey, who invaded the North with his fiery rhetoric. While assailing Douglas plentifully, Breckinridge men used their heavy ammunition against Lincoln. They presented his party as Black Republicans who would "spurn the pretence of peace" and "have none of your conciliatory counsels." Since, as they asserted, "the South could not, ought not to, submit," [4] they stressed the acute peril which the country faced in the event of Lincoln's election, though predicting an entirely peaceable dissolution prior to inauguration which would give Lincoln and Hamlin "no South to reign over." [5] Even when admitting the existence of better and more moderate elements in the Republican party, they accused the party of monopolizing the territories for Northern benefit, playing second fiddle to Lovejoy, endorsing Helper, and approving the "bloody acts of John Brown." [6] The party was represented as promoting equality of the races and their movement was advertised as a threatened "revolution in our social organization." [7]

The dread word "socialism" was hurled into the arena of words as a devastating characterization of Republican policy. "Socialism in its worst form," it was said, "including . . . women's rights, the division of land, free love and the exaltation of the desires of the individual over the . . . family, and the forced equality of all men in phalansteries . . . are a part of the logical chain of ideas that flow from . . . the soul of black republicanism." [8]

As for Breckinridge arguments in full, they would be a composite of all that was said by Breckinridge men—by a South Carolinian editor who predicted the time when "the President shall . . . proscribe every man who dares to raise his voice in favor of the constitutional

[4] Howard C. Perkins, ed., *Northern Editorials on Secession,* I, 32.
[5] Dwight L. Dumond, ed., *Southern Editorials on Secession,* 180.
[6] Perkins, *Northern Editorials,* I, 33, 37. [7] *Ibid.,* I, 36.
[8] *Ibid.,* I, 36 (quoting N. Y. *Herald,* Sep. 19, 1860).

rights of the South," [9] by Wigfall of Texas who ridiculed "the twaddle about the fathers," [10] by Yancey of Alabama who insisted that the fathers intended the increase of slavery and denounced Lincoln and Seward for proposing "to take them away from us by infamous legislation," [11] by a sensational New York newspaper which declared that by Lincoln's election "all . . . opposed to him will be ground to powder." [12]

While thus delivering their full arsenal of denunciation against Lincoln, Breckinridge leaders found little better to say of Douglas, whom they accused of "catering for Republican success and sympathy" and giving "cordial support to the [future] administration of Abraham Lincoln." [13] Bell, Douglas, Lincoln—they were all utterly unsatisfactory to Breckinridge supporters. "In contrast to the three" an Ohio editor presented Mr. Breckinridge—"a Union-loving man, . . . a faithful supporter of the constitution as interpreted by the Supreme Court—a man of fine talents, . . . beloved and admired by those who know him best." [14]

III

Douglas swung about with great energy, visiting nearly every Northern state and some Southern ones, projecting his powerful voice over huge outdoor multitudes, overtaxing his strength, courageously appearing in centers of tense hostility, and bearing as best he could the canards of abuse that floated throughout the land, such as the rumors that he was a drunkard, had received the sacraments from the Pope, and was the tool of the Rothschilds.[1]

The Douglas line of argument was to stress the note of compromise and appeal to an earlier statesmanship of adjustment and moderation. There could, however, be angry indignation on the part of pro-Douglas editors and speakers. Toward Lincoln at one extreme and

---

[9] Dumond, *Southern Editorials,* 155. [10] Quoted in Fite, *Campaign of 1860,* 162.

[11] *Ibid.,* 305.

[12] Perkins, *Northern Editorials,* I, 46 (quoting N. Y. *Herald,* Oct. 1, 1860).

[13] *Ibid.,* I, 41. (quoting Boston *Post,* Sep. 26, 1860). The accusation here was that Douglas, by favoring the maintenance of Federal authority *"in any contingency,"* meant that Republicans could do their worst and he would still support them.

[14] *Ibid.,* I, 60 (quoting the Columbus *Daily Capital City Fact,* Oct. 19, 1860).

[1] Milton, *Eve of Conflict,* 496.

Breckinridge at the other, both of whom they accused of defeating the cause of friendly adjustment, their language was severe and bitter. The Republicans, whom they identified with fanatical abolitionism, and the Breckinridge party, whom they denounced for seeking to impose slave codes upon the people of the territories, were equally assailed as promoters of disunion. Recognizing that fire-eaters were not all Southern and Cassandras of irrepressible conflict not all Northern, they hurled their epithets equally against "Northern negro-lovers and Southern nullifiers." [2] They did not fail to recognize that secessionist threats at the South were directed not only against Lincoln, but against Douglas as well. "As a dernier resort," declared the Peoria *Daily Democratic Union,* "the people of the South are made to believe that a dissolution of the Union, in case of the election of a northern man, will be an easy process . . . . This is an old trick . . . and must . . . result in humiliating defeat. The dissolution of this Union, . . . however much desired by . . . scoundrels . . . , is a moral, physical, and financial impossibility. A common language, a common religion, and the ties of consanguinity . . . forbid it. A common interest forbids it." [3]

Lincoln, it was argued, could not conduct a national administration on the basis of his 1858 principles. "When he shall have torn these States asunder," it was asked, "destroyed the internal trade of the country—and provoked a servile war, and flooded the whole North with fugitive blacks . . . —will he . . . have abolished slavery? Will he have made the negro the political equal of the white man? We can confidently answer, No!" What would be the result if Lincoln was elected? It would be "all anarchy and blood-shed where peace and prosperity reigned so long." The free states would force their abolition views "at the point of the bayonet." They would "subjugate the white men of the South." Revering the memory of John Brown, they would "follow his example and . . . revenge his death." [4]

The doctrine and policy of Douglas were forcefully developed by the senator himself at Raleigh, N. C., August 30, 1860.[5] Self government throughout the land, determination of local institutions by the people in every case, and, above all, adherence to the Union, were his points of emphasis. What he favored was the simple right of every

[2] Perkins, *Northern Editorials,* I, 51.
[3] *Ibid.,* I, 49.
[4] *Ibid.,* I, 53.
[5] Fite, *Campaign of 1860,* 276–300.

people to make its own laws. Two classes of politicians, he said, opposed this: the abolitionists on the one hand, and the interventionists or "Southern Secessionists" on the other. There would be no hope of electing Lincoln, he declared, except for the secessionists of the South.

On Lincoln's house-divided declaration the senator took bold issue. In a great and diverse country "there must necessarily be a corresponding variety of interests, requiring separate and different laws in each locality." This right, he said, "lies at the very foundation of our government." Uniformity in disregard of the wants and conditions of the people he considered neither possible nor desirable.

> The Revolutionary struggle [said Douglas] began in the defense of the right of the dependent colonies . . . to exercise . . . self-government as well as sovereign states. . . . George III . . . and his Tory friends . . . all denied the right of the people of these colonies to regulate their own domestic affairs. . . . Our fathers of the Revolution told the king that they did not get their rights from the king, but . . . from God Almighty. And the people of the territories will be likely to tell you that they do not get their rights from Congress, they get them from a purer source. (*Laughter.*) . . . There is no other argument used against squatter sovereignty, as they term it, that they have not copied from the Tories of the Revolution . . . . (*Applause.*) [6]

With telling effect he denounced the attitude of "the Secessionists of the South" toward the Cincinnati platform of 1856, which favored non-interference by Congress with slavery in the states and territories.

> At Charleston [he said] every friend I had from the Northwest offered to take the Cincinnati platform, word for word . . . . They [i. e., the anti-Douglas leaders] said it was not good Democracy. How came that platform to be adopted in 1856, if it was not sound? You know it was adopted at the suggestion of the Alabama legislature, on four propositions drawn by Mr. Yancey, and when introduced into the Cincinnati convention received the vote of every delegate from every state in the Union, free or slave. They proposed it and we of the North said it was fair and just, and we took it. It was adopted by a unanimous vote, and four years after you are told that a man is a traitor to the South who stands by the pledge we all made at Cincinnati. . . . I cannot change as rapidly as that. (*Applause.*) [7]

No topic in Douglas's speeches received stronger emphasis than his insistence upon recognition of whatever candidate was to be consti-

---

[6] *Ibid.*, 292–293.

[7] *Ibid.*, 293–294.

tutionally elected and his upstanding declaration that he would do all in his power to uphold the laws and sustain the Union. The strongest point he scored against Breckinridge was that disunionists were using and supporting him. When he was speaking at Norfolk he was presented with two written questions from electors on the Breckinridge ticket: would the Southern states be justified in seceding if Lincoln was elected; and if so, would he advise resistance? He answered emphatically that it was the President's duty to enforce the laws of the United States and that he would do all in his power to *"aid . . . in maintaining the supremacy of the laws against all resistance . . . , come from whatever quarter it might."* "The mere inauguration of a President," he said, "is not such a grievance as would justify revolution or secession." [8] When at Raleigh a gentleman asked him to repeat this declaration, he did so with great force, stating that if any man, after the election of Lincoln or Breckinridge, should attempt to violate the Constitution of the country, he would "hang him higher than Haman, according to law." [9]

IV

Since there were many voices to speak for Lincoln, who was not speaking for himself, the arguments for his party were somewhat diverse. Sometimes the issue was presented as a high moral crusade, but expediency often demanded that emphasis be shifted to other matters, such as free homesteads, a tariff for protection, a railroad to the Pacific, a glowing prospect of Republican prosperity, and the need for a change of administration. To Democrats it was suggested that parties come and go, that the time might come when existing parties ought to be dissolved and new associations formed. The Republican party was represented as embodying the vigorous spirit of the coming age. "The spirit of radical democracy," it was said, "will always exist and work in the country. That spirit has passed out of the old democracy into the new. To many the republican party looks radical, but it cannot look more so than the old democratic party did twenty five years ago when it had a life, a soul and a purpose. And the time was when the old republican [Jeffersonian] party of 1800 was reproached

[8] Milton, *Eve of Conflict*, 492–493.

[9] Fite, *Campaign of 1860*, 294–296. Reported in a slightly different version in Milton, 493.

with the name 'democrat,' just as the modern republican party is with the term 'abolitionist!' "[1]

The Republican party was thus pictured as "radical" to those to whom the word connoted upstanding reform and democratic progress. In this sense the fact that the Democratic party was once called "Republican" was not overlooked. Sincere Democrats were in fact asked to embrace the party of the Chicago wigwam, to realize that their own party was dead, and to consider the new organization a kind of modern Democratic party.

On the other hand, and more importantly, the party of Lincoln was presented as eminently conservative. Sometimes the argument under this head involved a delicate balancing act. This was illustrated in the tiny campaign biography by Vose, wherein Lincoln was praised for "the conservative tendencies of his mind" and held up as a man under whom all factions and "every section" could unite, not excluding "Americans" (nativists); yet in another passage in the same book Lincoln was commended for having "left the ground that Mr. Clay occupied, of compromise and concession to slavery," and manfully taking "the stand of open opposition and unyielding resistance to all the . . . aggressions of the slave power."[2] It seemed to be the special concern of this writer to relieve the Republican party of the odium of being merely a prolongation of the Whig party; indeed it was amazing to note how large a part of this midget of a book was written in the anti-Clay sense. Yet in other publications Whig principles were approved, and Lincoln, rightly enough, was held up as a true Whig. Whatever might be the effort to dissociate Lincoln from the Clay tradition, which was strong among Whigs as late as 1850, it was also true that the Republican candidate was pictured as all things to all men—moderate, conservative, patriotic, a man of the people, honored lawyer, popular orator, industrious and intelligent, "a personification of the distinctive genius of our country and its institutions."[3] The tradition of Lincoln as America, as democracy, was thus beginning to take form at the very outset of his larger career.

---

[1] Perkins, *Northern Editorials*, I, 60–61 (quoting Hartford *Evening Press*, Oct. 25 and 26, 1860).

[2] Reuben Vose, *The Life and Speeches of Abraham Lincoln and Hannibal Hamlin*, v, xiii–xiv.

[3] *Ibid.*, ix. The writer continued: "Whatever is peculiar in the history and development of America, whatever is foremost in its civilization, . . . finds its best expression in the career of such men as Abraham Lincoln."

It was characteristic of the Republican campaign that practical politics were dominant. The idea of a moral crusade against slavery was muted, while emphasis was placed on such economic issues as free homesteads for western settlers and a tariff for protection of industry. The tariff question was complex [4] and the tariff "plank" in the Republican platform of 1860 was most cautiously worded. It *seemed* to favor a tariff primarily for protection, and was so understood by protectionists,[5] but the word "protection" was omitted, while references to "revenue for the . . . government" and "remunerating prices" to agriculture, together with the vaguely expansive verbiage of the whole paragraph, would enable others to interpret it quite differently.[6] Expediency dictated the tariff policy of the party at a time when "protectionist sentiment mounted to fever heat in Pennsylvania" while it was feared that the Republicans could not win the presidency without the electoral vote of that state.[7] There were, however, elements within the party that looked to freedom of international trade as the key to widely based economic welfare, particularly former Democrats who "resented their new party's tendencies toward protectionism." [8] As to Lincoln's own position, he favored "a moderate, carefully adjusted protective tariff," so long as it would not be "a perpetual subject of political strife, squabbles, changes, and uncertainties"; [9] yet he showed excessive caution in avoiding a public statement on the subject in 1859 and 1860.

That the cause of antislavery was not regarded by Republicans as sufficient for their 1860 appeal is abundantly shown in contemporary records. Greeley knew that the country was "not Anti-Slavery." [10] James G. Blaine showed that the tariff had a "controlling influence"

---

[4] For an elaborate treatment, see Reinhard H. Luthin, "Abraham Lincoln and the Tariff," *Amer. Hist. Rev.*, XLIX, 609–629 (July, 1944).

[5] The tariff paragraph was especially slanted toward Pennsylvania. When that part of the platform was read at Chicago, "Pennsylvania went into spasms of joy . . . , her whole delegation rising and swinging hats and canes." Halstead, *Caucuses*, 135.

[6] Though the twelfth paragraph of the Republican platform was supposed in Pennsylvania and elsewhere to favor protection, yet such was the juggling of words at Chicago that it could be given just the opposite interpretation. This is shown by a statement in the Pittsburgh *Post* of October 10, 1860, that "a tariff for protection" had been "formally abandoned in their Chicago platform." Quoted in Perkins, *Northern Editorials*, I, 51–52.

[7] Luthin, "Abraham Lincoln and the Tariff," 613–614. [8] *Ibid.*, 624.

[9] *Works*, V, 256 (Oct. 11, 1859). For further statements concerning Lincoln, the Republicans, and the tariff, see below, pp. 280–281, 314–315.

[10] Luthin, "Abraham Lincoln and the Tariff," 615.

on the 1860 result.[11] Democrats, viewing the shift away from anti-slavery emphasis, were disturbed. One of them complained that in their speeches the Republicans were saying nothing of the Negro question, "but all is made to turn on the Tariff." [12] Along with the tariff were various questions of national finance, western expansion, rivers and harbors, and the like. As the Philadelphia *North American* remarked: "We have seen that slavery was not the dominating idea of the Presidential contest . . . ." [13]

V

In the raucous discord of party bickering the Bell-Everett plea was like a polite parlor conversation persisting in the midst of a riot. Why should we quarrel, they asked. Why all the sparks? Here is earth's paradise—here the kind uses of friendship with all the bright spots of national memory. We might have been a mighty and prosperous nation, a happy and contented people. In the days of the fathers we had our petty grievances but they did not rule us. We grew in harmony. The Constitution covered the nation as a blanket. We were National then. We were the people of one State. As a nation we were content, honest, flourishing. Why cannot we be so now? Love of country was once the universal theme. Now look at us—tangled in a maze, bewildered, angry with disputation, brothers no longer, pursuing a phantom, an *ignis fatuus* of demagogues. Surely we have a better destiny, a higher calling than that. From Maine to Georgia why can we not be united? Why not return to the happy days? [1]

Every one of the presidential candidates in 1860 was for the Union. To Bell and Everett the Union and the Constitution were the only issue. Douglas wanted no disunionist to vote for him.[2] In Lincoln's mind the Union was perpetual and fundamental, though he had to endure the distress of hearing Republicans accused of disunionism. "Many," he said, "charge upon us hostility to the Union"; then he added: "we claim that we are the only true Union men . . . ." [3] Even

[11] *Twenty Years of Congress*, I, 207.

[12] Luthin, "Abraham Lincoln and the Tariff," 621. [13] *Ibid.*, 624.

[1] Cincinnati *Daily Times*, Sep. 22, 1860, reprinted in Perkins, *Northern Editorials*, I, 38–39. The author has condensed and slightly paraphrased this patriotic pro-Bell editorial.

[2] Milton, *Eve of Conflict*, 492.

[3] *Works*, V, 345–346 (speech at New Haven, Mar. 6, 1860).

Breckinridge took pro-Union ground; indeed his support in the North was largely based on the supposition that, of all the candidates, his election would be likeliest to avert disunion. This was the theme song of the New York *Herald,* while in Kentucky it was editorially asserted that the "charge of disloyalty to the Union against Mr. Breckinridge and his party is as groundless, as false and infamous a slander as ever emanated from a political pen." [4]

VI

Except for saner elements which seemed inadequately vocal, the campaign was waged in an emotional atmosphere of abnormal intensity. It was unreality made real—a conflict made inevitable by repeatedly and vociferously declaring it so. Social psychology of the time partook of the pathological. Examples could be adduced on both sides. In the North Carl Schurz spoke harshly of "slavery despotism," [1] while the language of Wendell Phillips in this period, discarding reason, became a kind of grandiloquent, self-righteous raving.[2] In the South, though restraining voices were not absent, the campaign was conducted amid luridly sensational accounts of violent plots against Southerners on the part of Yankee incendiaries, poisoners, and murderers in their midst. Especially in Texas there were charges of deep-laid schemes for "a gigantic servile uprising, when at a given signal the slaves would rise against their masters, burn towns and dwellings, and murder their owners and families." [3]

The stories grew. Monsters were said to be abroad in the South, concocting the vilest of crimes. There was to be systematic arson and treason. Negro cooks were to add strychnine and arsenic to their masters' diet. The South was said to be infested with hundreds of

[4] E. M. Coulter, *Civil War and Readjustment in Kentucky,* 22, quoting *Kentucky Statesman,* Aug. 28, 1860.

[1] Quoted in Fite, *Campaign of 1860,* 261.

[2] The trend of Phillips's oratory is illustrated by a speech at Brooklyn on November 1, 1859. Praising John Brown and approving insurrection, he poured out violent abuse against Virginia. Soldiers and civilians concerned in the apprehension of Brown were denounced as "only a mob fancying itself a government." "Virginia, the Commonwealth of Virginia!" cried Phillips. "She is only a chronic insurrection. . . . She is a pirate ship, and John Brown sails the sea a Lord High Admiral of the Almighty, with his commission to sink every pirate he meets on God's ocean . . . ." Wendell Phillips, *Speeches, Lectures, and Letters,* 272, 283.

[3] Ollinger Crenshaw, "The Psychological Background of the Election of 1860 in the South," *N. C. Hist. Rev.,* 260–279 (July 1942). For the quoted passage see pp. 263–264.

abolition agents. In night meetings Negroes were to be impressed with the blessings of freedom. Abolition scoundrels were reported as being hanged all over Texas. So it went on. Orators and Southern political leaders took it up. Yancey painted a horrible picture of Southern conditions if Lincoln were chosen. Senator Albert G. Brown of Mississippi, James L. Orr of South Carolina, and Henry A. Wise of Virginia, even John C. Breckinridge, made political capital of these senseless canards. Southern audiences or readers were stirred up by stories of "untiring fanatics," "abolition fiends," a "hellish" conspiracy, "poison [predicted] in the wells of Texas," slaves incited to murder and arson, "poison, knives & pistols, distributed among our slaves," and a "covert, dark, unholy, and fanatical, insidious" scheme cooked up by peddlers and teachers from the North.[4]

A few publications in the North, such as the intensely Republican Chicago *Democrat* edited and owned by John Wentworth, accepted these frightful Southern rumors, but wholesome skepticism was expressed by the more sober and moderate journals of the South. A Douglas journalist in Georgia referred to such gruesome accounts as "wholesale lies," [5] and Southerners were warned that stories of Negro insurrections were manufactured for political purposes; in Mississippi a newspaper supporting Bell declared that the reports had no basis,[6] while a Baltimore paper printed a statement from Texas showing that "the fires had not in a single case been connected with an abolitionist emissary." [7]

Reckless statements are to be found in almost any quadrennial election campaign in the United States. To the extent that they are appraised as party propaganda and discounted as such, they may perhaps not be particularly dangerous. There are always, however, some people who believe such violent and provocative literature; the real basis for worry was not that Northern-inspired violence was going to burn out and destroy the people of Texas or any other Southern state, but that the repetition of such wild stories would aggravate an already grave psychological malady in sectional relationships. The history of Lincoln's election is incomplete unless one recognizes the seriousness of a comment by a Southern observer shortly before that

[4] *Ibid., passim,* esp. pp. 261, 267–268.
[5] *Ibid.,* p. 266, quoting Augusta *Daily Constitutionalist,* Aug. 28, 1860.
[6] *Ibid.,* 267, quoting Raymond (Miss.) *Hinds County Gazette,* Nov. 7, 1860.
[7] *Ibid.,* 267, with citation to Baltimore *American,* Nov. 1, 1860.

election that "the minds of the people are aroused to a pitch of excitement probably unparalleled in the history of our country." [8]

VII

The campaign was not waged in all states with equal intensity. In the South, the Lincoln ticket being non-existent except for weak support in Kentucky and Virginia, voters usually had three choices, though in Texas only two, for in that state there was no Douglas ticket. Those three choices, of course, were Douglas, Breckinridge, or Bell; yet in practice it narrowed down still more, because the Douglas ticket had little chance of carrying any Southern state. Breckinridge captured the more strongly sectional vote, while the less sectional or pro-Union vote, which Douglas might have been expected under normal circumstances to have received, went chiefly to Bell, who was both Southern and pro-Union, while Douglas was only pro-Union. Bell had been a Whig, which meant something in the South; he was a conservative; he was the complete opposite of the disturbing agitator; he made harmony throughout the country the paramount issue. Teamed with the eminently moderate Everett, he could be relied upon to favor, as did Crittenden, a compromise that would safeguard "Southern rights" while averting disunion and war.

Only a few of the states of the South could have been called strongly pro-Breckinridge; these were South Carolina, Mississippi, Texas, and Florida. Other Southern or border states, it is true, would go for Breckinridge in the election, but only with heavy opposition —Alabama, Arkansas, Delaware, Georgia, Louisiana, Maryland, and North Carolina.

In the North there were certain states considered so safely Republican that the contest was not really in doubt: Maine, Michigan, Minnesota, and Vermont. In other predominantly Republican states the Democrats had sizable, though minor, strength: Connecticut, New Hampshire, and Wisconsin. In all the other Northern states the contest was keen, especially so in the populous yet doubtful states of Illinois, Indiana, Ohio, Pennsylvania, New Jersey, and New York. As the campaign proceeded there was a panicky alarm over the growing prospect of Lincoln's election, with all that it would probably

[8] *Ibid.*, 279, quoting Natchez *Daily Free Trader*, Nov. 2, 1860.

mean in national chaos, financial loss, and war. This effect was magnified by the circulation of threats—real ones—of disunion in case of Republican success.

Except in South Carolina, where presidential electors were still chosen by the legislature, popular ballots were cast for the electors. Their specific function—voting for President and Vice President—was constitutional, but their popular mandate as to casting their votes in the Electoral College was inescapable. It would not be a complete statement to say that that mandate came from party groups. Those groups set up the nominations, but the people had no other choices before them, so that the popular election was conditioned and limited by the party nominations, made in conventions of delegates. When, therefore, an election had been held and the people had expressed themselves, the electors' mandates were from the people. A vote for a ticket of electors was intended only as a vote for a nominated presidential candidate; electors had no other significance. In no other way could the voters over the land, in going to the polls, know that they were voting for Lincoln, for Douglas, or for any other declared candidate. When electors were chosen, it was clearly understood that they had no discretion; the rules of the game as actually practiced were the controlling fact. Even in South Carolina the electors were instructed, though by the legislature, not the people. Nowhere in the country were they considered free agents whose performance of a constitutional function was in their own hands. Deliberately the people of America, or politicians for them, had made the Electoral College a mere tool through which parties operated, and by which people voted for President.

VIII

With such complications and limitations the American people on Tuesday, November 6, 1860, cast their ballots in the most disturbing election the nation has ever known. Lincoln "carried" seventeen of the free states, all but one. In that one, New Jersey, the electoral strength was divided; four for Lincoln and three for Douglas.[1] Breckinridge carried the second largest number of states. Besides all the states of the lower South (South Carolina, Georgia, Alabama, Florida, Mis-

[1] See below, p. 196.

sissippi, Louisiana, and Texas), he captured the electoral vote of Arkansas, Delaware, Maryland, and North Carolina. John Bell and Edward Everett, with their stress on the Union, came through with a significantly large vote in the South, carrying the important states of Kentucky, Tennessee, and Virginia, and obtaining large minorities in Alabama, Arkansas, Georgia, Florida, Louisiana, Maryland, Mississippi, Missouri, and North Carolina.

In addition to the three in New Jersey, Douglas obtained only the nine electoral votes of Missouri. Thus the electoral count stood: Lincoln, 180; Breckinridge, 72; Bell, 39; Douglas, 12. Viewed thus, it looked like a Lincoln landslide.

Quite different from this showing for the Electoral College was the popular vote: Lincoln, 1,866,452; Douglas, 1,376,957; Breckinridge, 849,781; Bell, 588,879.[2] These figures have been analyzed up and down and across the country in search of their significance in terms of popular opinion and sectional attitudes in a day of momentous crisis. The most striking fact was the great discrepancy between the popular vote and the electoral vote, this discrepancy being truly amazing in the case of Douglas, whose electoral vote was less than one-third that of Bell, though his popular vote was far more than twice the Bell total. Or, taking Douglas and Lincoln, their relation in the popular vote was, roughly speaking, in the proportion of 180 to 130, while the electoral vote was 180 to 12.

Electoral totals did not make sense as indications of popular preference. Despite his tiny representation in the Electoral College, Douglas towered high above Bell and also above Breckinridge in the ballots over the country. Taking only the Douglas and Bell votes together, they outnumbered Lincoln by nearly 100,000; add that of Breckinridge, and Lincoln's opponents surpassed him in the popular voting by 949,000 in a total of less than five millions.

Thus Lincoln became a minority President. While this would have been true of any of the others, had he been elected, Lincoln's support was much more sectional than that of any rival. In the area that was later to be included in the Southern Confederacy Lincoln received not one ballot in the popular voting except in Virginia; even there most of his vote came from the panhandle, which was not to be a

[2] Edward Stanwood, *History of the Presidency from 1788 to 1897*, 297.

part of the Confederate South.[3] The popular vote for Breckinridge was much less sectional than Lincoln's; in the North, not counting the border states, he received over 278,000 votes.[4]

It is a curious fact that, of the four presidential candidates, only Bell carried his home county (Davidson County, Tennessee—county seat, Nashville). Douglas's home county (Cook County, Illinois, whose county seat was Chicago) went for Lincoln; [5] Breckinridge's (Fayette County, Kentucky—county seat, Lexington) for Bell; Lincoln's (Sangamon County, Illinois—county seat, Springfield) for Douglas.[6] That Lincoln failed of a majority, or even a plurality, in his home county was but an illustration of the intensity of the campaign, the perplexity of voters confronting grave issues, the high regard for Douglas, the strong Democratic tradition in Illinois, and the vigor of Douglas's important organ, the *Illinois State Register,* edited by the Little Giant's close friend, Charles H. Lanphier.

One comes now to a further complication in the election of 1860 —the matter of "fusion." This was a term applied to a device used in a few states—a departure from custom—by which it was expected that Douglas-Bell-Breckinridge forces would be consolidated for one "ticket" of presidential electors. This fusion idea encountered difficult obstacles: angry factional hostility between Breckinridge men and Douglas men, the necessity of party and interparty conferences, differences of view as to how fusion electors should be instructed, search for party advantage by each group, and suspicion by Douglas's

---

[3] Lincoln received a few votes in the border states: 3815 in Delaware; 1364 in Kentucky; 2294 in Maryland; 17,028 in Missouri; 1929 in Virginia. The Virginia votes were chiefly in what became the West Virginia (non-Confederate) area; more than half came from two Ohio River counties—Ohio and Hancock—both in the panhandle.

[4] To figure Breckinridge's vote in the North is a technical problem, involving a conjectural apportionment of "fusion" votes to particular candidates. If one follows Stanwood (p. 297), the Kentuckian's Northern vote, not counting border states, is in round numbers 278,000; if these figures are modified by Paullin and Wright's apportionment (*Atlas of the Historical Geography of the United States,* 99) it would be 279,000. Stanwood counts nothing for Breckinridge in New Jersey and New York while assigning him 178,871 in Pennsylvania; Paullin and Wright assign him 50,000 in New York, 30,000 in New Jersey, and 100,000 in Pennsylvania. There is little difference in the over-all result.

[5] In Cook County the popular vote was: Lincoln, 14,589; Douglas, 9,846; Bell, 107; Breckinridge, 87. "Record of Election Returns, 1850–62," Illinois State Archives, 253.

[6] There was a close vote in Sangamon County as follows: Lincoln, 3,556; Douglas, 3,598; Bell, 130; Breckinridge, 77. *Ibid.,* 254. In Springfield, however, Lincoln had a majority: 1395 votes to 1326 for Douglas. Angle, *"Here I Have Lived,"* 253.

followers that the device was chiefly a maneuver to favor the Breckinridge faction, whose bitter enmity to Douglas could not be easily forgotten. The device of fusion meant that coöperating party groups would join in naming a ticket of presidential electors whose voting instruction would be such as to suit the multiparty combination; the avowed object of such instruction would be to defeat Lincoln; fusion electors would, of course, be instructed, but the terms of their instruction would not come from any one party.

It is necessary to glance at the manner in which fusion operated in four states—New York, New Jersey, Rhode Island, and (partly) Pennsylvania.[7] The New Jersey situation was peculiar. A "fusion" ticket was put before the voters which represented a combination among the Bell, Breckinridge, and Douglas forces, three of the presidential electors on this ticket being earmarked for Douglas, two for Bell, and two for Breckinridge. In addition, as a minor affair there was a separate Douglas ticket in the field, and, as a very tiny affair, a separate Bell ticket. The three Douglas men on the fusion ticket received in round numbers 62,000 votes, whereas the Lincoln totals (which differed as to particular electors) ran in the neighborhood of 58,000. It seems obvious that if the Douglas supporters had gone down the line solidly for the fusion ticket, the whole of New Jersey's strength (seven electors) would have been carried against Lincoln and for fusion. The difference between full fusion success and the partial success which occurred was traceable to the unwillingness of several thousand Douglas men to vote for the four non-Douglas electors. The whole story of this election shows the confusion which faced the voters as well as the intense bitterness between the Douglas and the Breckinridge elements. The fact that Lincoln obtained four electors in the state and Douglas three—this being the only state in which the electoral vote was divided—indicated a chaotic condition in which party and factional lines were uncertain and shifting.[8]

---

[7] To a minor extent, which need not detain us, fusion was also tried in Connecticut and Texas. Paullin and Wright, *Atlas*, 99.

[8] Stanwood, 297; Paullin and Wright, *Atlas*, 99 (bottom of c. 1). New York *Herald*, Nov. 15, 1860, p. 4, c. 5, and the New York *Tribune*, Nov. 16, 1860, p. 5, cc. 3–4; C. M. Knapp, *New Jersey Politics during the Period of the Civil War and Reconstruction*, 34–37; W. S. Myers, "New Jersey Politics from the Revolution to the Civil War," *Americana*, XXXVII, 444–449; James M. Scovel to Stephen A. Douglas, Camden, N. J., Dec. 10, 1860, Douglas MSS. The Scovel letter reveals the intense personal devotion felt by Douglas's followers, their deep sense of the public issues involved, their

In Rhode Island the fusion movement meant that there was only one anti-Lincoln ticket; that ticket was defeated at the polls; Lincoln obtained the entire electoral vote of the state.

Special interest attaches to the fusion movements in New York and Pennsylvania. In New York, after a series of conferences among party leaders, a consolidated ticket of electors was placed before the people comprising the Breckinridge, Bell, and Douglas elements (eighteen electoral nominees adhering to Douglas, ten to Bell, and seven to Breckinridge),[9] instead of full separate tickets of thirty-five for each of these three men. Had the voters of New York chosen this fusion ticket, there was small prospect that Breckinridge, or Bell, or Douglas, would have had a majority in the whole Electoral College, but neither would Lincoln, for fusion would have prevented the Republican candidate from carrying New York, without whose thirty-five votes he would have lacked the 152 necessary for an electoral majority. This fact revealed the strategy of fusion. Its main object was, by a massing of otherwise scattered votes, to defeat Lincoln in the Electoral College; the next step—choice by the House of Representatives voting by states—was still to be worked out in detail, but among fusionists there was hope of anti-Lincoln victory there. The first battle of fusion men would have been won if they had carried only New York. This being so, the fact that Lincoln carried New York by a majority of 50,000 over the fusion ticket was a decisive factor in the result.

In Pennsylvania, where rivalry between Breckinridge and Douglas factions was exceedingly bitter, the common hostility of these two groups to Lincoln was strong enough so that their fusion was arranged by the Democratic state committee.[10] As it finally worked out, however, there was a Douglas ticket and a Bell ticket in Pennsylvania in addition to the "fusion" ticket, which was interpreted as chiefly a Breckinridge affair. The Bell group in the state was not a party to the fusion. Many Douglas followers accepted fusion, but some of them,

---

distrust of the Republicans, and their angry resentment toward the Breckinridge element in the Democratic party. For valuable information on this subject the author is indebted to Mr. Sidney Goldmann, State Librarian, New Jersey State Library.

[9] D. S. Alexander, *Political History of the State of New York,* 331. For fusion and its complications, see also S. D. Brummer, *Political History of New York State during the . . . Civil War,* chap. iii.

[10] On the complex Pennsylvania situation, which cannot be discussed in full, the author has been assisted by Mr. R. N. Williams, 2d. of the Historical Society of Pennsylvania.

led by John W. Forney, able Philadelphia editor, declined to fuse and supported a separate ticket of all-Douglas electors. The Buchanan (pro-Breckinridge) element was powerful in the state, and against their controlling voice in Democratic counsels the Douglas men had little chance. Breckinridge men in Pennsylvania, with great intensity of purpose, were out to beat Lincoln, though this did not involve all the anti-Union implications attributed to some of the Breckinridge men in the South.[11] It is significant of the die-hard Douglas element in Pennsylvania that its most prominent leader, Forney, took pleasure after the election in claiming that by supporting Douglas instead of going along with fusion he had done much to assist Lincoln's victory. This claim has little substantial validity if one considers the importance of the tariff issue in Pennsylvania and the large vote which Lincoln polled in that state (268,030) as compared with that of all his opponents (208,412). The significant point is not so much the solid basis for the Forney assertion as the fact that a sincere Douglas man could make such a claim with evident satisfaction. In the violent war years that followed, Forney, with his Washington *Chronicle* and Philadelphia *Press,* was to become a vigorous supporter of the Lincoln administration.

John Cabell Breckinridge, reputed to be the secession candidate despite assurances of his devotion to the Union, failed to carry the popular vote of the slave states. There were fifteen such states; he carried eleven, but in some he had mere pluralities, the majority of the voters being opposed to him. If one takes Stanwood's figures for the fourteen slave states in which popular votes were cast, it appears that Breckinridge votes numbered a bit over 571,000, while non-Breckinridge votes (for Bell, Douglas, and Lincoln) numbered a bit under 706,000. The story is different, however, for what was to become the Confederate South; Breckinridge commanded an over-all popular majority in that area. Taking the ten states of the future Confederacy in which popular votes were cast, and making a needed cal-

---

11 William Bigler, prominent Democrat of Pennsylvania, wrote in this period to President Buchanan. Mentioning Southern "pronunciamentoes," he said that "the South will not be sustained in producing the election of Lincoln, and then making it cause of separation." Bigler to Buchanan, Aug. 13, 1860, MS., Hist. Soc. of Pa. (For calling his attention to this letter, and for informative comment on the Pennsylvania situation, the author is indebted to P. G. Auchampaugh of the University of Nevada, authority on Buchanan.)

culation as to Virginia,[12] the Breckinridge vote was 416,000 while the non-Breckinridge vote was 394,000. The Breckinridge advantage is greater when one conjecturally adds a figure to represent the popular vote that South Carolina might have cast. In all such calculations, however, in trying to determine whether the "secession candidate" [13] carried the South, one must not forget that Breckinridge's considerable number of Kentucky supporters (53,143) probably included many who voted for him in a pro-Union sense, since both Breckinridge himself and his advocates made pledges of Unionism, which was an important principle in Kentucky. In Virginia, where Breckinridge received 74,323 votes (53,703 in the portion that later adhered to the Confederacy), as well as in other states, the same principle must have had considerable application.

It can at least be said that if Southern secessionists had a candidate, it was Breckinridge; it could have been no other. What it amounted to was that the issue of Union or anti-Union was not clear-cut in his candidacy; on this question he was receiving opposite types of votes. The failure of secessionists to carry the whole South in the election of 1860 may therefore be stated thus: Even on the extreme assumption, which is obviously incorrect, that all those who voted for Breckinridge favored secession, disunion failed to carry "the South"; [14] much more did it fail to do so if one bears in mind the possible pro-Union interpretation of the Kentuckian's candidacy. While the trend of the Breckinridge ticket might be under question on this point of Union-

---

[12] Without any correction as to Virginia—i. e., including all the Virginia counties—the Breckinridge vote for these ten states was 436,000, the non-Breckinridge vote 419,000. Since, however, one is speaking of what was to become the "Confederate South," it is logical to subtract the votes of those forty-eight counties (Jefferson and Berkeley being not yet added) which were included in Lincoln's proclamation of April 1863 declaring the establishment of the state of West Virginia. In the figures given above, this calculation has been made, using Stanwood, 297, and *Tribune Almanac for 1861*, 50–51, in which some of the details of Lincoln's vote in Virginia are incomplete.

[13] The view that Breckinridge's candidacy had a secessionist tendency is a familiar part of the history of the time. Douglas said: "I do not believe that every Breckinridge man is a disunionist, but I do believe that every disunionist in America is a Breckinridge man." Frank E. Stevens, *Life of Stephen A. Douglas*, 623. When Douglas was speaking in Raleigh in August 1860 a gentleman in the audience referred to a Breckinridge elector as "an elector on the seceders' ticket." Fite, *Campaign of 1860*, 294. Such a statement came naturally to people's lips in 1860.

[14] The Southern border is of course included here; what is meant is that Breckinridge failed of a majority of the popular vote in the region south of the Mason-Dixon line.

ism, there could be no such doubt as to Douglas or Bell; their combined command of the popular mind south of the Mason and Dixon line in 1860 is therefore a significant thing to remember.

IX

Since by a very wide margin Lincoln was a minority choice in the popular voting, the question arises whether he could have been defeated by union among his opponents—i. e., by fusion tickets that would actually have united these opponents in a great many of the states instead of the ineffective "fusion" effort seen in only a few. The supposition that comes naturally to mind is that such union would certainly have defeated him, and superficial history has sometimes been written in those terms, but on closer examination one finds the curious fact that if all the opposing popular ballots had been cast for anti-Lincoln tickets (by which is meant tickets for presidential electors set up by states), Lincoln would still have obtained a majority in the Electoral College. The electoral vote would have been changed only in a few non-populous states; the shift would not have affected the whole election.[1] (One is speaking here of pro-Lincoln and anti-Lincoln votes actually cast. As above noted, if fusionists had gained enough votes, for instance, to have carried New York, Lincoln could not have had a majority in the Electoral College.)

Lincoln's three opponents could have defeated him hands down if popular votes could have been counted *in Federal totals,* disregarding states, and if all the anti-Lincoln popular votes could then have been united for one man in the Electoral College; but the existing system did not permit such a procedure. A statement that it could have happened under these conditions is intended only as an indication of relative strength as between Lincoln and his opposition.

Lincoln's opponents made much of state rights, but in this par-

---

[1] The difference between what Lincoln carried in the Electoral College and what he would have carried if fusion by states (within the existing electoral system) had enabled all the votes cast against him to have been concentrated, consisted only of California where fusion would have meant a Republican loss of four electoral votes, Oregon with a loss of three, and New Jersey with a loss of four (since in that case all seven of New Jersey's votes would have gone against the Republican ticket). Lincoln would then have had eleven fewer electoral votes, but he would still have had a clear majority in the Electoral College—i. e., 169 votes as compared to 134 for the opposition. Dumond, *Secession Movement,* 271; Nicolay and Hay, *Lincoln,* II, 295.

ticular the emphasis upon doing things by states, and by factions, worked against them. National election procedures, with consolidation of forces, would have helped them. The "general ticket" aspect should always be borne in mind. Electors in a commonwealth were not chosen by districts, nor apportioned to harmonize with ballots cast by the people. Each individual voter voted for a full slate which included all the state's electors. Except in New Jersey, only full slates, all alike, were chosen.

The fact that the winning ticket got *all the electoral strength*—all the legal voting power—of a state, though it might have only a slight superiority among the contenders, worked a pronounced inequality. Popular minorities in large doubtful states could not be thrown into a general total; they became wasted. In this Lincoln had an enormous advantage. He had practically no wasted votes. In ten states of the South he had not one popular vote; in three others (Kentucky, Virginia, and Maryland) his vote was small; in Missouri his wasted votes numbered only 17,028; in Delaware, only 3815; in New Jersey he actually obtained a majority of the presidential electors while receiving fewer votes than his opponents.

On the other hand, Douglas's wasted votes were tremendous. Taking his popular total, and counting out the vote of Missouri which he carried and of New Jersey which he partially carried, there were about 1,255,000 popular votes for Douglas that found no representation in the Electoral College.[2] It was, therefore, the peculiarity of the American system in the choice of President which gave Lincoln the election in spite of the fact that almost a million more voters cast ballots against him than for him.

Those whose views have not been firmly fixed in the anti-Douglas sense will find in the campaign and election of 1860 reason to note the unfriendly tricks of fate played upon the Little Giant. Since he was no trimmer, since people knew where he stood—for self-determination in the territories as well as in the states—he suffered woefully in a day when his own party was split in the North (between the Buchanan

[2] This calculation of Douglas's wasted support is based upon totals of popular votes as tabulated by Stanwood, 297. Douglas's vote should be figured somewhat differently if one follows Paullin and Wright, *Atlas*, 99. In that case one must add a considerable figure for Douglas for Pennsylvania, but this is much more than offset by what he must subtract from Stanwood's report of Douglas strength in New York and New Jersey.

and Douglas elements), while his hope of bridging the widening gap between North and South was crushed under the weight of sectional agitation. It was his unhappy destiny that in the South he was distrusted as pro-Northern, while in Northern Republican circles he was denounced as pro-Southern. Just what there was in his policy that in any way hurt the true interests of the Southern people, is hard to see now; while the Republican accusation that he was playing the game of slaveholders is entirely inconsistent with the furious opposition directed against him by Southern politicians at Charleston and Baltimore. That accusation is also contradictory to the well known fact that Greeley and others of the party thought favorably of Douglas as a possible Republican presidential candidate.

Douglas took into view the whole nation. It was neither his strategy nor his principle to appeal merely to one section. If his approach comprehended all sections, and if that fact worked against him, it was a sad commentary on the times; but it should not be taken as a disparagement of Douglas himself. Opposition to the foisting of slavery upon the people of Kansas against their will was a thing upon which Lincoln and Douglas agreed. In Lincoln it was counted a virtue; in Douglas it brought only grief. For Lincoln to take such a stand was to agree with his party in its campaign arguments to the extent that the party was emphasizing antislavery.[3] For Douglas to take the same position—against imposing slavery where the people did not want it—was to get little credit while incurring resentful opposition and proscription on the part of Democratic regulars. Douglas sacrificed more for the stand he took than any Republican, though opposition to the proslavery Lecompton constitution in Kansas was equally a Republican and a Douglas principle. The Republican party, searching in its early days for a name, was even for a time called the anti-Lecompton party. It would be easy in this troubled period to mention leaders whose tendency was sectional, but it would be hard to name any prominent statesman in either of the major parties—Democratic or Republican—who made a sturdier effort than did

[3] As to Lincoln developing such arguments, one is referring to the period from 1854 to February–March of 1860, not to the presidential campaign of 1860, in which Lincoln was silent while his party was giving much less emphasis to the antislavery issue. Lincoln's silence meant no retreat on his part, but it is fair to remember that Douglas kept repeating the same things throughout 1860 that he had been saying in previous years.

Douglas to discourage disruptive agitation and to build up those forces, widespread and sound though sadly inarticulate, that were tending to hold the nation together.

X

In retrospect there are several matters pertaining to Lincoln's election that appear a bit singular. All the emphasis in regular Republican efforts was upon the avoidance of what was called radicalism; perhaps it could better have been called excessive abolitionist agitation or unenlightened but self-righteous anti-Southernism. Yet in a few short years it was the radicals that captured the Republican party. In doing so, they assuredly went counter to Lincoln's wish. Again, Lincoln was anti-Knownothing and profited by it; yet Seward was anti-Knownothing and suffered by it. Lincoln gained by the fact that New Jersey support for Seward was lukewarm. One reason why it was lukewarm was that Seward was anti-Knownothing. Lincoln had the substantial support of those who were anti-Knownothing; yet when it came to voting, according to S. D. Brummer, there were "indications . . . that the greater part of those who supported Fillmore in 1856 voted for Lincoln in 1860." [1] Chase also was unpalatable to the nativists, as was Lincoln, yet no sheaves of political gain were garnered by the Ohioan because of this attitude.

Republicans in 1860 were appealing for the votes of Democrats. In doing so, as it turned out, they wanted it both ways: they cheerfully accepted Democratic support; then in later years they unfairly promoted the stereotyped charge that it was only the Republicans who had saved the country and that the Democrats had been anti-Union and disloyal amid war, which was the opposite of the truth. This latter charge, persisting for hate-filled postwar decades, was to be known as "waving the bloody shirt."

Parties give up something when they go out in pursuit of votes. Often, instead of taking a clear stand, they represent themselves as all things to all men. Their managers become vote brokers. They seek support in every quarter, then use the victory for party purposes. It is commonly the marginal, or border-line, appeal that sets the pattern of politician emphasis. Where in 1860 a state, a region, or a group

[1] *Political History of New York State during the . . . Civil War*, 96.

was known to be safely Republican, less attention was paid to it. Republican managers did not cater so actively to their known supporters—i. e., to groups that were likely to have pronounced Republican proclivities—as to those regarded as doubtful. They tried to win over men who distrusted or disliked them. The more they did this, the less clear-cut did their appeal become. Seeking the votes of doubters, they said things (or practiced silences) which caused their position to seem doubtful. If they made vote-seeking professions, the citizen might not sufficiently realize that professions are not all, and that an element that does not set the pattern openly at election time may exploit the results of the election and seize the reins when it comes to the business of government.

Questionable control of patronage and spoils was a factor whose true character in 1860 is not easy to analyze. Those among the Republicans who were most conspicuously associated with the deliberate use of partisan spoils were Seward and Cameron; their reputations in this respect worked against them and for Lincoln. Yet both Seward [2] and Cameron were brought into the cabinet; in the case of Cameron the Lincoln administration assumed a deadweight, an embarrassment, and, as to army contracts and the like, a taint of corruption.[3] In their 1860 platform the Republicans declared that the people "view with alarm the . . . extravagance which pervades . . . the Federal Government" as well as the "frauds and corruption at the Federal metropolis." [4] Their remedy was "an entire change of administration."

XI

One hears much of the perennial question: Who elected Lincoln? Answers are diverse: The great Northwest did it; New York did it; the "October states" did it, especially Pennsylvania.[1] The idea that

---

[2] It was not that Seward himself was responsible for such a reputation, but in practical politics the Seward movement was virtually identical with that of the boss, Thurlow Weed.

[3] See vol. II, 54–61.

[4] Johnson, *Proceedings*, 131–132.

[1] Though state elections usually coincided with the national presidential election, there were several states which held earlier elections for governor, etc. When Maine elected a Republican governor in September by a big majority, and when in October the Republicans elected governors in Pennsylvania and Indiana, while showing considerable gains in Ohio, these indications served to presage, perhaps partly to produce, Republican national success in November.

Carl Schurz made Lincoln President has had plausible support, being by no means denied by Schurz himself.[2] Southern secessionists, thought Douglas, were responsible. On a previous page the eccentricity of American election machinery, in its 1860 bearings, has been noted. It has also been argued that the foreign-born element, especially the Germans, elected Lincoln. Already the influence of German-Americans on the nomination at Chicago has been observed; in addition, it has been urged that they enabled Lincoln to carry doubtful states without which he could not have had an electoral majority. For the Northwest as a whole the case for the decisiveness of foreign-born influence has been presented by Donnal V. Smith.[3] For Illinois, populous and closely contested, the situation has been analyzed in similar terms by Jay Monaghan.[4] Yet this pattern of decisive German influence in the Republican sense has been significantly questioned. In a notably revisionist study, Joseph Schafer, whose Domesday Book for Wisconsin is a triumph of detailed historical scholarship, has carefully analyzed the familiar contention that the Germans turned the scale for Lincoln in 1860; he finds that no such conclusion is at all tenable, so far as Wisconsin is concerned.[5] It had been concluded by a former writer that there were 60,000 German voters in Wisconsin and that 40,000 of them voted for Lincoln. Since Lincoln's plurality over Douglas was 21,000, it had been concluded that the German vote was essential to this majority.[6]

By careful calculation, however, Schafer finds that the potential voting strength of Wisconsin Germans was something like 33,000, not 60,000; then he demolishes the facile assumption that two-thirds of

[2] *Amer. Hist. Rev.*, XLVII, 52–53.

[3] Donnal V. Smith, "The Influence of the Foreign-Born of the Northwest in the Election of 1860," *Miss. Vall. Hist. Rev.*, XIX, 192–204 (Sep., 1932).

[4] Jay Monaghan, "Did Abraham Lincoln Receive the Illinois German Vote?," *Journal*, Ill. State Hist. Soc., XXXV, 133–139 (June, 1942).

[5] Joseph Schafer, "Who Elected Lincoln," *Amer. Hist. Rev.*, XLVII, 51–63 (Oct., 1941).

[6] Even taking this assumption at its face value, it could not mean that Wisconsin would have been carried for Douglas if the German vote had been omitted altogether. If one subtracts 40,000 from Lincoln's Wisconsin vote and 20,000 from that of Douglas—i. e., if one leaves out the Germans as allegedly measured—Lincoln would still have carried the state by a safe margin over Douglas. The only way this claim makes sense even in its own falsely exaggerated terms is to suppose that the imaginary 40,000 German voters-for-Lincoln had voted the other way. If this had happened—i. e., if there had been such a large German element and it had shifted—Douglas would have carried the state. The claim, however, presented by a writer named Hense-Jensen, is shown by Schafer to be "fantastic." *Ibid.*, 57.

these German voters supported Lincoln.[7] Examining specific counties (there being, of course, no records in which voting totals are broken up in terms of racial groups), he found that those which showed a great preponderance of German family heads also showed a very strong predominance of Douglas votes, while Lincoln's majorities are found in counties whose population was simply part of the westward movement from older eastern portions of the United States. It was in "Yankee counties" in Wisconsin that Republican support was heavy, not in counties populated largely by foreign-born. Schafer notes that the same was true in New York. The New England element thus appears to have had a great effect in building up the Lincoln vote in the Northwest.[8] If one considers factors "without which" the result would not have happened, it must be remembered that various factors could qualify in that respect. It is much truer to say that the Yankees elected Lincoln than that the Germans did it.[9] German support for him, which in some states was large though it is difficult to measure, should of course be recognized. It should be properly credited and its significance correctly appraised, but it should not be overstated.

---

[7] Concerning the vote in Wisconsin Schafer writes: ". . . it is so certain that a large majority of Germans voted for Douglas as to make the Lincoln majority . . . a sure proof of the Germans' inability to alter the result. If all the Germans had voted for Douglas, Lincoln would, nevertheless, have won the state." *Ibid.*, 61.

[8] *Ibid.*, 56–57.

[9] Schafer concludes: ". . . it appears all but certain that the assignment of a dominant influence to the foreign born in the election of 1860 is 100 per cent wrong; . . . ." *Ibid.*, 63. This conclusion, based on close study for Wisconsin, is also supported, in Schafer's opinion, as to Indiana, Ohio, Michigan, and Iowa. In each of these states he finds Lincoln's majority greater than the probable total of German voters. As to Illinois, however, he concedes that the German vote may have made the difference between Lincoln's success and defeat.

CHAPTER IX

THE VEXED QUESTION

I

MANY and various were the threats, solutions, and panaceas that rose in answer to the question "what to do" as the result of Lincoln's election. Withdraw immediately and form a Southern government, declared the active secessionists. Meet Lincoln with a President of our own. Never live again with free-soil states.[1] Call a border-state convention, asked moderates of the Virginia-Kentucky area. Frankfort, Kentucky, was proposed as the place for such a gathering.[2] Call an official national convention broadly representative of the nation, was the wish of some of Buchanan's advisers. The President and also Lincoln favored the idea in principle. Call a peace conference of state representatives, said John Tyler and his associates of the Virginia legislature. Have nothing to do with such an Old Ladies Convention, said Republican radicals and Southern hotspurs; they are only tinkerers from the border states trying to save the Union. Accept disunion, said Mason of Virginia, though he would not have promoted it. When a state secedes, he said, let the President recognize the fact by proclamation and let Federal laws be suspended within the state.[3] Let the cotton states go in peace, said Horace Greeley. Secession may be revolutionary, but the right exists. "We hope never to live in a republic whereof one section is pinned to the residue by bayonets."[4]

[1] *Annual Report,* Am. Hist, Assoc., 1911, II, 529, 531.

[2] Edward McPherson, *Political History of the . . . Rebellion,* 6.

[3] *Ibid.,* 86.

[4] New York *Tribune,* Nov. 9, 1860. Perhaps the go-in-peace declaration was no more than an editorial flash. If it was a policy, it probably involved somewhat of hedging in the sense that its editorial sponsor never expected it to become a reality. It has even been contended that the hint of peaceable separation was a kind of trick, a

Have four unions by a rearrangement of the fragments of the United States, urged Winfield Scott, head of the army.[5] Let the slave states be trustees of the national territory south of 36° 30′, was another suggestion, and let the free states be trustees of the territory north of that line. Admit New Mexico and Arizona as slave states, declared a border spokesman; after that, prohibit the acquisition of any additional territory by the United States.[6] Hold to the Union if compromise can be obtained, urged upper Southern and border-state leaders.[7] Promote compromise and meet this wish, was the policy of Buchanan, of Douglas, of the Douglas Democrats, and of such Republicans as Seward and Weed.

"Patriots ought to stand loyally and patiently in the Union," urged the Louisville *Daily Journal* (November 8, 1860). There are checks on Lincoln. He can do no harm. House, Senate, and Court will restrain him. These checks are insurmountable. Only a cabinet of temperate views will be confirmed. No "unconstitutional law adverse to slavery" can be enacted "since both branches [of the Congress] are Anti-Republican." Lincoln is at the mercy of his opponents. If he commits an aggression, impeach him. Above all, quell disunion; "curb Yancey and Rhett." [8]

Let Lincoln electors save the day, advised some of the Northern "doughfaces," by casting their votes for Breckinridge and Lane, thereby pacifying the fire-eaters.[9] Let Breckinridge go South, said some who labored to defeat him, and let him "use his influence as the man who, of all others, can do most to quiet the disaffected States." [10] It was assumed that Breckinridge, not yet a secessionist, would use that

forestalling of that type of compromise which was designed to save the Union without war. This comes close to saying that the go-in-peace proposal tended (as the event proved) to produce war, either because its advocates did not foresee consequences, or because they actually preferred war to the kind of bargains that meant concession to slavery. See David M. Potter, *Lincoln and His Party in the Secession Crisis*, 51–57. Dr. Potter writes (p. 57): "The fictitious go-in-peace alternative continued to obscure the situation until the occasion for compromise had passed and war remained as the only means by which the Union could be maintained."

[5] Scott even suggested boundaries and capitals for these new confederacies. C. W. Elliott, *Winfield Scott: The Soldier and the Man*, 676.

[6] McPherson, *Rebellion*, 74–75.

[7] In early February 1861 the Kentucky legislature passed resolutions calling for a national convention, at the same time protesting alike against Southern revolution and Federal coercion. *Ibid.*, 8.

[8] D. L. Dumond, *Southern Editorials on Secession*, 218–220.

[9] Chicago *Tribune*, Dec. 3, 1860, p. 1, c. 1.

[10] New York *Herald*, Nov. 17, 1860, p. 6, c. 1: Dumond, *Southern Editorials*, 255.

influence for the preservation of the Union. Let the people elect the President directly, declared a North Carolinian who at once added that this would require an adjustment or weighting to allow increased strength to Southern states because of non-voting slave population.[11] Choose the President by districts, advised Andrew Johnson; elect a President from the free states and a Vice President from the slave states, and *vice versa,* every four years; choose senators by popular vote; limit Supreme Court tenure to twelve years; *elect* [12] one-third of the Court every fourth year.[13] Have two Presidents, said R. M. T. Hunter of Virginia. Let each section elect its President, the chief of one section succeeding that of the other every fourth year. Barring the overriding of vetoes (with sectional safeguards) no law should be valid, he thought, unless signed by both Presidents. He would also readjust the Court, increase its membership, and add various elements of interstate retaliation not then allowed.[14] Secession, thought Hunter, ought to be adopted only if approved by a majority of the states *of the section concerned.*[15]

While these suggestions and proposals showed the serious dislocations produced by the election of a sectional President in a day of overwrought sectionalism, they showed also the wish of a vast majority of Americans North and South to preserve the Union. Far different were the steps taken by the secessionists. Working with the semblance of popular support these leaders carried one redoubt after another, beginning directly after the election when the South Carolina legislature passed its convention bill, until their movement swept seven states out of the Union a month in advance of Lincoln's inauguration. No incoming President had ever faced so difficult a situation. It should be added that no outgoing President was ever placed "in a more trying and responsible position" than Buchanan.[16] To understand the subject is not merely to recatalogue "facts" and incidents. It is to restudy a many-sided situation whose complex character still baffles

---

[11] McPherson, *Rebellion,* 75. [12] Italics supplied. [13] McPherson, *Rebellion,* 73.

[14] *Ibid.,* 86–88. Hunter's proposal was: "That each section shall elect a President, to be called the first and second President: the first to serve for four years as President, the next to succeed him at the end of four years . . . ." He proposed further "That no law should be valid which did not have the assent of both Presidents, or in the event of a veto by one of them, the assent of a majority of the Senators of the section from which he came."

[15] Italics supplied.

[16] James Buchanan, *Mr. Buchanan's Administration on the Eve of the Rebellion.* 109.

complete unraveling and still claims the attention of revisionist scholars. Published writings, reminiscences, biographies, newspapers, state studies, voluminous public documents, social and economic monographs must therefore be sought by the reader who would comprehend the factors that were moving in the whole wretched crisis.

It could hardly be said that Lincoln was the center of these moving factors. While the President Elect remained inconspicuously at Springfield, others were steering Republican policy; determination of events was but slightly in Lincoln's hands. The drama of the time was in truth a series of simultaneous dramas out of which few writers have produced a comprehensive picture. There was the drama of South Carolina rushing ahead with its little revolution, of other cotton states pausing in momentary doubt and then taking similar action, of Southern senators and congressmen acting with the same effect as their opponents (the Republicans) for the defeat of compromise efforts at the nation's capital. All this assisted those who had already turned their backs upon the very thought of compromise and were moving in the lower South for the launching of a rival government that would present Lincoln with a *fait accompli*. There was the episode of Buchanan's changing ministry, overdramatized as a "cabinet row" but in truth serious enough. It involved the resignations of Cobb, Floyd, Cass, and Thompson. After their withdrawal the cabinet was strengthened by the appointment of firmer secretaries. As the new order in the lower South was boldly inaugurated there was striking contrast between those who took it as settled fact, not even open to argument, and those who continued to speak in familiar and established terms. Such a contrast was shown in the Buchanan administration's refusal to be stampeded by South Carolina into admitting the collapse of Federal authority. The same contrast appeared when Congress, whose main item on the agenda was conciliation, had to witness the spectacle of Southern solons rising in Senate and House to discharge parting oratorical shots. Through all this there was the homely drama at Springfield which is even yet viewed by Lincoln devotees as primarily a kind of success story of a local son who made good.

II

It is hard to convey an impression of the explosive effect of secession in the American scene. A complete reorientation was effected, with new shibboleths, thought patterns, phrases, loyalties, governments, and standards. In the lower South the bare events were as follows.

South Carolina passed its ordinance of secession on December 20. This was the first secession, the only one in 1860. On its own avowal the palmetto state was now a separate nation. Baffling governmental questions posed by this isolated status were never to be solved; the status was temporary and misleading. Completely separate existence was nominal. The Mississippi convention passed its ordinance of secession on January 9. In the electing of convention delegates the Mississippi vote was only sixty per cent of the presidential vote in 1860. The canvass for this purpose "did not command the active . . . interest of the voters of Mississippi"; the "time . . . for reflection . . . was exceedingly short"; "thousands stayed away from the polls because they were confused"; when the election was over the "Union forces felt that . . . they had been overwhelmed by the intemperate views of the Secessionists, and that the . . . country . . . was 'drifting into . . . anarchy . . . and ruin.' "[1]

Secessionists in Mississippi had the convention votes. Yet those who were actively promoting disunion showed no desire to have the question of secession submitted to the people. An amendment to this effect was submitted by Walter Brooke of Vicksburg but decisively defeated; the secessionists refused to submit to this popular test.[2] For this refusal the passing of the ordinance was denounced by the Natchez *Courier* as the work of a "dictatorial oligarchy."[3]

Florida's ordinance was passed on January 10, that of Alabama on January 11. In Georgia, where there was a keen contest and where the misleading argument of "better terms" out of the Union was effectively used,[4] the struggle was longer and the decision closer. On the main test of strength in the Georgia convention—a motion to substitute

[1] P. L. Rainwater, *Mississippi, Storm Center of Secession, 1856–1861*, 196–197.

[2] *Ibid.*, 211.

[3] Quoted in *ibid.*, 215.

[4] Unionists were enlisted in the secessionist cause, being assured that by a kind of temporary secession gesture they could get "better terms"—i. e., recognition of their "rights" in the Union—after which there could be a ready return to the old allegiance. For documentation, see Randall, *Civil War and Reconstruction*, 191.

coöperation among the Southern states in place of separate secession —the division was 133 for coöperation, 164 for secession. When an absent delegate later recorded his vote, it was 134 to 164; a change of sixteen votes would have defeated secession.[5] Finally the die was cast, January 19, by the passing of the ordinance. "I never felt so sad before," wrote Herschel V. Johnson.[6] It was his view that the election of Lincoln did not justify secession. Laboring actively against disunion, he believed that a fair canvass would have shown a majority of the Southern people against the policy of separation. The issue, he thought, was not fairly presented. Secessionists insisted "that it would be peaceable—that it would not bring war—that . . . the Yankees . . . would not fight—and that, at the worst it would be a short war . . . ."[7]

Two more states—Louisiana and Texas—completed the action of the lower South. The Louisiana convention voted secession on January 26, that of Texas on February 1. Secession in Texas was contrary to the loyalties of Sam Houston, its distinguished governor. On March 18, 1861, he was deposed.

Taking the journal of the Confederate provisional Congress and presenting its recital in condensed paraphrase, the legal birth of the Southern Confederacy was as follows. In the year of Our Lord one thousand eight hundred and sixty-one, in the Capital of Alabama, in the city of Montgomery, there assembled certain delegates from the several independent Southern States of North America, to wit: Alabama, Florida, Georgia, Louisiana, Mississippi, and South Carolina, the said delegates being assembled by virtue of divers ordinances adopted by conventions of the peoples of the independent states aforenamed. (Full texts of the secession ordinances appear in the record at this point.) A prayer to Almighty God was offered in behalf of the Congress of the States. Thirty-seven delegates presented their credentials and signed the roll (elaborate state papers giving credentials are here inserted in the journal). Howell Cobb of Georgia was chosen president of the Congress by acclamation, rules were adopted, and on February 7 a "Constitution for the Provisional Government of the Confederate States of North America" was presented. Stephens of Georgia moved that the word "North" be stricken out. It was agreed to.

---

[5] P. S. Flippin, *Herschel V. Johnson of Georgia*, 188–189.
[6] *Ibid.*, 192.
[7] *Ibid.*, 158, 170–171.

On February 8, fifth day of the Congress, the constitution was unanimously adopted. Next day, the vote being taken by states for President, the Hon. Jefferson Davis of Mississippi received all the votes cast, being six, and was thus unanimously elected President of the Provisional Government. With like unanimity the Hon. Alexander H. Stephens of Georgia received all six votes for Vice President.[8]

These fundamental measures were understood to be the solemn acts of sovereign Southern peoples, not directly but through chosen representatives. Only in Texas among the states of the lower South was the ordinance of secession submitted to popular vote, this being done after its adoption. It was argued, however, that the delegates who voted for secession had just been chosen with plenary powers by the people and that no later popular ratification was needed.

The Southern cause now had a new and exciting focus. In the initial stages it had all been accomplished with astonishing ease. The national government at Washington permitted this rival government to be set up without interference. The convention at Montgomery was not an all-Southern gathering. Of the fifteen slave states, only six were represented in the body that launched the Confederacy, created its constitution, and chose its high officials. In these early proceedings Texas was not represented, nor the states of the upper South, nor any of the states of the Southern border. The important state of Virginia had no part in the proceedings by which the Confederacy was set up. At Montgomery, of course, there was no debating of secession. No gathering of delegates from any grouping of Southern states for that purpose occurred in 1860–61, nothing comparable to the Nashville Convention of 1850. Withdrawal having already been decreed in the six states represented, the Montgomery Congress proceeded from there as an instrument for an independent Southern nation. By the time it met the secession movement had gained such momentum in separate-state terms that unionists such as Walter Brooke of Mississippi and Alexander H. Stephens of Georgia became supporters, one might say charter members, of the new Southern government.

Such men by the thousands might have willed a different result, but their states had acted, they had to share the fate of their people, the matter was considered beyond recall, and the spirit of state

[8] *Journal of the Congress of the Confederate States of America, 1861–1865* (Senate Document No. 234 [U. S.], 58 Cong., 2 sess.), I, 7–40 *passim*.

loyalty as well as the necessity of maintaining order was understood to require the support of all citizens of all groups. Constitutionally, in the Southern view, there was no doubt about the right of secession. Even unionists in the South, in that brief period when the matter was in process of decision, had not challenged the right, but rather the wisdom and desirability, of withdrawal from the United States.

With a stirring sense of revolution and military preparation in the air, but also with the manner of statesmen quietly altering their government in the midst of peace and in the exercise of well known American functions, Jefferson Davis was inaugurated provisional President of the Confederacy in the stately capitol at Montgomery on February 18, 1861. Lincoln, on his way to the seat of government, arrived that day in Albany, New York.

Davis and Lincoln were to stand at opposite extremes. Was there to be any middle ground? Practically, in terms of action open to American individuals and communities, there was not. Secession either had to be favored, at least admitted, or it had to be opposed. A state had to be either in or out of the union. Opposing a government, however, even a new "provisional" one, is no easy matter. Men of the time, knowing this, and realizing how quick was the pace from deliberation to irrevocable action, spoke of the casting of the die, the crossing of the Rubicon. No state of the South could balance itself somewhere in between the United States and the Confederate States. Even on the border that was impossible, as Kentucky was soon to discover.

When the consequences of secession unfolded, those who had been conspicuously in front as secessionist leaders—Rhett, Yancey, and the like—made very little contribution to the Southern Confederacy. Support for the Confederacy came rather in large part from men who had not favored secession, such as R. E. Lee and A. H. Stephens. According to Stephens's own statement directly after the war, his position in the Confederate government was retained after he "clearly saw that the great objects in view . . . in accepting it were not likely to be obtained even by the success of the Confederate Arms." [9] In the phase that followed Lincoln's election, when action was being hastily shaped in the lower South, Jefferson Davis had been "far from placing himself at the head of those who wished to precipitate . . .

[9] Alexander H. Stephens to President Andrew Johnson, Ft. Warren, June 8, 1865, Johnson MSS.

secession by separate state action." As matters were racing toward a climax in Mississippi, Davis "was opposed to such a program and was counselling delay and co-operation . . . ."[10]

III

Already the recital is both behind and ahead of the event. When a revolutionary thing happens on a vast scale with the tempo of impatient change, it may not be easy to view all its facets at once, or to see at a glance its background, incidents, exhibitionist phases, repercussions throughout the country, impact upon the established order, and consequences. Springfield was distant from Charleston, Washington from Montgomery; yet in reality the distance was deceptive. People and government were soon to find that they were all parts of the same interrelated American world. What South Carolina did was to have its effect in Virginia; December would show its results in April. The clarity of seeing consequences that were about to appear was given to some, but they were helpless to stem the current; the onrushing of events compelled on the part of millions a kind of horrified drifting. Debates in Congress, conventions in the farther South, popular explosions, proposals and remedies, conferences among leaders—all these, however opposite and conflicting, were parts of America in the tragic crisis of 1860–61. The action of South Carolina, taken with astonishing ease in its own setting, had brought reverberations everywhere. There were secessionist demonstrations at New Orleans, Mobile, Norfolk, Wilmington (Delaware), Baltimore, Petersburg, and even Washington. Elsewhere there were indignation meetings as at Pittsburgh where the threatened removal of artillery from the arsenal produced intense excitement.[1] By the end of December disunionists at Charleston were in possession of the post office, the Federal courts, the custom houses, and some of the forts (Castle Pinckney and Fort Moultrie) in the harbor. Taking their cue from this most truculent of the commonwealths, disunionists elsewhere, sometimes in advance of withdrawal by their states, took over Federal arsenals, forts, and custom houses. When on December 29 the resignation of Secre-

[10] Rainwater, *Mississippi*, 162 n.; Jefferson Davis to Rhett, Nov. 10, 1860, in Dunbar Rowland, *Jefferson Davis Constitutionalist: His Papers* . . . [etc.], IV, 541–542.

[1] Frank Moore, ed., *The Rebellion Record: A Diary of American Events, with Documents, Narratives,* . . . [etc.], (Diary), I, 6.

tary of War Floyd showed how deeply the crisis was cutting into the President's official family, people associated this action with Federal evacuation of Fort Moultrie and the removal of the garrison to Sumter.[2] By the middle of January such forts as Pulaski at Savannah, Fort Morgan at Mobile, and Fort Barrancas at Pensacola had been seized. Meanwhile Southern agents were abroad in the North purchasing munitions and other war material and having it shipped South. As these matters, or such as were not clandestine, were reported in the papers, the effect was registered in mass meetings, editorials, parades, and public resolutions. When Judah P. Benjamin of Louisiana declared in the Senate on the last day of 1860 that the South could never be subjugated, he was greeted with "disgraceful applause" and "screams" from the gallery and his admirers were overheard to say "That's the talk," "Now we will have war," "Abe Lincoln will never come here."[3] For every such event there was a pro-Union demonstration, as in the celebration held by the New England Society of New York which was addressed by Vice President Elect Hamlin and Senator Seward.[4]

To say that "the South" had acted to produce secession and form the Confederacy would be a doubtful generalization. Not only did the important states in the upper South and border have no part in the movement, as above noted; even in the deep South, which in population constituted a minority of the slaveholding section, every effort toward coöperation among the states in choosing between secession and union was avoided by secession leaders.[5] Had coöperation been likely to produce combined secession, Rhett and Company would have welcomed it; that it was expected to produce the opposite result

---

[2] It was also stated that Floyd's position in the cabinet had become untenable and that the Sumter garrisoning gave him a good excuse. It was even suggested that Buchanan eased the way by helping Floyd to resign in the best public light. *Ibid.*, I, 7–8; P. G. Auchampaugh, *James Buchanan and His Cabinet*, 97.

[3] New York *Times*, Jan. 1, 1861, p. 1, c. 1. It was not that Benjamin's manner was explosive. He spoke with calmness and deliberation. In his farewell speech, properly so called, delivered in the Senate on February 4, he even expressed affection for men of "other skies" with whom he was parting. *Cong. Globe*, 36 Cong., 2 sess., 212–217, 721–722; Robert D. Meade, *Judah P. Benjamin, Confederate Statesman*, 149, 152–153.

[4] Moore, *Rebellion Record* (Diary), I, 4.

[5] In the earlier sectional crisis of 1850–51 Rhett and other active secession leaders had been frustrated because coöperation among the Southern states had been the method. "Never did the Rhetts lose sight of the lesson . . . . In a struggle between separate state action and coöperation a second defeat was to be expected. This time there should be no such struggle." Laura A. White, *Robert Barnwell Rhett*, 172.

was admitted by Governor Gist of South Carolina who undemocratically warned against an all-Southern gathering because he thought "the Border and non-acting States would outvote us and thereby defeat action." [6]

Though secessionists had laid their plans well in advance and were ready to strike promptly after Lincoln's election (which they were said to hope for, since it could be taken as a factor making for disunion), the actual election of Lincoln fell so far short of swinging Southern sentiment against the Union that coöperative effort was still considered undesirable as a method of promoting secession. At a later stage commissioners were sent to other Southern states by South Carolina, and these commonwealths, whose coöperation on the main matter had been spurned, were now appealed to for secessionist support by a state that would otherwise have been left out on a limb. While seeking pro-secession assistance the South Carolina legislature on January 27, 1861, rejected Virginia's proposal for cooperative action, declaring that they had "no desire or intention to promote" the object Virginia had in view.[7]

There were evidences that secession as the answer to Lincoln's election by no means commanded the preponderant support of the Southern people. "Peaceful secession is a myth," declared the New Orleans *Picayune*. "It is a mere phrase to conceal the sad train of events that are inevitably to follow." [8] What is "the extent of the wrongs . . . that so arouse the . . . passions . . . as to obliterate . . . patriotism," asked the same editor. In answer he rejected the plea that the election of the chief of a sectional party could justify revolution.[9] How do "the Yanceyites propose to sustain the government they are engineering to impose upon us," inquired the New Orleans *True Delta*.[10] Secession would mean "a baptism of blood," warned a Wilmington editor who sarcastically asked whether the people of North Carolina wished "to be dragged into revolution and anarchy . . . to please the State of South Carolina, who, by her insufferable arrogance, . . . has been a constant source of annoyance . . . to the whole country, North and South, for the last thirty years?" [11]

"Stop and think," cautioned the *Daily Nashville Patriot*. Going out

---

[6] Dumond, *Secession Movement*, 137. [7] McPherson, *Rebellion*, 2 n.
[8] Dumond, *Southern Editorials*, 200. [9] *Ibid.*, 214. [10] *Ibid.*, 214. [11] *Ibid.*, 227–228.

of the Union "does not absolve the . . . citizen from the obligation to obey the laws of the Union . . . ." [12] To say that the people have no other recourse against oppression was "untrue," said the same editor; the government belonged to the people and they had the power to alter it in a peaceable manner. To try such peaceful redress, he said, was "our duty here in Tennessee." [13] "Let us meet in common council," urged the *Kentucky Statesman*. "Let us have a Southern convention, and let the slave States take counsel together as to the best mode of preserving their rights in the Union. . . . We see nothing else to save the Union than a Southern Convention; and we believe that will." [14]

There were some in the South who were not greatly outraged at the election of Lincoln. Many agreed that his election was not a just reason for disunion.[15] Large numbers of conservatives dreaded secession and preferred to await an "overt act" before undertaking it. The whole background of Lincoln's relation to the Republican party suggested that he himself would take the conservative side, and as for the fear that his party was abolitionized and would push him into radical measures (assuming there had been no secession and no war) the answer was that, if a further trial of preserving "Southern rights" within the Union were thought desirable, there was a convenient instrument for this purpose in the national Congress wherein the Republicans would not have had a majority in either house if the Southern states had retained their congressmen at Washington.[16] Thus even if measures hostile to the South had been attempted by the Republicans in opposition to Lincoln's well known wish for moderation as shown in his Cooper Union speech and elsewhere, such hostility could have been checked by the obvious device of a majority vote in Congress. As to the Lincoln threat being viewed as an attack upon

---

[12] *Ibid.*, 250–252. [13] *Ibid.*, 252. [14] *Ibid.*, 254–255.

[15] "A very large number of our citizens have joined in a call for a Mass Meeting . . . opposed to the secession movement . . . ." A. Burwell to S. A. Douglas, Vicksburg, Miss., Nov. 16, 1860, Douglas MSS. A broadside is enclosed which carries sixty-six names, including Thomas S. Dabney, but it is stated that in addition to the printed names there were "many others." The appeal reads in part: "The Union men of Mississippi ought to meet together, not as partisans . . . but as citizens of the same country, bound to a common destiny."

[16] The Chicago *Tribune* (a Republican paper) referred at the opening of Congress in December 1860 to the "fact that the Democracy control both branches" of that body (Dec. 3, 1860, p. 2, c. 1). See also Dumond, *Secession Movement*, 130–144; Dumond, *Southern Editorials*, 209, 255; Randall, *Civil War and Reconstruction*, 231–232.

slavery, it is significant to note that even Yancey himself, with his diplomatic colleagues Rost and Mann, later declared that fear of emancipation was not the cause of secession for the simple reason that the party of Lincoln did not intend to impose emancipation upon the South.[17]

It is a significant thing to call the roll of those Southerners who opposed secession during the hectic crisis of 1860–61. Ignoring many minor names the list included H. S. Foote, W. C. Rives, John Minor Botts, John B. Baldwin, G. W. Summers, Alexander H. H. Stuart, Robert E. Lee, Jubal A. Early, Jonathan Worth, Andrew Jackson Hamilton, J. W. Throckmorton, Sam Houston, Herschel V. Johnson, Benjamin H. Hill, Alexander H. Stephens, Andrew Johnson, Winfield Scott, George H. Thomas, John J. Crittenden, George D. Prentice, Benjamin Fitzpatrick, William L. Sharkey, Benjamin F. Perry, John A. Gilmer, John Tyler, John C. Breckinridge, William Aiken, J. L. Petigru, Emerson Etheridge, Thomas S. Dabney, and James Moore Wayne. This group contained thoroughbred Southerners mindful of the rights of their section but unconvinced that disunion was a remedy made necessary by any denial of those rights.

"[S]hall the people of the South secede from the Union in consequence of the election of Mr. Lincoln?" asked Alexander H. Stephens. "I tell you . . . candidly . . . that I do not think that they ought. . . . Were we to make a point of resistance to the Government . . . on that account, the record would be . . . against us." [18] Stephens went further; he actually spoke favorably of Lincoln. "In point of merit as a man I have no doubt Lincoln is just as good, safe and sound a man as Mr. Buchanan, and would administer the Government . . . just as safely for the South . . . . I know the man well. He is not a bad man. . . . I consider slavery much more secure in the Union than out of it . . . ." [19]

Much of the whole struggle of secessionists versus moderates in the South was illustrated by the difference between the diminutive Stephens and his burly colleague Toombs. Stephens regretted that the South had forced the issue at Charleston in 1860.[20] He would have avoided the assault upon Douglas and would have kept the Democratic

[17] Owsley, *King Cotton Diplomacy*, 66–67.
[18] McPherson, *Rebellion*, 21.
[19] *Annual Report*, Am. Hist. Assoc., 1911, II, 487.
[20] U. B. Phillips, *Life of Robert Toombs*, 190.

party intact. In the election of 1860 he supported the Douglas ticket. After that he labored to avert secession by his state, though admitting the constitutional right. His was the language of adjustment, compromise, and union. In this respect Stephens resembled Gilmer of North Carolina who wrote during this crisis: "We have had so much talk from . . . politicians about Southern Rights, that many honest Southern[ers] . . . have got it into their heads that they are already by the North deprived of some great . . . right, and are in immediate danger of losing others of still more vital importance. The people are beginning to open their eyes. They need aid. If they can be armed with a little plain common sense . . . they will pursue . . . those who have been deceiving them . . . ." [21] Toombs, on the other hand, used the harsher tones of truculence and sectional antagonism. He scored the "Black Republicans," identified them with abolitionists, denounced "intervention . . . by squatters" (meaning popular sovereignty in the territories), and declared that he would resist Douglas to the bitter end, though in doing so he could see "nothing but disaster and defeat in the future." [22] To judge from his language one would have supposed that Toombs would as soon have seceded against Douglas as against Lincoln. Some of his fiercest invective was aimed at men of his own party, Northern Democrats whom, on one occasion, he called "a lot of rogues." [23]

IV

As Congress began its session in early December of 1860 President Buchanan addressed the body in a message which denounced secession, stressed a Union that rested on public opinion, and favored the adoption of "peaceful constitutional remedies." The message has been more often denounced than read. Such writers as Nicolay and Hay and J. F. Rhodes have set the pattern of traditional criticism of Buchanan. Emphasizing the President's "weakness," they have harped upon the contrasting example of Andrew Jackson, and this contrast has become part of the stock-in-trade of Lincoln biographers who unhistorically imply that Jackson's menace of force "solved" the nullification problem and that his sternness turned the trick in averting

---

[21] John A. Gilmer to S. A. Douglas, Greensboro, N. C., Mar. 8, 1861, Douglas MSS.
[22] *Annual Report*, Am. Hist. Assoc., 1911, II, 469, 477. [23] *Ibid.*, 470.

a serious disaster threatened in his time by South Carolina. It is but a step from that to the denunciation of Buchanan for his avoidance of force. In view of the familiar assumption that a Jackson in the presidency in 1860 would have cleared up the whole situation, it is of interest to read contemporary comments by the sturdy New England ex-President John Quincy Adams who at the time of the nullification episode referred to Jackson's policy in terms of disgust, declaring that he was surrendering the Union "to the nullifiers of the South and the land-robbers of the West." [1]

In truth the nullification episode showed the success of compromisers, and it should not be forgotten that Calhoun of South Carolina as well as Clay of Kentucky and others, worked for compromise and union.[2] If one were so minded he could easily quote Jackson in the pro-Buchanan sense as when he declared in his "farewell address" (March 4, 1837) that the Union rested upon "the affections of the people" and was not to be maintained by the "exertion of the coercive powers confided to the General Government." [3] In the traditional criticism of Buchanan that has become a shopworn stereotype it is obvious that the critics place small value upon the avoidance of war and that the whole discussion is a matter of reading back after the fact of war to the supposition that no such avoidance was possible.

But Republican-minded critics were not alone in denouncing Buchanan. Jefferson Davis regarded his treatment of South Carolina as "perfidious" and furiously assailed him for not granting the demands of South Carolina's representatives who sought to negotiate with him.[4] "The President's message is condemned by the extremists from both North and South," declared a well known Republican paper, "while conservative members . . . approve . . . the general principles enunciated." [5]

In endless post-mortems Americans have been accustomed to view the Buchanan interval against a background of South Carolinian events, or cotton-state events. But the same interval can also be viewed from the background of the United States, of which Washington was still the capital. Buchanan did not lose this larger view. He believed

---

[1] C. F. Adams, ed., *Memoirs of J. Q. Adams*, VIII, 503.

[2] Randall, *Civil War and Reconstruction*, 32–33.

[3] Buchanan, *Mr. Buchanan's Administration*, 112; Richardson, *Messages . . . of the Presidents*, III, 297.

[4] Rowland, *Davis*, IV, 565.

[5] Chicago *Tribune*, Dec. 6, 1860, p. 4, c. 7.

that arbitration of the vexed issue rested with Congress. The message which is usually taken as the text for assailing him was delivered before any state had seceded and was presented to a Congress whose absorbing preoccupation was the avoidance of armed conflict. "The stake involved was no less than the peace and perpetuity of the Union." [6] Certainly in early December of 1860 the guarding of that stake was, in the eyes of moderates, a matter of adjustment. The issue could have been dramatized as a race between the precipitate action of the lower South and the peaceful policy that was being urged in the general latitude of Virginia, Kentucky, and Washington. That the secessionists of the cotton states controlled the event does not signify that theirs was the stronger position. It was a matter of playing the cards and of forcing the issue. As schemes to save the nation swarmed and multiplied it became necessary to create some device of parliamentary procedure to handle them; thus there arose the committee of thirteen in the Senate and a committee of thirty-three in the House, the latter being a special grand committee of one from each state. While these committees were delving into the problem of compromise, the President was hardly free to take measures that might have inaugurated war, nor to snatch the decision out of the hands of Congress.

The position of prominence belonged to the Senate committee, of whose distinguished membership much was expected. Including such men as Davis, Toombs, Seward, Douglas, Wade, Doolittle, Trumbull, Grimes, and Crittenden, the committee not only represented the elite of the nation's statesmen; it seemingly contained a leaven of mediatory influence. Created simultaneously with South Carolina's secession, it held its first meeting on the day after that first fateful ordinance, but a week before this the anti-compromisers had, as the journalist would say, stolen the front pages. On December 13 a group of Southern members of the House of Representatives, having assembled in the rooms of Reuben Davis of Mississippi, issued a manifesto "To our Constituents" as they called it, which declared that all hope of relief in the Union was exhausted and that Southern safety could be found only in a Southern Confederacy, which could be ob-

---

[6] Buchanan, *Mr. Buchanan's Administration,* 113. See also Frank Wysor Klingberg, "James Buchanan and the Crisis of the Union," *Jour. of So. Hist.,* IX, 455–474 (Nov., 1943).

tained only by separate state secession.[7] It is only fair to add that Southerners defended this course on the ground that no reliance could be placed in compromise plans because of the attitude of the Republican party, but it is also true that the manifesto was deliberately used as a secessionist propaganda device at a time when the congressional search for compromise had hardly begun. It is further true that both the Northern radicals and Southern secessionists were vigorously opposed to compromise. What was back of the manifesto seems almost to have been a fear that compromise would be successful. An adjustment at Washington that would satisfy the upper South and the border was precisely the thing which disunionists of both extremes dreaded. Senator Toombs as early as November 14 wrote that he would sustain South Carolina in secession,[8] and on December 23 he issued his address to the people of Georgia in which he did his best to close the door, or declare the door closed, to compromise before adjustment plans could ever be launched. Charging that the Senate compromise committee was "controlled by Black Republicans, your enemies," he warned his people not to be "deceived" by peaceful efforts and concluded: "Secession by the fourth of March next should be thundered from the ballot-box by the unanimous voice of Georgia . . . ."[9] Equally uncompromising statements by Northern extremists could be cited.

Under these circumstances the task of the committee of thirteen, whose proceedings Lincoln constantly watched, became well nigh hopeless. Its utter failure was formally announced eleven days after its appointment. On December 31, an early day for such a failure, the committee reported its inability to agree upon any plan of adjustment. No other act of his public life, said Douglas, had caused him so much regret.[10] There have been times when the Senate has failed the country in an hour of need, or in a challenge to greatness; this was one of the times.

---

[7] Rhodes, *Hist. of U. S.*, III, 177–178; McPherson, *Rebellion*, 37.

[8] Phillips, *Toombs*, 203. On December 13 Toombs "sounded a different note," proposing delay until compromise amendments could be considered (*ibid.*, 203–204), but on that day the anti-compromise address "To Our Constituents" was made public with an indication (which may not have been correct) that Toombs, absent from Washington, would have signed. On December 23, as seen above, Toombs emphatically opposed further compromise efforts.

[9] *Annual Report*, Am. Hist. Assoc., 1911, II, 525.

[10] *Annual Cyclopaedia*, 1861, 175.

In the general futility that marked the mechanics of compromise the record of the House committee of thirty-three need not be given in detail. Ultimately it reported a series of proposals, a goodly number of which passed the House, but none of them became law or shaped the situation in the direction of sectional appeasement. The committee as appointed contained a majority of Republicans, including Adams of Massachusetts, Corwin of Ohio, Kellogg of Illinois (mouthpiece of Lincoln), and Morrill of Vermont. Prominent Democratic names were absent. The committee's report, delayed until January 14, contained a series of proposals, but none commanded a majority of its members. Concerning the work of this group Charles Francis Adams stated that the recusant states would accept no form of adjustment that did not involve the Federal obligation to protect and extend slavery.[11]

Two of the committee's proposals may be specially noted here. One was a resolution denouncing state laws that hindered the return of fugitive slaves and recommending the repeal of such laws. It passed the House by more than five to two (136–53).[12] The other was a curious "unamendable" amendment to the Constitution which read as follows: "No amendment shall be made to the Constitution which will authorize . . . Congress . . . to abolish or interfere, within any State, with the domestic institutions thereof, including that of persons held to labor or service by the laws of said State."[13] In the House this amendment was approved by a vote of 133 to 65, in the Senate by 24 to 12.[14] Its supporters thus barely mustered the necessary two-thirds, yet two-thirds was a heavy majority. To become effective it would have required ratification by three-fourths of the states. This never came about, but action concerning the amendment is significant because it registered the sentiment, even after the withdrawal of many Southerners, that Congress should never interfere with slavery in the states. One should also mention the earlier action of the House in adopting without a dissenting voice (161–0) the resolution of John Sherman of Ohio declaring that neither Congress nor the people of

---

11 McPherson, *Rebellion*, 57.

12 *Cong. Globe*, 36 Cong., 2 sess., 1263 (Feb. 27, 1861).

13 *Ibid.*

14 The vote was taken on February 28, 1861, in the House and on March 2 in the Senate. *Ibid.*, 1285, 1375.

the non-slaveholding states had the constitutional right to legislate upon or interfere with slavery in any of the states.[15]

Looming higher than all the committees was one man, the venerable John J. Crittenden of Kentucky, compromiser by nature, spokesman of the great border, political heir of Henry Clay, and fit representative of the nation's elder statesmen. It is easy to pick flaws in the specific proposals of this distinguished Kentuckian, but it is impossible to escape a sense of the patriotic earnestness of his efforts to stave off civil war. Harking back to previous compromises in the days of 1820 and 1850 which he personally remembered, Crittenden thought that Southern apprehension could be quieted by concessions concerning slavery in the territories and in interstate relationships. Extending the Missouri line (36° 30′) to the Pacific, he would, as it were, give the West a Mason and Dixon line, prohibiting slavery in the territories on the Northern side, and protecting (not merely permitting) slavery on the Southern side. He further proposed that Congress disclaim the power to abolish slavery in a state, that there be no abolition in the District of Columbia without the consent of Virginia and Maryland, and that full guarantees be given for the protection of Southern rights in escaping slaves. By amendments to prevent future amendments he would assure the South in the most solemn manner that a changed Constitution would never allow Federal abolition of slavery within the states, nor change the ratio by which three-fifths of a state's slaves were counted in the apportionment of congressional seats.[16]

Crittenden's proposal was furiously assailed by Republicans and its details sound unsatisfactory today, but the terms he offered were more of a restriction upon slavery than the existing policy of the Supreme Court. Moreover, before the session of Congress was ended the Republicans themselves, in specific territorial legislation, were to refrain from applying that Wilmot-proviso doctrine which constituted their chief basis of objection to the Kentuckian's formula of peace. Crittenden tried in vain to get his proposals adopted by the Senate committee of thirteen; later the Senate itself voted him down, 23 to 25.[17] That the proposals were solidly supported by the Democrats and

---

[15] *Ibid.*, 857 (Feb. 11, 1861).

[16] *Ibid.*, 36 Cong., 2 sess., 112–114.

[17] *Ibid.*, 409. The vote was on a motion to substitute a very different resolution for Crittenden's.

as solidly opposed by the Republicans was naturally emphasized at the South. On the other hand it has been urged that the failure was due to the refusal of six Southern senators to vote. It was charged that these senators did not want compromise.[18] There was truth in both these attributions of blame; intransigents on both sides, antislavery enthusiasts no less than ardent secessionists, opposed not only compromise "terms" but the very idea of any compromise whatever.

V

The Republicans of the time were not a close-knit party. Rather they were a mixture of differing groups. S. S. Cox declared that he did not know "where the head or the tail of the . . . party" was.[1] Among Republicans of Ohio, for example, Corwin had been an old-line Whig, Chase an antislavery Democrat, and Giddings a radical abolitionist. Between Sumner and Seward, or between Greeley and Weed, there was indeed a gulf fixed. Also there was a marked difference between Greeley's November attitude and his later belligerency. Perhaps it was the difference between Greeley couchant and Greeley rampant. The Republicans had no spearhead, no consistent spokesman, no fully recognized leader in those fateful weeks when Southerners were saying that all depended on the Republicans and that no settlement could even be considered unless it had the previous endorsement of the incoming administration. Such statements were used for propaganda purposes in the South where emphasis was placed upon the "Black Republicans" who, as was stated by Toombs, had treated compromise proposals with "derision or contempt." [2]

An analysis of the Republican attitude on compromise is therefore essential. When at the beginning of the congressional session it was proposed to create a compromise committee of thirty-three, the majority of the Republicans favored it; nevertheless all the thirty-eight votes in opposition were on the Republican side.[3] The committee was fully under Republican control, and it was futile as an instrument of compromise. Yet one cannot say that the committee favored no concessions. It was rather that its concessions did not avert the trouble,

---

[18] *Ibid.*, 37 Cong., 2 sess., 587–588.

[1] Samuel S. Cox, *Eight Years in Congress*, 78.

[2] McPherson, *Rebellion*, 37–38.

[3] *Annual Cyclopaedia*, 1861, 201; Dumond, *Secession Movement*, 156.

and if one seeks an explanation of why this was so he realizes how artificial difficulties had accumulated to make real obstacles out of shadow objections and how a problem that seems simple to a later generation was fraught at the time with sectional inhibitions till it was well nigh unsolvable. Even though they went a considerable distance, Republicans lacked that element which could make compromise take hold; on the other hand they could answer that the satisfying of the secessionists was an impossibility unless secession itself was to be admitted.

Nearly every generalization needs its qualifying corrective. In the midst of the sectional crisis there was noticed a "thinning of the ranks" among Republicans, which meant that a considerable number favored compromise.[4] Such men as Seward and Weed were willing to go far toward adjustment. In his influential Albany newspaper Weed came out with a formula of conciliation involving an effective fugitive slave law, repeal of the personal liberty laws, noninterference by Congress with slavery in the territories, and, if necessary, restoration of the Missouri line.[5] The last point involved a considerable retreat from the Chicago platform. The New York *Times* and the New York *Courier and Enquirer,* both Republican and pro-Seward, favored the Weed compromise.[6] On January 12, Seward, long the most prominent Republican in the country, made a notably conciliatory speech. He showed his entire willingness to satisfy the South concerning fugitive slaves and the unrestrained admission of future slave states.[7] Such Republicans as Grimes and Trumbull would not endorse the Crittenden compromise, though some Republicans would do so, yet they would make concessions. Grimes agreed to protection of slavery in the states, revision of the personal liberty laws, and the admission of slave states in the Southwest to offset the admission of Kansas free.[8] Trumbull would never agree to an open declaration making slavery perpetual, yet he disavowed any intention to interfere with Southern domestic institutions.[9] Cox of Ohio, ardent Democrat, was impressed with the extent of the things the Republicans would agree to, emphasizing that they

[4] David M. Potter, *Lincoln and His Party in the Secession Crisis,* 191.

[5] McPherson, 74. Greeley wrote: "Weed thinks he is saving the Union. I guess not." Greeley to Brockway, Dec. 8, 1860, Greeley MSS., Lib. of Cong.

[6] Rhodes, *Hist. of U. S.,* III, 156. [7] *Cong. Globe,* 36 Cong., 2 sess., 341–344.

[8] William Salter, *Life of James W. Grimes,* 137. [9] White, *Trumbull,* 132–133.

would have admitted New Mexico as a slave state. Controlling the patronage, he thought, they would "be content with the tricks" (jobs) and "allow us" the honors (concessions). Under "the lead of Bates, Raymond, Corwin, Ewing, Weed, ay, and Seward and Lincoln," they would "drown the Giddings crew" and would be "as harmless in office as most men are." [10]

By no means were the Republicans standing firm on any thorough antislavery principle. Many of them, especially urban dwellers, stood ready to support Weed.[11] The party in general supported the Adrian resolution "earnestly recommend[ing]" the repeal of the personal liberty laws, and this before any state had seceded.[12] They even agreed to the aforementioned constitutional amendment by which Federal action against slavery in the states should forever be prevented. It was common in these days for those Republicans who stood firm to express disgust or regret at the manner in which men of Lincoln's party were backing down. "It is sad," wrote Chase, "to think what is now yielded and by whom." [13] J. G. Blaine's account of Republican action on territorial legislation in the closing days of the Thirty-Sixth Congress should be carefully read in this connection. With Republican majorities in both houses of Congress (owing to the absence of Southerners) laws were passed organizing the territories of Colorado, Dakota, and Nevada without the prohibition of slavery. After seven years, declared Blaine, the Republicans abandoned the "cardinal principle" of their new-fledged party. Even Wade, Sumner, and Chandler joined in this action. It was not sufficient, said Blaine, to contend that there was no danger of slavery going into these territories: if the prohibition was proper for Oregon it was equally needful for Dakota; if for Kansas, then for Colorado and Nevada. References to the needlessness of the ter-

---

[10] Cox, *Eight Years,* 204, 206.

[11] "In our city & State some of their [the Republicans'] most prominent men are ready to follow the lead of Weed, and active agencies are at work to bring about a compromise." August Belmont to Herschel V. Johnson of Georgia, Dec. 30, 1860, Douglas MSS., Univ. of Chicago. As for the rural districts of New York the opposite opinion was reported. "Do not judge New York state by Mr Weed," wrote George E. Baker from Albany to Sumner. "He no longer speaks for her when he suggests a Compromise. . . . The rural districts repudiate the idea unanimously." Sumner MSS, Dec. 3, 1860.

[12] The Adrian resolution passed the House of Representatives on December 17, 1860, by a vote of 153 to 14. *Cong. Globe,* 36 Cong., 2 sess., 108.

[13] S. P. Chase to John A. Andrew, Jan. 26, 1861, Andrew MSS.

ritorial prohibition came strangely from Republican lips. They had heaped abuse upon Webster and even more upon Douglas for making the same point. Now they took action in Congress which seemed to Blaine a triumph for Douglas.[14] And, to make the victory complete and the futility of the territorial controversy crystal clear, Southerners themselves conceded "that the demand they had so loudly made for admission to the Territories was really worth nothing to the institution of slavery." The whole fuss and storm "related to an imaginary negro in an impossible place." [15]

It has been noted above how Douglas was able in 1861 to taunt the Republicans with abandonment of those principles on which the Lincoln-Douglas debates had been waged in 1858.[16] That point deserves further notice here. When the aforementioned acts organizing Colorado, Nevada, and Dakota were passed (February-March 1861), the prohibition or permission of slavery was not mentioned in these statutes, which left the question of slavery in the territories exactly where it was in Douglas's Kansas-Nebraska act of 1854, so far as congressional legislation was concerned.[17] In the Senate these bills were passed without division; this lack of challenge and of recorded vote indicated Republican consent. In the House the yeas and nays were recorded, and one may test the party attitude by the vote on the Colorado bill, which Mr. Sickles desired to have read "to see if the Wilmot proviso was in it"; he then pointed out that "that principle is abandoned." [18] The bill was passed with 90 yeas and 44 nays; 86 Republicans favored it and only ten were opposed.[19] After the proceedings had been completed regarding the three territorial bills, the only such measures pending at the time, Douglas could not refrain from making his comment. "This very

---

[14] J. G. Blaine, *Twenty Years of Congress,* I, 269 ff. Blaine wrote (p. 271): "Every prominent Republican senator who agreed in 1861 to abandon the principle of the Wilmot Proviso . . . had, in 1850, heaped reproach upon Mr. Webster for not insisting upon the . . . principle . . . ." He added: "It was . . . a day of triumph for Mr. Douglas. He was justified in his boast that, after all the bitter agitation which followed the . . . Kansas-Nebraska Bill, the Republicans adopted its principle . . . in the first Territory which they had the power to organize."

[15] *Ibid.,* I, 272.

[16] See above, p. 126.

[17] Colorado was organized by act of February 28, 1861, Nevada and Dakota by acts of March 2, 1861; except for such matters as boundaries and name, the acts were identical. *U. S. Stat. at Large,* XII, 172, 209, 239.

[18] *Cong. Globe,* 36 Cong., 2 sess., 1003 (Feb. 18, 1861).

[19] *Ibid.,* 1005 (Feb. 18, 1861); McPherson, *Rebellion,* 90.

session," he said, "the Republican party, in both Houses of Congress, . . . have backed down from their platform and abandoned the doctrine of congressional prohibition. This very week three territorial bills have been passed . . . without the Wilmot proviso, and no man proposed to enact it; not even one man on the other side of the Chamber would rise and propose the Wilmot proviso. . . . They have abandoned the doctrine of the President elect . . . . He said . . . that he had voted for the Wilmot proviso forty-two times, ... Not one of his followers this year voted for it once. The Senator from New York, [Mr. Seward,] the embodiment of the party, . . . did not propose it. . . . Practically, the Chicago platform is abandoned; the Philadelphia platform is abandoned; the whole doctrine for which the Republican party contended as to the Territories is abandoned, surrendered, given up; non-interference is substituted in its place." [20] Again he said: "What you . . . said before the election was one thing. What you felt it your duty as patriots to do . . . after the election is a very different thing. After having secured . . . power, you . . . organized all the Territories that we have now got, on the principle of . . . popular sovereignty." [21]

Douglas was careful to commend the motives that prompted the action of his opponents in 1861 when their doctrine meant peril to the country. "For years," he said, "that party has aimed shafts at my breast . . . ." Then he showed that on attaining power they had come round to the Douglas program, and added: "I rejoice . . . to say that they acted like patriots . . . in abandoning the ground on which they had stood for years, and coming over to the Democratic doctrine . . . . I do not refer to this in any spirit of . . . crimination. . . . I refer to it as an evidence of patriotism . . . for which all Union-loving men will give them due credit." [22]

Having been led to believe that the territorial issue concerning slavery was the pivotal and vital issue of the age, that it was the basis of the Republican party or the intolerable challenge to Southern rights, Americans of the time were witnesses of a scene in Congress in which "Mr. Seward waived the anti-slavery guaranty on behalf of the Republicans" while James Stephens Green of Missouri moved

---

[20] Douglas in United States Senate, March 3, 1861, *Cong. Globe*, 36 Cong., 2 sess., 1391.
[21] *Ibid.*, 1503 (Mar. 25, 1861). [22] *Ibid.*, 1460 (Mar. 15, 1861).

a corresponding waiver of pro-slavery guarantees "on behalf of the Breckinridge Democracy." [23] Republicans did not consistently adhere even to their own party ideology.[24] It seemed to an opponent that they were "like the man that drew the elephant in the raffle" and knew "not what to do with him . . . ." [25] To those who were firm in the antislavery faith it seemed that they were backsliders.[26] The truth was that their party was almost leaderless, that their leading men differed as to policy, and that their stickling at one or two points, though of little importance in itself, neutralized the effect of concessions offered, making it easy for opponents to overdramatize their position as the refusal of all compromise whatsoever.

For Union and peace the cards were wretchedly played. Such a valuable thing as the calling of a national convention was discarded. Secessionists were able by the bolder play of their hands to produce a result far beyond the cards they held. To change the figure, if politics be an art and mass emotions its medium, unionists were woefully unskillful in the technique by which the medium was handled.

VI

Lincoln's attitude on the vexed question was shaped in varying parts by Republican ideology, by his dislike of particular proposals, and by his none-too-perfect reading of popular sentiment. While controversy raged the thing most obvious to the public ear was Lincoln's silence. To write for publication, he said on October 23, "would do no good." "If I were to labor a month I could not express my conservative . . . intentions more clearly . . . than they are expressed . . . in my many speeches already in print and before the public." Any public statement, he thought, would be "useless." He could say nothing which he had not already said. To speak again

---

[23] Blaine, *Twenty Years of Congress*, I, 271.

[24] "I need not say how anxious I am that our friends . . . shall stand firm . . . . I am sorry to find so many cowards even among republicans." Joshua Giddings to Charles Sumner, Dec. 3, 1860, Sumner MSS.

[25] R. W. Massey to S. A. Douglas, Paola, Kan., Nov. 28, 1860, Douglas MSS.

[26] "There has been a great cave in by the Republicans in the [Pennsylvania] Senate. Today they voted virtually to extend slavery if the 'border states' demanded it." Thus wrote one of William Lloyd Garrison's correspondents who referred in the same letter to "Republican backsliders." E. W. Capron to W. L. Garrison, Harrisburg, Pa., Jan. 28, 1861, Garrison MSS. This note of disgust at Republican concessions runs all through the correspondence of Garrison, Sumner, and other antislavery men.

would give the opportunity for further garbling and misrepresentation. This he regarded as a situation to be prudently faced not "in a spirit of complaint or resentment" but as a guide to policy. He was not at liberty to shift his ground and he saw no reason for mere repetition. Indeed he thought a repetition "would do positive harm." "The secessionists *per se* . . . would clamor all the louder." While saying all this, however, he indicated that there should be no apprehension in the country that his course would be "other than conservative." [1]

When the Republicans planned a huge celebration of the election of Lincoln and Hamlin at Springfield on November 20, 1860, Lincoln was strongly urged to share the platform with such men as Trumbull, Yates, and Palmer, and to use the occasion to allay the growing distrust of his incoming administration. Such a meeting would have offered a sounding board for a repetition of his conservative views at an early stage in the crisis, and there were those who felt that a restraining and reassuring statement from him along conservative Union lines was a solemn public duty. Lincoln not only refused to make a speech at this Republican gathering but declined even to appear, confining himself to a few sentences of greeting to some Wide Awakes who stormed his home. Though joining in party rejoicing he counseled against "any hard feelings toward any citizen who . . . has differed with us." [2]

Not altogether, however, did he let the occasion pass without an expression of his views. He wrote out a passage to be incorporated into Trumbull's speech, so that the Illinois senator was actually using Lincoln's own words when he declared that all the states would have "as perfect liberty to choose and employ their own means of protecting property . . . within their . . . limits, as . . . under any administration." [3] Again he was using Lincoln's words when he declared that secessionists *per se* were "in hot haste to get out of the Union" because they could not continue to "maintain an apprehension among the Southern people that their homes and firesides [were] . . . to be endangered by the action of the Federal Government." [4]

---

[1] For statements quoted in this paragraph, see *Works*, VI, 63–71 (Oct. 23, to Nov. 16, 1860).

[2] *Ibid.*, VI, 72. [3] White, *Trumbull*, 109. [4] *Ibid.*, 110.

The flight of this trial balloon was not propitious. A week later Lincoln knew of no newspaper having made the Trumbull statement a basis for quieting anxiety, while the Boston *Courier,* correctly attributing Trumbull's remarks to Lincoln, used them as the text for denunciation of the President Elect for abandoning Republican ground. On the other hand the Washington *Constitution* held the speech up to the South as an open declaration of war against them.[5] All this served to confirm Lincoln in the view that nothing he could say could ease the troubled situation.

Even when expressing views of a sort to quiet the country in his correspondence with close friends, Lincoln insisted upon secrecy. One may take his published works from November to March, 1860–61, and find pithily worded, even eloquent expressions of good will, common sense, and restraint in letters that provokingly carried the heading "private," "confidential," "private and confidential," "strictly confidential," or for "your own eye only." It was in this manner that he wrote secretly to George D. Prentice, A. H. Stephens, John A. Gilmer, and Henry J. Raymond.[6] In the same period one may take the Trumbull manuscripts and note frequent inquiries as to why Trumbull, understood to be Lincoln's spokesman, did not speak out. Lincoln's words in correspondence were so conciliatory and reassuring that they seem to the present view precisely the kind of pronouncements which the emergency demanded from the President Elect. Why, then, did he let only a few favored friends have these salutary words from his pen while his public monosyllables were both colorless and rare? Possibly we have the explanation in a letter to George D. Prentice of Kentucky shortly before his election. His abstinence from speaking out, he wrote on October 29, 1860, was not punctilio. It was a conviction that speaking out would only "do harm." For the good men of the South, and he regarded "the majority of them as such," he would repeat his stand "seventy and seven times," but he had bad men to deal with, "both *North and* South;[7] men . . . eager for something new upon which to base new misrepresentations . . . ." These men were ready to accuse him of "timidity and cowardice" and "would seize upon almost any letter . . . [he] could write as being 'an awful coming down.' "[8]

---

[5] *Works,* VI, 74–75 (Nov. 28, 1860).
[6] *Ibid.,* VI, 66, 74, 79, 85 (Oct. 29 to Dec. 22, 1860).
[7] Italics supplied.
[8] *Works,* VI, 66–67.

This sounds very much as if Lincoln's silence was due, at least in large part, to a fear of men of his own party. It was they, not Southerners, who would convict him of cowardice. If he spoke it would be for conciliation, but this would be branded as timidity and a "coming down" from those elements of Republican ideology which after all represented only a minority of the people. Thus early did the force of Northern radicalism, which was to plague Lincoln's whole administration, make itself felt in the pre-war crisis. This tendency to call Lincoln timid was due less to any actual "coming down" than to the extremists' inherent dislike of compromise (let one go over the manuscripts and published sources of the time if he doubts this), and to the persistent attitude of rebel-baiting which was one of the foremost emotional factors of the time. Again and again it reveals itself in abolitionist denunciation of such men as Weed and Seward for their moderate views. Where radicals thought Lincoln leaned toward moderation they denounced Lincoln too. The words of William Lloyd Garrison in this connection were expressive of the extremist attitude, which sometimes went to the extent of favoring disunion. "Would to God," wrote Garrison, "that the people of the North, without distinction of party, could see that the time has come for a separation from the South . . . in obedience to the 'Higher Law'! Is it not self-evident that we are, and must be, with slave institutions in one section and free institutions in the other, two nations?" [9]

In spite of his studied reticence it is possible to reconstruct Lincoln's actual position touching the sectional crisis. He favored enforcement of the fugitive slave law. While he believed that such enforcement should be relieved of "vindictiveness," [10] he also thought that Northern personal liberty laws ought to be repealed to the extent of their conflict with the fugitive-slave clause of the Constitution.[11] It may fairly be said that he stood ready to make every reasonable concession to Southern sensibilities on this point. Suspected fugitives when caught, he thought ought to have a fair trial.[12] Unlike abolitionists Lincoln had favored a decision of the Ohio supreme court (1859) upholding the Federal courts in the enforce-

---

[9] W. L. Garrison to Sumner, Feb. 26, 1861, Sumner MSS.
[10] J. Dixon to Gideon Welles, Dec. 3, 1860, Welles MSS.
[11] *Works*, VI, 81 (Dec. 15, 1860).
[12] White, *Trumbull*, 112.

ment of the fugitive slave law. Writing on July 28, 1859, to Samuel Galloway, who called himself the first Ohioan to write to him suggesting his name for the presidency,[13] Lincoln had objected strenuously to the action of the Ohio Republicans in repudiating this decision and favoring a repeal of the fugitive-slave law. Hannibal Hamlin, who conferred personally with Lincoln in November 1860, stated that the new chief insisted that the law concerning fugitives must be executed in good faith and that no one who thought otherwise ought to enter his cabinet.[14]

On other points Lincoln's views showed a like conservatism. He had, as President Elect, no thought of recommending the abolition of slavery in the District of Columbia even on the safeguarding conditions outlined in previous declarations. Abolition of the slave trade among the states he did not contemplate. These were matters he cared little about [15] but he knew even if he were to recommend such abolition it was "quite clear Congress would not follow" him.[16] Nor did he care much about possible extension in New Mexico, "if further extension were hedged against." [17] Often he said he would do nothing to anger the people of the South, nothing to harass them.[18] "Rest fully assured," he wrote to Samuel Haycraft, "that the good people of the South . . . will find no cause to complain of me." [19] To Alexander H. Stephens he wrote: "Do the people of the South really entertain fears that a Republican administration would, directly or indirectly, interfere with the slaves, or with them about the slaves? If they do, I . . . assure you . . . that there is no cause for such fears. The South would be in no more danger in this respect than . . . in the days of Washington." [20] In particular he would not use the patronage against Southerners, would not discriminate against

---

[13] Samuel Galloway to Andrew Johnson, April 21, 1865, Johnson MSS. For the letter to Galloway see *Works*, V, 136–138 (July 28, 1859).

[14] After having consulted with Lincoln, Hamlin talked with James Dixon of Connecticut concerning the possibility of bringing Gideon Welles into the cabinet. The Vice President Elect "then said Mr. Lincoln & himself agreed that the fugitive slave laws must be executed in good faith— . . . that an agreement on that point was indispensable—that his cabinet could not act harmoniously unless they agreed with him . . . ." Lincoln had to be satisfied as to Welles's views on this matter, and in writing, before appointing him. Dixon to Welles, Washington, Dec. 3, 1860, Welles MSS.

[15] *Works*, VI, 103–104 (Feb. 1, 1861).

[16] *Ibid.*, VI, 80 (Dec. 15, 1860).

[17] *Ibid.*, VI, 104 (Feb. 1, 1861).

[18] *Ibid.*, VI, 81 (Dec. 15, 1860).

[19] *Ibid.*, VI, 69–70 (Nov. 13, 1860).

[20] *Ibid.*, VI, 85 (Dec. 22, 1860).

non-Republicans or slaveholders, and would not force carpetbag appointments upon an unwilling section. Not only did he make this clear in letters;[21] he told a New Orleans merchant who interviewed him just after his election that he would not send Northern men to fill Southern offices.[22]

This did not mean weakness in the matter of law enforcement. Lincoln is reported to have told Weed that "he did not quite like to hear Southern journals and . . . speakers insisting that there must be no 'coercion'; that while he had no disposition to coerce anybody, yet after he had taken an oath to execute the laws, he should not care to see them violated."[23] In similar vein he was quoted[24] as saying that he was opposed to "buying" the privilege of taking his rightful office.

On one point, slavery in the territories, which Republicans deemed "vital" (until they came to legislate upon it in 1861),[25] Lincoln repeatedly said that he would be unyielding. To Weed he wrote (for a convocation of governors) that he would be "inflexible" on the territorial question. He explained why. Either "the Missouri line extended, or Douglas's and Eli Thayer's popular sovereignty," he said, "would lose us everything we gain by the election; . . . filibustering for all south of us and making slave States of it would follow . . . ."[26] On secession he said little before he became President, but said enough to let it be known that in his opinion "no State can in any way lawfully get out of the Union without the consent of the others."[27] The President and other Federal officers, he thought, ought "to run the machine as it is." To balance this he gave repeated assurances that he had no intention of interfering with slavery as a state institution. He even stood ready to approve the contemplated constitutional amendment closing the door to any such future interference. "So far as we know," declared the Chicago *Tribune,* "all Republicans deny the power of Lincoln's or any other Administration to interfere with slavery in

---

21 "As to the use of patronage in the slave States, where there are few or no Republicans, I do not expect to inquire for the politics of the appointee, or whether he does or [does] not own slaves. I intend in that matter to accommodate the people in the several localities . . . ." Lincoln to Gilmer, Dec. 15, 1860, *Works,* VI, 80–81.

22 New York *Herald,* Nov. 9, 1860, p. 2, c. 5.

23 *Autobiography of Thurlow Weed,* edited by his daughter, Harriet A. Weed, 606.

24 McPherson, *Rebellion,* 67.

25 See above, pp. 229 ff.

26 *Works,* VI, 82 (Dec. 17, 1860).

27 *Ibid.*

the States, to oppress . . . communities upon which the institution is saddled, or to use the Federal arm for destroying . . . property declared . . . such by the local law." [28] Referring to the charge that Lincoln was an abolitionist the same paper declared the accusation "so baseless that it ought never to have been credited for a moment," though it was "widely spread over the South" and was "the cause of much of the bad blood in that section." [29]

Aside from the maintenance of the government itself, the territorial matter was almost the only point on which Lincoln spoke the language of inflexibility. His statements to Hale, Weed, Seward, Kellogg, and Trumbull all carry the same note of conviction. If we surrender this, he said, "it is the end of us and of the government." [30] He would support no compromise which would permit the extension of the institution "on soil owned by the nation." Acquiring territory and then letting some local authority spread slavery over it, he thought, would "put us again on the highroad to a slave empire." He would watch compromise measures to avoid such a "trick." [31] On this matter Lincoln was less yielding than Weed and Seward, and this has led to the conclusion that among high placed Republicans it was Lincoln especially who blocked the road to adjustment. As if specifically to influence action in Congress Lincoln advised Kellogg and Washburne, Illinois congressmen, to entertain no compromise of any sort concerning slavery in the territories.[32]

VII

It is significant to note how far sectional agitation by politicians was concerned with two points—the fugitive slave question and slavery in the territories—and then, by analysis of the contemporary situation, to find how utterly inadequate each of these factors was as *casus belli* or ground for disunion. There is, of course, the broader explanation of the Southern movement on cultural lines, and volumes have been written on the economic background of the crisis.[1]

---

[28] Chicago *Tribune*, Nov. 24, 1860, p. 2, c. 1.

[29] *Ibid.*, Nov. 26, 1860, p. 2, cc. 1–2.

[30] *Works*, VI, 93 (Jan. 11, 1861).

[31] *Ibid.*, VI, 103 (Feb. 1, 1861).

[32] *Ibid.*, VI, 77–79 (Dec. 11 and Dec. 13, 1860).

[1] In Randall, *Civil War and Reconstruction*, especially 110 ff., the economic background is sketched. For bibliography, see *ibid.*, 887 ff.

The economy of a great nation, however, has many facets, and one does not exhaust economic truth by noting disruptive tendencies. Sections with diverse interests could logically have treated those interests as supplementing factors making for a well rounded nation. As for a Southern shift of economic control in banking, trade, cotton dealing, and the like, this was a business matter; if the ways of business had tended in that direction such a shift could have been accomplished within the Union. Economic interpreters ought not to be afraid of their own subject. It was economic factors which had placed New York where it stood in the financial and commercial life of the whole nation, as well as placing the South where it stood in agrarian specialization. The year of the beginning of secession, 1860, found a tariff law on the books which was not at all anti-Southern. As to the fear of an adverse law being passed in the new situation, historians have not pinned down enough evidence to show that this fear, nor any similar economic or cultural factor, actually moved a majority of Southern people to the point of demanding secession. If there was a group in the South who insisted upon secession for cultural motives, it was that group known at the time as secessionists *per se,* and all the evidence tends to show that this group was a minority. Even the men of this group, however, used slavery "grievances" to make their case, denouncing low-tariff Northern Democrats as well as Republicans, so that the stock complaints of the time cannot in any case be ignored if one is studying factors of agitation.

In this agitation the traditional "grievances" were used out of all proportion to their solid content. If "Nothing is more real than an emotional reaction," [2] it is also true that when emotions are whipped up the actual stuff of controversy may often be amazingly thin. Assuredly slavery in the territories, represented to be a cardinal factor in the formation of the Republican party, was a constant theme of intersectional bickering, and the same may be said of the fugitive slave issue. Remembering this, it is ironical to note how these "issues" were not only less of a stickling point than agitators represented them to be, but in practice utterly insignificant. If the Civil War was fought because of fugitive slaves or on account of slavery

[2] R. S. Henry, *The Story of Reconstruction,* 72.

in the West, the American people were miserably hoodwinked by the demon of strife. The census of 1860 numbered escaping slaves at 803, which was approximately one-fiftieth of one per cent of the total number of slaves in the country. By no means all of these eight hundred fugitives escaped to the North, but the number of free Negroes kidnapped in the North and brought South was considerable; thus the actual loss to the South was exceedingly small. The fugitive slave clause of the Constitution was implemented by a law that was so drastic as to be shockingly one-sided. Stephens of Georgia declared that the South had not made sufficient effort to negotiate with offending states concerning the rendition of fugitives.[3] The law of 1850 showed that Congress had gone a long distance to meet Southern objections. The Supreme Court was sustaining Federal law in this field. Some of the states had prohibited kidnapping and had sought otherwise to temper the fugitive-slave arrangements with a reasonable regard for civil rights, but even these laws were to be given up on Republican advice.[4] The personal liberty laws were a "remediable complaint" [5] and it was recognized by such a moderate Southerner as John A. Gilmer that no genuine grievance existed on this score. "With a perpetual guaranty against Congressional interference with slavery in the States," wrote Gilmer to Douglas, "and the Territory under . . . organization without the Wilmot proviso, . . . and . . . the free States repealing their personal liberty laws as rapidly as they can, what more does any reasonable Southern man expect or desire?" [6] S. S. Cox, ardent Democrat, was of opinion that prevailing sentiment in the House of Representatives was such as to encourage those who sought to cure sectional evils.[7] A considerable group of leading men of Massachusetts joined in a printed public declaration favoring repeal of their personal liberty laws, not under

[3] McPherson, *Rebellion*, 23.

[4] As one of many evidences on this point one may cite the following letter. "The only weak point in our position is the Personal Liberty bills which have never impeded the surrender of any fugitives yet, and probably never will, but which are used as justification of all kinds of wrong doing on the other side. And these would undoubtedly be repealed in every State, except perhaps Wisconsin, if some humane & proper modification of the Fugitive Law were made by Congress." Colfax to Yates, Dec. 10, 1860, MS., Chicago Hist. Soc.

[5] Rhodes, *Hist. of U. S.*, III, 147.

[6] John A. Gilmer to S. A. Douglas, Mar. 8, 1861, Douglas MSS.

[7] Cox, *Eight Years*, 196.

threat, as they said, but "under our own love of right . . . ." [8] Nor did the Southerners have any valid complaint against Lincoln on the fugitive matter. As has been seen he wanted less vindictiveness in the system, but stood unequivocally for fulfillment of the Federal obligation to promote the return of the fugitives. A number of Northern governors had urged the repeal of the fugitive laws of their states to which Southerners objected,[9] Banks of Massachusetts even going so far as to call the law of his state "unnecessary to the public service, . . . detrimental to the public peace, [and] . . . an unexcusable public wrong." [10] Even if runaways had been numerous it by no means appears that the number could have been decreased by the erection of an independent slave nation in the South. At one stroke this would have deprived the South of a powerful constitutional guarantee. Such a remedy for the fugitive grievance would have been like moving Canada down to the Ohio. The main result of Northern state and Federal action as to fugitives had been to facilitate rather than hinder their recovery. Abolitionist rescues, though sensational, were of less effect than the regular operation in the North of legal processes favorable to slaveholders. Practically it does not make sense to say that the South had to secede because of fugitive slaves.

As to the territorial question it is well known that Kansas and Nebraska had been written off for freedom by 1860 for the reason that Southerners did not care to take slaves into those regions, and that the prospect of slavery taking hold in New Mexico (then including Arizona) was negligible. Federal law permitted slavery in Kansas, but since the census of 1860 showed only two slaves in that territory,[11] which contained a population of over 100,000, it may be

[8] When one considers the Southern emphasis upon Northern personal liberty laws as a grievance (these being state laws to obstruct the return of fugitive slaves as required by Federal statute) it is important to note how these leading men of the Bay State urged that by their own free will and as an act of right the people of that commonwealth ought, in view of the excited condition of the country, to repeal this legislation, after which recovery of fugitives would proceed according to Federal process. The appeal was made by men "of different political parties" and the whole paper breathes conciliation with the South. Among the signers were Lemuel Shaw, Benjamin R. Curtis (former justice of the United States Supreme Court), Joel Parker, Joseph Grinnell, George Ticknor, Jared Sparks, Levi Lincoln, Theophilus Parsons, and a number of other prominent men. B. R. Curtis MSS., Lib. of Cong., no. 4319.

[9] Rhodes, *Hist. of U. S.*, III, 252–253.

[10] *Annual Cyclopaedia*, 1861, 576.

[11] For the census report of only two slaves in the territory of Kansas and fifteen in the territory of Nebraska, see *U. S. Census, 1860*, Agriculture, 227, 246. When the

truly said that the colossal quarrel concerning slavery in Kansas had practically nothing to do with Kansas itself. Many Republicans said they would not yield on slavery in the territories; but, leaving aside the opportunity of the South to vote down the Republicans by staying in the Union, it is to be repeated that the Republicans themselves dropped the freedom principle as a matter of actual enactment in the Dakota, Colorado, and Nevada laws. Speaking on the eve of Lincoln's inauguration, Douglas asserted in the Senate that the South had, by the action of a Republican Congress, the full right to emigrate into all the territory of the United States, and showed that the Republicans had in fact abandoned their Chicago platform.[12] In the completed legal arrangements of 1860–61 slave interests were given a heavier, not a lighter, weighting than the broad nineteenth-century situation would naturally have provided. Southerners themselves said that sectional agitation had strengthened slavery. Some of them also said that no grievances pertaining to slavery existed which could form a valid basis for disunion.

VIII

Public leaders ought to be viewed against a background of public opinion, but opinion in the sectional crisis was of many colors. It followed no constant pattern; it was only in part vocal; its mouthpieces were often false; its gauges as they remain after eight decades are unsatisfactory. Selections could be made to "prove" the most diverse generalizations. There were Northern secessionists, there were Southern unionists, there were plain citizens pouring out petitions for adjustment, there were other citizens spurning any thought of compromise. There were manufacturers concerned only with such a matter as the tariff, there were business men alarmed at the economic

---

slavery struggle had waxed hot in the 1850's the number had not been notably large. A census taken by persons appointed by the governor of Kansas in February 1855 showed 192 slaves in a total population of 8601 (*House Rep. No. 200*, 34 Cong., 1 sess., p. 72). If this figure was correct, the slaves in 1855 numbered slightly above two per cent of the total. By 1860 the free-state element had gained control of the legislature, so that slaveholders left the territory or sold their slaves outside of Kansas. For some time after the Civil War Kansas remained anti-Negro in the sense that its people voted down Negro suffrage and maintained separate schools in many districts, including Lawrence, of New England Emigrant Aid Company notoriety. (In these matters the author has been assisted by Professor James C. Malin, University of Kansas.)

[12] *Cong. Globe*, 36 Cong., 2 sess., 1391 (Mar. 2, 1861).

depression that accompanied the crisis and pleading for reason and peace from the merchant's point of view. There were conservatives in the North who were ready to go as far as necessary to satisfy the South and avoid war.[1] There were army men, and others expecting to be called, looking anxiously on while politicians held not only their personal fate but the shaping and twisting of the cause for which they would have to fight. There were Lincoln men who repented of their votes when they viewed the consequences. And there were Democrats who declined to "thrust Republican wrongs down the throats of the South at the point of the bayonet." [2]

People were stirred by a crisis psychology. "These are times," wrote a New Englander, "to develope manhood. We have had none finer since 1776." "It is encouraging, and ennobling," he added, "to see true patriotism warm up—and the political conscience purge itself." [3] The literary perception of Edward Everett Hale did not miss the dramatic significance of the days through which he was living. A letter he wrote to Sumner the day after South Carolina's secession closed with the words: "Dec. 21, 1860—And of the Disunited States the first day." [4] The crisis, however, was not as painful to Hale as to others; he took secession calmly and thought "the Northwest . . . [would] take charge of the country and make us all keep the peace." In that sense he thought Abe Lincoln "a typical man."

Some were impressed by the head shaking, the "spinal paralysis" of the dominant party, and lamented the "doleful" uncertainty, the business stagnation.[5] At a moment when compromise seemed possible a grandson of William Ellery Channing wrote of the "demoralization of the Republican party" and declared that he felt "summoned to its obsequies." It was "an awful time for merchants," wrote a Bostonian. He saw more than half of them in his city facing ruin and he wished "every member of Congress from the North could keep

---

[1] In this crisis Henry Grinnell of New York City wrote earnestly to a friend insisting that if the South were to remain united with the North Lincoln would have to "renounce and denounce the issue on which he was elected." He added: ". . . if Mr. Crittenton's proposition was submitted to the people of New England it would be carried by a large majority.—People begin to believe that . . . a Slaveholder will be admitted into Heaven." Grinnell to Wm. Gooding, New York, Feb. 1, 1861. MS. (copy) loaned to the author by H. E. Pratt.

[2] S. S. Cox, *Eight Years in Congress*, 206.

[3] Joseph Sargent to Charles Sumner, Worcester, Mass., Dec. 30, 1860, Sumner MSS.

[4] Sumner MSS.

[5] Frank W. Ballard to Sumner, New York, Feb. 6, 1861, *ibid.*

silent." [6] Fearing loss of trade with the South and animated by general sympathy for Southerners, the mayor of New York City made the fantastic suggestion that the metropolis become a "free city," an independent city-state, "with but nominal duty on imports, . . . free from taxes, . . . [with] cheap goods nearly duty free . . . [enjoying] the whole and united support of the Southern States." [7] Again it was urged that the true policy of New York City was to "throw the weight of her influence in favor of a convention of the States." [8] To J. M. Forbes writing from Boston the question of the hour was the tariff. In contradiction to the demand for free trade he wanted "to increase the schedules generally." [9] While some deliberately intensified the quarrel and "feared" compromise, others were for avoiding the slavery question, as when a Philadelphia group cautioned those who addressed them to avoid the topic of slavery and antislavery.[10]

Sumner's correspondents often struck the note of heroics. Firmness was the word. Let there be no flinching. Meet the consequences of Lincoln's election. Compromise was "mean and degrading." The danger was not struggle and war, the senator was told; it was that some miserable compromise would be patched up. Let statesmen be steadfast; the Republican platform was law. It was better that the crisis had come. People should be glad of it. The cause of antislavery was reaching its triumph, its culmination. Friends in Great Britain were looking to us. Let them not be disappointed. Peace should not be preserved by selling out the liberties of the African race. If Seward and Adams bow to slavery, we are come upon evil times. If we are only to be saved by a Crittenden compromise, every dictate of patriotism demands that we perish.[11]

While these heroic demands were heard in some areas, pleas for peace, compromise, and union were no less numerous and their sources no less respectable. From Massachusetts came a petition of more than 22,000 citizens urging Congress to adopt the Crittenden compromise,[12]

---

[6] George G. Channing to Sumner, Brooklyn, Conn., Feb. 6, 1861; George Livermore to Charles Sumner, Boston, Dec. 12, 1860; *ibid.*

[7] McPherson, *Rebellion*, 43. [8] New York *Herald*, Nov. 17, 1860, p. 4, c. 2.

[9] Forbes to Sumner, Boston, Feb. 2, 1861, Sumner MSS.

[10] W. H. Allen of the People's Literary Institute of Philadelphia, to Sumner, Dec. 17, 1860, *ibid.*

[11] For the material of this paragraph the basis is to be found in the Sumner MSS., vol. 47, items 22, 29, 33, 54, 58; vol. 49, items 4, 17, 22, 51.

[12] C. N. Feamster, *Calendar of the Papers of John Jordan Crittenden*, 248, 256.

and while Sumner claimed that many signed it in ignorance,[13] the Northern voice in favor of adjustment with the South was full and vigorous. Another mammoth petition earnestly demanding compromise came from Pennsylvania, signed by citizens who had voted for Lincoln and Hamlin and who "earnestly desire[d] a prompt adjustment of our National difficulties." [14]

It is a difficult problem to pass judgment on the failure of compromise efforts. Republican leaders have been charged with grave responsibility for this failure. Though they yielded some ground, it is contended that they did not yield enough, and that since theirs was the incoming executive administration, they were "at the center of the problem." [15] But it is to be remembered that the secessionists, who were equally at the center of the problem, did all they could to prevent compromise. In the critical months of the disunion crisis the Republican party was tending toward conservatism; antislavery radicals within the party were out of touch not only with its main emphasis, but also with its management. On close study it becomes evident that in this prewar period the Republican party was only in a very slight degree an antislavery party. On broad racial matters and on state rights Lincoln was closer to the attitude of Southerners than to that of extreme abolitionists. No one formula will serve in dealing with complex questions of sectional tensions, frenzied politics, and party propaganda; nor did it help the situation that bold stands were taken prematurely before even the chances of adjustment had been explored.

A leader clothed with public office cannot be a mere agitator. He must find solutions and in doing so must consider the claims of more than one class or section. Analysis of Lincoln's part in the crisis narrows down to the problem whether a greater emphasis on conciliation, seeing that conciliatory measures were favored by many Republicans, might not have defeated disunion efforts by keeping eight of the fifteen slave states in the Union. Many supposed that, had these eight been kept, a minority of Southern states could not permanently have main-

---

[13] Signers were much offended by the allegation that they signed in ignorance. *Ibid.*, 261.

[14] Papers of the House of Representatives (MSS., Library of Congress), boxes 161 and 162.

[15] D. M. Potter, *Lincoln and His Party in the Secession Crisis*, 60. On this subject of Republicans and compromise, see also pp. 155, 174, and *passim*.

tained their Confederacy. Looking ahead in mid-December, the Chicago *Tribune* declared that the seceding states would desire to return in a few years.[16] If such a thing was possible, then by not keeping the upper South Lincoln bore a heavy responsibility. Such a criticism, however, belongs not to the Rhett-Yancey-Toombs school of thought on one side nor to the Garrison-Phillips school on the other. It is faulty reasoning to assail Lincoln because he did not grant all that the secessionists wanted. He could hardly have been expected to please the Rhetts and Yanceys, nor could even a Southern President of the United States have pleased them. South Carolina was not asking redress nor seeking conciliation. Not the wiping out of causes of complaint, but the playing-up and exaggeration of "grievances" was the game of aggressive cotton-state leaders. Nor could Lincoln have been expected to please Garrison or Phillips at the North, both of whom welcomed disunion.

The criticism that does claim attention is the earnest complaint of the upper South and border, whose people wanted Union and peace as much as did Lincoln. What the people of this area desired was more the fact of compromise than the particular terms that would have nationalized slavery. They wanted adjustment, and they agreed with Lincoln in wanting to defeat the extremists who refused adjustment and wanted discord. In the November-to-March phase these Southern Union men were severely disappointed; in April, as will be seen later, their resentment and the dilemma of actual war was to carry four additional commonwealths all the way out of the Union. Republicans were unskillful in their courting of upper Southern states. They repudiated Sumner and the abolitionists without effectively dramatizing the fact or making the repudiation count in terms of accomplished results. Moderates to the contrary notwithstanding, Lincoln and his party continued to be advertised as Black Republicans and haters of the South.

---

[16] Chicago *Tribune*, Dec. 15, 1860, p. 1, c. 3. This comment was made before any state had seceded. It is one of many examples to show that secession was not taken with the gravity that it deserved. Yet to express apprehension as to dissolution might have been regarded as alarmist and as involving a certain truculence toward the South. Unionists, North and South, were making secession easier.

CHAPTER X

PRESIDENT ELECT

I

IN THE frenzied period between his election and his departure for Washington Lincoln remained continuously at Springfield except for brief visits to Chicago to confer with Hamlin and to Coles County where he visited his stepmother. The governor's office in the Illinois state house had been turned over to him and he kept regular hours there through November and December. As visitors poured in—statesmen, politicians, old friends, newspaper correspondents, office seekers, and casual callers—Lincoln met them with cordial informality. Those who saw him were favorably impressed by his witty conversation and unaffected friendliness, albeit they learned little to allay their concern as to the new leader's position and policy. Lincoln would appear quite early at the governor's office; beginning at ten he would hold a reception till noon, meeting all callers. "Altogether, probably no other President-elect was as approachable for everybody," was the comment of Henry Villard.[1] In the afternoon he was again at his office attending to correspondence with the help of secretaries and meeting men of importance by appointment. "In the evening old friends called at his home for the exchange of news and political views. At times . . . he would go to the telegraph or newspaper offices after supper, and stay there till late." [2]

His mail was "immense." Letters poured in from autograph collectors, place seekers (including some Southerners), anxious citizens, and politicians of many grades.[3] Republican politicians who had labored to defeat him now sought his confidence on the supposition

[1] Villard, *Memoirs*, I, 142. [2] *Ibid.*
[3] New York *Herald*, Nov. 12, 1860, p. 1, c. 3; Nov. 16, p. 1, c. 6; Nov. 17, p. 7, c. 1.

that Lincoln had "forgotten their treachery" and would "accept them as his advisers." [4]

On the most devastating question of the day, the disintegration of the nation by the progress of secession, Lincoln maintained an attitude of such calmness that he was thought by some to be either unaware of the true situation or lacking in policy.[5] Readers of the Chicago *Tribune* were told that Mr. Lincoln "does not . . . believe that any of the States will . . . go off and organize a Confederacy" and further that "Abraham Lincoln and the Republican party will not interfere with the rights of the South." [6] He was reported to have expressed "doubts as to the practicability of holding the Slave States in the Union by main force, if they were all determined to break it up." [7] Up to the time of his departure for Washington, according to Villard, he "did not dream that his principal duty would be to raise great armies and fleets . . . for the suppression of . . . rebellion . . . ." [8] He found abolitionists a constant embarrassment, both because of their importunity and on account of the deliberate misrepresentation of himself as a "*confrere* of Garrison, Phillips, and Company." [9] When these abolitionists called on him it was with a sense of proprietorship and usually with the zeal of an exhorter. In a letter to Charles Sumner written at Springfield, Illinois, on December 3, 1860, Joshua Giddings wrote: "I . . . expect to meet him [Lincoln] today. I shall do what I can to strengthen his faith and nerve him to the business before him." [10]

That Lincoln, while commanding the respect of moderates, did not quite repel and offend antislavery radicals seems now something of a miracle. Perhaps the truth was that even though repelled they sought still to exert influence. The most common comment from abolitionists was an almost savage opposition to compromise. Jubilating over Lincoln's election as "a great . . . victory of Liberty over Slavery, of Freedom over Despotism," an Illinois radical declared: "I do pray . . . that he will make no compromises with the South on the slavery question." [11]

---

[4] *Ibid.*, Nov. 12, 1860, p. 1, c. 3.

[5] "This unusual silence derived not so much from native taciturnity, as from Lincoln's firm conviction that sectional antagonism fed upon discussion . . . , and . . . upon misconstruction of what he had said." Potter, *Lincoln and His Party*, 135.

[6] Nov. 17, 1860, p. 2, c. 1. [7] Villard, *Memoirs*, I, 145. [8] *Ibid.*, I, 146.

[9] Chicago *Tribune*, Nov. 26, 1860, p. 2, c. 1. [10] Sumner MSS., vol. 47, no. 5.

[11] W. Kitchell to Lyman Trumbull, Trumbull MSS., Nov. 28, 1860.

Both Weed and Seward saw Lincoln in this pre-presidential period at Springfield, but their visits were in marked contrast. Seward's was not even a stop-over. Returning from Kansas, he passed through Springfield (October 1) and exchanged a few trivial words with Lincoln who turned up at the station to greet him.[12] He was in Springfield only as long as his train stood there. Concerning this incident a caustic journalist remarked that "the meeting . . . was conventional and formal, as if each was afraid of his own virtue in the presence of the other." [13] Weed paid two visits to Springfield in 1860. The first was on May 24 directly after the Chicago nomination which left the New York manager so disappointed "as to be unable to . . . talk on the subject." [14] This conversation lasted five hours. According to Weed's later account dressed up for public display, its main significance was that Weed admired Lincoln's good sense and left the interview prepared to work "with a will" for his election.[15] It was Gideon Welles's belief, however, that the full story did not appear in these reminiscences and that Weed was "intrusive to impertinence in presenting and pressing his claims." [16] Welles goes on to relate that Lincoln's Illinois friends were at special pains to make friends with the gentleman from New York, that they invited him to visit Springfield after the nomination, and that Weed "greedily availed himself of the courtesy" while postponing his visit until after the first rush from Chicago was over, reaching Springfield by a roundabout course involving a boat trip on the Mississippi. Lincoln made no commitments in the interview, and, contrary to the roseate picture in Weed's memoirs, Welles was of the opinion that the New York politician returned to Albany in "not a very complacent state of mind." [17] All the evidence leads to the supposition that in this period Weed expected, if nothing else, at least to be a kind of patronage dispenser and political manager for the new administration, as he had certainly expected to be in the event of Seward's election.

Weed's second visit to Lincoln, which was the object of a special trip from Albany, coincided with the secession of South Carolina (December 20, 1860). According to his memoirs, which again have the

---

12 P. M. Angle, *Lincoln, 1854–1861*, 353.

13 New York *Herald*, Nov. 12, 1860, p. 4, c. 4.

14 Thurlow Weed, *Autobiography*, 602–603; *Illinois State Register*, May 25, 1860.

15 Weed, *Autobiography*, 603.

16 Welles MS. (postwar recollections), Ill. State Hist. Lib., 12.

17 *Ibid.*, 15.

quality of public rationalization, Weed found Lincoln amusing, quaint, agreeable, and full of anecdotes. He stated specifically that Lincoln did not tell indelicate stories to his knowledge,[18] but Villard, who saw much of him, asserts precisely the contrary.[19] The substantive matters on which Weed and Lincoln conferred were chiefly two: compromise proposals to deal with the sectional crisis, and cabinet-making.[20]

The President Elect's visitors included many other notables: Giddings, Trumbull, Cameron (December 30), Chase (January 4), Bates, Amos Tuck, Francis P. Blair, Jr., Browning, Judd, William Kellogg, David Wilmot, George Opdyke, Hiram Barney, Judge Hogeboom, M. Romero (Mexican minister), and Horace Greeley. Sometimes Lincoln would call on such men at their hotels; at other times they would meet him in his home or state-house office.[21] While the new leader was secretive as to his plans the identity of his visitors could not be concealed, and journalists, as at present, spun out their stories accordingly. Rumors and guesses clustered round these interviews, and special emphasis was placed upon those visitors who came upon Lincoln's invitation, such as Chase and Bates. Some of the visitors wore homespun as in the case of an old man from Mississippi who was given an interview and expressed the wish that every Southerner could talk face to face with the President Elect.[22] "Offensively democratic exhibitions of free manners occur every once in a while," wrote the *Herald* reporter. "Churlish fellows will obtrude themselves with their hats on, lighted segars and . . . pantaloons tucked into their boots. Dropping into chairs, they will sit puffing away and trying to gorgonize the President with their silent stares, until their boorish curiosity is . . . satisfied." [23]

In the harassment and strain of a cruelly difficult position these visitors found a man who displayed little showmanship and lacked

---

[18] Weed, *Autobiography*, 605, 611–612. [19] Villard, *Memoirs*, I, 143–144.

[20] "You know that Mr. Weed has been at Springfield. I can state positively, that, in the only two interviews he held with Mr. Lincoln, a third person was present at the request of Mr. L. That third person is here, & I think I can hardly be mistaken in saying that one of those interviews was . . . devoted to . . . the slavery question, . . . compromises, &c, . . . that the other was devoted to talking about men, offices, &c., . . . [and] that his [Weed's] line of remark drifted . . . towards Seward & Cameron." H. B. Stanton to S. P. Chase, Jan. 7, 1861, Chase MSS., Lib. of Cong.

[21] Angle, *"Here I Have Lived,"* 257.

[22] Angle, *Lincoln 1854–1861*, 366. [23] New York *Herald*, Nov. 22, 1860, p. 3, c. 4.

dramatic exuberance but who kept an even keel and exhibited outward calm, often illuminated by flashes of prairie humor. Gloom and sadness characterized his features as he "perceived . . . the danger of the situation," but in spite of this, when in company, he was "as jovial and . . . droll as usual." [24] "Of Mr. Lincoln the politician," wrote an interviewer, "I say nothing; but Lincoln, the man, I was delighted with." [25] Lincoln's reticence in this period was counted a virtue. "The singularly small amount of self-revelation that he has given since his nomination" was mentioned as "one of the best . . . indications." [26] This democracy of manner stayed with Lincoln after he left Springfield and there was comment on the "perfect identity, in all his broad, shrewd, western rusticity of style between President Lincoln and good Neighbor Lincoln of Springfield aforetime." It was felt that his new importance made "not the slightest impression on his nerves, proving that the great office [was] not too much for him." [27] From *The Times* in London came the comment that "Mr. Lincoln can do anything he sets his mind to, partly from natural pliability, partly by an immense power of fixing his attention on whatever is before him." [28]

Young Henry Villard, perhaps because he was employed by the New York *Herald,* found the Illinois leader in many ways unsatisfactory. He disliked what he called his coarse "license" in telling stories and confessed a feeling of "disgust" and "humiliation" toward a man whom he was far from worshiping as hero. "I could not have persuaded myself [he wrote] that the man might possibly possess true greatness." [29] Earlier he had been "no great admirer of the Republican standard-bearer" though he had desired his election. This same observer wrote of Mrs. Lincoln as imprudently taking presents from office seekers.[30] "She does not appear to realize [said the *Herald* writer] that she has been elected to preside at the White House the next four years." [31]

---

[24] Gustave Koerner, *Memoirs,* II, 116.
[25] Chicago *Tribune,* Dec. 17, 1860, p. 1, c. 2.
[26] New York *Sun* as quoted in *Weekly Illinois State Journal,* Feb. 27, 1861.
[27] *Ibid.*
[28] Quoted in Chicago *Tribune,* Dec. 19, 1860, p. 2, c. 5.
[29] Villard, *Memoirs,* I, 144.
[30] *Ibid.,* I, 138, 148.
[31] New York *Herald,* Nov. 16, 1860, p. 1, c. 6.

II

As Lincoln read the papers and viewed the national scene he witnessed an ominous succession of events. The January pace was so rapid that early February presented a picture startlingly different from that of late December. Sometimes a little thing contained the whole picture, as when a Charleston bookseller returned his package of *Harper's Weekly* because it contained a picture of the President Elect.[1] Some days later in the same city every Episcopal clergyman omitted the usual prayer for the President of the United States. As one fort after another fell into the hands of secessionist authorities, attention was centered upon "incidents" at Charleston where ominous rumblings followed the removal of the Federal garrison (December 26) from Fort Moultrie to Fort Sumter, and where a United States merchant vessel carrying military supplies and troops was fired upon with no formality of hostilities and without producing war (January 9). Shortly afterward Colonel Hayne of South Carolina called on the President of the United States and demanded (unsuccessfully) the "unconditional withdrawal" of the Sumter garrison.[2]

Whether such happenings were only "brag and bluster" as Edward Bates thought[3] or whether they meant the collapse of the nation he was called to lead, was a matter to give Lincoln pause. There were, it is true, other developments which seemed calculated to check secession and keep the road to compromise open. In the upper South Lincoln noted that the people voted against secession in Arkansas, Tennessee, and Missouri,[4] and that moderates were keeping the helm in Kentucky and Virginia. Through February the upper South and border were resisting the secession fever and efforts toward adjustment continued to be pushed at Washington where the Virginia-inspired Peace Convention, with Lincoln's friend Stephen T. Logan as an Illinois member, gave evidence that the desire for Union was not dead in the South. Those favorable to Union could also point to the stiffening of Buchanan and his cabinet as above noted, to Southern anti-secession editorials, to the heartening attitude of Douglas, to popular Union demonstrations in the South, and to the refusal of the Mary-

---

[1] Chicago *Tribune*, Nov. 20, 1860, p. 1, c. 2. [2] *Ibid.*, January 18, 1861, p. 4, c. 4.
[3] Bates, *Diary*, 157. [4] Randall, *Civil War and Reconstruction*, 251, 253, 326.

land governor to receive a pro-secession commissioner from Mississippi.[5]

Throughout these days it was easy for Republicans to believe the worst of Buchanan and it was even rumored in December that the outgoing administration was using the whole power of the Federal government to fill the South with arms and munitions.[6] It became a stereotype of the period to attribute the blackest treachery in this respect to the Southern secretary of war, John B. Floyd of Virginia, but altogether aside from the alleged action of Floyd there was the undeniable fact that Northern individuals and firms were contributing in these anxious weeks to the military preparation of the South. Not only were Jefferson Davis's emissaries successful in obtaining a great variety of war supplies in Northern factories in this February-March period, but even Kentucky, which never joined the Confederacy, was busy arming itself in an anti-Lincoln sense. Simon B. Buckner, later a Confederate general, wrote in March 1861 of a trip from Louisville to New York via St. Louis "to attend to our arms." He told of "shipments every week," indicating that he could be addressed in care of General A. E. Burnside at the office of the Illinois Central Railroad Company, New York City.[7] If he looked westward Lincoln had also to consider wild doings in Kansas where even Republicans found it necessary to denounce "Free State men" who were invading Missouri in as brutal a manner as any border ruffians.[8] This was the period of James H. Lane and his "jayhawkers." Taking advantage of the turbulent conditions of the time, some of the free-state Kansans took their own revenge upon Missourians for their hostility in border-ruffian days. It was an ugly kind of irregular or private war, and it tended to reflect discredit upon Lincoln's party by reason of the tendency to associate the Republicans with everything that pertained to John-Brownism and kindred tactics in Kansas and Missouri.[9]

The question of Southern military preparation thrust upon Lincoln the trying problem of what announcements to make and what arrange-

[5] Moore, *Rebellion Record* (Diary), I, 3.

[6] Chicago *Tribune*, Dec. 29, 1860, p. 2, c. 1.

[7] Buckner to Magoffin, Mar. 8, 1861, MS., Ill. State Hist. Lib.

[8] Chicago *Tribune*, Nov. 26, 1860, p. 2, c. 1.

[9] For the jayhawkers see Hildegarde Rose Herklotz, "Jayhawkers in Missouri, 1858–1863," *Mo. Hist. Rev.*, XVII and XVIII (1922–1923). For John Hay's reference to jayhawkers appearing among early volunteer fighters in Washington (April 18, 1861), see Tyler Dennett, ed., *Lincoln and the Civil War in the Diaries and Letters of John Hay*, 1.

ments to promote for the maintenance of the government's authority. These questions were everywhere asked. Occasionally they were embarrassingly answered by a self-appointed Lincoln "spokesman." On the other hand it became a stock argument with a certain type of Southern editor to predict what Lincoln would do, as when the Richmond *Enquirer* pictured the day, soon to come, when Lincoln's "free-soil mirmidons" would be conveyed by Northern ships through Hampton Roads so that they could run off slaves, pillage the country, and insult the state of Virginia.

In this overwrought period even a gesture toward Federal military preparedness, if traced to Lincoln, would inevitably have been denounced and distorted by Southern extremists. Shortly after his election Lincoln received a statement of "views" from the head of the army, General Winfield Scott, which he answered with a noncommittal but respectful compliment to the "distinguished . . . military captain." [10] On November 20 he referred to "all American citizens" as "brothers of a common country." [11] On December 21, the day after South Carolina's secession, he indirectly sent his respects to General Scott with the confidential request to be "prepared . . . to either hold or retake the forts, as the case may require, at and after the inauguration." [12] In January he was similarly complimentary, cautious, and noncommittal in his correspondence with Scott, and on January 14 he wrote to General Wool with equal caution indicating that he had given "little attention to the military department of government" and saying that he would have to rely upon Scott and Wool for advice as to "how far the military force of the government may become necessary to the preservation of the Union, and more particularly how that force can best be directed to the object." [13] In all this he restrained himself from truculent declarations that would inflame Southern feeling while prudently leaving the way clear for a proper defense of Federal authority. The truth was that the manner of meeting the South Carolinian and later the lower Southern challenge was a problem of the utmost difficulty in which the processes to be chosen would have to be worked out after inauguration and after existing peace efforts had been allowed to develop.

---

[10] *Works*, VI, 68 (Nov. 9, 1860).
[11] *Ibid.*, VI, 72.
[12] *Ibid.*, VI, 84–85.
[13] *Ibid.*, VI, 92–93, 98.

III

Of the two trips which Lincoln made outside Springfield in the pre-presidential interval the first was political and the other intimately personal. On November 21, 1860, he took train at Springfield in the presence of a large crowd and proceeded to Chicago for a conference with Hannibal Hamlin. Mrs. Lincoln accompanied him and Senator Trumbull was also in the party. Lincoln was dodging ovations and avoiding speech-making for reasons already noted, and just before his departure he had disappointed Republican jollifiers by refusing to speak at their grand celebration. The train stopped at Lincoln and Bloomington; at each place Lincoln made a brief platform appearance, giving a sentence or two of greeting. Dealing only in generalities, these remarks were those of a leader who had decided to make no speeches but who could not refuse the courtesy of greeting friends and expressing appreciation. At Bloomington he stepped out on the platform of his car and thanked the people of "Old McLean" (County) for their part in placing him in his present position, declaring that the people will do well when they are well done by and that it was his intention to "do well by the people." Retiring into the car amid cheers he shook hands with acquaintances, while Trumbull added a few remarks, commending the people for supporting the "whole Republican ticket." [1]

At Chicago Lincoln discussed cabinet matters with Vice President Elect Hamlin, visited the Republican wigwam and other buildings, and held a reception which occupied the morning of November 23. He attended church in company with Isaac N. Arnold, spoke briefly at a mission Sabbath school, and spent an uneventful rainy day on the return to Springfield.[2] Real business had been transacted, for shortly after this Hamlin confidentially quoted Lincoln as saying that Gideon Welles's appointment to the cabinet was more probable than that of any other New Englander.[3] In this consultation Lincoln conferred upon Hamlin a unique distinction. In the case of no other

[1] Bloomington (Ill.) *Pantagraph*, Nov. 22, 1860, p. 3, c. 2.

[2] Typical reporters' accounts of Lincoln's Chicago trip are to be found in the Chicago *Tribune*, Chicago *Journal*, and New York *Herald*, November 22–27, 1860. For summaries see Angle, *Lincoln, 1854–1861*, 360–361; Charles E. Hamlin, *Life . . . of Hannibal Hamlin*, 366–375; Baringer, *A House Dividing*, 76–90.

[3] James Dixon to Welles, Dec. 3, 1860, Welles MSS.

statesman did he make a trip for the purpose of an interview while President Elect.

At the end of January Lincoln made an arduous two-day trip via Charleston, Illinois, to a remote spot in Coles County to see his aged stepmother, Sarah Bush Johnston Lincoln, widow of Thomas Lincoln. Besides the rail trip to Charleston there was a ten-mile rural drive which even then stopped short of the Thomas Lincoln cabin, for the more accessible frame house of a neighbor, with a convenient location on the highway, had been placed at Lincoln's disposal. Among the reminiscences pertaining to this occasion is that of James A. Connolly, a Charleston lawyer who stated that Lincoln missed the regular passenger train at Mattoon where a change of cars was necessary and arrived a number of hours later on a freight caboose. Those who met Lincoln at Charleston had a long wait. "Presently," said Connolly, "we saw a tall man . . . make his way through the long expanse of slush and ice beside the track . . . . [Q]uite a crowd of natives were gathered on the platform to see him. I confess I was not favorably impressed." In this bit of reminiscence we have glimpses of Lincoln dropping formality and addressing his old friend A. P. Dunbar as "Aleck," spinning out backwoods stories, delighting those who chatted with him, but disappointing some who merely glimpsed his "awkward, if not ungainly figure." [4] Herndon records that on this visit, besides seeing his stepmother, Lincoln met members of the Johnston and Hanks families, visited his father's grave, gave directions for a suitable stone marker, and made a brief public address at Charleston.[5] If fully recorded the episode would offer a picturesquely quaint and pathetic incident in Lincoln's personal life. There was drama in the homespun rusticity of the surroundings, the informality of the President Elect, the painful lowliness of relatives contrasted with the distinction of the illustrious son, and the genuine affection of Sarah Lincoln for the boy of whom she had seen little in thirty years. It was characteristic of Lincoln and of the time that the deep human interest of the visit was not played up in public print.

---

[4] Jesse W. Weik, *The Real Lincoln: A Portrait,* 294–297.
[5] Herndon (Angle ed.), 387–388.

IV

A necessary labor for every President Elect is the selection of a cabinet, and for many a chief this problem offers a bewildering and unpleasant eye-opener to the ambitions and tricks of politicians. In the case of Lincoln a please-all cabinet would have been an amazing thing. It would have recognized every section, comprised diverse elements of the winning though minority party, embraced opposites who refused to fraternize, allowed no place to an endorser of Helper's *Impending Crisis,*[1] included Democrats and Southerners along with New Englanders and abolitionists, contained no more than one from a state while pleasing quarreling factions within states, and, as a kind of afterthought, would have assigned to each post a man adapted by training and experience to its duties. To be "ideal" the cabinet would have to offend no politician, editor, or party worker, and lose no votes in coming elections. To do as much of this as possible within the limits of a seven-man ministry, to choose the manner of doing it so as to avoid premature leaks and embarrassing complaints, and after doing it to soothe the feelings of the disappointed, was an assignment that would have taxed Lincoln's utmost skill even if he had been as "consummate" a "politician" as some have supposed.

Two weeks after the election a writer in the New York *Herald* published his prediction of the new cabinet in which every one of the seven guesses was wrong. The following was the *Herald's* list: Secretary of State, John McLean of Ohio; Secretary of the Treasury, William L. Dayton of New Jersey; Postmaster General, Fitz-Henry Warren of Iowa; Secretary of War, Cassius M. Clay of Kentucky; Secretary of the Navy, Emerson Etheridge of Tennessee; Secretary of the Interior, Galusha A. Grow of Pennsylvania; Attorney General, Henry Winter Davis of Maryland.[2] Had Lincoln justified this prediction he would have been defended by a sufficiently belligerent minister of war, but he would have had a decrepit secretary of state, an inland secretary of the navy, and a ferocious hater of the South as attorney general. He would have had no one from New York nor New England, and nearly half his advisers would have come from south of the Mason and Dixon line.

---

[1] New York *Herald,* Nov. 17, 1860, p. 6, c. 6. [2] *Ibid.,* Nov. 20, 1860, p. 1, c. 6.

That he was hounded almost to distraction by this cabinet problem was suggested by his own statement that he deferred the final selection as long as possible "to avoid being teased to insanity to make changes." [3] When asked for public statements on cabinet questions he would usually evade the issue, sometimes with a quirk about cabinet-making of the saw-and-hammer variety, sometimes with a solemn platitude. An example of the latter was a statement quoted by the Chicago *Tribune* as follows: "Gentlemen, in the formation of my Cabinet, I shall aim as nearly as possible at perfection. Any man whom I may appoint . . . must be, as far as possible, like Caesar's wife, pure and above suspicion, of unblemished reputation, and undoubted integrity." [4] The search for such paragons, however, was not easy, for, as he is reported to have said, "while the population of the country had immensely increased, really great men were scarcer than they used to be." [5]

It has been noted in a former chapter how Lincoln was not uninfluenced by agreements in the party convention of 1860 which have been construed as promises of cabinet appointments to Simon Cameron of Pennsylvania and Caleb B. Smith of Indiana.[6] In addition to these obligations, he had so profited by the friendliness of certain men that they may naturally have thought they had claims upon his favorable consideration. Among such were Gideon Welles of Connecticut, Montgomery Blair of Maryland, and Cassius Clay of Kentucky. Thus the bestowal of rewards for party service for which the successful candidate had reason to be personally grateful was a potent, though unwelcome, element in Lincoln's choice.

But these "conditions . . . fairly implied" [7] were only the beginning of Lincoln's worries. The very nature of his party, precarious, unrepresentative of the whole nation, never before victorious in a presidential election, presented complications. Already it was a party of factions, and these factions cut deep into practical Republican affairs in every important state.[8]

---

[3] This statement was in a letter to Seward, January 12, 1861. In the same letter Lincoln said he expected trouble "with every other Northern cabinet appointment," politely making an exception in the case of Seward himself. *Works*, VI, 94–95.

[4] Chicago *Tribune*, Feb. 7, 1861, p. 1, c. 2.

[5] Weed, *Autobiography*, 606.

[6] See above, pp. 169–170.

[7] Lincoln's own words; see above, p. 170.

[8] See vol. II, 222–223.

V

Nor were the factions merely intrastate. The severe antipathies between the Seward element and the Chase element, and between Seward and Welles, related precisely to those problems of broad national policy that were to become the peculiar harassment of the incoming administration. To all this was added the task of recognizing Southerners in a "black Republican" cabinet while keeping due regard for other sections, especially New England, whose claims were natural enough but whose chances of genuinely agreeing on a selection were slight. It was not merely a question of "a New England member" but *what* New England member, and so on throughout the country. Cabinet positions meant power. To politicians they meant plums. By many they were regarded as doors to patronage.[1] The question of a man's special fitness for a particular job in governmental administration was exceedingly difficult to work into the cabinet-making pattern; it was a subordinate factor in Lincoln's actual selection.

The New York situation, which was tied in with the national situation, was perhaps the point of departure, and it was one of the thorniest of Lincoln's problems. As Whig overlord and later as Republican "boss," Thurlow Weed had built up a powerful machine but had covered himself with discredit because of alleged "corruption at Albany during the last session of the legislature, in which many Republicans were implicated." [2] No account of the politics of this period would be complete without mention of "agents of vested wealth" (influential in both parties), the "lobby," "railroad and canal interests," and many a party manipulation behind the scenes.[3] Seward had benefited over the years by the support of Weed who has been called his Warwick.[4] The New York statesman's commanding position in the party, together with the almost pathetic grief of "Weed, Seward, & Co." at the May nomination, made it virtually imperative to choose him. Once that decision was faced, however, the incoming President

---

[1] ". . . Mr. [W. C.] Noyes expressed the opinion that Seward did not desire to go into the Cabinet unless he could control the patronage and thus serve his friends." White, *Trumbull*, 140.

[2] *Ibid.*, 140.

[3] P. G. Auchampaugh in A. C. Flick, ed., *History of the State of New York*, VII, 65.

[4] "While Seward sounded high idealism at Washington, Weed stoked the . . . fires at home." *Ibid.*

was confronted with two stubborn facts: the opposition of a high-minded New York element to such a choice, and the dislike of many Republicans outside New York to Seward himself [5] and even more to the prospect of Weed in "control" at Washington. For Weed was first and last a politician and thought in terms of control and intrigue. Those under his lead—"robbers" they were called by their critics—were said to hate Lincoln, while at the same time they planned to use him as a fulcrum for efforts at patronage control.[6] It was customary for such managers as Weed to draw upon the metropolitan police force and custom house of New York City (involving hundreds of appointments) for delegates to party conventions, the purpose being to keep such conventions in the hands of boss and machine. Weed was reported to be connected with "schemes of plunder" involving the national government,[7] and opposition to such tactics caused an indignant New York official to declare that "no human power . . . [could] make a majority of the electors of this state *bow* down to the corruption of the Weed dynasty." [8] From the same source we have a description of Weed's methods as embracing control of party primaries throughout the state, "assessments upon candidates and incumbents seeking and holding office," and the mustering of a "horde of political pensioners . . . which he has quartered upon our party" by which "every wish of the better portion" of the party had been "defeated." [9]

Friends of Seward were, as Gideon Welles saw them, "very officious in giving advice" and at the same time "vehemently opposed" to Mr. Chase,[10] who held as important a place in Lincoln's cabinet plans as did Seward. Their insistent advice to Lincoln covered much of the whole cabinet field. Besides opposing Chase they objected to Blair, sought to exclude Welles, and were ready with selections for the New England secretary.[11]

The effort of Weed to reach far beyond New York was certainly a factor with which Lincoln had to contend; it was thought that with Chase out and Seward in, the New York member would have "little

---

[5] Francis P. Blair, Sr. considered Seward a nightmare to the administration, and John A. Andrew shared this antipathy. Blair to Bigelow, Oct. 26, 1861, Blair MSS.; Andrew to Montgomery Blair, May 28, 1866, *ibid.*

[6] A. G. Tillinghast to S. P. Chase, June 18, 1862, Chase MSS., Lib. of Cong.

[7] John Jay to S. P. Chase, May 3, 1861, *ibid.*

[8] R. Campbell to S. P. Chase, Apr. 8, 1861, *ibid.*

[9] R. Campbell to S. P. Chase, Mar. 27, 1861, *ibid.*

[10] Welles MS. (postwar recollections), Ill. State Hist. Lib., 6.

[11] *Ibid.*, 10.

difficulty in shaping the policies of the Administration." [12] One of Weed's intrigues was a kind of Seward-Cameron deal behind Lincoln's back. Illinois friends of Lincoln, especially David Davis and Leonard Swett, considering Weed a big man and realizing his bitterness at the Chicago outcome, had joined with Weed and some gentlemen from Pennsylvania in a meeting at Saratoga in the summer of 1860 at which it was said to have been "arranged" that Seward should have the state department and Cameron the treasury.[13]

Such maneuvers have their significance in the development of Lincoln's personality. There were efforts to get him, while President Elect, to go to Auburn and confer with Seward in his home. Had he gone it would have been a good deal like launching his administration with Seward and Weed in command. But, as Welles relates, Lincoln "knew too much of the proprieties of his position . . . to put himself in the keeping of any man or men." [14] It was after Lincoln's refusal to come to Auburn that Weed made his December visit to Springfield with its disappointing results in terms of large control. The difference between Lincoln going to Auburn and Weed coming to Springfield was considerable. Under trying circumstances the new and untried leader had made a real decision. He had taken on Seward, though with more reluctance than is generally realized,[15] but, in the matter of unofficial advisers, he had virtually refused to take on Weed.

VI

At the outset of his cabinet studies Lincoln had reached the decision that Salmon P. Chase ought to be included. The appointment of the Ohio leader would put into the cabinet an able administrator, a former Democrat who was also a member of the "Old Liberty Guard" (i. e., a leader of the Liberty party), an antislavery man untainted with abolitionist excess, and a rival for the nomination. Joshua Leavitt considered that the great danger of the Republican party was that it was "alleged to be nothing but an elongation of the Whig party" with the dismal prospect of sharing Whig fate.[1] That some of the cabinet should have non-Whig antecedents was thus desirable. Chase went to Springfield on Lincoln's invitation and Lincoln paid him the cour-

---

[12] *Ibid.*, 16. [13] *Ibid.*, 15. [14] *Ibid.*, 18.

[15] For a fuller discussion of this subject, see Baringer, *A House Dividing*, 87, 135 ff.

[1] Joshua Leavitt to S. P. Chase, Jan. 19, 1861, Chase MSS., Lib. of Cong.

tesy of calling at his hotel.[2] It was predicted by the *Herald* that Chase would be offered the foreign office, but on January 7 Lincoln wrote that in his opinion it was a *"necessity"* that Chase should take the treasury.[3] Chase's own comments on the matter of a cabinet appointment were in his usual tone which was that of an unwilling recipient of public office. Stating that Lincoln had talked over with him the question of the treasury appointment, Chase wrote to a friend: ". . . if he . . . thinks I ought to take it (which I hope will not be the case) I shall consider the offer with an anxious wish to do whatever may be . . . best for the general interest." [4]

The Weed faction made a determined effort to eliminate Chase and in particular they were anxious to exclude him from the treasury department which they wanted for Cameron. The most important factor, however, was that radicals were rallying to the Chase standard and to their way of thinking the Weed opposition was a very good reason for including him. The fact of having made the choice served at the start as a salutary example of independence from Weed domination. Among those who took delight in the Chase appointment was Horace Greeley who wrote that it took a desperate and intense fight to achieve the appointment of "the ablest Republican living, who (so Gen. Dix said) was almost indispensable to the treasury, . . ." [5] It was not until shortly after Lincoln's inauguration that Chase's appointment was officially made and unanimously confirmed. In resigning his senatorship Chase continued the role of reluctant acceptance, writing the governor of Ohio that he would have preferred to remain where the people of his state had placed him.[6]

For the New England member various men were suggested. The Weed element favored Charles Francis Adams, John A. Andrew, N. P. Banks, Amos Tuck, or J. P. Hale, while objecting strongly to Welles of Connecticut because they preferred not to see too much recognition of the former Democratic element of the party.[7] Welles attributed his success with Lincoln largely to the efforts of N. P. Banks, Senator Dixon, and Preston King, who worked against the "Albany

[2] Chase arrived in Springfield on January 4, 1861. Angle, *Lincoln, 1854–1861,* 366; Schuckers, *Chase,* 201.

[3] Lincoln's italics. Tracy, *Uncollected Letters,* 174.

[4] Chase to G. W. Julian, Jan. 16, 1861, Giddings-Julian MSS.

[5] Greeley to B. Brockway, Mar. 12, 1861, Greeley MSS., Lib. of Cong.

[6] Schuckers, *Chase,* 207–208.

[7] Welles MS. (postwar recollections), Ill. State Hist. Lib., 10.

clique" and the "intense partisanship" of Seward.[8] New England's importance in shipping made it appropriate to give the naval secretaryship to that region.

Welles believed that he had been the first in Lincoln's thoughts for this appointment, but George S. Boutwell reported otherwise. He records an interview with Lincoln about the time of his inauguration in which the President was said to have told him that had Banks remained in New England instead of moving to Chicago, "there would have been no second man thought of," that Banks's name "was in the first list that he ever made," but that removal from the state "put it out of his power to do what he should otherwise . . . have done without a suggestion from any one." [9] In this piece of cabinet making Lincoln gracefully allowed Hamlin to take a part, thus recognizing a species of "custom" that the Vice President, too likely to be a cipher, should have the chance of naming one cabinet member. Lincoln's conference with Hamlin in Chicago, the only one of its kind, was devoted to this subject. Before selecting Welles Lincoln made sure of his position on the fugitive-slave matter; in this he recognized that cabinet members ought to be in agreement with the President on matters of policy and that to the public his choice of advisers was sure to be regarded as a barometer of his future course as President.[10]

The choice of Edward Bates of Missouri caused little difficulty. In this bearded elder statesman it was recognized that the claims of regional recognition, presidential rivalry, individual worth, and personal agreeableness were united in one person. Bates was, perhaps, more similar to Lincoln in his general approach to public questions than any other member of the cabinet. Born in Virginia, he had carried into Missouri "many of the traditions of Virginia planterdom." [11] His Missouri career had been that of a conservative antislavery Whig whose legal aptitude had been particularly apparent. Though associated with the Republican party he was "never an orthodox Republican." [12] Like Lincoln he admired both Jefferson and Clay, pursued a moderate course, and regarded slavery as chiefly

---

[8] *Ibid.*, 22, 24.

[9] G. S. Boutwell to N. P. Banks, Boston, Mar. 8, 1861, Banks MSS.

[10] See above, p. 235.

[11] Howard K. Beale, ed., *Diary of Edward Bates, 1859–1866 (Annual Report,* Amer. Hist. Assoc., 1930), xi.

[12] *Ibid.*, xii.

a state matter. Also like Lincoln he opposed slavery in the territories. On the crisis of the day he vigorously opposed secession and favored a strong policy for the suppression of any revolt against the government. He considered Southern politicians and newspapers "absolutely demented" and wrote caustic comments in his diary denouncing South Carolina for her "preposterous egotism" and her intention to "drag down into the pit . . . the *Cotton States* at least, if not all the *South*." [13]

At first, though this was quite unusual, Lincoln offered to go to St. Louis to see Bates, but the latter felt it to be more fitting for him to come to Springfield, which he did on two occasions. On December 15 he had two long conversations with the new chief, with the result that Lincoln offered and Bates accepted a cabinet appointment, with a kind of understanding that it would probably be the attorney-generalship, though if a certain difficulty were out of the way, meaning Seward, it would have been the state department.[14] Being fully determined, even to the point of permitting public announcement, Lincoln arranged to have "a little editorial appear" in the *Missouri Democrat* saying that Bates would be offered a place in the cabinet.[15] Two weeks later, being summoned by telegraph, Bates turned up again at Springfield where he found himself in company with "General" Cameron in whose room he talked with Lincoln for two hours on the night of December 30, while on the next day he had two long conversations with the President Elect. In these conversations, of which we have only hints, Lincoln showed his "liberality," his friendliness toward the South, and withal his difficulties in the cabinet problem.[16] Until shortly before inauguration Lincoln withheld a definite statement as to the particular office Bates should fill; thus it came about that military men were pressing to have him made secretary of war.[17] By making him attorney general Lincoln chose a conservative legal adviser indisposed to push the enforcement of severe wartime laws. He thus gave a mild tone to those executive functions that have to do with the preparation and conduct of prosecutions in the courts.

---

[13] *Ibid.*, 162.

[14] *Ibid.*, 164–165.

[15] *Works*, VI, 83 (Dec. 18, 1860). The *Missouri Democrat*, published at St. Louis, was a Republican newspaper of the radical type.

[16] Bates, *Diary*, 170–171.

[17] F. P. Blair, Jr., to Montgomery Blair, Feb. 12, 1861, Blair MSS.

VII

Bates had shown a modest willingness to "relieve" the new President by withdrawing if that should seem desirable.[1] This was in vivid contrast to the greed of Cameron in ignoring an out-and-out request of Lincoln to withdraw from the picture. Most of the comments that have come down to us have been unfavorable to this Pennsylvania leader. Trumbull considered him "a trading, unscrupulous politician," a "manager" interested in "schemes," who had "not the confidence of our best men." [2] Welles stated that he had "no . . . devotion . . . to political principles of any kind" and did not command the full support of his own state.[3] He has been described as a politician interested chiefly in a "smooth-running party machine" for which object he used methods that were "often circuitous," building up a "patronage" that amounted to "political despotism." [4] For a time he had been a Democrat; later for "political" reasons he became a Republican, but it was remarked that he "had not . . . zealously espoused the . . . republican ticket." [5] Always he had been involved in factional politics; there was a Pennsylvania "cabal" both *pro* and *contra* Cameron.[6] His keenness in party dickering together with his espousal of a protective tariff served to explain his influence in Republican circles.[7]

By the Chicago "bargain" and the Saratoga arrangement Cameron was slated for the cabinet, but a remarkable series of developments ensued before the final selection. It was evident that Cameron was all mixed up with the Seward-Weed connection, so that if Lincoln made the appointment he would offend some of the best men of his party, who opposed both Cameron and Seward.[8] It was through David Davis, Lincoln's manager, that a cabinet post had been offered to Cameron,[9]

---

[1] "Seeing Mr. L[incoln]'s difficulties . . . I told him . . . I was ready to relieve him . . . and that if he could fill the places without me, it would be a relief rather than a disappointment. He answered promptly—'No . . . —that State [stake?] cant [*sic*] be pulled up.'" Bates, *Diary*, 172 (Dec. 31, 1860).

[2] White, *Trumbull*, 146.

[3] Welles MS. (postwar reminiscences), Ill. State Hist. Lib., 17.

[4] A. Howard Meneely, *The War Department, 1861*, 82–83. According to Blaine his field was that of a "party manager" in which he was an "indefatigable worker." Blaine, *Twenty Years*, I, 196.

[5] Welles MS. (above cited), 17.

[6] Villard, *Memoirs*, I, 147.

[7] For Lincoln's cautious treatment of the tariff question, see below, pp. 280–282.

[8] White, *Trumbull*, 146–147.

[9] *Ibid.*, 142.

but trouble was encountered with the new chief when it came to fulfillment of the promise. Lincoln was reluctant to have Cameron come to Springfield, but an invitation was arranged, says Horace White, through Davis and his *"Fidus Achates,"* Leonard Swett.[10] Cameron turned up inevitably in Springfield, Davis and Swett put on the pressure, and Lincoln with obvious reluctance sent the Pennsylvanian a brief note (December 31) promising him either the treasury or the war portfolio.[11] Willy-nilly, Lincoln was thus partly caught in the Chicago-Saratoga net.[12]

It became known that the appointment was promised and the knowledge produced a shock and a storm in Pennsylvania and elsewhere. From Washington H. B. Stanton, husband of Elizabeth Cady, wrote: "The strongest protests have gone from here, & from Pennsylvania, to Mr. Lincoln, against Mr. Cameron being called to the Treasury. Senators . . . have written most pointedly to that effect. So have Representatives, & others." [13] Lincoln was soon aware that the Cameron selection was anathema to such men as Trumbull, A. K. McClure, A. G. Curtin, W. C. Bryant, Preston King, Horace Greeley, Ebenezer Peck, Gustave Koerner, N. B. Judd, S. P. Chase, David Dudley Field, and Hiram Barney.[14] Accounts of Cameron's alleged corruption reappeared in the papers, and so great a stir was produced that it was thought necessary to keep Cameron from the treasury if the party was to be saved from ruin. In the correspondence of the time there was indignant denunciation of the "Cameron and Weed gang," while the choosing of the Pennsylvanian was referred to as an "error," a "calamity," and an occasion for "urgent protest." [15] "If Lincoln do appoint Cameron he gets a fight on his hands," wrote William H. Herndon, "and if he do not he gets a quarrel deep . . . & lasting. . . . Poor Lincoln. God help him." [16] At this time Lincoln is said to have told his old friend William Butler that the Cameron affair had given him

---

[10] *Ibid.*, 144.

[11] *Works*, VI, 90.

[12] Welles ". . . always understood that Mr. Lincoln became committed to this [Weed-Seward] scheme in a measure, though it was unlike him." Welles, *Diary*, II, 389–390.

[13] H. B. Stanton to S. P. Chase, Jan. 7, 1861, Chase MSS., Lib. of Cong.

[14] Harry E. Pratt, "Simon Cameron's Fight for a Place in Lincoln's Cabinet," in *Bulletin No. 49*, Abr. Lincoln Assoc., 6–7 (Sep., 1937); White, *Trumbull*, 147–148.

[15] White, *Trumbull*, 147–148; E. B. Washburne to S. P. Chase, Jan. 10, 1861, Chase MSS., Lib. of Cong.

[16] William H. Herndon to Trumbull, Jan. 27, 1861, Trumbull MSS.

"more trouble than anything . . . he had yet encountered." [17]

Lincoln was so impressed with the arousing of public conscience and with the quality and extent of the opposition to Cameron that he reconsidered his offer. On January 3 he wrote to Cameron that "things had developed" which would make it "impossible" to take him into the cabinet. An interview at Springfield with A. K. McClure of the anti-Cameron faction in Pennsylvania was one of the factors in this decision, but the "more potent matter" was outside Pennsylvania. Lincoln bluntly suggested that Cameron write him "declining the appointment," adding the further request that he do it "at once," signifying such intention by telegraph "instantly." [18] Shortly after this E. B. Washburne wrote to Chase that "Lincoln's administration is likely to escape a great calamity." Cameron, he said, "will *not* have a place in the cabinet, either by his declining the appointment, or by a withdrawal of it by Lincoln." [19] Washburne's statement of the case was precisely correct in terms of Lincoln's intentions and expectations in early January.

That any man could have ignored these expectations or have declined so pointed a request from a President Elect is difficult to comprehend, but Simon Cameron did just that. He neither wired nor wrote the declination that Lincoln demanded. Even had he done so, Lincoln still had the pro-Cameron men and the protectionists to consider. On January 12 Lincoln was visited by two of Cameron's emissaries, J. P. Sanderson and Edgar Cowan,[20] whose solicitations were buttressed by a telegram from members of the Pennsylvania legislature insisting that Cameron be included in the cabinet and Chase excluded. The next day Lincoln did a thing which showed how a marked regard for Cameron's feelings combined with a continuation of his sincere effort to resist the Cameron pressure. He wrote to Cameron expressing regret for what he had said on January 3, assuring him that he had intended "no offense," and suggesting, not definitely that he would give him a department, but that Cameron would be consulted if he should make a "cabinet appointment for Pennsylvania" before reaching Washington. Lincoln accompanied this with a letter pre-dated to

[17] White, *Trumbull*, 148. Ebenezer Peck is quoted as stating that the Chicago delegation in the Illinois legislature all worked to prevent Cameron's appointment, "believing him not to be a proper man for any place in the Cabinet." *Ibid.*, 147–148.

[18] *Works*, VI, 91–92; H. E. Pratt, "Simon Cameron's Fight," 6–7.

[19] Jan. 10, 1861, Chase MSS., Lib. of Cong. [20] Pratt, "Simon Cameron's Fight," 8.

January 3 in which, in more tactful tones, he asked the Pennsylvanian to "relieve" him from "embarrassment" by allowing him to "recall the offer." [21]

At this point it was evident that Lincoln still hoped to keep Cameron out of the cabinet, but he had failed to get the declination which would have avoided embarrassment, while he had made friendly gestures toward the Cameron group.[22] It seemed, however, that as long as Cameron's ambitions were not met Lincoln was to have no peace. "Delegations of Cameronites from New York and Pennsylvania descended almost daily upon Lincoln in the last two weeks of January," [23] while David Davis at this time was said to be "quite huffy" because of the objections raised to Cameron.[24] There was further hauling and tugging, and Lincoln, still hesitating, told clamoring politicians in New York in February that he would have to take the responsibility,[25] which he did by making Cameron his secretary of war. As will appear later, this was but the beginning of further grief.

Lincoln particularly wanted a Southerner in his cabinet and it is not at all impossible that he might even have chosen a slaveholder. Of his own desire to appoint a Southerner there is clear evidence. On December 12, 1860, there appeared in the *Illinois State Journal* a cautious editorial supplied by Lincoln in which the new President's "supposed purpose . . . to call into his cabinet two or three Southern gentlemen from the parties opposed to him" was mentioned and queries were put as to whether any such "gentleman of character" would accept a place and whether such acceptance would involve "surrender" of political views or "open opposition" within the administration.[26] Among the Southerners mentioned for the cabinet were Winfield Scott, Robert E. Scott, John Minor Botts (all from Virginia), John A. Gilmer and William A. Graham of North Carolina, and from Tennessee such men as Emerson Etheridge, Andrew Johnson, John Bell, and T. A. R. Nelson. After conferring with Lincoln on the South's share in the cabinet, a Virginia Republican reported

---

21 *Works*, VI, 96–97.

22 Lincoln's hesitations, perplexities, and embarrassments on the Cameron matter are well treated in White, *Trumbull*, esp. 142–148, and Baringer, *A House Dividing*, 131–136, 166–174, 255, 288–291.

23 Pratt, "Simon Cameron's Fight," 9.

24 E. Peck to Trumbull, Feb. 2, 1861, Trumbull MSS.

25 Pratt, "Simon Cameron's Fight," 10.

26 *Works*, VI, 78.

that he seemed disinclined to appoint the more outspoken type of Southern Republican such as Cassius M. Clay or John C. Underwood, who represented a small Republican minority in their states, but was more favorably disposed toward a well respected moderate such as Gilmer.[27] In January Frank P. Blair, Jr. wrote to his brother Montgomery that Dr. Gitt of Virginia was at Springfield "on a special mission in behalf of C. M. Clay [of Kentucky] and Underwood of Virginia who it seems aspires to a seat in the Cabinet." [28]

To make the selection was not easy and on January 3 Lincoln wrote to Seward of his uncertainty whether he could "get any suitable men from the South, and [if so] who, and how many . . . ." [29] In this phase of Lincoln's search he indicated that if a man was "farther South" than another it would make him preferable, also that it would be better for a man to have "a living position in the South." [30] Lincoln definitely sought the inclusion of Gilmer of North Carolina, who, he hoped, would take a cabinet post "on a fair understanding." [31] While the Gilmer matter was pending Lincoln concluded that it was unwise to take "more than one who opposed us in the election" for fear of losing friends.[32] Gilmer as well as others, however, proved unavailable, cabinet posts meanwhile had to be filled, and, though ultimately three men from the region south of the Mason-Dixon line served him as ministers,[33] the out-and-out "Southerner" was lacking.

VIII

The appointment of Caleb B. Smith to the cabinet was a fulfillment of a Chicago bargain and a recognition of the importance of Indiana. Here again intrastate rivalries embarrassed Lincoln. Schuyler Colfax as well as Smith was pressing for the appointment, but Smith brought to bear a greater organized influence. Playing the office-seeking game, Smith asked George W. Julian to write Lincoln in his

---

[27] W. W. Gitt to W. P. Fessenden, Feb. 17, 1861, W. P. Fessenden MSS.

[28] Blair MSS. Underwood was a Virginia radical Republican who became a Federal judge, serving in war time and after. His views resembled those of Thaddeus Stevens. Lincoln had no intention of appointing such a man to his cabinet.

[29] *Works*, VI, 91.

[30] *Ibid.*, VI, 94 (Jan. 12, 1861).

[31] *Ibid.*

[32] *Ibid.*

[33] Edward Bates of Missouri, Montgomery Blair of Maryland, and (later) James Speed of Kentucky.

behalf,[1] and Lincoln's friend Davis kept him reminded of the "pledge." By mid-January Colfax, having written unacknowledged letters to Lincoln, realized that "the game is up" and that Smith was preferred.[2] Lincoln seems to have had little enthusiasm for the Smith appointment which was deferred until a "late hour,"[3] and the Indianian was placed only after Norman B. Judd of Chicago had been definitely excluded. This latter gentleman, a former Democrat, Chicago friend of Lincoln, and contender for the governorship, had the support of leading men such as Trumbull,[4] Grimes, Chandler, and Wade. Lincoln, however, hesitated to take any cabinet member from his own state,[5] and the choice of Judd would have offended the Seward-Weed-Cameron element as well as many influential Illinois Republicans. It appears that Mrs. Lincoln intervened against Judd, but this is not to say that petticoat influence was actually the factor that controlled Lincoln's decision.[6]

The name of Montgomery Blair of Maryland, a conservative emancipationist of Dred Scott fame,[7] had suggested itself to Lincoln at the outset of his cabinet studies,[8] yet it was not until shortly before the inauguration that Blair was actually determined upon. No one would have accused the Blairs of backwardness in office seeking, and Lincoln was kept steadily aware of the Marylander's availability.[9] Though the position of postmaster general has sometimes been considered a minor one, yet any cabinet place under Lincoln was im-

---

[1] Smith to Julian, Jan. 21, 1861, Giddings-Julian MSS. (Julian did not do as Smith asked. Baringer, *A House Dividing*, 179–180.)

[2] Colfax to Yates, Jan. 12, 1861, MS., Chicago Hist. Soc.

[3] Welles, *Diary*, II, 390.

[4] White, *Trumbull*, 150.

[5] "We . . . hope . . . Lincoln will not make such a mistake as to appoint Judd." O. H. Browning in his *Diary*, I, 448 (Jan. 13, 1861).

[6] Mrs. Lincoln wrote to David Davis urging him to advise Mr. Lincoln to make up his cabinet without Judd. Mary Lincoln to David Davis, Jan. 17, 1861, Davis MSS., cited in H. E. Pratt, "David Davis" (ms. dissertation, Univ. of Ill.), ch. vii, n. 27; Welles, *Diary*, II, 390. On January 24, 1861, F. P. Blair, Jr., just returned from Springfield, wrote his brother that Judd was not out of the question, that Lincoln wanted him and he wanted to be in (Blair MSS.).

[7] Blair had served as counsel for plaintiff when the Dred Scott case was tried in the Supreme Court, and had indeed done much to "make" this *cause célèbre*. He was "the only West Point graduate and the only one with any military experience in the Cabinet." William E. Smith, *The Francis Preston Blair Family in Politics*, II, 2.

[8] Welles MS. (postwar recollections), Ill. State Hist. Lib.

[9] Two letters of F. P. Blair, Jr. to Montgomery (January 24–25, 1861) refer to Frank's visit to Springfield to see Lincoln about cabinet matters, including, of course, the Blair claim (Blair MSS.).

portant, and this office, whether rightly or not, was referred to as involving "the casting vote of the new Cabinet." [10] Blair was much more conservative than Henry Winter Davis, a Maryland rival for cabinet place; thus the choice of Blair was an indication that Lincoln preferred to steer a middle course.

When the cabinet was made up it was found that Lincoln had representatives from populous states such as New York, Pennsylvania, and Ohio (though not from his own), that Massachusetts was unrepresented, that he had no Southerner as usually understood though he had two from the border region, and that diversity of political views rather than uniformity was the cabinet's most obvious characteristic. Writing in nautical figures a correspondent of Governor Andrew said that Lincoln's officers did not all look the same way: his "first officer (Seward) looks one way and rows the other, talks compromise and peace, but votes the Chicago platform . . ."; his second officer (Chase) "thinks the true way to sail a ship is to look and row in the same direction" ; his third (Cameron) "gives no indictation as to which direction he will be inclined to pull." This hopeful individual added that Captain Lincoln would summon them all into the after cabin and make known that he was master of the ship and that all his officers had to do was to "obey orders." [11]

No one consistent principle, unless that of opportunism, had been followed in the selection of the cabinet. Its members did not agree with Lincoln nor among themselves; they did not pull the same way. Only a study of the conflicting influences bearing upon Lincoln can explain how each appointment came about, and then the explanation becomes clear. The idea that the President was selecting a nonpartisan or "all parties" cabinet, though often put forward, is a misconception. Active Democrats such as Douglas, Reverdy Johnson, or Horatio Seymour were left out, and while some former Democrats were chosen, each and every member of the original cabinet had supported the Republican ticket in 1860. The differences between cabinet members were differences within the Republican party. Lin-

---

[10] Nicolay and Hay, *Lincoln*, III, 369. If one considers the other six members of the cabinet as three former Democrats and three former Whigs, then a preponderance of one or the other group would be involved in the appointment of postmaster general. The fact that, in appointing Blair, Lincoln actually chose four Democrats (by former affiliation) and only three Whigs, is treated below.

[11] L. B. Comins to J. A. Andrew, Mar. 6, 1861, Andrew MSS.

coln is said to have been reminded that he had appointed "four Democrats and only three Whigs" upon which he replied that he himself was an old-line Whig, making the parties even.[12]

Such statements are misinterpreted if they are understood to mean that Lincoln was taking party opponents as of 1860 as well as party supporters into his cabinet, or that he was creating a coalition of antagonistic parties. As noted above, Lincoln indicated his own doubts as to taking into the cabinet those who had opposed the Republican party in the elections.[13] What is often overlooked in comments on Lincoln's alleged all-parties cabinet is that former Whigs in the Republican party derived from a political organization that was dead in 1860, while the Democratic party was very much alive. This being the case, it is entirely misleading to speak of Lincoln appointing "Democrats" in 1861 in the sense of taking opponents into his official family. The four were only former Democrats; they were good Republicans who had drawn away from the Democratic party.

As constituted in 1861, Lincoln's cabinet was as follows: William H. Seward of New York, secretary of state; Salmon P. Chase of Ohio, secretary of the treasury; Simon Cameron of Pennsylvania, secretary of war; Gideon Welles of Connecticut, secretary of the navy; Edward Bates of Missouri, attorney general; Caleb B. Smith of Indiana, secretary of the interior; Montgomery Blair of Maryland, postmaster general. Of the seven secretaries only two (Seward and Welles) were still at their cabinet posts when Lincoln died in office. Cameron was appointed minister to Russia and was succeeded by Edwin M. Stanton of Pennsylvania on January 20, 1862. Chase resigned June 29, 1864, his place being filled by W. P. Fessenden of Maine until March 4, 1865, then by Hugh McCulloch of Indiana. Bates resigned in 1864 and was followed by another border-state man, James Speed of Kentucky. Blair resigned amid clamorous intraparty disputes in September 1864 and was succeeded by William Dennison of Ohio. Smith resigned in December 1862, accepting a position as Federal circuit judge under Lincoln's appointment. In January 1863 the department of the interior was placed under John P. Usher of Indiana; he served only until the end of Lincoln's first term and was followed in March

---

12 Nicolay and Hay, *Lincoln*, III, 369. Seward, Bates, and Smith were the former Whigs; Blair, Chase, Cameron, and Welles the former Democrats.

13 *Works*, VI, 94 (Jan. 12, 1861).

1865 by James Harlan of Iowa. This résumé omits the short service of Buchanan's ministers who held over for a few days after March 4, 1861, until Lincoln's men could be confirmed and assume control. Disregarding these cases there were thirteen men who served in Lincoln's cabinet. Yet there were only seven cabinet positions and six departments, the department of justice being a post-Lincoln establishment. Contenders for cabinet place who failed of selection were in a number of cases "cared for" by diplomatic or consular posts. Gustave Koerner went to Madrid, Dayton to France, C. F. Adams to London, Judd to Berlin, C. M. Clay to Russia. Had Cameron not been chosen to the cabinet it is likely that he would have received a rather choice foreign assignment.[14]

---

[14] The pre-presidential phase is ably treated by William E. Baringer in *A House Dividing: Lincoln as President Elect* (1945).

CHAPTER XI

LINCOLN TAKES HOLD

I

AS THE time for Lincoln's departure from Springfield on the long way to Washington approached, his last hours at home were occupied with official cares, social obligations, and homely incidents of a peculiarly western or Lincolnian flavor. A public reception was given at his home on the night of February 6, 1861; it was described as a large affair, made brilliant by beauty, fashion, and the political elite, with hundreds in attendance.[1] Vacating their home, "breaking up housekeeping," the Lincolns stayed a few days at the Chenery House. The chores of packing were partly performed by Lincoln himself; the personal trunks, tied with his own hands, bore his label: "Lincoln, Executive Mansion, Washington." On Sunday, February the tenth, his last day in Springfield, he turned up at the Lincoln-Herndon office for a talk with his partner and chatted easily of incidents in his early practice. On departing he asked that the old sign be permitted to hang so that clients might understand "that the election of a President makes no change in the firm of Lincoln and Herndon." [2] Next day there was enacted one of the most touching scenes of his life as he took his departure from Springfield, bound for untold anxieties in Washington. Friends had gathered despite the stormy weather and the early hour, and Lincoln, rising to a level that was rare among rear platform appearances, spoke his few words of parting; they were as perfectly fitted to the occasion as any of his more formal speeches:

My Friends [he said]: No one, not in my situation, can appreciate my feeling of sadness at this parting. To this place, and the kindness of these

[1] New York *Tribune*, Feb. 7, 1861.

[2] Herndon (Angle ed.), 390.

people, I owe everything. Here I have lived a quarter of a century, and have passed from a young to an old man. Here my children have been born, and one is buried. I now leave, not knowing when or whether ever I may return, with a task before me greater than that which rested upon Washington. Without the assistance of that Divine Being who ever attended him, I cannot succeed. With that assistance, I cannot fail. Trusting in Him who can go with me, and remain with you, and be everywhere for good, let us confidently hope that all will yet be well. To His care commending you, as I hope in your prayers you will commend me, I bid you an affectionate farewell.[3]

Synchronous with the beginnings of the Confederacy, the presidential journey came at a time of widespread apprehension for the new chief and for the government itself. Extra precautions were taken in dispatching the presidential train. The time card of the Great Western (Wabash) Railroad Company, printed under date of February 11, 1861, for the use of its employees, contained the following injunction: "It is very important that this train should pass over the road in safety . . . . Red is the signal for danger, but any signal apparently intended to indicate alarm . . . must be regarded, the train stopped, and the meaning of it ascertained. Carefulness is particularly enjoined." [4]

Of the President's traveling party some went all the way, some made only the trip from Springfield to Indianapolis, others joined the train en route for rides of varying length. To enumerate all that were in the party, with information as to where they got on and off, is quite unnecessary. Robert Lincoln was on the train as it left Springfield. Mrs. Lincoln, with the other two boys—William and Thomas—boarded it at Indianapolis. The party also included the private secretaries, John G. Nicolay and John Hay; Elmer E. Ellsworth, Lincoln's young friend who would soon fall at Alexandria; army officers (Col. E. V. Sumner, Major David Hunter, Capt. George W. Hazard, Capt. John Pope); relatives of the Lincolns (Dr. W. S. Wallace, Lockwood Todd); men of political prominence in Illinois (David Davis, Norman B. Judd, Orville H. Browning, Governor Richard Yates,

[3] *Works,* VI, 110–111. Henry Villard claims to have prevailed upon Lincoln to write down this speech and to have been the first to give it out for publication (*Memoirs,* I, 149). Nicolay and Hay (*Lincoln,* III, 291 n.) state that it was written down immediately after the train started (partly by Lincoln and partly by his private secretary at his dictation), and that it was first "correctly printed" in the *Century* for December 1887.

[4] Broadside, Ill. State Hist. Lib.

Ward H. Lamon); and others so slightly known that their presence seems wholly incidental. (In this latter group were such unknowns as J. M. Burgess, George S. Latham, and B. Forbes. For all that they mattered, they could have been there merely for the fun or the ride.) W. S. Wood, an eastern railway official, was present in a managerial capacity. The army officers, who took very seriously their duty of guarding the President without satisfying others on this point, were there by action of the war department. David Davis joined the party at Indianapolis, while Yates and Browning traveled only as far as Indianapolis. From Browning's pedestrian diary one gets the impression that he by no means regarded the journey as a notable episode. At first he declined, then later accepted, Lincoln's invitation to accompany him. At the end of the first stage he "determined to go no farther." "The trip to Indianapolis," he wrote, "has been very pleasant, but is just about as much of that sort of thing as I want." [5]

While Lincoln was en route there were numerous expressions of apprehension among his friends and threats among his enemies. The day after his departure his Springfield friend J. C. Conkling wrote Trumbull: "If he is inaugurated on the 4th March . . . I do hope the most . . . vigorous . . . policy will be adopted." [6] Some of the newspaper assurances that all would be well served only to register a feeling of insecurity, as when the Chicago *Tribune* unconvincingly declared that the "timid, who fear that a mob will prevent Mr. Lincoln's inauguration, do not stop to think that the inauguration ceremony . . . is an invention of the people," and added: "We have no doubt that he will be President of the United States and Commander-in-Chief of the Army and Navy, before he leaves Springfield." [7] It was feared that the spread of secession would extend to Virginia and Maryland, or at least one of these states, producing a direct threat of violence at the inauguration. "[I]f Virginia and Maryland *do not adopt measures to prevent Mr. Lincoln's inauguration at Washington,*" declared the Richmond *Enquirer,* "their discretion will be . . . a subject of ridicule . . . ." [8] "Beneath all this talk [declared the reassuring *Tribune*] . . . unquestionably lurks a scheme for the assas-

[5] Browning, *Diary,* I, 454–455.

[6] Conkling to Trumbull, Feb. 12, 1861, Trumbull MSS.

[7] Jan. 3, 1861, p. 1, c. 1. Legally, of course, Lincoln's term could not begin until March 4; he could perform no act as President before that.

[8] Quoted in Chicago *Tribune,* Jan. 4, 1861, p. 3, c. 3.

sination of Lincoln and Hamlin . . . ." [9] Not all the apprehended or imagined violence was directed against Lincoln. Greeley wrote from Springfield in February 1861: "I was engaged to arrive at St. Louis tonight, but do not, because my friends fear a mob." [10]

Much will be missed in recapturing the psychological setting of the inauguration if Lincoln's own calm is not remembered in contrast to the keen apprehension of danger to him and to the government on or about March 4. The substantial danger is hardly the main point. Even if this be dismissed as an exaggeration it is important to recognize that the feeling of danger was real and that it affected the most sober minded of the nation's leaders. Charles Francis Adams wrote in early January to the governor of his state: "It is beyond a doubt that the revolutionists have determined to take forcible possession of the Government at Washington before the fourth of March, and perhaps within thirty days." [11] "I am anxious . . . about the safety of the Capital," wrote Neal Dow a few days later. "The fear is, that Scott cannot collect force enough for its protection." [12] In this state of mind those who would rise up and save the country by unsolicited military help were an annoyance to the outgoing President and to General Scott. When Governor Andrew wrote to Scott offering help from Massachusetts the old general made it known that he was "much embarrassed" and was in a position where even an answer to Andrew's letter would be considered a "gross assumption" on his part. Further he thought that volunteers beyond the District would not be needed in the near future.[13] This was at the middle of January, but a few days later Sumner, having passed an hour and a half with Scott, reported that the general was "not without solicitude with regard to the capital." Sumner told of newly received information which confirmed the idea "of a wide-spread conspiracy." [14] The subject was the more annoying because of the inexactness and mystery that attached to it. Having conferred with the attorney general on January 27 "for a long time till after midnight," Sumner wrote to Andrew:

[9] *Ibid.*, Feb. 13, 1861, p. 1, c. 1. Lincoln was en route as this was printed.

[10] Greeley to L. U. Reavis, Feb. 6, 1861, Reavis MSS.

[11] C. F. Adams to John A. Andrew, Washington, Jan. 4, 1861, Andrew MSS.

[12] Neal Dow to John A. Andrew, Jan. 19, 1861, *ibid.*

[13] Winfield Scott to Henry Wilson, Washington, Jan. 15, 1861, *ibid.*

[14] Sumner also wrote of Scott being unable to ride his horse, but being determined to ride in the inaugural procession in a carriage. Charles Sumner to John A. Andrew, Jan. 23, 1861, *ibid.*

"I know from him what I cannot communicate." Then he added: "Suffice it to say, he does not think it probable, hardly possible that we shall be here on the 4th of March. . . . General Scott is very anxious. It is feared that the Departments will be seized and occupied as forts." [15]

Trans-Mississippi fears matched or perhaps exceeded those of the Bay State. "What I fear," wrote S. T. Glover of St. Louis, "is the utter over throw of the government in all the slave states and a new government in successful operation before the 4th March." For his own locality he feared mobs, minute-men, and lynching.[16] Frank Blair the younger was much concerned about reënforcing the St. Louis arsenal, fearing that the enemies of the government would try to disarm the Northwest after arming themselves "by robbing the Southern arsenals." [17] A part of the "conspiracy," it was said, was "to withhold money from the Government, so as to place it at the mercy of the Seceders and their allies." [18] Provide against treachery was the burden of John Jay's advice from Katonah, New York. Keep Maryland open, he said. Watch out for the taking up of rails and the destroying of bridges. Let telegraph wires be guarded with religious care. "If we are to have war, let the Gov. shew not only moral but . . . military strength from the start." [19] In these matters he would have "no trusting to state honour" but would supply "a sufficient force . . . to crush on the instant the first effort at interference." He would "stand on the defensive," but he would restore the people's belief in the "sovereignty of gov[ernment]." [20]

In the deep South secessionist threats were both wildly exaggerated and exultant. A Mississippi man had written in December that his state would go out of the Union "with a perfect whoop," and would be followed "by all the Cotton States . . . , & if an army of 1.000.000 . . . do not take possession of Washington City before the 4th of March, I am very much mistaken." [21] J. M. Ashley wrote to Chase that Ohioans returning from Richmond declared in December that

---

[15] Sumner to Andrew, Jan. 28, 1861, *ibid.*
[16] Glover to Montgomery Blair, Jan. 18, 1861, Blair MSS.
[17] Frank Blair, Jr., to M. Blair, Jan. 24, 1861, *ibid.*
[18] Gustave Koerner to Lyman Trumbull, Feb. 19, 1861, Trumbull MSS.
[19] John Jay to Charles Sumner, Feb. 8, 1861, Sumner MSS.
[20] Jay to Sumner, Feb. 4, 1861, *ibid.*
[21] J. W. Williams to S. A. Douglas, Holly Springs, Miss., Dec. 10, 1860, Douglas MSS.

the capital would be captured by Virginia and Maryland and Lincoln's inauguration "resisted by force" unless some compromise was worked out.[22] The "numerous stories of the intended assassination of Mr. Lincoln" that were "constantly promulgated" added to public apprehension while giving a text for partisan denunciation, for without any basis whatever these plots were attributed to the Democrats.[23]

If the alleged danger was a bluff, the government would err as well as aggravate the situation by taking it seriously. Cassius M. Clay wrote: "The South is weak and she knows it! She bullies again!" [24] It was felt that military assistance would have to be invited by the general government. Any marching of troops from Massachusetts in minute-man spirit would have been regarded as a "first move" toward "hostilities." [25]

In Lincoln's own mind the inauguration was "not the most dangerous point," for, said he, if the two houses of Congress refused to meet for the counting of the electoral votes on the legally fixed day (February 13), or if a quorum should fail, "where shall we be?" [26] Though the counting was only a legal formality, yet without it the President's title would have been faulty, and it was thought that his opponents would not scruple to interfere at this point by a parliamentary trick if they saw the chance. Whatever Buchanan's detractors might say about "imbecility" at Washington, the truth was that Federal authority was respected; people breathed more freely when on February 13 it was announced that the ceremony of counting the presidential votes had been uneventfully completed.[27] On the same day there met in Richmond a Virginia convention known to be predominantly unionist, and there was now less fear that this important state, whose efforts were still tied up with the Peace Convention, would secede before the fourth of March.

---

22 Ashley to Chase, Washington, Dec. 18, 1860, Chase MSS., Lib. of Cong.

23 Chicago *Tribune*, March 1, 1861, p. 2, c. 6, quoting Buffalo *Commercial Advertiser*.

24 C. M. Clay to Andrew, Jan. 16, 1861, Andrew MSS.

25 Sumner to Andrew, Jan. 17, 1861, *ibid.*

26 *Works*, VI, 90–91 (Jan. 3, 1861).

27 The full Congress being assembled in the House chamber, certificates of the electors were opened by the Vice President and the vote was counted and announced. Lincoln had 180 electoral votes in a total of 303. "Whereupon the Vice-President declared that Abraham Lincoln of Illinois, having received a majority of the whole number of electoral votes, is duly elected President of the United States . . . ." Senator Trumbull and Representatives Washburne and Burlingame were then appointed to notify Lincoln and Hamlin of their election. *Sen. Mis. Doc. No. 5*, 44 Cong., 2 sess. (1876), pp. 53–54. (This 1876 document gives a history of the counting of electoral votes.)

II

Never again was Lincoln to make so many speeches in so few days as on his presidential journey. If at times the speeches seem mediocre, the reasons are to be found in a continuance of the policy of silence, a prudent caution to avoid misrepresentation, a wish to make no mistake before taking further bearings, and a deferment of difficult public questions for appropriate and matured treatment in the coming inaugural. The point of his speeches en route was to show himself, acknowledge ovations, and satisfy the many who pressed forward to see and hear him. The crowds did not expect magic answers to questions of policy so much as they wanted to gaze upon the President Elect and hear his voice. Few leaders have met such a situation with better grace than Lincoln. The generalities were pardonable and there was as little triteness as could have been expected in this weary itinerary. Certainly the new leader could not treat fundamental national questions at each place where his train stopped. If the speeches are re-read with these conditions in view they will be found to contain pithy Lincolnian expressions and not to lack gracious elements of fitness to the local occasion. That they were not his most distinguished utterances is readily admitted.

Often Lincoln struck the note of self-depreciation. He referred to himself as an old man; once he had a passage read by "younger eyes"; at times he confessed that he had not the "voice" nor "strength" for longer speaking. He called himself "without mock modesty" the "humblest of all individuals that have ever been elevated to the presidency,"[1] and declared that "without a name, perhaps without a reason why . . . [he] should have a name," there had fallen upon him "a task such as did not rest even upon the Father of his Country."[2] Repeatedly he showed his sense of the heavy responsibility that rested upon him; without cant he called upon the Supreme Being for help and invoked the undivided support of the people to sustain him. His thanks had a personal, genuine ring, yet he kept saying that honors and demonstrations were not for him; they were tributes to the cause he represented, to "the majesty of the nation," to the "perpetual liberty of the people of this country," to "something . . . more than

[1] *Works*, VI, 140 (Feb. 18, 1861).

[2] *Ibid.*, VI, 121 (Feb. 13, 1861).

any one man, . . . or ten thousand men," to "the elected representative of a free people." [3] With real eloquence he spoke from his pioneer heart of "civil and religious liberty for all time to come," of the fundamental processes of democracy, of the people rising in mass, of the business of preserving "the liberties of this people." In no other land, he said, could men come together as in America in the enjoyment of "free institutions." [4] Often he repeated that the demonstration was not for any political party. It would have been the same if Douglas or Bell or Breckinridge or "any citizen" had been "constitutionally elected." [5] "If Judge Douglas had been chosen President," he gracefully said at Cleveland, "and had this evening been passing through your city, the Republicans should have joined his supporters in welcoming him just as his friends have joined with mine to-night." [6] When "an election is past" a "free people . . . should be one people." [7] It was not often that he struck a false note, though perhaps he did at Indianapolis, where his sentences about coercion and state rights were of the sort to irk the Southerner, and where his metaphor of "free love" and of an "arrangement . . . maintained only on 'passional attraction' " hardly fitted his own Victorian age.[8]

Though more than vignettes, his speeches were fittingly brief. The longest and driest was at Pittsburgh where he rose painfully to the Republican duty of saying something about the tariff, "the specialty of Pennsylvania" which had been of more influence in obtaining the support of this area than slavery and antislavery. If a student searches the speech for economic wisdom or even for serious commitment on protection versus free trade, he will search in vain.[9] Plainly the tariff was not Lincoln's forte. He frankly confessed that he had no "thoroughly matured judgment" on the subject and was "not posted" on

---

[3] *Ibid.*, VI, esp. pp. 110, 111, 121, 129, 130, 143.

[4] *Ibid.*, VI, 141, 112, 116.

[5] *Ibid.*, VI, 115–116 (Feb. 12, 1861).

[6] *Ibid.*, VI, 131–132 (Feb. 15, 1861).

[7] *Ibid.*, VI, 139 (Feb. 18, 1861).

[8] Lincoln referred unfavorably to those who professed love for the Union, yet spoke of maintaining it as if that amounted to unjustifiable "coercion." Then he added: "In their view, the Union as a family relation would seem to be no regular marriage, but rather a sort of 'free-love' arrangement, to be maintained only on 'passional attraction.' " *Ibid.*, VI, 114 (Feb. 12, 1861). For the occasion of the Indianapolis speech, see below, pp. 284–285.

[9] "It proved him to be the veriest novice in economic matters, and strengthened my doubts as to his capacity for the high office he was to fill." Villard, *Memoirs*, I, 152. For the Pittsburgh speech, see *Works*, VI, 124–129 (Feb. 15, 1861).

the provisions of the Morrill bill then pending. Referring in homely fashion to the tariff as "housekeeping" and as "replenishing the meal-tub" (which would apply to a revenue producer, not to protection) he asked his secretary to read the platitudinous plank in the Republican platform, after which he admitted that there might be "differences in construing" its meaning and expressed the hope that every member of the next Congress would "post himself thoroughly" (as Lincoln said he had not done) "so as to contribute his part" to an adjustment that would "produce a sufficient revenue, and . . . be just and equal to all sections . . . and classes of the people," a phrase which could hardly describe a protective tariff. That the speech was taken as advocacy of protection at all was perhaps due to the fact that people were already used to generalities and verbalisms from politicians on this topic.

One of Simon Cameron's main interests had been to get a national administration that would favor protection, and he thought that Pennsylvania had "the power in her hands," by which he meant that the state's vote should be used for the benefit of manufacturing interests in the election of 1860.[10] When Cameron wrote to Lincoln (August 1, 1860) stating that he was gratified with "notes of speeches" (Lincoln speeches) which a "Mr. Lesley" had showed him, Lincoln replied with one of those cautious and embarrassed letters that a candidate not infrequently has to write. Briefly stating that "Yours of the 1st" was received, Lincoln wrote that David Davis would by that time have called upon Cameron and have shown him "the 'scraps' mentioned . . . by Mr Leslie." Then he added that "Nothing about these must get into the newspapers" and took care to mark the whole letter "Private." [11] Next month Lincoln sent G. Yoke Tams a letter that was both "Private and confidential" concerning an inquiry as to whether he favored a tariff of protection. Without specifically saying that he approved of protection he referred to the Republican platform, said he was not free "to publicly shift the position by adding or subtracting anything," for then the convention might "displace" him as their candidate, and remarked that his questioner would not wish him "to give private assurances to be seen by some and kept secret

[10] Cameron to W. D. Lewis, Dec. 14, 1859, Cameron MSS.

[11] Lincoln to Cameron (not in Nicolay and Hay, *Works*), Aug. 6, 1860, *ibid.*

from others." He enjoined "that this shall by no means be made public." [12] Neither publicly nor privately was Lincoln speaking his whole mind on economic matters.[13] Once he did comment on the " 'respectable scoundrels' " who "got . . . up" the "financial depression" that coincided with his election, hoping they would be "less greedy to do the like again," but this letter he also marked private and confidential in a headline at the top, repeating in the letter that it was "strictly private" and that he had no "declaration for the public." [14]

III

The main burden of Lincoln's speeches en route was preservation of the Union; to this theme he recurred continually. To the people of the South he showed conciliation and recognition of local rights. He referred to what would now be called the tyranny of words and declared that there was "nothing going wrong," "nothing that really hurts anybody." [1] As the context plainly indicates, this often misinterpreted statement showed no lack of anxiety and no callousness toward the ugly crisis that was shaking the country. What Lincoln meant and said was that in whipping up an unnecessary quarrel "men wrangle by the month with no certainty that they mean the same thing, while using the same word." [2] It was a matter not of essential invasion of rights, but of misunderstanding and misrepresentation. The crisis was "artificial." [3] It is strange that Lincoln was assailed [4] for this correct divination of the existing situation. It was almost as if he had captured for his time the dispassionate and realistic interpretation of a later age. The analysis given in a previous chapter [5] agrees with Lincoln's divination; on such matters as runaways and slavery in territories the fuss was about things that did not count. In such an emergency it behooved the people North and South to keep their temper, get all the light possible, and wait till clouds could be dispelled. A year previous to his election Lincoln had assured Kentuckians, as well as all Southerners, that he meant no interference; now he said: "Fellow-

---

12 Lincoln to Tams, Sep. 22, 1860, *Works*, VI, 58.

13 Reinhard H. Luthin, "Abraham Lincoln and the Tariff," *Amer. Hist. Rev.*, XLIX, 609–629 (1944).

14 Lincoln to Truman Smith, Nov. 10, 1860, *Works*, VI, 68–69.

1 *Ibid.*, VI, 122 (Feb. 13, 1861).

2 *Ibid.*, VI, 113 (Feb. 12, 1861).

3 ". . . there is no crisis but an artificial one." *Ibid.*, VI, 125 (Feb. 15, 1861).

4 Rhodes, *Hist. of the U. S.*, III, 303–304.

5 Above, pp. 229 ff., 237 ff.

citizens of Kentucky!—friends!—brethren! may I call you in my new position? I see no occasion, and feel no inclination, to retract a word of this." [6]

At times his speeches on the journey were mere apologies for not speaking. This was true at Rochester, Syracuse, and Troy. At Syracuse he declined going upon the "handsome platform" prepared for him, passing it off with a cryptic and noncommittal reference presumably to the Chicago platform. At New York City, being introduced by one of his bitter opponents, Mayor Fernando Wood, he managed to capitalize the fact of party disagreement among those who welcomed him. Always he had a word for the occasion and the locality. At Albany he referred to "the great Empire State." At Cincinnati he addressed Germans with a note of sympathy for foreigners generally, saying that when people were "borne down by . . . shackles" he would not add to their burdens nor do aught to prevent their coming to the United States. On this occasion he hailed the working men as the "basis of all governments," voicing the hope that "every poor man . . . [might] have a home" and favoring measures to "give the greatest good to the greatest number." [7]

The impression made by these speeches was varied. At the Ohio capital it was thought by a friend of Chase that he had "impressed every one . . . favorably," but that he was making a "great *mistake* in making speeches all over the country." [8] The Indianapolis speech was given the twisted interpretation that the Republican party was only waiting the end of the existing administration to begin the war and that Lincoln's speech was really a signal for massacre and bloodshed.[9] Lincoln was accused of showing "ignorance" concerning the revolutionary happenings of the day and a lack of capacity to grapple with existing dangers.[10] It was remarked, however, that the Buffalo speech was totally different from preceding ones and that there was hope of Lincoln and Seward making history in the conservative sense. In this speech Lincoln had referred to the difficulties threatening the country, but he had done so most unprovocatively, stressing the note of calmness and predicting that when he should speak out on this subject

---

[6] *Works*, VI, 118 (Feb. 12, 1861).

[7] *Ibid.*, VI, 119–120 (Feb. 12, 1861).

[8] R. C. Parsons to S. P. Chase, Feb. 18, 1861, Chase MSS., Lib. of Cong.

[9] New York *Herald*, Feb. 13, 1861, p. 4, cc. 2–3; Feb. 14, p. 4, c. 4.

[10] *Ibid.*, Feb. 15, 1861, p. 4, c. 6. This was a reference to the statement that nothing was going wrong, that nothing was happening that hurt anyone.

he hoped "to say nothing inconsistent with the Constitution, the Union, the rights of all the States, of each State, and of each section of the country . . . ."

IV

Policy making was offering a fearsome challenge to the nation's new leader, but long hours of travel, ceremonial duties, parades, and numerous public appearances were claiming his time and strength. Not only was there an official welcome at each major scheduled visit; there were dozens of minor stops where Lincoln had to show himself on the platform, frequently with what the papers called "a few pleasant remarks." [1] To give an account of these appearances in detail would be pointless, though for thousands the seeing of the Rail Splitter with his son, the "Prince of Rails," was then and thereafter a high spot in their lives. A few selected instances must suffice to suggest the scenes that characterized this moving pageant.

When Lincoln's train stopped at Indianapolis at 5:00 p.m. on Monday, February 11, some blocks short of the union depot, it was greeted by a surging multitude headed by Governor Morton, together with public functionaries and "distinguished citizens," members of the legislature, committees from neighboring cities and states, and the ubiquitous firemen. Zouaves and militia, brass bands, streaming banners, the roar of saluting artillery, and the deafening cheers of the multitude signalized this first visit of a President Elect to the Hoosier capital.

At the very point of Lincoln's alighting from the train Governor Morton did the honors in a speech that was more than an address of welcome; it was a policy declaration and even an exhortation to the President Elect to stand firm for the Union and for the upholding of ballot-box decision. Replying to Morton, which he had to do without anticipation, Lincoln expressed hearty thanks for the "magnificent reception" and told the crowd that the salvation of the Union was in the "hearts of a people like yours." Preservation of the nation's liberties and of the Union, he said, rested "not with politicians, not

[1] For example. it was reported that on the first day "Crowds greeted the train at every station between Lafayette and Indianapolis, and at every plaee where it stopped Mr. Lincoln showed himself on the platform of the cars and spoke a few words to the people." Indianapolis *Daily Journal,* Feb. 12, 1861, p. 2, c. 2.

with Presidents, not with office-seekers, but with you." It was a well phrased brief speech, undistinguished but fitting in every way, though bearing the marks of impromptu utterance.[2]

Through dense crowds Lincoln passed through the streets, standing in his carriage and bowing to the people, till the procession ended at the Bates House, where a reception was held including members of the legislature, and where later Lincoln delivered to a large crowd a prepared address which constituted one of the major declarations of this itinerary. Deploring the prevailing confusion of words, he quoted Solomon's admonition as to "a time to keep silence"; then he gave a definite hint of coming policy—one of the few en route—in a rhetorical question which suggested that holding government property and collecting import duties could not properly be regarded as coercion or invasion.[3]

Because of this and other matters people were to hear a good deal of newspaper comment on this "Solomon speech." It is therefore interesting to note as a historical problem that Nicolay and Hay in their edition of Lincoln's *Works* give an erroneous statement as to the date, place, and occasion of this address, placing it on February 12 before the Indiana legislature,[4] whereas in fact it was given, perhaps contrary to plan, on the night of February 11 at the Bates House.[5] The matter is not of great importance in itself, yet it serves to show that correctness of detail was by no means always achieved by Lincoln's secretary-biographers who edited his *Works*.

From Indianapolis the President Elect traveled to Cincinnati to

---

[2] *Works*, VI, 111–112.

[3] The end of this day (February 11) which began with the poignant farewell to his neighbors at Springfield was thus described in a newspaper of the time: ". . . the President's weariness induced him to retire [at the Bates House], although the rush to see and congratulate him continued unabated." Washington *Daily National Intelligencer*, Feb. 14, 1861, p. 3, c. 3.

[4] *Works*, VI, 112–115.

[5] Since the "Solomon speech" is reported in certain morning newspapers—e. g., the Chicago *Tribune*, New York *Tribune*, and New York *Times*—on February 12, and for other reasons, it appears that it was given to the crowd at the Bates House Monday night, February 11. In the hurried activities of Tuesday morning, February 12, no speech to the legislature occurred. This is confirmed by contemporary accounts, including the legislative journals. The above account of the Indianapolis visit is based on the Indianapolis *Daily Journal* and various other newspapers. The author has also been assisted by the diary of Calvin Fletcher, prominent Indianapolis citizen, and other material supplied by Margaret Pierson of the Indiana State Library. See also George S. Cottman, "Lincoln in Indianapolis," *Ind. Mag. of Hist.*, XXIV, 2–11 (Mar. 1928).

be greeted by another large reception (at the Burnet House) "where large crowds . . . called upon him." [6] At Buffalo ex-President Fillmore headed the delegation of citizens who greeted him; at Albany the honors were done by mayor, council, legislative committees, and Governor Morgan.[7] His speaking at New York City, already noted, was but an incident of his visit, which included meeting mayor and council, greeting citizens for long hours in parade and reception, conferring with politicians, receiving delegates at the Astor House with brief speeches, parrying insistent demands concerning his cabinet, and attending the opera at the Academy of Music. The long line through which his procession passed (February 19) "was densely crowded with spectators, almost equaling the turn-out to witness the pageant of the Prince of Wales." [8] The traveling Chief faced the public at close quarters, and some of the incidents en route were unpleasant. Crowds "almost crushed" Lincoln at Columbus; one of his party had to withdraw because of bodily injury. At the little town of Hudson near Cleveland, Ohio, he made an appearance to satisfy a large crowd, but he "was so hoarse that he was almost inaudible to people beyond the front row." [9] There was such "wearisome sameness" as the days wore on that one of the correspondents asked to be relieved of the "travelling show," detaching himself at New York.[10]

V

The last three days of Lincoln's journey, with their plots, rumors, and detective foils, would make a "thriller" if fully told; at least some attention must be given to this episode. Without an understanding of what went on, one might fail to appreciate the excitement of these pre-inauguration days and wrongly interpret a change of schedule which caused undeserved public censure.

Thursday, February 21.—The presidential party traveled from New York to Philadelphia with a scheduled stop at Trenton where Lincoln

[6] Washington *Daily National Intelligencer*, Feb. 14, p. 3, c. 3.

[7] *Ibid.*, Feb. 20, 1861, p. 3, c. 4.

[8] *Ibid.*, Feb. 21, 1861.

[9] John H. Cramer, "Lincoln in Ohio," *Ohio Archeol. and Hist. Quart.*, LIV, 167. In this article Mr. Cramer has given a fresh study of Lincoln's speech-making journey in Ohio, basing it on obscure and formerly unused newspaper articles. Concerning Lincoln's fatigue at Hudson, Mr. Cramer writes: "Thirty-seven speeches in five days was enough to tire any man."

[10] Villard, *Memoirs*, I, 152.

spent some hours, visiting the legislature of New Jersey and making speeches to the senate and house of representatives. He recalled his childhood reading of Washington's crossing of the Delaware, recognized again that he was addressing party opponents, and suggested amid prolonged cheers that for the preservation of "peace" it might be necessary "to put the foot down firmly."

The party traveled on to Philadelphia and put up at the Continental Hotel. In the evening Lincoln spoke at the mayor's reception. Meanwhile behind the scenes there had been close and anxious consultation between S. M. Felton, president of the Philadelphia, Wilmington and Baltimore Railway, Allan Pinkerton, head of a Chicago detective agency, and N. B. Judd, Lincoln's Chicago friend. The gist of it all was that Pinkerton's agents and spies reported a conspiracy to murder the President Elect as he passed through hostile Baltimore on February 23. Meeting secretly with Lincoln at the Continental, Pinkerton, Judd, and Felton explained the danger and urged him to cut remaining engagements and travel to Washington that night. At this point Judd alone of the presidential party knew of these consultations and suggestions as to change of plan. Lincoln cross-examined his interviewers and listened to their warning. Then, though facing possible assassination, he refused to abandon his Friday engagements at Philadelphia and Harrisburg.

About noon of this Thursday a page touched the arm of Frederick Seward as he sat in the Senate gallery at Washington. Soon he was informed by his father, Senator Seward, that General Scott had independent reports of the Baltimore plot and that Lincoln must be found and his arrangements changed. Colonel Charles P. Stone, a man of high reputation (which radicals were later to smear), had reported the plot to Scott, who had conveyed the information to Seward for transmittal to Lincoln. Traveling to Philadelphia, Frederick Seward managed with the help of Ward Lamon to see the President Elect alone, and Lincoln was given to know that "different persons . . . pursuing separate clues" [1] had concluded that the plot against his life was real. Judd states that he and Pinkerton devoted nearly the whole of that night, with railway and telegraph officials, to the task of arranging the difficult details of what was to follow.

---

[1] Frederick W. Seward, *Reminiscences*, 137.

Friday, February 22.—Lincoln's day began and ended at Philadelphia with a side trip to Harrisburg. In the early morning of this Washington's Birthday the new executive officiated in a scheduled flag-raising at Independence Hall, speaking to a group in the building and to a crowd outside. In this setting, where thought inevitably reverted to the Declaration of Independence, he offered the hope "that in due time the weights would be lifted from the shoulders of all men, and that all should have an equal chance." If the country could not be saved without giving up that principle, he added, "I was about to say I would rather be assassinated on this spot than surrender it." Speaking with "deep emotion" and giving rein to sentiment, he recalled the dangers and toils of Revolutionary soldiers, and stressed his belief that the Declaration was vital in 1861. There would be no giving up, he said; yet he particularly explained that his policy did not involve "bloodshed and war." [2]

Lincoln kept all his Friday engagements, traveling laboriously to Harrisburg, making two solid public speeches there, greeting a large crowd in a reception at the state house, and attending a hotel banquet given by Governor Curtin. At Harrisburg the men of the presidential party were informed by Judd of the suspected plot, and Lincoln was confronted with the problem of a night ride that would avoid the Baltimore danger. Unlike other cities and states Maryland and Baltimore had extended no official invitation to Lincoln and had arranged no speeches or receptions. The authorities had even failed to supply adequate police protection. Marshal George P. Kane described the plot rumors as a "political *canard,* receiving a . . . coloring of reality from the . . . expressions of a class of people who . . . are mostly to be found . . . in public bar-rooms." [3]

It had been publicly announced that about mid-day of Saturday the 23rd Lincoln would pass through Baltimore and that he would arrive at Washington that evening. To omit passing through the streets of an inhospitable city was a less serious matter than cutting the speaking engagements of Friday, and the President Elect, despite danger of ridicule and misunderstanding, reluctantly yielded to his advisers and consented to a secret night ride. With one companion,

---

[2] *Works,* VI, 156–158.

[3] *Annual Cyclopaedia,* 1861, 419. There is a tendency now to discredit rumors which, in this excited period, weighed heavily with Pinkerton.

Ward Lamon, he took a special train at Harrisburg with precautions to evade notice, entered the sleeper of a regular train at Philadelphia about eleven at night, and passed unnoticed through Baltimore in the early hours before daylight.

Saturday, February 23. Lincoln pulled into Washington at six a.m., and was met at the station by Congressman E. B. Washburne of Illinois. Though one finds conflicting claims as to this detail, Washburne stated that it was he who met Lincoln as he stepped off the train in company with Pinkerton and Lamon, that the four men entered a carriage and drove rapidly to the Willard Hotel, that they were shown into a receiving room, and that Seward then entered, "out of breath and . . . chagrined to think he had not been up in season to be at the depot on the arrival of the train." [4] The previous night ride had involved elaborate arrangements for cutting wires, intercepting messages, holding the night train at Philadelphia until a "package" was delivered (a Pinkertonian touch), preventing fire, putting guards at bridges and at a railway ferry, and creating the illusion that Lincoln had spent the night as planned at Harrisburg.[5]

The activities hinted at in this curtailed chronology must not be set down as mere nervousness. Events were soon to show that Maryland and Baltimore were capable of violence. Though some of the wildest rumors were canards (especially regarding a suspected *coup d'état* by which the "rebel" government would seize the capital), yet

[4] Statement by Washburne in Rice, *Reminiscences of Abraham Lincoln,* 37–39. Other statements, seemingly not so trustworthy, indicate that Seward and Washburne met Lincoln at the depot and were with him in the carriage as it arrived at Willard's. (Nicolay and Hay, *Lincoln,* III, 315; Chittenden, *Recollections of President Lincoln,* 65.) Pinkerton's postwar reminiscent writings were more popular than accurate. His *Spy of the Rebellion* (1883), p. 98, gives a faulty account with an incorrect illustration showing Lincoln leaving the depot escorted by Washburne *and* Seward. Pinkerton's MS., however, giving a contemporary record, states that "Washburne said . . . he was at the Depot . . . and that Gov. Seward was to have been at the Depot also, but that he (Washburne) did not see him." (The date is Feb. 23, 1861; Herndon-Lamon Collec., Huntington Lib., LN 2408, III: 305). In these matters the author gratefully acknowledges the assistance of Miss Norma Cuthbert of the Huntington Library.

[5] The following are among the references for the melodramatic episode of Lincoln's change of plan and secret ride: *Annual Cyclopaedia,* 1861, 416–419; Ward H. Lamon, *Life of Lincoln,* 511–526; Ward H. Lamon, *Recollections of Abraham Lincoln, 1847–1865,* ed. by Dorothy Lamon; Nicolay and Hay, *Lincoln,* III, 302–316; S. M. Felton, in William Schouler, *Mass. in the Civil War,* I, 59–65; *History . . . of the Passage of Abraham Lincoln from Harrisburg . . . to Washington . . .* (Republican print, undated); Charles W. Elliott, *Winfield Scott,* 693 ff.; Arthur Edwards, *Sketch of the Life of Norman B. Judd.* See also Chittenden, *Recollections,* and Rice, *Reminiscences.*

there was official information which could not be known to be so false as to be ignored. Secret service men of the Federal government were not then in the President Elect's party; had they been, Lincoln would have had even a poorer chance of resisting the demands for a change of schedule. The American method did not involve a pervasive national police, nor even an embryonic one; local police systems were uncoördinated, and it was, governmentally speaking, nobody's business in particular to see the President through in safety. Neither Lamon, Judd, Felton, nor Pinkerton had any governmental authority to act. Had President Buchanan detailed a military force to escort the President Elect, it would have added to the trouble besides being out of line with precedent. Had Lincoln been assassinated anywhere but in the District of Columbia, the national government would have been without authority even to punish the guilty party. Assurances of safety in Baltimore were unconvincing. George P. Kane, marshal of Baltimore, emphatically denied that there existed in his city any danger of mob action or of violence toward any public functionary, but his statement was dated January 16,[6] while Lincoln was to pass through on February 23. Kane himself was anti-Lincoln and feeling was at high pitch. Earlier in this narrative it has been shown that apprehension was real and widespread. The papers for many days had been full of serious talk of suspected violence. It was not as if Lincoln had evaded danger in the line of duty. He did not even have any ceremonial appointments in Baltimore; the passing through the streets was intended only as a necessary link in the itinerary. After he left Harrisburg his next duties were in Washington. He changed his plan not merely on the basis of Pinkerton's reports (Pinkerton having been brought into the picture on private arrangement by Felton and Judd) but on independent advice from the capital. In such matters a public chief is neither a free agent nor at liberty to take the public into his confidence.

What leaders have to suffer from, however, is not so much the essential situation as the manner in which it is publicly viewed. There were sorry consequences of Lincoln's night ride. He was reported going through Baltimore in a fictitious "Scotch plaid cap and . . . long military cloak," a fabricated description that has been traced to a journalist later imprisoned for forgery.[7] Cartoonists were particularly

[6] *Annual Cyclopaedia*, 1861, 419

[7] Nicolay and Hay, *Lincoln*, III, 315.

devilish in their caricatures of this imagined disguise. Opposition papers spread themselves on the subject and even Lincoln's friends were humiliated at the manner of his arrival in Washington.[8]

VI

The nine days between Lincoln's entry into the capital city and his inauguration were wearisome and difficult. On the day of his arrival he called upon President Buchanan and was introduced to members of the outgoing cabinet. With severe stress behind the scenes he had to make many public appearances. Congress, the mayor of Washington, hotel throngs, serenaders, members of the Supreme Court, and delegates to the Peace Conference had to be greeted, smiled upon, and in some cases addressed with an appropriate speech. Of more than common significance were the polite calls of his three 1860 rivals: John Bell, Stephen A. Douglas, and John C. Breckinridge. At Willard's the pressure was terrific, allowing "hardly . . . a chance to eat or sleep." Springfield, the harassed leader is reported to have said, was "bad enough . . . , but it was child's play compared with this tussle here." "I am fair game for everybody of that hungry lot." [1] The horde of office seekers [2] and the round of greetings and appearances allowed little time for public problems, yet his cabinet was not yet formally announced nor his inaugural address finally revised. To make things worse a major crisis in cabinet plans threatened at the very time of inauguration. Lincoln was informed that Seward could not serve in the same cabinet as Chase, and on March 2 Seward actually asked "leave to withdraw." [3] To lose Seward would mean seriously weakening the administration. The New York statesman and his friends were not of the sort to let the matter end there. Too radical a cabinet would not do; Lincoln found Seward indispensable. Yet it was not till the day after the inauguration that the matter was settled when Seward yielded to Lincoln's insistence that his eleventh-hour withdrawal be countermanded.[4] A matter of state was thus settled

[8] Rudolph Schleiden, minister resident of Bremen at Washington, reported on February 26 to his government that "like a thief in the night, the future President arrived here on the early morning of the 23d." R. H. Lutz, ed., in *Annual Report*, Amer. Hist. Assoc., 1915, 210.

[1] Villard, *Memoirs*, I, 156. [2] For the rush of office seekers, see below, pp. 311–312.

[3] Nicolay and Hay, *Lincoln*, III, 370; Bancroft, *Seward*, II, 43–44.

[4] *Works*, VI, 185 (March 4, 1861); Nicolay and Hay, *Lincoln*, III, 371–372; Baringer, *A House Dividing*, 327–329.

by Lincoln and in Lincoln's favor.

That form of studiously favorable publicity which modern journalists turn on or off at will had been denied to Lincoln. In general it cannot be said that he had a "good press" at the threshold of office. Showmanship failed to make capital of his rugged origin, and there faced the country a strange man from Illinois who was dubbed a "Simple Susan," a "baboon," or a "gorilla." Writers of this period labeled Lincoln an "ape" (this being a favorite term in the South), a "demon," or an "Illinois beast." On one occasion it seemed to a Washington correspondent that his "attempt" at speaking was "crude, ignorant twaddle, without point or meaning." [5] There was the preposterous rumor that he had avoided a train because he feared a wreck and had then counseled his wife and sons to take it.[6] Publicity was unfortunately given to a trivial act of the traveling President Elect in kissing a little girl, described by Charnwood as the "dreadful young person" [7] who claimed credit for those ill-designed whiskers which now disfigured Lincoln's face. To Charles Francis Adams the younger it seemed that while Sumner "talked like a crazy man" and Seward "was laboring under a total misconception," the "absolutely unknown" Lincoln was "perambulating the country, kissing little girls and growing whiskers!" [8] An impertinent journalist linked the whiskers theme with the choice of a New York hotel: "Mr. Lincoln, having . . . brought his brilliant intellectual powers to bear upon the cultivation of luxuriant whiskers . . . , has now . . . concentrated his mental energies upon the question—what hotel he shall stop at in New York." [9] Though Lincoln's social *faux pas* have been exaggerated, there were men in the East who thought him lacking in polite ways and innocent of *savoir faire*. From this it was an easy step to consider him deficient in sagacity and qualities of statesmanship. This was one aspect of the matter that gave point to the criticisms apropos of the night ride to Washington. It was a lowering of a prestige that at best was none too high. " 'What brought him here so suddenly?' was

---

[5] Villard, *Memoirs*, I, 152. This was the tariff speech at Pittsburgh. The quoted statement was written later by Villard, but it presumably represents his contemporary attitude.

[6] Chicago *Tribune*, Feb 27, 1861, p. 2, c. 1. [7] Charnwood, *Abraham Lincoln*, 204.

[8] C. F. Adams, *Autobiography*, 74–75, 79, 80, 82. This Adams was the son of the one who was soon to be minister to England.

[9] Albany *Atlas and Argus*, Feb. 15, 1861, p. 2, c. 4.

on everybody's tongue." [10] Yet some of the comments on the secret ride were favorable, recognizing that a calamity or at least an insult had been averted, that Lincoln had taken the advice of good counsellors, and that, even from the standpoint of Baltimore, the change was fortunate.[11]

VII

President Buchanan, Secretary of War Holt, and General Scott had paid heed to the possible danger of violence, and March 4, 1861, found Washington under unusual military protection, with guns commanding Pennsylvania Avenue, cross streets under guard, riflemen on housetops, new-drilled volunteers on parade, and "brawny young Republicans" on hand, "determined to see . . . [Lincoln] installed in office." [1] The militaristic touch had aroused the suspicions of the House of Representatives which had formally asked the reason for "so large a number of troops in this city." [2] In answer Secretary Holt referred to disorders in the South and to the belief of "multitudes" in a conspiracy to strike at the government, which belief he "fully shared." The general apprehension of a "raid upon the capital," and the open threat that Lincoln would never be inaugurated, he thought, could not be ignored.[3] Buchanan explained that, on March 1, there were only 653 "troops" in Washington exclusive of marines stationed at the navy yard, that these troops were there "to act as a *posse comitatus,* in strict subordination to civil authority," and that the existing condition of "high excitement," with rumors filling the air and threats freely expressed, was such that he "could not hesitate to adopt precautionary defensive measures." [4] Of course the protection of the government was not a mere matter of these 653 men. Contemporary accounts speak of a city full of troops, of "[t]housands of young men . . . well armed," [5] and especially of District of Columbia volunteers. These latter were organized by Colonel Charles P. Stone, charged with the defense of the capital, but they were not yet mustered into the Federal service and would not be Federal "troops" in the sense of

---

[10] Chicago *Tribune,* Feb. 26, 1861, p. 1, c. 2.
[11] *Ibid.,* Feb. 26–27, 1861.
[1] C. W. Elliott, *Winfield Scott,* 695.
[2] *Annual Cyclopaedia,* 1861, 750.
[3] *Ibid.,* 751.
[4] Richardson, *Messages . . . of the Presidents,* V, 669–670.
[5] G. Koerner, *Memoirs,* II, 117.

Buchanan's message. When thanked in Lincoln's behalf by Leonard Swett for his precautions, Stone replied that Lincoln should not be grateful to him, that he had opposed his election, and that his efforts were for "saving the Government." [6] Very much the same attitude toward Lincoln characterized the great majority of those who then held national office.[7]

Amid these military and quasi-military activities Lincoln performed the exacting duties of inauguration day. He entered President Buchanan's carriage at Willard's, and these diverse individuals rode side by side, in company with other "distinguished citizens," along the historic avenue.[8] Buchanan was described as grave and silent, Lincoln "calm and but little affected by the excitement around him." [9] For hours the human stream poured on toward the Capitol, the majority being Northerners according to the quaint remark of a reporter who noted the "lack of long haired [i. e., Southern] men in the crowd." [10] Part of the pageantry was a car decorated to symbolize the Union, the states and territories being represented by girls in white, the float being drawn by six white horses whose housing bore the word "Union." The parade was a Republican affair; marching delegations were politically sympathetic toward the incoming President. It was reported that Lincoln had to kiss the thirty-four states of the Union.[11] Arm in arm Lincoln and Buchanan entered the senate chamber where they faced crowded and brilliant galleries, while surging and heaving masses struggled in vain to view them. Here they attended a brief ceremony, Buchanan sighing "audibly, and frequently," Lincoln "impassive as an Indian martyr." [12]

On a temporary platform at the east front of the unfinished Capitol Lincoln faced an immense outdoor throng as he swore to "execute

---

[6] C. P. Stone, in *Battles and Leaders of the Civil War*, I, 22–23.

[7] It was reported that at the inauguration "nearly twenty of the . . . military companies of the District of Columbia were out, comprising . . . more than two thousand men under arms." Washington *Daily National Intelligencer*, Mar. 5, 1861, p. 3, c. 3.

[8] *Ibid.*

[9] New York *Herald*, Mar. 5, 1861, p. 1, c. 2. Buchanan wrote: "It is due to President Lincoln to state, that throughout his long progress in the same carriage with the late President, both on the way to the Capitol and the return from it, he was far from evincing the slightest apprehension of danger." Buchanan, *Mr. Buchanan's Administration*, 170.

[10] New York *Herald*, Mar. 5, 1861, p. 1, c. 2.

[11] Moore, *Rebellion Record* (Diary), I, 18.

[12] New York *Times*, Mar. 5, 1861, p. 1, c. 2.

the office of President of the United States, and . . . defend the Constitution . . . ," the oath being administered by Chief Justice Taney, whose court and whose opinion Lincoln had criticized. Near Lincoln on the platform were Buchanan, Breckinridge, and Douglas. In later accounts one finds of the dramatic story of how Senator Douglas held Lincoln's hat as he spoke his inaugural message, a fascinating and beautifully symbolic bit of Lincoln-Douglas biography for which a strictly contemporary source—i. e., an account written by a witness in March 1861—is difficult to find. None of the newspaper reports or other accounts written *at the time,* within the knowledge of the author, mentions the hat incident. A writer in the *Atlantic Monthly* in August 1861 described Douglas's sympathetic behavior at the inauguration without mentioning the hat.[13] The reference commonly given for the incident is "The Diary of a Public Man," published in 1879, but this diary, while rich in picturesque detail concerning Lincoln, has become a *cause célèbre* among historians and must be used with reservations. It purports to have been written in 1860–61 (December to early March), but as research on the subject now stands it is untraceable. Its authenticity is unproved, not to say doubtful.[14] (Those who accept the diary as authentic need look no further.) J. G. Holland referred to the hat incident, and his account has value, but his book did not appear until 1866.[15] Nicolay and Hay give only a passing reference to the holding of the hat, relegating it to a minor position in a footnote and offering it not as their own statement, but merely as part of a quotation from the post-war Holland account.[16] If they knew of the incident from direct observation or from contemporary statements, they give no sign of it. This is not to assert that the hat incident did not occur. The point is rather that a careful biographer looks for contemporary evidence, and where such evidence is lacking, or has not yet been found, it is his duty to say so. Henry Watterson reminiscently repeated the hat-holding story, reporting it as a witness, but his ac-

---

[13] *Atl. Mo.,* VIII, 212.

[14] "The Diary of a Public Man" appeared in four installments in the *North American Review* in 1879. For the hat incident see *ibid.,* CXXIX, 383. The present writer has commented briefly on the historical problem of the diary in *Amer. Hist. Rev.,* XLI, 277–279 (Jan. 1936). See also *The Diary of a Public Man . . . ,* Prefatory Notes by F. Lauriston Bullard, Foreword by Carl Sandburg, pub. by Abraham Lincoln Book Shop, 1945.

[15] J. G. Holland, *Life of Abraham Lincoln,* 278.

[16] Nicolay and Hay, *Lincoln,* III, 326 n.

count has by no means the value of a strictly contemporary record.[17]

Much more could be said of the vast crowds, of the incidents of inauguration day, of the hand-shaking, of the relief that came when no violence occurred, and of the President's ball that night. Lincoln's voice was described as "strong and clear," the cheers "loud and long." [18] "The opening sentence, 'Fellow-citizens of the United States,' was the signal for prolonged applause . . . . Again, when, after defining certain actions to be his duty, he said, 'And I shall perform it,' there was a spontaneous, and uproarious manifestation of approval, which continued for some moments." [19]

VIII

It is a mistake to suppose that prior to his inaugural Lincoln's attitude on resistance to secession, maintenance of the government, and like questions was altogether a cipher or an interrogation point. His policy had been one of caution and avoidance of public statement, but he had watched the situation, had kept in touch with Washington, and had at least made his position known to friends and counsellors. As noted in a previous chapter,[1] he had written in private letters that he would not persecute the South, would respect state rights, and would not push abolition measures. He had sought Southerners for his cabinet and had disclaimed any use of the patronage against the South. He had written to Weed that in his opinion "no State can . . . lawfully get out of the Union without the consent of the others," and that it would be his duty to "run the machine as it is." [2] He had cautioned General Scott to be ready to "hold or retake" the forts if necessary. He had protested against the interpretation that enforcement of the laws meant unjustifiable "coercion" or "invasion" [3] and had questioned the right of a "fiftieth part" of the nation to break up the whole.[4] He had been quoted as saying: ". . . I should regard concession in the face of menace as the destruction of the government

---

[17] *Marse Henry*, I, 78.

[18] Thurlow Weed, writing to Albany *Evening Journal*, Mar. 4, 1861, Weed's Book of Clippings, Division of Manuscripts, Lib. of Cong.

[19] New York *Times*, Mar. 5, 1861, p. 1, c. 3.

[1] Above, pp. 234–236.

[2] *Works*, VI, 82 (Dec. 17, 1860).

[3] *Ibid.*, VI, 113 (Feb. 12, 1861). For the "hold or retake" see *ibid.*, VI, 85 (letter to Washburne, Dec. 21, 1860).

[4] *Ibid.*, VI, 114 (Feb. 12, 1861).

itself . . . ." [5] He had said in February that there had been nothing (he meant no completed act of the Federal government against the South) "that really hurts anybody." [6] He had eloquently pledged allegiance, his life if need be, to free institutions, had praised the genius of American democracy, and had newly invoked the memories and principles of the Declaration of Independence. He had eschewed partisanship and uttered repeated expressions of friendliness toward the South and toward political opponents. If some were dissatisfied, he had nevertheless argued that "the defeated party . . . [were] not in favor of sinking the ship," but would "wait in the hope of . . . setting it right next time." He had summoned opponents to help pilot the ship, lest there "be no pilot ever needed for another voyage." [7] While avoiding a position from which he might later "be disposed . . . to shift," he had hinted that his known attitude would go far toward explaining his coming policy so far as the Union and the preservation of American civil liberties were concerned.[8] Though promising efforts toward a "peaceful settlement," [9] he had suggested that for this very object firmness might be needed. On vital and essential points he had expressed himself, yet his inaugural address came with real freshness and with the force of actual office-taking after important Washington consultations.

Proceeding without delay to the Southern fear that their security was endangered, Lincoln made it clear that he had no purpose "to interfere with . . . slavery in the States where it exists." [10] In doing this he underscored an attitude already announced, so as to make his pronouncement "the most conclusive . . . of which the case is susceptible." The peace and security of no section, he said, were endangered by the now incoming administration. Treating very guardedly the constitutional clause for the reclaiming of fugitive slaves, he declared that members of Congress must "keep good" their "unanimous oath" to support the Constitution, though he desired safeguards so that no free man would be surrendered as a slave. Applying historical perspective as against momentary or temporary agitations he referred to the "fifteen . . . distinguished citizens" who had

[5] Chicago *Tribune*, Feb. 5, 1861, p. 1, c. 1.
[6] *Works*, VI, 122 (Feb. 13, 1861).
[7] *Ibid.*, VI, 143, 154 (Feb. 19 and 21, 1861).
[8] *Ibid.*, VI, 147–148 (Feb. 19, 1861).
[9] *Ibid.*, VI, 153 (Feb. 21, 1861).
[10] *Works*, VI, 170. The quotations which follow are from *ibid.*, VI, 169–185, being the Nicolay-Hay edition of the inaugural address.

administered the executive branch in the seventy-two years since Washington's first inauguration. This sweep of time he contrasted with "the brief . . . four years" of the term on which he was entering. The "Union of these States," he said, "is perpetual." He dwelt in an extended passage on this theme, turning it over in its legal implications, declaring that the Union is "older than the Constitution" and concluding that the "Union is unbroken."

Lincoln did not dodge the problem of maintaining Federal authority in Southern areas where it was defied. His statement on this knotty subject had more in it than most writers have yet seen, though the address has been re-read and analyzed innumerable times. Just what did Lincoln say on this point, and how did he say it? These were his words:

> I . . . consider that . . . the Union is unbroken; and to the extent of my ability I shall take care . . . that the laws of the Union be faithfully executed in all the States. Doing this I deem to be only a simple duty on my part; and I shall perform it so far as practicable, unless . . . the American people . . . shall withhold the . . . means, or . . . direct the contrary. I trust this will not be regarded as a menace, but only as the declared purpose of the Union that it will . . . defend and maintain itself.
>
> In doing this there needs to be no bloodshed or violence; and there shall be none, unless it be forced upon the national authority. The power confided to me will be used to hold, occupy, and possess the property and places belonging to the government, and to collect the duties and imposts; but beyond what may be necessary for these objects, there will be no invasion, no using of force against or among the people anywhere.

Thus remembering his inescapable duty of seeing that the laws be faithfully executed, the new-sworn President nevertheless put in a modifying phrase or a conciliatory qualification at every possible point; this factor becomes especially impressive as one carefully rereads the address with knowledge of the consultations back of it and the elaborate revisionary care devoted to its final wording. To miss this point is to fail to understand the inaugural. The very source of his authority, the Constitution of the United States, said Lincoln, expressly enjoined upon him the simple duty of enforcing the laws. This statement itself was conciliatory; it was intended to emphasize that his thought about the laws was in terms of his oath, of the American system, of the President's obligation to the people, of his own unavoidable need to be amenable to their mandate. Even at this point, however, he added the qualifying phrase; ". . . I shall perform it [the duty of seeing that the laws be observed] so far as practicable, unless my rightful masters, the American people, shall withhold the . . . means, or . . . direct the contrary. I trust this will not be regarded as a menace, but only as the declared purpose of the Union that it will constitutionally defend and maintain itself." With meticulous care he was emphasizing defense, omitting any suggestion of *re-possessing* strongholds that had fallen, avoiding the word "forts" (choosing rather the words "property and places belonging to the government"), and taking care repetitiously to give assurance that there need not be any violence, any trouble with the people in any locality. Then, having said this, Lincoln felt that an additional word, a further clarification, was needed. The unprovocative nature of his program is especially evident in his next statement:

> Where hostility to the United States, in any interior locality, shall be so great and universal as to prevent competent resident citizens from holding the Federal offices, there will be no attempt to force obnoxious strangers among the people for that object. While the strict legal right may exist in the government to enforce the exercise of these offices, the attempt to do so would be so irritating . . . that I deem it better to forego for the time the use of such offices.
>
> . . . So far as possible, the people everywhere shall have that sense of perfect security which is most favorable to calm thought and reflection. The course here indicated will be followed unless . . . events . . . shall show a modification . . . to be proper, and . . . my best discretion will be exercised according to circumstances actually existing, and with a view and a hope of a peaceful solution of the national troubles and the restoration of fraternal sympathies and affections.

The President was insisting on upholding governmental authority in principle, but as a practical matter this was not possible in certain troubled areas. This being so, the new leader actually went so far toward peace as to say that in regions where opposition was "great and universal" the performance of Federal functions would be suspended. The strict legal right existed, he said, but he deemed it better to "forego" that legal right for the time being. Government, as Lincoln saw, was more than a legal science; it was an art. Precise legality was not all. There must be due allowance for "discretion . . . according to circumstances actually existing." A bad situation must not be made worse by a wrong stroke from Washington. Confronted with a choice of evils, the nation's chief thought it better to yield the exercise of Federal authority than to do the thing which would be both irritating and fruitless of any favorable result. It was not a matter of meeting defiance with force, but of changing the mood, forgiving a certain truculence on the other side, having regard for an atmosphere conducive to conciliation, and preserving "a view and a hope" of peaceable adjustment.

In a scholarly study of the sectional crisis by David M. Potter this passage of Lincoln's inaugural has been referred to as a formula and a plan. Lincoln was doing more than uttering words. He was studying solutions. The plan was to assert Federal authority with all cogency and firmness and then, where such authority was angrily challenged, to suspend its actual enforcement. Further "places and property" were not to be yielded; yet Lincoln's policy, in practice, was shaped more in terms of suspension than of enforcement. Where such enforcement occurred it was to be non-truculent; it was to be off-shore; people in the interior were not to be molested. The off-shore positions, of course, were Pickens and Sumter. To surrender these was not promised, but in matters pertaining to the customs, the national courts, the forts and arsenals already seized, and the post offices, "obnoxious strangers" (Federal officials) would not be forced upon the people. In such a matter of daily life as the mails a qualifying phrase was used; the mails would be continued "unless repelled." As to customs duties, if collected at all, this was to be done by an off-shore process; as it turned out, even this effort was dropped, while collection at customs houses was also avoided. Writing of this general subject, but with special attention to the question of the forts, Dr. Potter remarks that "Lincoln's attitude toward this problem shows how completely he had abandoned a policy of force." [11]

It is significant that Lincoln took this prominent occasion to deliver a striking pronouncement concerning the Supreme Court. He by no means admitted the authority of the Court to settle constitutional questions and went much farther than most liberal legal commentators in limiting the effect of the Court's decisions to the "particular case" and to the "parties to a suit." Having said this much he proceeded:

[11] David M. Potter, *Lincoln and His Party in the Secession Crisis*, 327. For the wretchedly complicated questions of disunion, compromise, peaceable separation, and rumblings of war that pertained to the crisis following Lincoln's election, Dr. Potter's scholarly monograph offers a competent marshaling of material and a capable analysis.

At the same time, the candid citizen must confess that if the policy of the government, upon vital questions affecting the whole people, is to be irrevocably fixed by decisions of the Supreme Court, the instant they are made, in ordinary litigation between parties in personal actions, the people will have ceased to be their own rulers, having to that extent practically resigned their government into the hands of that eminent tribunal. Nor is there in this view any assault upon the court or the judges. It is a duty from which they may not shrink to decide cases properly brought before them, and it is no fault of theirs if others seek to turn their decisions to political purposes.

For grievances he recognized in general the peaceful processes of constitutional amendment, and in particular (though this was a hard concession) he indicated his consent to the pending amendment which would have made an "express and irrevocable" declaration "that the Federal Government shall never interfere" with slavery in the states.

In closing he begged for "patient confidence in the ultimate justice of the people" and asked "Is there any better or equal hope in the world?" To "dissatisfied fellow-countrymen" he said: "You can have no conflict without being yourselves the aggressors. You have no oath . . . to destroy the government, while I shall have the most solemn one to 'preserve, protect, and defend it.' " From reason and logic he turned in his last paragraph to sentiment and affection. "I am loath to close. We are not enemies, but friends. We must not be enemies. Though passion may have strained, it must not break our bonds of affection. The mystic chords of memory, stretching from every battlefield and patriot grave to every living heart and hearthstone all over this broad land, will yet swell the chorus of the Union when again touched, as surely they will be, by the better angels of our nature."

A significant chapter could be written on the composition of this inauguration speech. Privately printed in Springfield, it had undergone elaborate and careful revision en route and in Washington. The "original" soon became a patchwork of pastings, deletions, insertions, and printed residue; it was this patchwork which Lincoln held as he read, and a reproduction of it was given to the press. There had been in the earlier version a weak and embarrassed reference to the Chicago platform and an unenthusiastic promise to "follow" its "principles" while repeating none of its "aspersion[s] or epithet[s]." Deleting this limping passage on Seward's advice, Lincoln avoided anything like blanket approval of the Republican platform whose binding effect was already disputed among Republicans themselves, while the great popular majority of voters in 1860, being anti-Republican, had deprived the platform of all force as a "mandate." The clause in the platform which Lincoln did emphasize and endorse was that which recognized state rights in the American "balance of power" and promised noninterference with slavery in the states.

In one of his alterations Lincoln produced a passage which offered Federal assistance to the states ". . . as cheerfully to one section as to another." Where the earlier version had said the disruption of the Union had been ". . . on paper . . . effected" Lincoln made it read ". . . formidably attempted." A reference to the perpetuity of the Union was strengthened by a statement that the faith of all the states had been "expressly plighted." The word "revolutionary" was substituted for "treasonable" in a passage concerning Southern ordinances of secession. On the suggestion of his friend O. H. Browning, to whom he gave a copy of his printed draft while at Indianapolis, Lincoln made probably the most important change of all by deleting a statement that his power would be "used to reclaim the public property and places" already fallen, and confining himself to a pledge that he would "hold, occupy, and possess" the government property.

There were many other changes, an insertion assuring Southerners of reciprocal citizenship rights, an emphasizing of the pledge against aggressive use of force, and an underlining of his "hope of a peaceful solution." The passage referring to "destruction of our national fabric, with all its benefits, its memories, and its hopes" was an addition to the earlier printed version, as was also the notable passage deploring a situation by which vital policy could be "irrevocably fixed" by the Supreme Court. Finally, the peroration was a Lincolnian transmutation of a passage written by Seward. More high-flown than Lincoln's usual style, it nevertheless conveyed a sentiment so deeply moving that exalted rhetoric became its fitting medium.[12]

---

[12] Among the manuscripts in the Library of Congress is found the earlier printed version with secretarial reproductions of the many handwritten changes. This library also has a photostat of the letter of John Hay to Charles Eliot Norton (March 29, 1889) explaining how the address was revised. See also Nicolay and Hay, *Lincoln*, III, 327–343 (footnotes); Browning, *Diary*, I, 455 and n.

IX

Comment on the President's address ranged widely. There was reasoned praise, fulsome adulation, denunciation, ridicule, and caricature. Much of the comment was concerned with elements read into the address rather than with its explicit contents. For Americans of a later day it is interesting to note that Lincoln was not then regarded as a master of style and that the literary form of his speech received unfavorable comment. The Toronto *Leader* could not admire the "tawdry and corrupt schoolboy style" of the address, though giving "credit" for its "good sense" and abstention from threats of coercion.[1] J. C. Welling asked Sumner what he thought of the inaugural. "Is it a clear . . . and homogeneous paper, or is it, like the Cabinet, a little 'mixed,' as well in point of thought as of style?" He thought the style "exceedingly *plain,* not to say *hard-favored.*" He was sure the concluding sentence was written either by Seward or Sumner. He thought Lincoln "would have done better if he had submitted the whole document to the revision of . . . [Sumner's] scholarly taste." [2] This very plainness, however, seemed a virtue to the Chicago *Tribune,* which admired the "*freshness* of Mr. Lincoln's utterances" and their "freedom from diplomatic vagueness and hackneyed political phrases." [3] Some of the comments were merely noncommittal. It seemed to a *Herald* writer that the address was received by Republicans with a lack of enthusiasm.[4] The Boston *Post* could not determine from the speech whether the new chief meant coercion or conciliation, and sagely remarked that time only could show whether the country's difficulties were to be adjusted or whether "rashness . . . [would] plunge it into the abyss of war." [5]

Part of the rejoicing over the inaugural was relief and pleasure over the fact of a successful inauguration. The Chicago *Tribune* referred to Monday, March 4th as "the day of deliverance." [6] Bells were rung and thirty-four guns fired at Wyandotte, Kansas, to express "general rejoicing" in the inauguration as an event.[7] In Hartford, Connecticut,

---

[1] Toronto (Canada) *Leader,* quoted in New York *Tribune,* Mar. 7, 1861, p. 7, c. 3.
[2] J. C. Welling to Charles Sumner, probably Mar. 5, 1861, Sumner MSS.
[3] Mar. 5, 1861, p. 1, c. 1.
[4] Villard, *Memoirs,* I, 158.
[5] As quoted in New York *Tribune,* Mar. 7, 1861, p. 7, c. 1.
[6] Mar. 4, 1861, p. 1, c. 1.
[7] New York *Times,* Mar. 6, 1861, p. 8, c. 2.

a national salute was fired on the afternoon of inauguration day.[8] "I felt a hundred fold better and stronger the moment it [the inaugural] was delivered," wrote one of Governor Andrew's friends. Already, he said, the "public pulse" showed signs of "returning national health." "What an audience! . . . Every word was heard, & the most perfect quiet & order prevailed—this is a great day." [9] "A truer, or safer, or more patriotic policy it would be impossible . . . to inaugurate," was the judgment of the Newark *Mercury*.[10] "The whole civilized world [thought the Hartford *Courant*] will echo Lincoln's Inaugural, and agree that it is fair to both sides, and worthy of a patriot statesman." [11]

Some of the comment generalized as to the quality of the new leader. A Plymouth paper saw reason to hope "that Abraham Lincoln will prove a wise, prudent and fearless president, unbiased by the fanaticism of his party, ..." [12] Praising the "ability, directness, candor and purpose" of Lincoln's address, the New York *Tribune* found all doubt removed "concerning his success as Chief-Magistrate." [13] To the New York *Evening Post* it was evident that Lincoln was becoming "a great favorite with all classes" and was winning "universal popularity." [14] The sincerity and manliness of his address "extorted the praise even of his enemies," [15] and "Republicans of all shades" were "delighted" with the incoming leader.[16] An Illinois admirer thought the address was "endorsed by all parties" and that nothing could have been added or taken from it unless it might have been a sentence declaring that a free people should have remunerative employment and that the government should protect the results of labor.[17]

Some of the praise was at a discount with Lincoln's conservative supporters. Where the papers commending him were radical, praise was an embarrassment. Such papers stressed Lincoln's firmness of purpose, his emphasis upon his oath to defend the government, his alleged resemblance to General Jackson, and his determination to "hold"

---

[8] *Ibid.* [9] I. Z. Goodrich to John A. Andrew, Mar. 4, 1861. Andrew MSS.
[10] Newark (N. J.) *Mercury*, as quoted in New York *Tribune*, Mar. 6, 1861, p. 6, c. 5.
[11] Quoted in New York *Tribune*, Mar. 7, 1861, p. 7, c. 1.
[12] *Plymouth Rock* (Plymouth, Mass.), Mar. 7, 1861.
[13] New York *Tribune*, Mar. 5, 1861, p. 5, c. 4.
[14] Quoted in Chicago *Tribune*, Mar. 4, 1861, p. 1, c. 3.
[15] *Ibid.*, Mar. 8, 1861, p. 2, c. 4. [16] *Ibid.*, Mar. 7, 1861, p. 1, c. 4.
[17] W. H. Thomas to Lyman Trumbull, Mar. 12, 1861, Trumbull MSS.

the forts.[18] It is not true, however, that the radicals were completely satisfied, and the statement of the Chicago *Tribune* that the mere holding of the forts was "not enough" [19] suggested that if Lincoln were really to please such men he would be sure to offend multitudes of others. One of the most interesting comments, because it did not repeat the commonplace, was that of Elizur Wright of Boston, who admired the address as a "masterly piece of generalship." "I hardly know which most to admire [he wrote], the adroit . . . use of the rotten plank in the Chicago platform, or the sound argument which puts the supreme court back into its proper place." [20]

Adverse comments in the North served to underline the hazard of American presidents as of all leaders in democratic states—namely, running the gantlet of press criticism. That such criticism was expected, was even protected by the government itself as an indefeasible right, and was usually considered in relation to its source, was after all, perhaps, the most comforting factor in the situation. There was no suppression of such criticism. "The Inaugural, as a whole," declared the Baltimore *Sun,* "breathes the spirit of mischief. . . . It . . . intimates the design to exercise . . . authority to any extent of war and bloodshed, qualified only by the *withholding* of the requisite means . . . by the American people. . . . There is no Union spirit in the address, ..." [21] An Albany paper dealt out sarcastic paraphrase, thus: ". . . Mr. Lincoln declares: 'The minority have given me power, and I will use it . . . against the dissatisfied States; and the responsibility of civil war will rest upon the insurgents who resist.' " [22] Lincoln's policy of collecting the revenue and enforcing the laws in the South was held "impracticable, if not impossible" by the *Herald* and his position declared "pitiable." It was pointed out that no Federal court in the South would uphold him and that the only solution would be for Congress to give him despotic power.[23] The President, thought the

---

18 Chicago *Tribune,* Mar. 5 to 11, passim.

19 Apr. 11, 1861, p. 2, c. 1.

20 Elizur Wright to S. P. Chase, Boston, Mar. 7, 1861, Chase MSS., Lib. of Cong. Wright appears to have objected to the Republican platform as not sufficiently abolitionist. Lincoln's use of the platform in his address had been to quote and stress the conciliatory passage renouncing interference with slavery ("domestic institutions") in the states.

21 Quoted in New York *Tribune,* Mar. 7, 1861, p. 7, c. 1.

22 Albany *Atlas and Argus,* as quoted in New York *Times,* Mar. 7, 1861, p. 4, c. 4.

23 Editorial, New York *Herald,* Mar. 6, 1861, p. 4, cc. 2–3.

Herald, showed deliberate ignorance of the issue. Some of his words meant war, in others there was an attempt at mediation. His government was probably undecided. In particular he was assailed for attacking the Supreme Court.[24] The Chicago *Times* denounced the whole message as "a loose, disjointed, rambling affair" and concluded that the Union was "lost beyond hope." If the message was carried out, this paper expected civil war in thirty days.[25] To the New York *Staats Zeitung* it appeared that Lincoln had shown himself more the lawyer than the statesman, and that his success lay more with words than with accomplishments. Commenting on Lincoln's suggestion that nothing was to be lost by taking time, this German-American journal suggested that the Republican party had made poor use of its time by refusing compromise and cutting off the chances of reconciliation.[26] In the same spirit the St. Louis *Republican,* representing the Douglas Democrats, said: "We hoped for a more conservative and more conciliatory expression of sentiments." [27]

X

It was no surprise to find that the inaugural was unfavorably received in the South. As printed in New Orleans papers the address was, said the Chicago *Tribune,* "horribly botched" and its words so twisted as to give the opposite of the meaning intended.[1] A Savannah paper facetiously referred to the suggestion that people pray for Lincoln and remarked that he was "past praying for." [2] A Kentuckian, resenting the Republican refusal to compromise and the inaugural pledge to "collect revenue from . . . an independent Government," suggested capturing Lincoln and "showing him around the country as a curiosity." This same gentleman declared that he could raise ten thousand men in a week and have them "on the road to join Davis' forces the moment a blow is struck against him." [3] Charles J. Faulkner, a Virginia diplomat writing from the American legation at Paris, could

---

[24] Mar. 5, 1861, p. 4, cc. 2–3.

[25] As quoted in New York *Times,* Mar. 6, 1861, p. 8, cc. 1–2.

[26] As quoted in New York *Tribune,* Mar. 6, 1861, p. 6, c. 5.

[27] Reprinted in New York *Times,* Mar. 6, 1861, p. 8, c. 1.

[1] Chicago *Tribune,* Mar. 11, 1861, p. 2, c. 1.

[2] Savannah *Daily Morning News,* Mar. 5, 1861.

[3] B. Duncan, Louisville, Ky., to S. A. Douglas, Mar. 7, 1861, Douglas MSS. This Kentuckian ended with the impudent wish that Mrs. Douglas might be his wife.

see nothing in the inaugural calculated to tranquilize the South or to indicate whether the President meant peace or war.[4]

The denunciation of the inaugural as a call to arms was the commonest and most typical of the Southern comments. Dispatches from Montgomery brought the news that in the capital city of the new Confederacy war between North and South was now considered inevitable.[5] In North Carolina, where secession was yet resisted, the cry of the disunion leaders that the address was a "war message" was having its effect.[6] A Savannah journal predicted that Lincoln's program left little doubt that the volunteer military companies would have opportunity to serve the South.[7] At Nashville opinion was reported as unsettled, with an inclination toward the unfavorable. Jackson and Columbus, Mississippi, and Tuscumbia, Alabama, were reported as considering it a declaration of war, New Orleans condemned it, and Vicksburg dubbed it a "silly production." [8] In Richmond both the secessionist *Enquirer* and the conservative *Whig* deplored the address.[9] To the Richmond correspondent of the New York *Tribune* it seemed that in the latitude of Virginia the message was regarded as strengthening the hands of the secessionists, whereas this element had been but a few days previously a small minority.[10]

The Columbia *South Carolinian* caught up some hope (disunion hope) from the pledge to commit no aggressive act and felt assured that Lincoln would see the impracticability of exacting unjust tribute from the Confederate States.[11] The *Mercury* (Charleston) referred to Lincoln's "insolence" and "brutality," and declared that the United States had become "a mobocratic Empire." To this paper the policy of the South was now one of "war strategy." [12] While waiting for the inaugural, palmetto-state spokesmen had prepared their people for a

[4] C. J. Faulkner to W. H. Seward, U. S. Legation, Paris, April 5, 1861, MS., Ill. State Hist. Lib.

[5] New York *Herald,* Mar. 6, 1861, p. 4, c. 1.

[6] Q. Busbee to S. A. Douglas, Raleigh, N. C., Mar. 11, 1861, Douglas MSS.

[7] Savannah *Daily Morning News,* Mar. 5, 1861.

[5] New York *Herald,* Mar. 6, 1861, p. 4, c. 1.
Times.

[9] *Ibid.*

[10] "The Secessionists [in Virginia] now . . . say . . . 'We told you so.' . . . There is but little doubt *now* that henceforth the Secessionists, who a few days ago were but a small minority, will have things pretty much their own way." Statement of *Tribune* correspondent writing from Richmond, in New York *Tribune,* Mar. 9, 1861, p. 6, c. 2.

[11] Quoted in New York *Times,* Mar. 9, 1861, p. 1, c. 6.

[12] Charleston *Mercury,* Mar. 5, 1861.

Southern proclamation of a state of hostility between the cotton states and the North if the President promised a retention of the few remaining lower Southern forts.[13] Among some South Carolinians, however, there appeared to be a feeling of regret that the inaugural was not more bellicose, and that it contained so little "blood and thunder." This was reported as "annoying to the Rebels, who hoped to find in the address a provocation for extreme action." [14] In Georgia also it was reported that the lack of truculence in the President's address knocked the props from under the secessionists.[15]

Though, as the New York *Times* remarked, it would have been impossible for Lincoln to have delivered a message that would please the secessionists,[16] yet among Southerners who did not approve of secession the address did meet with some favor. After talking with Southern men a friend of Governor Andrew wrote that Lincoln's inaugural had broken the backbone of secession.[17] John Letcher, governor of Virginia, wrote that there was a sobering down, that conservatives intended to think calmly, and that they were turning their thoughts to a border-state conference.[18] An Alabama friend wrote Douglas that the inaugural was "not very warlike"; it was the papers, he said, that were "one and all making it out coercive in the extreme." [19] Jubal A. Early, speaking in the Virginia Convention, referred to Lincoln's intent to execute the laws as "a guarantee that he would perform his duty" and put the blame for the "perilous condition" of the country upon the states that had seceded "without having consulted our views." [20] John A. Gilmer, the North Carolinian whom Lincoln wished to bring into his cabinet, ably expressed the Southern unionist point of view. Mentioning the guarantee against interference with slavery in the states together with the other pledges of the President, and also the repealing by the Northern states of their personal liberty laws "as rapidly as they can," he asked: ". . . what

[13] Statement of *Tribune* correspondent at Charleston, Mar. 2, 1861, New York *Tribune*, Mar. 7, 1861, p. 6, c. 1.

[14] *Ibid.*, Mar. 9, 1861, p. 6, c. 1.

[15] Statement of *Tribune* correspondent at Savannah, in New York *Tribune*, Mar. 11, 1861, p. 6, c. 2.

[16] Mar. 7, 1861, p. 4, c. 2.

[17] L. B. Comins to John A. Andrew, Washington, Mar. 6. 1861, Andrew MSS.

[18] John Letcher to J. D. Davidson, Richmond, Mar. 9, 1861, Davidson MSS., McCormick Library, Chicago.

[19] Joseph C. Bradley to S. A. Douglas, Huntsville, Ala., Mar. 8, 1861, Douglas MSS.

[20] Quoted in B. B. Mumford, *Virginia's Attitude toward Slavery and Secession*, 266.

more does any reasonable Southern man expect or desire?" "Are not . . . these . . . cheering assurances enough to induce the whole South to wait for the sober second thought of the North?" [21] Unfortunately the mild and quieting comments just quoted from Letcher and Gilmer were conveyed in private correspondence, while the comments in Southern newspapers and in the published statements of politicians were usually of the truculent sort.

Neither South nor North had an adequate mirror of itself at the time, but it is significant that trouble-making comments traveled faster and attained far more publicity than moderate ones. Every clue to Lincoln's attitude confirms the conclusion that he spoke truth in saying he had no aggressive design whatever upon the South. Secessionists, as shown above, regretted the lack of blood and thunder in his address, thus admitting its unthreatening character, while moderates saw in it a basis upon which even Southerners could stand. It is interesting to note that Lincoln in Washington was more moderate than Lincoln in Springfield. Whether this was due to the influence of Seward or to a combination of various contacts and reflections en route and at Willard's, the fact remains that, aside from literary revision, the controlling motive in the extensive alteration of the inaugural in these days was that of friendliness, nonaggression, and adjustment with the South.

In short, if one would justly appraise Lincoln's first presidential state paper, this inaugural of 1861 deserves both to be read as delivered and to be set over against the alternative statements that Lincoln avoided or struck out in revision. Statements pledging maintenance of Federal authority were toned down and shorn of truculence, while promises of conciliation were emotionally underlined. Even in enforcing the laws Lincoln held himself subject to his "masters," the American people. Men who would destroy the Union were referred to as "persons in one section or another." Protection to the states was offered "as cheerfully to one section, as to another." The Republican platform was quoted not for anything the South might resent, but for the pledge of non-interference with slavery. The new chief would seek a "peaceful solution." He would stress "fraternal sympathies." As to military policy he showed special care in the choice

[21] Gilmer to Douglas, Mar. 8, 1861, Douglas MSS. Later in the letter he referred to "the sober second thought of a majority of those who voted for Lincoln."

of nouns and verbs. His statement was not that he would "recapture" the "forts," but that he would "hold, . . . and possess the property and places belonging to the government." Even this holding and possessing was qualified; it involved no need of bloodshed, no invasion, no use of force anywhere. This was decidedly not a promise to withdraw from Sumter, but it was a promise not to use Sumter for aggressive attack upon South Carolina. Maintenance of the Union was conceived as adjusting difficulties within the Union. Physically there could be no separation. Relations could be no more satisfactory after separation than before. One could not fight always. When fighting ceased the old questions were still to be faced. In the very words of Gilmer the President asked his countrymen to think calmly. The Union was not merely to be supported; it was to be cherished. Memories were bound up with it. In contrast to the remediable and trivial character of existing grievances, he warned of the gravity of "the destruction of our national fabric, with all its benefits, its memories, and its hopes." Could anyone hazard such a step "while the ills you fly from have no real existence?" Newspapers might denounce the "war message," but these were the concepts that the new President begged the nation to ponder.

CHAPTER XII

SUMTER

I

THE transition from the Buchanan to the Lincoln administration meant just one thing to politicians—offices and spoils. "The change from a long Democratic to a Republican régime involved a sweeping change of functionaries." [1] When a reporter noted that the new President was "about the busiest person in Washington" and that he was "working early and late," he indicated that most of this was due to office seekers.[2] Edwin M. Stanton wrote that the scramble for office was "terrific," as had been said at Willard's, and that Lincoln was reported to be "seeing no strangers alone." [3] It was also stated that Lincoln was doing the appointing himself, undertaking to handle "the whole patronage small and great leaving nothing to the Chiefs of Departments." [4] Joseph Medill of the Chicago *Tribune,* who was in Washington at this time, wrote of a "mob of candidates" and feared that they would "neutralize the strength of the Tribune folks with Mr. Lincoln." The case of the Chicago post office was typical of the hundreds of positions that Lincoln had to fill, for it was assumed that incumbents would be put out all over the country and that places would be made for Lincoln's friends. "To us the P. O. would be of great value," wrote Medill to Trumbull. "If Mr S. [John L. Scripps] had it the country Post Masters of the N. West would work to extend our circulation . . . . You observe that the office would be vastly more beneficial to us than to any individual . . . . The Republican people of Chicago expect . . . the 'Tribune'

[1] Nicolay and Hay, *Lincoln,* III, 443.
[2] Chicago *Tribune,* Mar. 14, 1861, p. 1, c. 2.
[3] E. M. Stanton to James Buchanan, Mar. 10, 1861, Buchanan MSS.
[4] Stanton to Buchanan, Mar. 16, 1861, *ibid.*

to have the P. O." [5] But Lincoln had not only to satisfy the *Tribune,* which considered the post office its proper quarry; he was expected to reward every element that helped him at Chicago, including, for example, a vigorous contingent of Germans.[6]

New York also had its *Tribune,* and its editor was no less interested in offices. On this subject Greeley felt deeply. "I tell you [he wrote] the chances are three to one against an honest man getting anything. The thieves hunt in gangs, and each helps all the rest. Three-quarters of the post-offices will go into the hands of the corruptionists." [7] So it went. In the eyes of party workers it was the local offices that counted, which meant rivalries, perplexities, and pressure from all over the country. This was the first phase of Lincoln's duty as executive; it made cruel demands on his time at the outset, and with an increasing number of offices to fill it remained an unending source of annoyance throughout his presidency.

The cabinet should have been an instrument to assist and sustain the President, but under Lincoln it was never that. It has been seen that his administration began with a cabinet crisis before the official council was installed,[8] and, had Lincoln known it, this might have been taken as a warning that his period of rule would be a series of minor cabinet crises, with now and then a major one. Confirmation of cabinet appointments by the Senate came with little difficulty on March 5, except for a few Southern votes cast against Bates and Blair. Senator Mason of Virginia opposed the confirmation of Blair on the ground that no Southern man ought to hold office under Mr. Lincoln.[9] When confirmation was announced it was remarked that Weed made no concealment of his chagrin, that Cameron took the event as a bitter pill, and that Greeley strode about with the air of a conqueror.[10] "Yes, we *did* [wrote Greeley], by desperate fighting, succeed

---

[5] Medill to Trumbull, Mar. 4, 1861 (marked "Private"), Trumbull MSS. Scripps was appointed; thus the *Tribune* got the post office.

[6] G. Koerner to Trumbull, Mar. 13, 1861, *ibid.*

[7] Greeley to B. Brockway of Watertown, N. Y., Mar. 12, 1861, Greeley MSS., Lib. of Cong.

[8] See above, p. 291.

[9] Senators Mason, Bragg, Clingman, and Mitchell (Southerners) voted against confirming Blair; Hunter, Wigfall, and others refused to vote. There was the same opposition in the case of Bates. New York *Tribune,* Mar. 6, 1861, p. 4, c. 6. This Southern attitude offers a significant commentary on Lincoln's problem so far as it related to intersectional compromise.

[10] New York *Herald,* Mar. 6, 1861, p. 1, c. 1.

in getting four honest . . . men into the cabinet—by a fight that you never saw equalled . . . . Gov. Chase, the ablest Republican living, . . . indispensable to the treasury, got it at last . . . . All the Kitchen Cabinet, including the Senate President, were dead against him . . . ." [11] Yet the satisfaction of Greeley, due to the choice of Chase, should not be understood to indicate that the cabinet was radical, or even particularly forward in its firmness for the Union. It was reported as a "common saying" in Washington that Lincoln's cabinet "did not contain three as absolute and strong defenders of the Union as Dix, Holt, and Stanton, who had just retired with Mr. Buchanan." [12] Under these circumstances the sterner type of Republicans looked to Chase to preserve the country "from dissolution," [13] while another type within the party looked to Seward to save it from wild radicalism. At the first meeting of the cabinet, which occurred on the night of March 6, it would appear that virtually nothing happened. At any rate Edward Bates recorded that the occasion was "formal and introductory only—in fact, uninteresting." [14]

In the first month or so the new administration was watched for indications of its direction or policy, and a surprising amount of the Northern comment was distrustful or unfavorable. Editors inevitably pronounced their pontifical judgments, and among these Bennett of the *Herald* was particularly caustic, declaring that the Lincoln government was interested only in spoils and in pursuing an antagonistic attitude toward the South.[15] Edwin M. Stanton reported to Buchanan: "Every day affords proof of the absence of any settled policy, or harmonious . . . . action, in the administration. Seward, Bates, and Cameron, form one wing, Chase, Welles, Blair the opposite wing. Smith is on both sides, and Lincoln sometimes on one, sometimes on the other. There has been agreement on nothing." [16] Stanton noted a diminishing of loyalty to the government and thought the administration did not

[11] Greeley to B. Brockway of Watertown, N. Y., Mar. 12, 1861, Greeley MSS., Lib. of Cong.

[12] Blaine, *Twenty Years of Congress*, I, 285–286. "We have great faith in . . . our President but none in the majority of his Cabinet." W. B. Plato to Lyman Trumbull, Geneva, Ill., Mar. 29, 1861, Trumbull MSS.

[13] John Jay to S. P. Chase, Katonah, N. Y., Apr. 8, 1861, Chase MSS., Lib. of Cong. Similarly, an Ohio man wrote to Chase: "How deplorably has Mr. Seward mistaken the temper . . . of the Northern people. . . . We *Republicans* of Ohio look to you . . . to redeem us." W. D. Bickham of Columbus, Ohio, to Chase, Apr. 2, 1861, *ibid.*

[14] Bates, *Diary*, 177.

[15] New York *Herald*, Mar. 21, 1861, p. 4, c. 2.

[16] Stanton to Buchanan, Mar. 16, 1861, Buchanan MSS.

have the confidence of the people. "Seward," he said "rented a house 'while he should continue in the Cabinet,' " but five weeks after the inauguration he had not opened it, nor had his family come. They all acted as if "they meant to be ready 'to cut and run' [thought Stanton] at a minute's notice." Their tenure, he said, was "that of a Bedouin on the sands of the desert." Among the people Stanton observed "a strong feeling of distrust in . . . Lincoln personally, and of his Cabinet . . . ." [17]

Amid distrust of Seward, growls about Scott's "imbecility," [18] complaints of moneyed men, and disappointment at the adjournment of a Congress which had neither provided for defense nor promoted compromise, Stanton found a kind of grim comfort for Buchanan, whose administration he now considered vindicated.[19] As if other troubles were not enough, the new tariff bill (the partially protective Morrill act of February 20, 1861, favored by Republicans and passed after withdrawal of Southerners in Congress) was giving "great trouble"; [20] "The Republicans . . . [were] beginning to think that a monstrous blunder was made in the tariff Bill; and that it . . . [would] cut off the trade of New York, build up New Orleans, . . . and leave the government no revenue—they see before them the prospect of soon being without money, and without credit." [21] Pennsylvanians were reported "angry about the threatened repeal of the tariff" and saying that they voted for Lincoln with the "explicit understanding" that they would be satisfied on this point.[22] There was much to confirm the close connection between Pennsylvania Republicanism and the tariff. While the Morrill bill was pending, a Philadelphian had written Congressman John Sherman that a mere "loose aggregation" could be "knit together and crystalised into a genuine republican party" by the passage of the tariff bill; if not, he added, the state would relapse

---

[17] Stanton to Buchanan, April 11, 1861, *ibid.* Stanton wrote: ". . . no one speaks of Lincoln or any member of his Cabinet with respect or regard." *Ibid.*

[18] Stanton to Buchanan, Mar. 16, 1861, *ibid.*

[19] Stanton to Buchanan, Apr. 3, 1861, *ibid.* These letters of Stanton were written at Washington.

[20] *Ibid.* Stanton added: ". . . luckily it is a measure of their own." Stanton was thinking in anti-Republican and anti-Lincolnian terms.

[21] Stanton to Buchanan, Mar. 16, 1861, *ibid.*

[22] Chicago *Tribune,* Apr. 1, 1861, p. 4, c. 4. As an example of the opposite point of view, Joshua Leavitt wrote from New York to Chase, February 18, 1861: "I do hope we are not to be sacrificed to sordid Pa on the tariff," adding that duties were needed for revenue. Chase MSS., Lib. of Cong.

into the control of the "Bogus democracy." His advice was: "Save the Bill and you *make* a party in Penna." [23]

II

Cabinet troubles, post offices, and tariff worries might loom large in other administrations. For Lincoln the abnormality of the American situation left no time to settle down to a regular round of executive duties. At the very beginning there was thrust upon him an inescapable dilemma as to Charleston Harbor, where an early decision had to be made, but where any conceivable choice of conduct would be dangerous and bitterly distasteful. For it must be noted that the calamitous difficulty of the Sumter question, involving the most vexatious decision that Lincoln ever had to make, was inherent in the dilemma itself. It existed in the nature of the ugly factors of the problem as presented in March and April of 1861. Lincoln could not hope to avoid trouble; he could merely choose between alternatives of trouble. It was not merely a matter of inheriting Buchanan's dilemma, though it was partly that; under Lincoln an almost immediate decision had to be made, whereas Buchanan could deal in understandings, deferments, and status quo.

While conciliation seemed still possible and the avoidance of war supremely important, Buchanan had permitted Southern occupation of the great majority of the Federal forts, arsenals, navy yards, and custom houses within seceded areas. In this respect secessionists, instead of having a cause of complaint, achieved an easy success far beyond what might have been reasonably expected. Cards were placed in their hands. The list of the forts and places seized before Lincoln took hold is much too long to be given here, but any student of the period will find the list full of interest.[1] To mention but one aspect of this situation under Buchanan, the Federal military force then available was entirely inadequate to garrison the forts. To have attempted it would have exposed the weakness of the government and might thus have provoked war. Reënforcing the forts in December 1860, wrote Buchanan, "would have been little short of madness . . . with the small force at his [the President's] command. . . . Our army

[23] T. Webster to John Sherman, Philadelphia, Feb. 18, 1861, John Sherman MSS.

[1] As to Texas alone the list fills a closely printed page. *Offic. Rec.*, 1 ser., I, 502.

was still out of reach on the remote frontiers, and could not be withdrawn, during midwinter, in time for this military operation. . . . [T]he inhabitants on our . . . frontiers would have been . . . exposed to the . . . scalping knife of the Indians." [2]

This was the general situation, but in very few exceptional cases forts were still held. Lincoln himself referred to them as follows: "Within these States all the forts, arsenals, dockyards, custom-houses, and the like, . . . had been seized, and were held in open hostility to this government, excepting only Forts Pickens, Taylor, and Jefferson, on and near the Florida coast, and Fort Sumter, in Charleston Harbor . . . ." [3] Taylor and Jefferson were of no crisis value. Pickens was susceptible of adjustment. Sumter, on the other hand, was packed with psychological dynamite, being located in the proud port of the imperious little state that had led in secession, where coöperation of sister Southern states had been spurned and where restraint even by Confederate authorities was difficult and doubtful. Of the three forts in the harbor (Sumter, Moultrie, and Castle Pinckney), only Sumter remained in Federal hands; for on December 26, 1860, Robert Anderson, commanding harbor forces, had evacuated Moultrie and moved his force to Sumter. This was after the United States had strengthened Moultrie [4] while Sumter was yet unfinished and some of its guns unmounted. The forts were so placed, however, that Anderson thought Moultrie could be "very easily carried" if attacked,[5] while the more detached location of Sumter was considered less likely to invite attack.

Of the three men who had most to do with the removal from Moultrie, President Buchanan was a conciliatory and non-aggressive sympathizer with the South, Floyd was a Southern secretary of war at Washington, and Anderson, a Kentuckian, was above all anxious to avoid provocation and violence. South Carolina quickly seized Pinckney and Moultrie, and commissioners from that state demanded that the Federal authorities move back from Sumter to Moultrie, though on the latter fort the palmetto flag was then flying. Also they demanded complete evacuation of the harbor. Buchanan resisted these demands, and in early January he sent an unarmed merchant ship with men and munitions to strengthen the Sumter garrison. On January 9, 1861,

---

[2] Buchanan, *Mr. Buchanan's Administration,* 169. See also Crawford, *Genesis of the Civil War,* 167–168.

[3] *Works,* VI, 297–298 (July 4, 1861). [4] *Offic. Rec.,* 1 ser., I, 92. [5] *Ibid.,* 99.

this United States ship, the *Star of the West,* was fired upon by South Carolinian guns. Prior to that date South Carolina alone had seceded from the Union. This might have been considered the "first shot" of "the war," but the ship merely turned back and Buchanan preferred not to treat the incident as a provocation. From this point until Lincoln's inauguration the situation at Sumter continued with little change except that the Carolinians greatly strengthened their forces in the harbor, erecting sundry batteries in addition to the forts they had seized. Against these forces Sumter could hardly be said to have controlled the position. The main point, however, was that no Federal attack from Sumter was contemplated.

III

The Sumter pot of trouble had thus been filled before Lincoln took office and it contained the following elements: a complete impasse as to government status between Charleston-Montgomery and Washington, a trick of fate that threw the center of agitation in that part of the country that was psychologically most unstable, a trigger-like hazard that an incident might be magnified into a war, a surplus of unbending honor and legalistic logic, a shortage of statesmanship as a human art, a plethora of popular demonstrations that encouraged trouble makers and embarrassed conciliators, a time limit, and a change of administration that came at the most difficult stage of the developing quarrel. Another factor was an American democratic tradition in the direction of peaceable adjustment of internal quarrels combined with an inadequacy of standing force and a complete lack of trained reserves. This meant that the calling-out of troops would be provocative without being presently effective. As the imbroglio deepened there was a negotiation that proceeded in Washington which actually dealt with the Sumter question but which was considered irregular on one side though official on the other. There was also a looseness of official relations in the Lincoln administration which resulted in commitments—or seeming commitments—being made without regular authorization.

South Carolina first and the Confederacy later were making a demand that was logical enough to those who accepted the thesis that the Union was irrevocably dissolved and the new Southern nation already a foreign country. Lincoln had not thrown away the whole Union case by accepting this thesis; his inaugural indicated that he did not regard the government of the United States as merely that of the Northern people, but, as before, the government of the nation. The impasse was a clash of complete opposites; on the plane of governmental logic the Sumter question was the whole problem of status between the United States, an established government, and that of the Confederacy, struggling for recognition.

In the main neither side actually wanted war; yet vigorous American determination on both sides demanded opposite things. To the Confederacy and to South Carolina entire independence of the seceded area was a finality and the detaching of other areas an objective; to Lincoln the breaking of the Union was unthinkable. The deep South was not seeking any formula of settlement within the Union. In that area unilateral action had been taken; demands had been treated as accomplishments; *de facto* changes had been effected; full warrant was claimed for those changes; and leaders had proceeded from there as if the main question in dispute was already closed. While the upper South still thought of adjustment, it was far different with the cotton states; for them the die had been cast.

The eagerness of Charleston authorities presented difficulties at Montgomery. The Confederate Congress had resolved (February 12, 1861) to take "under its charge the questions . . . relating to the occupation of the forts, . . . [etc.]" within the seceded region,[1] but this was done over the protest of South Carolina, whose governor at once stated: ". . . it is due to us . . . to get possession of Sumter at a period not beyond the fourth [of March]." [2] He informed Montgomery that the "independence of the State [this was after South Carolina had joined in launching the Confederacy] carrie[d] necessarily with it the right to reduce Fort Sumter" and that soon "arrangements" would be completed "for its certain and speedy reduction." "The right to do so," he said, "has been considered the right of the State" and circumstances "remitted her to the necessity of employing force to obtain" that object. "Mr. Lincoln," said Governor Pickens, "can not do more . . . than Mr. Buchanan has done. . . . If war can be averted, it will be by making the capture of Fort Sumter a fact

[1] *Journal*, Confed. Cong., I, 47.
[2] *Ibid.*, 49.

accomplished during the . . . present [Buchanan] Administration . . . ." "Mr. Lincoln may not attack, because the cause of quarrel will have been . . . past." [3] It is of significance in recapitulating Governor Pickens's position to note the following points: (1) he treated the Sumter question as a problem for the state of South Carolina, rather than the Confederacy, to handle; (2) he predicted that Lincoln would not attack; (3) he asserted that South Carolina would be under the necessity of using force to take the fort; and (4) in the averting of war he gave far too little regard to restraint on the part of his own state.

It may be said that Governor Pickens had reason to believe that Lincoln would not attack, and that, from the standpoint of the state in its newly assumed status, acquisition of the fort under Buchanan was desirable. It can even be said that it would have been easier for Lincoln to have come into office with Sumter already fallen, as were nearly all the forts in the seceded area, than to be faced with the wretched problem of surrendering it under menace of civil war. Had Sumter been peacefully taken under Buchanan, all the indications are that Lincoln would not have attempted recapture. The tinderbox element at Charleston would thus have been eliminated and more time would have been allowed for cooling off, though one can only guess how far such cooling off would have promoted adjustment in terms of union. Tension at Charleston grew as March 4 approached, and the newspapers, especially the *Mercury,* were full of rumors and conjectures. While the supreme menace of a reënforcement of Sumter was harped upon, there was constant emphasis upon the alleged danger that such reënforcement would be stealthily attempted.

On March 6, 1861, Joseph Holt, for a brief time secretary of war under Lincoln (before Cameron took hold), met with Scott, Welles, and other officials, and it was then revealed that Anderson could not remain at Sumter more than six weeks longer because of insufficient food.[4] Here entered the fateful time limit; on or about April 15 Anderson's garrison would have to be fed or the fort evacuated. On March 7 President Lincoln held an anxious conference in the White House with various officials. While some urged reënforcement, it was pointed

---

[3] Governor Pickens to the President of the Confederate Provisional Congress, Feb. 13, 1861, *ibid.*, 56–58.

[4] Welles, *Diary,* I, 3–4.

out that successful resistance to attack would require a force of 20,000 at a time when the whole scattered army of the United States numbered less than 16,000. No decision was reached, but, as Welles recalled, Lincoln urged all to "forbear giving any cause of offense." [5] Knowing that he would either have to evacuate Sumter or feed the garrison, which could not be expected to rely upon the Charleston market for supplies, Lincoln on March 15 put the question of a provisioning expedition to his cabinet, requesting written opinions as to whether it was "wise to attempt" such an expedition.

Chase wrote a letter that looked both ways. He gave "an affirmative answer" to the question whether an expedition should be sent, but could not advise it if the attempt would "so inflame civil war as to involve . . . armies and the expenditure of millions . . . ." If, however, the attempt were accompanied by a statement of generous policy toward the disaffected states in harmony with the inaugural address, it seemed to Chase "highly improbable" that it would produce war.[6] Blair definitely favored the provisioning expedition and thought it "would completely demoralize the rebellion." All the others (Seward, Cameron, Welles, Smith, and Bates) emphatically counseled that the expedition would be unwise. General Scott agreed with his old Whig associate Seward, so that in mid-March Lincoln faced a situation where his army head and ministers of state, war, and navy, voted against the expedition, while his minister of finance had such doubts as to make his "affirmative" answer ineffectual. Only Blair of all the secretaries was clear-cut in advising retention of the fort,[7] but his advice hinged upon the illusion that Sumter could be "provisioned . . . with little risk."

This much appears in formal written opinions of cabinet members, all of which are readily accessible. When one gets behind the scenes via manuscript sources the near-unanimity for yielding the fort seems truly remarkable. On this matter the two "opposites," Seward and Chase, were very much alike. Seward favored conciliation, even "going in peace," and did not expect serious trouble. What is not so well known is that Chase also favored going in peace—i. e., letting the lower Southern states go their separate way. "It is true [wrote Chase

[5] *Ibid.*, I, 6.

[6] For these cabinet views, see Lincoln, *Works*, VI, 192–220.

[7] "[T]here was great opposition to any attempt at relieving Fort Sumter, and . . . Mr. Blair alone sustained the President in . . . refusing to yield . . . ." G. V. Fox, in *Offic. Rec.* (Nav.), 1 ser., IV, 247.

in 1862] that, prior to the attack on Fort Sumter, I shared a quite general opinion that . . . it would be better to allow the seven States . . . to try the experiment of a separate existence, rather than incur the evils of a bloody war . . . ." [8] On this point the elder Frank Blair wrote in 1864: "You know that while Chase was willing 'to let the South go in peace'— . . . not willing even to succor Fort Sumpter, . . . would have . . . consigned the blacks to eternal bondage & throw the Slave States out of the . . . Union that he might not have their votes to encounter, when looking to gratify his ambition by becoming President in the North, Montgomery withstood him at all points; . . . ." [9] Montgomery Blair stated that Chase openly advocated letting the South go at the time that Seward was advising the surrender of Sumter and Scott the surrender of both Pickens and Sumter. The postmaster general, holding out for firmness, nevertheless expected Sumter to be given up, and stated that he "had prepared . . . [his] resignation to be handed in in that event at the Cabinet meeting at which the President decided contrary to the opinions of all the other members . . . not to surrender that Fort." [10]

IV

Those aspects of the Sumter question that belong to the field of negotiation must now be examined. Three men (Martin J. Crawford, John Forsyth, and A. B. Roman) had been appointed in late February as commissioners from the Confederate States to the United States. Their credentials, instructions, and studiously correct diplomatic manner were all predicated on the assumption that Lincoln's Union policy had been completely defeated and that the Confederacy of the lower South was entirely and finally independent. The main subject of the commissioners' negotiation was Sumter; their instructions stated that it would be idle to talk of peaceful relations while the United States maintained a force obstructing entrance to one of the Confederacy's principal harbors. "Not even to avert war" would the Confederate government permit this; evacuation was a *sine qua*

[8] S. P. Chase to Elihu Burritt, Oct. 6, 1862, in Chase MSS., Hist. Soc. of Pa.

[9] F. P. Blair, Sr., to Simon Cameron, Silver Spring, Nov. 22, 1864, Cameron MSS. (Blair wrote this in urging his son's claims as against Chase's for appointment on the Supreme Court.)

[10] Rough draft of letter, M. Blair to President Johnson, Aug. 9, 1865, Blair MSS.

non; withdrawal of Federal troops from areas within the Confederacy was an indispensable condition.[1] To Robert Toombs, Confederate secretary of state, it seemed that the Washington government was "neither declaring war nor establishing peace," but he added that this afforded the Confederacy the advantages of both conditions and enabled them to provide for defense more expeditiously than otherwise. Hence, he said, "We . . . care little for Mr. Seward's calculations . . . ."[2] Confederates also felt that the "peace policy" of the war and state departments under Lincoln would be "beneficial to the Confederate States."[3]

On March 12 the three commissioners formally asked Seward to set a day for presenting their credentials to the President and stating the object of their mission. In this communication they referred to the Confederate States as "an independent nation, de facto and de jure, ..."[4] Seward avoided direct communication with the commissioners in order to avoid implied recognition of the Confederacy, but he managed to deal with them indirectly. He immediately wrote to Senator R. M. T. Hunter of Virginia (March 12) that he could not receive the gentlemen but had no "want of personal respect" for them.[5] Three days later he wrote a "memorandum" addressed to no specified person in which he indicated that he understood recent events in the South "very differently from the aspect in which they . . . [were] presented" by the commissioners, and pointed out that he could not "in any way admit that the so-called Confederate States constitute[d] a foreign Power . . . ."[6]

There now entered an element that was to cause endless controversy and misunderstanding—an episode of indirect and informal exchanges between the state department and the commissioners via intermediaries, especially John A. Campbell of Alabama, then a member of the Supreme Court of the United States. Campbell with his colleague Nelson talked earnestly with Seward and then reported to the commissioners the wish of Seward to preserve peace. The commissioners were given to understand in mid-March that Sumter would

---

[1] Confed. Gov't Instructions to Its Commissioners, Montgomery, Mar. 14, 1861, Pickett Papers (MSS., Lib. of Cong.).

[2] Secretary of State Robert Toombs to Confederate Commissioners, Apr. 2, 1861, *ibid.*

[3] Martin J. Crawford to Secretary Toombs, Mar. 6, 1861, *ibid.*

[4] Confederate Commissioners to Seward, Mar. 12, 1861, *ibid.*

[5] Bancroft, *Seward,* II, 112.

[6] McPherson, *Rebellion,* 108–109.

be evacuated in five days, and that Southern coöperation was desired in order to allow time for evacuation to have its beneficial effect.[7] There seems no reason for the claim that Campbell misrepresented Seward. Lincoln's so-called "premier" evidently believed that he was directing affairs, that the welfare of the country imperatively demanded avoidance of an outbreak at Sumter in order to prevent civil war, and that, considering the intentions of Montgomery and Charleston, such avoidance required Federal evacuation. Nearly the whole cabinet, as above indicated, agreed with Seward on this matter. When the five days passed and Sumter was not surrendered "as . . . promised," the commissioners again sought out Campbell, who conferred with Seward (March 21) and came back with the solemn assurance that there was no want of good faith on the part of the United States government. It was stated that governments could not move with "bank accuracy" and that delay was unavoidable without being serious. Campbell then put in writing the assurance that the United States government had no intention of hostile military action toward the Confederacy. Again on March 22 it appears that Seward, in the presence of Campbell and Nelson, gave a pledge that the vexatious fort would be given up.[8] At the same time it was indicated that the evacuation policy was exceedingly trying and was opposed by a powerful element in the North and the Republican party.[9]

There was yet another mediator, Baron de Stoeckl, the Russian minister. On March 24 Commissioner Roman conversed in French with Stoeckl, and his report confirmed the impression received from Campbell that a policy of conciliation would prevail so far as Seward was concerned. The Russian stated that Seward, whom he had just seen, had an earnest desire to preserve peace and that there would be no coercion of the South. No blockade, he said, was intended; the Confederate authorities would be permitted to collect duties at their custom houses. It was even reported by Stoeckl that Seward, while hoping the seceded states would return to the Union, was nevertheless of the opinion that if they refused to do so, they should be suffered to depart in peace and that, if sufficient time were allowed, an amicable separation could be arranged. To bring about this result Seward was reported as willing to fight the ultras of his own party.

[7] Report of commissioners to Toombs, Mar. 22, 1861, Pickett Papers.
[8] *Ibid.* [9] *Ibid.*

Stoeckl invited Roman to take a cup of tea with him on March 26 at which time Seward would drop in "by chance," Stoeckl would be compelled to go out, and the two men (Seward and Roman) would be left alone. Embarrassed, however, by the risk of newspaper publicity, Seward sent his regrets and the interview never took place.[10]

In terms of the later outcome these left-handed negotiations concerning Sumter were unfortunate. Though Lincoln himself made no promise to the commissioners that Sumter would be evacuated, they had the best reason to believe that it was the Lincoln administration which, through its secretary of state, had made a definite pledge of evacuation, for how otherwise could Seward's assurances have had any significance? In addition to the inherent difficulty of the Sumter question in all its complex relations there was thus the further difficulty of a new administration that had not found itself. The man who was directing "foreign" relations of the government was going to amazing lengths in assuming power on his own initiative, and President Lincoln had not brought administrative conduct within his control. In Southern eyes—and this included the upper as well as the lower South—the Lincoln administration began with a serious breach of faith. It is not pleasant to say this, but one is speaking here of the Southern view, and the evidence as to Seward's pledge and Southern understanding is incontrovertible. On this point the administration was not a unit nor a definite personality with one controlling will. In those March days when the Campbell interviews were proceeding, the President was feeling his way as to Sumter, but the secretary of state was assuming that the matter had been decided in the sense of his own desires.

In the vacillating period before Lincoln decided to attempt to hold Sumter there were various indications that the President himself was pondering the merits of evacuation. The importance of holding Virginia and the rest of the upper South in the Union was at stake and this required careful study. On February 4, with the Confederacy of the lower South already formed, the people of Virginia voted for the Union and against secession by electing a majority of unionists to the Richmond convention. This body was not authorized to act finally, but to consider whether secession should be adopted, subject to approval by vote in a general Virginia election. The convention as-

[10] A. B. Roman to Secretary Toombs, Mar. 25, 1861, *ibid.*

sembled at Richmond on February 13. Had it been controlled by secessionists Lincoln might have found the vitally important state across the Potomac out of the Union by the time of his inauguration. For two months the non-secession delegates at Richmond held the state in the Union, thereby performing a service of great value to Lincoln and to the cause of peace. In the March phase of the Virginia convention it was reported that an ordinance of secession could not pass that body, and that if it could have passed, it would have been defeated overwhelmingly by the people.[11] Instead of rushing into secession in the manner of the lower South, the Richmond body devoted itself to a careful study of state and federal relations, exploring methods of compromise and avoiding any action that would hamper the conciliatory efforts of the Peace Convention then in session in Washington under Virginia's sponsorship.[12]

It was realized south of the Potomac, however, that one condition was indispensable to success of Virginia unionists—the preservation of peace between Washington and the lower South. George W. Summers, prominent Union sympathizer and delegate to the Virginia convention, wrote to a Washington friend that the anti-secession members were in a majority and would have no trouble in holding Virginia in the Union "if not disturbed from abroad," but, he added, it was "of the essence . . . that a pacific course be continued"; if a collision occurred anywhere they could not answer for the result. Under the impression that Sumter was being evacuated, he stated that this "acted like a charm" and "gave us great strength." [13] There was every reason to believe that Virginia could be held in the Union if an outbreak at Sumter was avoided, and Lincoln himself so far realized this as to arrange and hold an interview with one of the unionist delegates of the Virginia convention. First seeking a consultation with George W. Summers, whom the President would have found useful as a Virginia

[11] New York *Times*, Mar. 14, 1861, p. 4, c. 1. "Until early April, nearly all of them [secessionists in the Virginia convention] realized that immediate separation was an impossibility, and that the submission of an ordinance to the people . . . would be unwise." Henry T. Shanks, *Secession Movement in Virginia, 1847–1861*, 188.

[12] As an example, the Virginia convention voted (108 to 16) to thank Senator Crittenden for his "patriotic efforts" toward "honorable adjustment." *Journal of the . . . Convention of . . . Virginia*, 96 (Mar. 11, 1861).

[13] George W. Summers to J. C. Welling, Richmond, Mar. 19, 1861, Blair MSS. Published in *Nation*, XXIX, 383–384 (1879). In a postscript Summers wrote: "What delays the removal of Major Anderson? Is there any truth in the suggestion that the thing is not to be done at all? This would ruin us."

Whig and former congressman, Lincoln accepted a substitute, John B. Baldwin, a like-minded Virginia unionist. The matter seemed almost to resolve itself into a kind of bargain—Sumter for Virginia, and Lincoln has been quoted as saying to Virginia "peace commissioners": "If you will guarantee to me the State of Virginia I shall remove the troops. A State for a fort is no bad business." [14] He might well have said four states for a fort, since the whole upper South was at stake in the Virginian sense.

Lincoln never left a statement of his consultation with Baldwin, and the somewhat labored and rationalized account by his secretaries, who show marked sarcasm toward Virginia unionism while disliking to admit that Lincoln might have yielded Sumter, is far from satisfactory.[15] Statements have been preserved, however, by Summers, Baldwin, John Minor Botts (a Virginia unionist in touch with Baldwin), and Allan B. Magruder, who served as messenger between Washington and Richmond.[16] Disregarding matters about which these accounts disagree, it appears that Lincoln, through Seward and Magruder, sought consultation with some responsible Virginia unionist, and that Summers, not wishing to leave Richmond, sent Baldwin. The conversation between Lincoln and Baldwin took place on April 4 [17] in a back room at the White House. It was secret and confidential; its main topic was Lincoln's urgent wish that the Virginia convention adjourn without passing an ordinance of secession. Baldwin stated that Lincoln received him "very cordially," that they conferred alone for an hour behind a locked door, that Lincoln feared Baldwin had come "too late," and that he asked why the Richmond convention did

[14] Lincoln is thus quoted by Schleiden, minister resident of Bremen (*Annual Report*, Am. Hist. Assoc., 1915, 211). Schleiden does not state that Lincoln said this to Baldwin specifically, and on this point Baldwin later wrote: "My . . . recollection . . . fails me if Mr. Lincoln used any such expression as that he 'would give a fort for a State any time' . . . ." Autograph statement by J. B. Baldwin, Staunton, Va., Aug. 26, 1869, from collection of Maj. Gen. S. W. Crawford, Catalogue no. 284, American Art Association sale, May 5–6, 1915. The Baldwin statement does not destroy the testimony of Schleiden, whose record is both impartial and close to the event. It seems to have been part of Baldwin's game to deny that a Virginia-Sumter bargain had ever been offered.

[15] Nicolay and Hay, *Lincoln*, III, 415–428.

[16] Baldwin's and Botts's accounts appeared as testimony before the committee on reconstruction in 1866. *House Report No. 30*, 39 Cong., 1 sess., pt. 2, 102–109, 114–123. Magruder's story appeared in the *Atl. Mo.*, XXXV, 438–445. Prior to publication Magruder wrote to J. S. Black (July 27, 1874) saying that Baldwin was his friend through A. H. H. Stuart and that he had Baldwin's full notes. J. S. Black MSS., vol. 62.

[17] *House Report No. 30*. 39 Cong., 1 sess., pt. 2, 102.

not adjourn. Did he mean sine die?, asked Baldwin. Yes, said Lincoln, sine die. To this Baldwin answered that unionists controlled the convention, that there was no need for adjournment, and that such a course would leave important matters unsettled, whereas the convention while in session could hold the state in the Union. According to Baldwin's recollection, Lincoln referred to the possibility of withdrawing from Sumter as a "military necessity," showing that such withdrawal seemed as late as April 4 to have been in the President's mind; the President strongly dissented when Baldwin predicted that the firing of a gun at Sumter would mean war and would lose the cause of Union and peace.

The main difference of evidence is on the question whether Lincoln made a "pledge" of evacuation in return for Virginia's avoidance of secession. Botts, trying to recall what Lincoln and Baldwin had told him, stated that Lincoln, anxious for peace and for keeping Virginia, made an offer to evacuate Sumter and take the chance of negotiating with the cotton states if the Union majority at Richmond would go home without passing an ordinance of secession.[18] According to Botts, Lincoln stated that Baldwin would not listen civilly to the suggestion. Baldwin, however, stated that no such pledge was made.[19] Much of Baldwin's report is made up of a kind of speech which he made to the President advising him what to do. He particularly suggested that Lincoln ought to withdraw from both Pickens and Sumter and call a national convention.

One reads of Lincoln's unsatisfactory contact with Virginia unionists with a sense of frustration. Had this contact been fully worked out at an earlier stage, the possibilities seemed highly significant, though Nicolay and Hay spurn the idea that it offered any satisfactory hope. The Baldwin interview came at a late stage in the Sumter muddle and it coincided with a conference of Northern governors at Washington whose chief object was to stiffen the President's position toward Sumter.[20] Also it came shortly after a memorable call of the older Francis P. Blair upon Lincoln. As related by W. E. Smith, Blair was told by the President (March 29) that he did not know whether he would withdraw Anderson, whereupon Blair sternly admonished the

---

[18] *Ibid.*, 114–116. Botts stated that on April 7 he talked with Lincoln concerning the Baldwin interview and that later he talked of the matter with Baldwin (*ibid.*, 114).

[19] *Ibid.*, 105.

[20] *Atl. Mo.*, XXXV, 444.

President that withdrawal would be treason, and that by such a course the administration would forfeit public confidence.[21] Taking these and other stiffening influences into account at the time of the belated Virginia negotiations, one can understand how the harassed President was swung over to the policy of provisioning Sumter; what one finds hardest to reconcile with evidence is the supposition that all the while the President was planning a war-provoking maneuver.

One will miss the point of the Sumter imbroglio if he underestimates the merits or sponsorship of the evacuation policy. If it was a military and naval question, evacuation was favored by Secretary Cameron, General Scott and other leaders of the army, and (at first) by Welles of the navy; if diplomatic, it was favored by Seward; if broadly political, the advocates of withdrawal included Douglas, Andrew Johnson, Thurlow Weed, and scores of other prominent men; if sectional, the vast border and the important upper South were overwhelmingly in favor of withdrawal.[22] Some even of the extreme antislavery radicals were ready to consent to withdrawal on the assumption that union with slaveholders was wicked and that the North would not care to fight to maintain such an unhappy connection.

V

In his study of the Sumter situation Lincoln sought information on the spot, and for this purpose several investigators were sent. Gustavus V. Fox, able assistant secretary of the navy, had a plan for relieving Sumter by running the batteries with steamers at night; partly to ascertain the practicability of this plan, Lincoln consented to a visit which Fox made to Charleston in March, arriving on March 21. Fox met Governor Pickens, visited Sumter, and conferred with Anderson, finding repeated indications that South Carolinians expected evacuation. He found the garrison short of supplies, and "it was agreed that . . . [he] might report that the 15th of April at noon would be the period" beyond which the fort could not be held "unless supplies were furnished."[1] He studied conditions at Sumter without making any

[21] Smith, *Blair Family*, II, 9–10.

[22] John M. Harlan of Frankfort, Kentucky, wrote on March 11, 1861, to Joseph Holt that immediate Federal withdrawal from Pickens and Sumter would kill secession in Kentucky and the upper South, adding that the great worry in the border area was that the Lincoln government would attempt "coercion." Holt MSS.

[1] *Offic. Rec.* (Nav.), 1 ser., IV, 247.

arrangements with Anderson "for reenforcing or supplying the fort." Anderson seemed to doubt the success of a relief expedition, while Fox thought it would have a fair chance. On his return to Washington, Fox conferred frequently with the President and was called upon, in the presence of cabinet members, to answer military objections to his scheme.[2]

If it should turn out that a relieving expedition were to be sent, the advice of the chief naval authority who favored such an expedition would be indispensable, but other types of advice were also sought. Two other investigators, both Illinois men of Southern antecedents, had a more personal task, being expected to sound out Charlestonian sentiment. Stephen A. Hurlbut of Belvidere, Illinois, a former Charleston lawyer, visited his native city and conferred with J. L. Petigru, stout Charleston unionist, from whom he learned that attachment to the Union, "always feeble" in South Carolina, had been "extinguished and overridden." The visit of Ward Lamon of Bloomington, Illinois, was even more significant. Not only was he a close friend of Lincoln, but by birth and general temperament he had a special sympathy with the Southern point of view. No Southerner could have been more fervent in detesting abolitionists, nor, it is hoped, more profane in cursing them, than this Virginia-born westerner. In Lamon's recollections, however, edited by his daughter, it is recorded that the burly Illinoisan was insulted as the representative of the hated Lincoln and that the hostility of a crowd in a Charleston hotel was unpleasantly manifest.[3]

Arriving in Charleston on March 25, Lamon had interviews with the chief leaders, including Major Anderson, Governor Pickens, and General Beauregard. In the minds of each of these important men the President's "messenger" left the definite impression that Sumter would be evacuated. Though various sources could be cited, the whole story is contained in the following statement of Beauregard to Anderson: "Having been informed that Mr. Lamon, the authorized agent of the President of the United States, advised Governor Pickens, after his interview with you at Fort Sumter, that yourself and command would be transferred to another post in a few days, and under-

---

[2] *Ibid.*

[3] Ward H. Lamon, *Recollections of Abraham Lincoln, 1847–1865,* ed. by Dorothy Lamon, 76.

standing that you are under the impression that I intended . . . to require . . . a formal surrender . . . , I hasten to . . . inform you that our countries not being at war, . . . no such condition will be exacted of you, ..." [4] Anderson received from Lamon the same impression as did Beauregard, for he wrote on April 1 to General Lorenzo Thomas, adjutant general, that "since the return of Colonel Lamon to Washington" he had been "in daily expectation . . . of receiving orders to vacate this post . . . ." [5] Again he wrote: "The remarks made to me by Colonel Lamon, taken in connection with the tenor of newspaper articles, have induced me . . . to believe that orders would soon be issued for my abandoning this work." [6] Though Lamon's trip was an exploratory visit, it was considered more than that by some of the principals in the controversy, and it is likely that Lamon exceeded his authority. It appears that his part was badly played, but at the time the Colonel left Washington evacuation was in the air. Lincoln himself was studying its possibilities.

Amid all this tension there were three things that Lincoln did not do. (1) He did not order what would now be called mobilization, nor the remotest equivalent of it. The precautionary assembling of any force, however inadequate, for operations in the South was, in the existing military system, out of the question. The fact that military forces were not raised is, nevertheless, significant as showing not only the utter unpreparedness for war but also the unmilitaristic nature of Federal policy. The lack of peacetime armed strength was not an oversight or accident. In 1861 it was an American pattern of long standing—a pattern that called for law and order being upheld without a sizable army. In time of peace America has always, throughout its history, been unprepared for war. (2) Lincoln issued no public statements designed to inflame passion or whip up antagonism against the South. He did issue statements in the opposite sense. (3) He did not attempt to retake any of the occupied forts in the seceded portion of the South, though Union logic required this as much as secession logic required reduction or Federal abandonment of Sumter. Logic is not always wisdom.

Lincoln's attitude of mind during March gave the appearance of vacillation; rather it was that of prudent hesitation and cautious study

[4] *Offic. Rec.* 1 ser., I, 222 (Mar. 26, 1861). [5] *Ibid.*, 230. [6] *Ibid.*, 237; see also 294.

of the Sumter question. The President was working toward a decision which would partly depend on circumstances yet to develop. As his secretaries expressed it, he did not deem it prudent to order the expedition, nor did his "sense of duty permit him entirely to abandon it." [7] There is no proof that his March attitude involved any intention to send an expedition to Sumter in expectation and acceptance of war, or with the purpose of deliberately maneuvering the South into firing the first shot. Avoidance of trouble while in some way maintaining Federal authority was his chief concern. That Lincoln weighed and tested the possibility of evacuating Sumter is now clear, and in this connection the relation between Fort Pickens and Fort Sumter attracted his particular attention.

What emerged from the President's study of the question was a decision to arrange for two expeditions, but their purposes and orders were dissimilar. Properly deeming Pensacola a less emotional and explosive area than Charleston, Lincoln moved for an expedition with definite reënforcing orders to Pickens, while for Sumter he planned a tentative expedition to be "used, or not, according to circumstances." [8] One expedition was positive, the other provisional. The fundamental decision of the President was not that Sumter could not possibly be abandoned. Feeling that an abandonment of Sumter "under the [existing] circumstances" would be "ruinous" because it would "not be fully understood" and would be "construed as a part of a voluntary policy," Lincoln nevertheless felt that Pickens might be reënforced as "a clear indication of policy" and that (in his own words) this would "better enable the country to accept the evacuation of Fort Sumter as a military necessity." [9]

On March 12 [10] Lincoln's direct orders were sent to reënforce Pickens without an "if." [11] Maintaining Federal authority there, he would feel that evacuation of Sumter could better be endured. On this matter, as on about everything else in regard to "the forts," the President's plans went wrong. There had been a quasi-truce under

---

[7] Nicolay and Hay, *Lincoln*, III, 388. [8] *Works*, VI, 302 (July 4, 1861).

[9] *Ibid.*, VI, 301 (July 4, 1861).

[10] Lincoln's order was issued through E. D. Townsend, assistant adjutant general, to Captain I. Vogdes, army officer on board the *Brooklyn*, then off Pensacola. *Offic. Rec.* (Nav.) 1 ser., IV, 90.

[11] No such orders were ever sent as to Sumter.

Buchanan which involved a Federal promise not to reënforce Pickens in return for a Florida promise not to attack.[12] The Lincoln administration had only "vague and uncertain rumors" concerning this "*quasi* armistice," [13] to which it was not a party, and did not consider it an official agreement of binding force after March 4; but Captain Vogdes, under Lincoln's orders to reënforce Pickens, was prevented from doing so by Captain Adams of the *Sabine,* to whom the troops had been transferred, Adams's reason being the truce, and what he considered insufficiency of orders for the undertaking.[14] Thus the informal truce arranged under Buchanan did tie Lincoln's hands, and the peremptory order to reënforce the Pickens garrison was not carried out. But Pickens and Sumter were related parts of Lincoln's policy concerning "the forts." The Sumter expedition was not a single item in the picture; it belonged to a combination of which the Florida situation was an essential part. Had Pickens been reënforced, we have Lincoln's own word for believing that his mind was ready to avoid using the tentative Sumter expedition, which did not sail till April 8–9, and which, unlike the Pickens plan, was made up at first without definite orders as to its use.

While matters were in this state (the reënforcing of Pickens having been ordered as a way of sugaring the possible evacuation of Sumter) Lincoln was advised by General Scott on March 28 that not only Sumter but Pickens also ought to be evacuated. When the President gave this information to his cabinet members at a state dinner that night, there was "blank amazement" in the group, followed by indignant denunciation on the part of Blair.[15] Next day the question of relieving Sumter was again put to the cabinet and again the answers were given in writing. Lincoln's secretarial biographers state that the former cabinet decision to evacuate was reversed,[16] but the record shows that only three of the seven secretaries (Chase, Welles, and Blair) were now unequivocally in favor of sending an expedition to Sumter.

---

[12] Under Buchanan a kind of "agreement" had been entered into between the United States government and that of Florida (through Senator S. R. Mallory and Colonel William H. Chase, commanding Florida forces). As late as April 1 Captain H. A. Adams wrote to Secretary Welles: "This agreement binds us not to reenforce Fort Pickens unless it shall be attacked or threatened. It binds them not to attack it unless we should attempt to reenforce it." *Offic. Rec.* (Nav.), 1 ser., IV, 110.

[13] *Works,* VI, 302 (July 4, 1861).

[14] *Offic. Rec.* (Nav.), 1 ser., IV, 110.

[15] Nicolay and Hay, *Lincoln,* III, 394–395; *Offic. Rec.,* 1 ser., I, 200–201.

[16] Nicolay and Hay, *Lincoln,* III, 429–433.

Seward and Smith definitely opposed it, while Bates contributed the illuminating advice that Sumter ought to be either evacuated or relieved! [17] Cameron gave no written advice at all. It does not appear in any case that Lincoln's action depended upon cabinet advice, but the consultation of the cabinet marks the end of March as a kind of crisis in Lincoln's own mind on this fearfully vexing subject. Nicolay and Hay state that on the night of March 28 Lincoln's eyes did not close in sleep.[18]

VI

As the fateful month of April 1861 opened, two expeditions, both army undertakings with naval coöperation, were being prepared, but orders and purposes as to the expeditions differed. Colonel Harvey Brown was put in command of an expedition "to reenforce and hold Fort Pickens" and was to "proceed with the least possible delay to that place . . . ." [1] The Pickens reënforcement was thus not allowed to depend upon the earlier order to Vogdes from whom no word had come. Sumter plans and orders were in very different terms. Instead of an expedition to move at once with orders to reënforce, Lincoln's order was "that an expediton . . . be got ready to sail" by April 6.[2] In the case of each expedition there was not merely one order, but a series of orders, since military and naval coöperation involved a number of officers and vessels. In these collateral orders as of April 1 the Pickens expedition was directed to proceed and to act for the reenforcement of the fort, while the ships meant for Sumter were given no positive orders to reënforce nor even to sail, but were directed to be "in readiness for sea service." [3] On March 30 the assistant secretary of the navy, Gustavus V. Fox, was sent to New York "with verbal instructions to prepare for the voyage, but to make no binding engagements." [4] To put it briefly, one expedition was *sent;* the other was *prepared.* One was definitive, the other tentative.

Not until April 6 did the Lincoln administration learn that the Vogdes order to reënforce Pickens (the order of March 12 which Lincoln had considered vital in his plans) had not been carried out.[5] If

---

[17] *Works,* VI, 227–231 (Mar. 29, 1861). [18] Nicolay and Hay, *Lincoln,* III, 395.
[1] *Offic. Rec.* (Nav.), 1 ser., IV, 107. [2] *Ibid.,* 227. [3] *Ibid.,* 228. [4] *Ibid.,* 248.
[5] Nicolay and Hay, *Lincoln,* IV, 7.

one follows Lincoln's own reasoning it appears that this put a new face on the Sumter plans.[6] The point was that Lincoln was reluctant to evacuate Sumter unless Federal authority could somehow be upheld in terms of his inaugural address, which he thought might have been done by a reënforcement of Pickens; but the news of April 6 now made it impossible to achieve a reënforcement of the Florida fort in time to offset the Sumter situation, since the deadline for withdrawing or feeding the garrison was fast approaching. Part of the difficulty was that plans and orders had to be prepared some days in advance of the actual sailing of an expedition to proceed from New York with ships that were yet to be put into commission, which meant manning, fueling, stocking, equipping, and recalling officers on leave. Even if an expedition was tentative, elaborate preliminary preparations had to be made.

Fox stated that on April 4 the President "said that he had decided to let the expedition go." [7] At that time Fox told the President that by the time he should arrive in New York he would have only nine days to prepare, sail, and reach Charleston, so that if Lincoln ever intended to avoid a decision by default he would have to act very soon. After April 4, however, there would be a short interval of several days before the expedition would actually sail, so that up to April 6 by schedule, and longer as the event proved, Lincoln could still hold back the expedition by telegraph. But it was on April 6 that the President learned that the Vogdes order to reënforce Pickens had not been executed. The predicament at this point has been stated by Lincoln himself:

> To now reinforce Fort Pickens before a crisis would be reached at Fort Sumter was impossible—rendered so by the near exhaustion of provisions in the latter-named fort. In precaution against such a conjuncture, the government had, a few days before, commenced preparing an expedition as well adapted as might be to relieve Fort Sumter, which expedition was intended to be ultimately used, or not, according to circumstances. The strongest anticipated case for using it was now presented, and it was resolved to send it forward.[8]

If the Sumter expedition had not been sent, could Lincoln have worried along with the sectional problem; rather, could he have

---

[6] *Works*, VI, 300–304 (July 4, 1861).

[7] *Offic. Rec.* (Nav.), 1 ser., IV, 248.

[8] *Works*, VI, 302 (July 4, 1861).

solved it in the Union sense? Could ballots, in the face of the spirited Southern movement, seemingly so irrevocable, have given the answer, as the President himself suggested? It was this question which gave significance to Lincoln's careful consideration of contingencies before he acted—contingencies or circumstances under which Sumter might have been surrendered without loss of face. Not only did this difficult conjecture confront Lincoln; he was also confronted by fortuitous circumstance in the exhaustion of supplies at Sumter. Still another fortuitous circumstance arose in the unexpected non-compliance with his Pickens orders. Transition from hesitation to decision was thus partly a matter of what went on in Lincoln's mind, and partly a matter of events beyond his control.

April 6 would seem to have been the key-date of this transition. It is true, as above stated, that some of Lincoln's preparatory orders for the Sumter matter were issued on April 4, but more significant orders were issued on the sixth, after which the act of sailing was still delayed. It was on April 6 that news came to Washington of the Pickens disappointment, requiring, as Lincoln said, a recalculation as to Sumter policy. April 6 was the date of readiness for possible sailing as indicated in Lincoln's order of March 29 when tentative Sumter preparations began. It was the date when the instruction to Anderson, telling him that an expedition would go forward, was sent by Lincoln, though it was dated April 4. It was the date of Lincoln's instructions to Chew to notify Governor Pickens that a supply fleet would be sent. It was the date beyond which vacillation as to releasing the expedition would hardly be possible because of the low condition of Anderson's supplies. Even then, it was not the date of sailings, which occurred mostly on April 8 and 9. In acting as to Sumter, Lincoln's reluctance is illustrated by his waiting not merely till the last day, but till the eleventh hour.

The reënforcement of Pickens succeeded. It was not chiefly a matter of an expedition from New York; rather it resulted from orders issued through Captain J. L. Worden and delivered on April 12. In obedience to these orders a reënforcement was achieved at once (April 12);[9] it was followed by a further reënforcement which brought the force at Pickens up to 1100 men. The unprovocative strengthening of the fort was accomplished "without the firing of a gun, or the spilling of

[9] *Offic. Rec.* (Nav.), 1 ser., IV, 115; Nicolay and Hay, *Lincoln*, IV, 17.

one drop of blood." [10] This showed that such a thing could be peaceably done. At Pickens as well as Sumter Union efforts were nonaggressive. Colonel Harvey Brown, U. S. A., informed General Braxton Bragg, C. S. A., that he would hold himself on the defensive.[11]

The Sumter expedition, when at last it was released, had even yet no peremptory orders to reënforce. The primary object of the undertaking was to provision Sumter, merely to avoid withdrawal by delivering food to the garrison. If the authorities at Charleston had permitted the fort to be supplied, so read Welles's instructions, no further service was to have been required of the vessels. Only in case of attack by the other side was the expedition under orders to attempt to place additional troops in the garrison.[12] To underline the element of nonaggression Lincoln took from it any aspect of hostile surprise by sending his own messenger, R. S. Chew (a clerk in the state department), to Governor Pickens of South Carolina, notifying that official that an attempt would be made "to supply Fort Sumter with provisions only; and that, if such attempt . . . [were] not resisted, no effort to throw in men, arms, or ammunition . . . [would] be made without further notice, or in case of an attack upon the fort." [13] The date of the instructions to Chew, drafted by Lincoln and signed by the secretary of war, was April 6; the order was to deliver the written message by personal interview with Pickens; the interview took place on April 8.[14]

Provisioning was to be attempted only if Major Anderson's flag was flying over the fort, the major being authorized to capitulate if that should in his judgment be necessary. The authorization of capitulation to avoid bloodshed (the opposite of successful reënforcement) was yet another indication of a non-violent enterprise on the part of the President, whose attention, at the trying moment of sending the expedition, had been given not to the details of a possible military

---

[10] N. Y. *Tribune*, May 2, 1861, p. 8, c. 1; Moore, *Rebellion Record* (Docs.), I, 162–163. Throughout the Civil War the Union flag remained at Pickens.

[11] *Offic. Rec.* (Nav.), 1 ser., IV, 129, 138.

[12] "The primary object of the expedition is to provision Fort Sumter . . . . Should the authorities at Charleston permit the fort to be supplied, no further . . . service will be required . . . , and . . . [the ships] will return to New York and . . . Washington." Naval order to Captain Mercer, *ibid.*, 235. On the purpose of the expedition, see also *ibid.*, 232, 234; Lincoln *Works*, VI, 302 (July 4, 1861). "Gov. Pickens was formerly [*sic*] notified that . . . our only object was to supply our men with food." Caleb B. Smith to R. W. Thompson, Washington, Apr. 16, 1861, MS., Lincoln National Life Foundation, Fort Wayne, Ind.

[13] *Works*, VI, 241 (April 6, 1861).

[14] *Offic. Rec.*, 1 ser., I, 251.

operation by an utterly inadequate garrison, but to a set of plans and circumstances by which such an operation could be avoided, the fort being peaceably held on the basis of assurances communicated with great care and deliberation to Charleston. The thing expected of Anderson was to hold out if possible till food should arrive, to give as much resistance as military pride and judgment required, and if necessary to capitulate on honorable terms.[15]

VII

Among the extraordinary features of the Sumter episode was an amazing muddle in regard to one warship, the *Powhatan*. Secretary Welles, whose interest was in the naval aspects of the Sumter enterprise while Seward's thought was concentrated on the Pickens fleet, gave orders that the *Powhatan,* commanded by Captain Mercer, be made the flagship of the Sumter expedition. The President gave his approval to instructions to Mercer, signed by Welles, to that effect. In direct conflict, Seward *in the President's name* had ordered David D. Porter to take over the *Powhatan* and attach it to Seward's specialty, the Pickens expedition. The overworked President was giving more attention to the Charleston aspects of the expedition (making sure that it should not bear the aspect of menace or aggression) than to the New York details, and it came about that he signed the Seward order without realizing specifically what was involved. When the flat conflict of the Mercer and Porter orders became known, Welles and Seward made a night sortie upon Lincoln who ruled that the *Powhatan* must be restored to the Sumter expedition. When Seward objected, the President, as Welles stated, was "imperative," and ordered Seward to make the necessary change of orders. Seward then muddled the

[15] Both the instructions to Chew for the interview with Governor Pickens and those to Anderson were first drafted by Lincoln in his own hand, though issued as orders signed by Cameron. It was the duty of Captain Theodore Talbot to deliver the instructions to Anderson, but on reaching Charleston the captain was refused permission to make such delivery. Nicolay and Hay, who got behind the surface record by their use of the Lincoln papers (deposited in the Library of Congress but closed to investigators), have done a useful service by pointing out that certain of these documents were Lincoln's own autograph manuscripts. Such records in the President's hand offer mute testimony concerning Lincoln's close personal attention to those aspects of the Sumter expedition that promised avoidance of trouble by giving assurance of non-aggressive intent at Charleston. Nicolay and Hay, *Lincoln,* IV, 27–28, 34–35; *Works,* VI, 239–241 (April 4 and 6, 1861).

thing further by countermanding in his own name the former order issued in the President's name. The countermanding order instructed the bewildered Porter to turn the ship over to Mercer and to the Sumter expedition. The *Powhatan* had sailed before Seward's countermanding telegram arrived in New York, and it became necessary to send a swift steamer to overtake her. By great exertion the warship was reached, but Porter refused compliance with the amended order, claiming that it was too late and that the countermanding order was merely signed by a cabinet secretary while the earlier order giving him the *Powhatan* had been that of the President. Thus the President's instruction was disobeyed, Seward had his way, and the *Powhatan* remained detached from the Charleston-bound fleet.

The amazing nature of the administrative methods employed in this Pickens-Sumter imbroglio are revealed in the diary and manuscripts of Montgomery C. Meigs, then a captain in the regular army with engineering duties in Washington. It was Meigs whom Seward used, in a secret and underhand manner, to promote the Pickens expedition, which was in a peculiar sense Seward's own scheme. Working with Seward, Meigs on April 1 was busy all day making orders for the signature of the President. He related that he was being asked to assume command far beyond the level of his captain's rank, that Porter was "in despair" when he received the change of order above indicated, and that Meigs, taking his cue from Seward, deliberately sought to obstruct the plans of the secretary of the navy. "I took the ground," wrote Meigs, "that Capt. Mercer had been relieved by orders signed by [the] President, . . . that no man, secretary or other, had a right to take her [the *Powhatan*], and that the secretary could not do it as I was by the President made responsible and told not to let even the Secretary of the Navy know that this expedition was going on." [1] The full audacity of these statements by Meigs, prompted by Seward, can only be appreciated when one remembers what it means to have naval ships sent on an expedition without even the knowledge of the secretary of the navy, and also that "the ground" Meigs took was flatly contrary to orders peremptorily issued by President Lincoln.

The significance of this *Powhatan* muddle for a biographer of Lincoln is not alone the weakening of the Sumter expedition. The episode revealed looseness of administrative methods, meddling by

[1] *Amer. Hist. Rev.*, XXVI, 300–302.

Seward in army and navy affairs, and eagerness of that official to justify his sobriquet of "premier" by assuming functions belonging to the President. Yet it need not be concluded that Seward's motive in this affair was mere personal ambition or greed for power. He honestly believed that evacuation of Sumter was of supreme importance to the country. Up to the beginning of April there had been much in the attitude of cabinet and army officials to give a basis for expecting evacuation, while even the President had at least been contemplating it. Coupled with a conviction as to the wisdom or necessity of evacuation was the "premier's" belief in his own ability to bring it about. Behind the scenes in this critical April, Lincoln had to struggle with Seward's complacent assumption of control. Even after making decisions, the President could not always know that his authority would be respected.[2]

Lincoln's notification to Governor Pickens of the intention to provision Sumter caused anxious consultation and some delay at Montgomery, but on the tenth Beauregard, Confederate commander at Charleston, was instructed to demand evacuation of Fort Sumter, and if that was refused, to "reduce it." [3] The communication of President Lincoln to Governor Pickens, wrote S. W. Crawford, "precipitated the issue." [4] In other words, from the standpoint of Charleston and Montgomery, where Southern independent sovereignty was considered final and dissolution of the Union a *fait accompli,* the sending of an expedition, though only to feed the garrison, left no choice but force to resist what was deemed invasion. On the 11th Beauregard's demand for surrender was conveyed by three officers to Anderson, who made the formal written reply that the demand was one with which his sense of honor prevented compliance. He added orally and informally, however, that he would await the first shot and that in any case, if not attacked, he would soon be starved out.[5]

Again on April 11 Montgomery was consulted, and orders came

---

[2] Seward's April daring is treated in vol. II, 29–31. Narratives and sources for the *Powhatan* muddle are found in *Offic. Rec.,* 1 ser., I; *Offic. Rec.* (Nav.), 1 ser., IV, especially 229–240; Welles, *Diary,* I, 21–28; Bancroft, *Seward,* II, 139–149; Welles MSS.; Nicolay and Hay, *Lincoln,* IV, ch. 1; "General M. C. Meigs on the Conduct of the Civil War," *Amer. Hist. Rev.,* XXVI, 285–303 (1921); S. W. Crawford, *Genesis of the Civil War,* 409 ff.

[3] Order of L. P. Walker, Confederate secretary of war, April 10, 1861; in Crawford, *Genesis,* 421; *Offic. Rec.* 1 ser. I, 297.

[4] Crawford, *Genesis,* 422.

[5] *Ibid.,* 423–424.

to withhold bombardment if Anderson would promise not to attack and to evacuate by a definite date, otherwise to "reduce the fort";[6] again a boat carried officers to Sumter (this being the night of April 11–12), and Anderson answered that he would evacuate Sumter by noon of the 15th and would not in the meantime fire upon Confederate forces unless attacked. He added, however, that evacuation was subject to the condition of receiving no "controlling instructions from . . . [his] Government or additional supplies."[7] Here was Anderson's conditional prediction of evacuation; here was his renewed offer not to attack. Could it have been taken as a basis for avoiding Confederate assault? The main responsibility in answering this question was with the Montgomery authorities, though in their decisions they could not ignore the position of the state of South Carolina and of Governor Pickens. Within the pattern of instructions from Montgomery the command at Charleston was that of Beauregard. Within this pattern also, certain last-minute matters were handled—perhaps "decided" is too strong a word—by the men who went on that night boat to Sumter. The function of these three Confederate messenger-aides (A. R. Chisolm, Stephen D. Lee, and James Chesnut, Jr.) was to visit Sumter, present to Anderson the Confederate demand for evacuation, and obtain his reply. Directly upon getting his reply, the purport of which has been noted, these aides (at 3:20 a. m., April 12) served notice on Anderson that Beauregard would "open the fire . . . on Fort Sumter" in one hour.[8] The notice of the aides was written at Fort Sumter and presented to Anderson without having been referred back to Charleston, but in this they considered that they were acting in conformity with their instructions from Beauregard who in turn was carrying out the will of the Montgomery authorities.

Among the slightly known documents of history is a manuscript journal by one of these aides, A. R. Chisolm.[9] He mentions various visits under flag of truce by Confederate officers to Sumter, characterized by military correctness and courtesy. When on the 11th the

---

[6] Order of Secretary Walker, April 11, 1861, *Offic. Rec.* 1 ser. I, 301. Confederate orders kept constantly emphasizing the condition that there be no attack upon Charleston from Sumter at a time when United States authorities had no intention of attacking.

[7] *Ibid.*, 1 ser., I, 14. [8] *Ibid.*

[9] This Chisolm manuscript was unknown to the author until recently. For a copy he is indebted to Mr. Vernon Munroe of New York City.

aides presented a note "demanding the surrender of Fort Sumter," Major Anderson "showed a great deal of feeling and stated that if we had not made the demand he would have been starved out in a few days." On hearing Anderson's answer, Beauregard sent the men back that same night; Anderson, wrote Chisolm, then told them that "if his flag was fired on again he should . . . open on our Batteries." [10] Chisolm added that this answer was not "satisfactory," that it was "discretionary" with the aides what to do next, and that "we informed him that in one hour . . . our Batteries would open fire." "The Major was very much affected and shoock [*sic*] us warmly by the hand and said he hoped if we did not meet again in this world we would in the better one." The Southern officers immediately proceeded to Fort Johnson and gave the firing order, which began with the discharge of the signal mortar at 4:30.[11]

From a boat in the harbor the aides "saw the red ball scribe a semicircle and explode immediately over the Fort." [12] At the moment they were on their way to report to Beauregard's headquarters.

Following the signal shot from Fort Johnson [13] there ensued a general intense bombardment from various forts and batteries in the harbor. For over thirty hours Anderson defended Sumter, by which time great damage had been done; then (April 13) he submitted to Beauregard's terms of evacuation, at which point Confederate officers concerned themselves with generous assistance to Anderson and his men. It is worth noting that Beauregard had been a pupil of Anderson in West Point days.[14] A poignant note in the whole Sumter in-

---

[10] This statement that if attacked he would fire back is mentioned by Chisolm as the "unsatisfactory" part, though, as shown above, the major's reply contained other elements. Essentially, the unsatisfactory matters in Confederate eyes were Anderson's refusal to surrender, and the knowledge that a relieving fleet was arriving. Chisolm MS. (see preceding note).

[11] *Ibid.* It is of interest to note the reference to the "discretionary" authority of the officers who issued the firing order on this fateful night. It is confirmed in the Chisolm narrative that the aides themselves, without referring the matter to headquarters, drew up the final reply to Anderson telling that firing would begin. This, he wrote, was done "in about five minutes . . . Col. Chesnut dictating Capt. Lee writing and I copying . . . ."

[12] *Ibid.*

[13] Crawford, *Genesis,* 427. The shell fired from Fort Johnson was a signal shot; the traditional "first shot" was fired by the aged Edmund Ruffin of Virginia from a battery on Morris Island. *Battles and Leaders of the Civil War,* I, 47.

[14] Anderson was an instructor of artillery at West Point from 1835 to 1837; Beauregard attended the Military Academy from 1834 to 1838. *Biographical Register . . . of the U. S. Military Academy,* I, 277; *Register of the Officers and Cadets of the U. S. Military Academy . . .* June, 1837, pp. 4, 9.

cident was the sense of brotherhood in military service and of honor among officers as between Northern and Southern army men thrust into antagonistic duties. On Sunday afternoon, April 14, the major marched out "with colors flying and drums beating, bringing away company and private property, and saluting . . . [his] flag with fifty guns." [15]

Though no use of Sumter for a Federal attack had been contemplated, the superiority of Confederate attacking power demonstrated that the Sumter menace had been overstated. The provisioning expedition had done nothing to assist Anderson. To have given such assistance would have been very difficult in view of the formidable Southern forces in Charleston Harbor. The little fleet was not equipped or designed as an adequate force to hold the one remaining Federal fort in the harbor against Southern attack. Landing of food was its main object; success in this object was, from the Lincoln standpoint, conditional upon the Southerners' taking the President's declaration of non-aggression at its face value. Even then, the problem of a broken Union was still to be solved. Thus Sumter was not in fact relieved, but in the act of sending the expedition Lincoln had made a decision; he had given up the Seward type of conciliation (if it was that) which was dependent upon voluntary Federal evacuation.[16]

VIII

There have been many post mortems on the Sumter affair, some anti-Lincoln, some otherwise. In the summer of 1861 there was an outburst against one James E. Harvey, recently appointed minister to Portugal, who was worried at Lisbon by attacks at home. Harvey was a Northern journalist with friendly connections at Charleston. His offending consisted in the fact that, while the Sumter situation was developing, he had telegraphed Charleston officials advising that Sumter would be evacuated. For example, on March 11 he wired A. G.

---

[15] Crawford, *Genesis*, 449.

[16] Fox's report of the Sumter expedition and of what preceded it is found in *Offic. Rec.* (Nav.), 1 ser., IV, 245–251. The lack of help from the relieving fleet is described on p. 249, where it is stated that S. C. Rowan, commander of the *Pawnee*, for instance, indicated "that his orders required him to remain 10 miles east of the light and await the *Powhatan*, and that he was not going in there to inaugurate civil war." For Rowan's orders from Welles (one of a series for the Sumter fleet), see *ibid.*, 235–236.

Magrath, former Federal judge, that Anderson would be withdrawn. After a series of such messages he wired on April 6 that supplies were being sent, supported by a naval force to be used if the landing of supplies were resisted. When in August Harvey was severely abused for this conduct, he wrote to Cameron explaining that his humble efforts to preserve peace had never been concealed and that Cameron himself had advised him of the necessity of evacuating Sumter. When informed that six members of the cabinet, including Cameron, had favored evacuation and that such a policy had been urged by Scott and other army officials, Harvey felt justified in assuming the withdrawal to be settled. His communication of this expectation to Petigru, Magrath, and others in Charleston was "with a view of preventing the attack on Fort Sumter . . . and the inauguration of Civil War." It is revealed in this letter that Cameron had resented Lincoln's hesitation "in failing to ratify the almost unanimous opinion of his cabinet," and attributed this attitude to Blair, who, according to Cameron as quoted by Harvey, "ought never to have been brought into the Cabinet . . . ." Harvey added that his aim was to save the border states and avert war, but that his patriotic efforts were tortured into the worst of crimes. One of the things clearly indicated in the Harvey episode was the fact that the Sumter expedition at the time of sailing was no secret. Lincoln himself had already notified the Southern authorities, and plans for the expedition had been noted in the Charleston papers.[1]

As early as August 1, 1861, a theory as to Lincoln's purpose was advanced which has become familiar in recent years. This was also from Lisbon, whence John L. O'Sullivan, New York Democratic politician and supporter of lost causes, wrote to Samuel J. Tilden concerning the "strange proceedings of the Administration about Fort Sumter." O'Sullivan was convinced that it was all an "adroit manouvre . . . to draw the fire of Beauregard's batteries and . . . precipitate the attack upon Sumpter [*sic*] . . . for . . . its expected effect upon the public feeling of the North." [2]

This same theory reappears in an independent and scholarly study of the subject by Professor C. W. Ramsdell, published in 1937. The

[1] Harvey to Cameron, Lisbon, Sept. 20, 1861, Cameron MSS.; N. Y. *Times*, Mar. 30, 1861, p. 4, c. 4; *Cong. Globe*, 37 Cong., 1 sess., p. 432–433 (Aug. 3, 1861); *ibid.*, 40 Cong., 2 sess., 1308–1310, 1402–1403.

[2] J. L. O'Sullivan to S. J. Tilden, Lisbon, Aug. 1, 1861, Tilden MSS.

essence of Professor Ramsdell's thesis is a question postulated as a query that "must have" arisen in Lincoln's mind: "Could the Southerners be *induced* to attack Sumter, to assume the aggressive and thus put themselves in the wrong in the eyes of the North and of the world?" [3] In this episode Lincoln's course is compared to the alleged conduct of Bismarck in the Ems dispatch. Certain rationalizations of Lincoln's secretary-biographers (Nicolay and Hay) are produced in support of this thesis as to Lincoln's intent, as well as a fragmentary reminiscent remark attributed to Lincoln by his friend Browning. On July 3 Browning recorded in his diary that he had talked with Lincoln that night and that Lincoln spoke thus as to Sumter: "The plan [sending supplies] succeeded. They attacked Sumter—it fell, and thus, did more service than it otherwise could." [4]

If this remark by Lincoln nearly three months after the event was correctly quoted and if it meant a deliberate maneuver to cause the South to fire the first shot, it is, as to Lincoln's motive, unsupported by contemporary evidence of March and April, 1861. It is significant that when two expeditions were preparing, the one that was given orders to sail and act was directed to that fort at which Southern attack was *not expected* (Pickens), while the one made "ready" in a tentative sense was concerned with the fort where trouble was more likely. The purpose of the Sumter expedition when sent was merely to maintain the status quo as nearly as possible by giving food to the garrison. Only in case of Southern attack was there to be a forcible effort to land troops. The nature of the announcement of the expedition to Southern authorities should also be noted. Had the purpose been to trick the South into firing the first shot, a leakage of information as to a supposedly secret expedition with hints as to hostile intent would have served better. Instead of this there was an official notification with emphasis upon non-hostile intent and with a pledge not to reënforce unless attacked. It would be going very far indeed to imply that this emphasis was insincere. Lincoln's note to Governor Pickens did not read like the message of a leader trying to induce the other side to make an assault, nor did his actions and orders in April, taken in their

[3] C. W. Ramsdell, in *Jour. of So. Hist.*, III, 272 (Aug., 1937). For the whole article, an able review of the Sumter imbroglio, see *ibid.*, 259–288. The idea that Lincoln meant deliberately to maneuver the Southerners into firing the first shot also appears in Edgar Lee Masters, *Lincoln the Man*, 391.

[4] Browning, *Diary*, I, 476 (July 3, 1861).

setting and without reading meanings back into them, indicate any such intention.

If conjecture as to Lincoln's purpose is to be reduced to a hypothetical question, it might be worded thus: Could Lincoln, after pondering evacuation and reluctantly reaching the point of sending the expedition to Sumter, have determined to manage the expedition in such a way as to avoid hostile provocation? If it were desirable to advance any thesis as to intent, an affirmative answer to this question might become a pattern into which authentic evidence of March and April could be fitted more validly than into the provocation pattern. When Lincoln sent the Sumter expedition he was not putting the country on a basis of war expectancy. His cryptic remark to Browning, assuming it to be properly and fully recorded, is only part of a conversation in which the President is also quoted as saying that "all the troubles and anxieties of his life had not equalled" those which preceded the fall of Sumter, also that it was he himself who "proposed sending supplies, *without* [5] an attempt to reinforce [,] giving notice of the fact to Gov Pickins [*sic*] of S. C." [6] Sending food, avoiding reenforcement, giving notice—such was the nature of Lincoln's plan as revealed in that very Browning record which has been quoted against him! Lincoln is quoted as saying that the plan succeeded. What this meant, if he said it, is not clear, but at least the United States had not bunglingly thrown the switch.

Whether Lincoln showed supreme wisdom in sending the Sumter expedition against the judgment of important advisers need not be argued in these pages. In the upper South, as will be seen in the next chapter, the sequel of the Sumter outbreak was most unfortunate to the Union cause. It is more to the point to appreciate the difficulty of Lincoln's task, and to note that feeding the garrison was not considered by him to be incompatible with a continuation of peace. It is easier now to say that Lincoln misread the probable Charleston and Montgomery reaction than to have known for a certainty, before the event, that the President's efforts to avert a hostile reaction would fail. Nor can one find sufficient evidence to conclude that these efforts were insincere and that Lincoln was descending to a mere trick. One must distinguish between the intent of the President's Sumter move and its effect—or, more correctly, the effect of the firing upon the fort.

[5] Author's italics.

[6] Browning, *Diary*, I, 476.

On July 4, 1861, Lincoln addressed Congress with a message in which he indicated something very different from deliberate hostile provocation. It is true that public papers of Presidents do not always give the last word as to motives, and the question arises whether Lincoln's message may be interpreted as rationalization after the event, but the Browning conversation (even if correctly reported) could also be so interpreted. So far as the conversation conflicts with the message on the disputed question of Lincoln's purpose, the message has the better corroboration in the March-April record. The Baldwin interview on April 4, for example, reveals Lincoln as seeking to avoid, not provoke, violence. The whole March-April story—Lincoln's orders and instructions, his conversations with Baldwin and Botts, his delay in sending the expedition, his notification to South Carolina, his non-aggressiveness in the final phase, his adherence to inaugural declarations in which avoidance of bloodshed was emphatically stressed, his studious distinction between Pensacola and Charleston, and his denial that provisioning Sumter would mean war [7]—are facts which the doubtful remark to Browning is inadequate to refute.

Lincoln was talking in familiar terms, while Montgomery and Charleston were speaking a novel language of changed allegiance, consummated dissolution of the Union, and rival federal authority in the lower South, where states other than the seven seceded ones were regarded as foreign nations. At times the new terminology became almost ludicrously awkward, as when a resolution was passed in the Confederate Congress "to enforce the existing revenue laws against all foreign countries, except the State of Texas." [8] That Lincoln should avoid such terminology and speak in terms of Federal authority was the thing expected of the President of the United States. Taking a completely opposite view of authority, Charleston and Montgomery spoke in terms of a dissolved union before the country had time to rub its eyes. In the face of these opposite positions Lincoln had to

[7] Lincoln does not appear to have been among those who considered war inevitable. Magruder and Baldwin testify that he rejected the idea that a Sumter expedition meant war. *Atl. Mo.*, XXXV, 443; *House Report No. 30*, 39 Cong., 1 sess., pt. 2, 104. On March 12, 1861, the Confederate commissioners wrote to Secretary Toombs that a gentleman from Louisiana talked privately with Lincoln that day and was assured by the President that there would be no war and that he, the President, was determined to keep the peace. Pickett Papers.

[8] *Journal*, Confed. Cong., I, 60 (Feb. 16, 1861).

watch his step as to concessions. His exploration of the potentialities gave him little reason to expect that withdrawal would promote restoration of seceded areas. He had already made a big concession in avoiding a retaking of fallen forts to which he considered the United States had a clear right. To go farther and even avoid keeping the few remaining forts was a bitter alternative, made no easier by the nature of Southern threats. Considering the novelty of its governmental situation, South Carolina could more easily have endured the continued retention of Fort Sumter in Federal hands than Lincoln could endure its surrender. Surrender would have involved the greater change of status. In spite of all this Lincoln examined the policy of evacuation. By his own account he contemplated it if the quiet strengthening of Pickens could have been accomplished at the time he wished; there is fairly good evidence also that he thought of it as a kind of price for Virginia's definite rejection of secession.

Circumstances failed to develop any bargain as to Virginia. The expectation as to Pickens also failed, but knowledge of its failure did not come until the wretched Sumter situation would admit of no further delay. Then the President sent ships with food to Sumter, but even yet it was known that Lincoln would make no attack. Even in the Southern view, in which the United States by preserving existing attitudes was considered the "invader" from the first instant of secession, Lincoln was no more aggressive than his predecessor. Each day of mere retention of the fort was, to Governor Pickens, an act of offense. In respect to Sumter Lincoln went no farther than Buchanan, the man who has been so roundly denounced for weakness.[9] Orders for the April expedition were no more of a challenge than orders for the *Star of the West*. Even before the sending of that ship South Carolinian language against Buchanan had been sharp and severe. In a communication directed to Buchanan himself, in which diplomacy and respect for high office might have been expected to soften language, South Carolinian commissioners referred to the President's refusal to "re-

[9] Buchanan not only approved Lincoln's policy in connection with the Sumter bombardment, but identified it with his own. "They chose to commence civil war [he wrote] & Mr. Lincoln had no alternative but to defend the country against dismemberment. I certainly should have done the same thing had they begun the war in my time: & this they well knew . . . ." Buchanan to J. S. Black, Wheatland, Mar. 4, 1862, Black MSS.

store the status you had pledged your honor to maintain," and added: "You . . . hold by force what you have obtained through our misplaced confidence . . . ." [10]

Contemporary Southern criticism represented Lincoln as an aggressor. Scurrilous newspaper abuse may be omitted, but even Jefferson Davis made it appear that the Unionists had refused a mutual agreement not to fire on either side, that the aggressive Union purpose was to place the Southern "forces at Charleston between the simultaneous fire of the fleet and the fort," and that therefore there remained no alternative but to "direct that the fort should be at once reduced." [11]

It is but a commonplace now to say that each side accused the other not only of causing but also of touching off the war, and even yet the subject is frequently discussed in these controversial terms. In addition to the familiar line of censure there is one point of criticism that appears in an almost unknown document of the time which, as it takes a different Southern tack, deserves at least a glance. In the papers of Governor Pickens [12] are letters and memoranda, from a friend in Alabama, John W. Lapsley of Selma, in which veiled references are made to a "proclamation" and an "apology" by President Lincoln, both of which were referred to as documents which the President prepared for the purpose of announcing and explaining the abandonment of the Sumter garrison. A circumstantial account is given of how printed proof sheets of these documents were discovered in the White House and indirectly, through a brother-in-law of Mrs. Lincoln, turned over to "a friend" who turned them over to Pickens's correspondent. It is alleged that the documents indicate that Lincoln intended to abandon Sumter, to proclaim this officially, and, in a sort of manifesto or apology, to justify it to the people.

The subject is too involved for full discussion here, but one comment by Lapsley may be quoted, in which he refers to "one of the foulest and wickedest plots on record," i. e., a plot "to *cause the*

---

[10] Reply of S. C. commissioners to the President, Jan. 1, 1861, *Offic. Rec.*, 1 ser., I, 123–124.

[11] Message of President Davis to the Confederate Congress, April 29, 1861, *Journal*, Confed. Cong., I, 164.

[12] John W. Lapsley to Francis W. Pickens, June 4, 1861 and July 30, 1861; Lapsley to I. W. Hayne, June 25, 1861, MSS., Duke University.

destruction of a brave and faithful garrison . . . for the *sole purpose* of exciting their whole people to a pitch of phrenzy so as to command their treasures, for the support of the vast armies they expected . . . to rally under . . . the same phrenzy, to be precipitated upon the South." From the context it appears that these words refer to Lincoln's supposed plan to abandon Sumter which is referred to as if it meant withholding help and leaving the garrison to its fate. In other words, here is a severe Southern criticism of Lincoln (on the basis of inadequately explained "documents") for allegedly doing exactly the opposite of what he did. Instead of abandoning Sumter he attempted to provision and hold it. Had he abandoned it without such an attempt, the Lapsley assault suggests that this very abandonment would have been vigorously criticized at the South as an effort to cause a frenzy at the North, as a sacrifice of a brave garrison, and as a cause of war! Any suggestion that the withdrawal from Sumter would have been conciliatory is lacking in these documents.[13] Criticisms of this nature make it appear that anything Lincoln might have done would in some way have been attacked and misrepresented by enemies.

The sequel of the Sumter expedition, or rather of the bombardment, was so disastrous and ghastly that attacks upon Lincoln for his part in it were inevitable. It was in this light that the provocation theory, as old as 1861, originated. A careful restudy of elaborate sources, published and unpublished, for the purpose of this book, does not, in the opinion of the present writer, reveal evidence to show that Lincoln calculated in terms of a maneuver and provocation designed to produce war by a precipitated "first shot" on the other side. Still less is it tenable to assert that an unsuccessful effort to feed the garrison was *per se* the inaugurating of war; in any case the attack upon Sumter had something to do with the matter. That Lincoln, under severest pressure from Northern advisers demanding firmness, and under pledge to maintain Federal authority with no need of bloodshed, was drawn by untoward circumstances into a reluctant and non-aggressive provisioning of the Charleston fort, which he sought to control in such a way as to avoid provocation and to preserve the status quo as he

[13] Lapsley sought to have the documents published by way of a "canard" which would attribute them to a "Junius" writing at Washington. He wanted it all done with elaborate precautions to put inquirers on the wrong scent and to prevent tracing the documents to their actual source.

found it, seems the more valid conclusion.[14] That he did this after carefully testing the potentialities of evacuation, a policy which offered to his mind little in terms of Union advantage (though the upper South and border thought otherwise) seems also likely. When war came it turned out that he had kept the non-aggressive record of his government clear, which assuredly is not to his discredit; but to say that Lincoln meant that the first shot would be fired by the other side *if a first shot was fired,* is not to say that he maneuvered to have the shot fired. This distinction is fundamental.[15]

It may be fitting to close this chapter with the statement of a Virginian who had glimpses of some of the "secret history" of the time. Allan B. Magruder, concerned with the Lincoln-Baldwin interview above mentioned, disagreed with Lincoln's Sumter policy while honoring his peaceful motives. The satisfactory solution, in Magruder's view, was "withdrawal . . . from Fort Sumter and an earnest appeal to the country . . . to stand by the Union . . . and stay the mad career of secession." As to Lincoln's purpose he said: "It seems clear that Mr. Lincoln had fully resolved on the policy of peace, and did not mean to permit the war to be inaugurated, if it were possible . . . to avert that calamity. . . . All of the facts of the case go to fortify this conclusion." [16]

---

[14] In these paragraphs the subject is not discussed by way of controversy with any particular writer. Despite variance of conclusion, the author has high respect for the scholarly and unprejudiced survey by Professor Ramsdell. His study (above cited) is welcomed as a real contribution to the Lincoln and Sumter theme.

[15] The writer has attempted a rather full analysis of the problem of Lincoln and Fort Sumter in "When War Came in 1861," *Abr. Lincoln Quart.*, I, 3–42 (Mar. 1940). A strongly anti-Lincoln account of the whole subject (Sumter and Pickens) is to be found in John Shipley Tilley, *Lincoln Takes Command* (Chapel Hill, 1941).

[16] Allan B. Magruder, in *Atl. Mo.*, xxxv, 445 (1875).

CHAPTER XIII

EIGHTY DAYS

I

QUESTIONS of state for President Lincoln in the days and weeks after Sumter covered all the usual vexations of a new President displacing a rival party, magnified a thousandfold by the demands of unprecedented emergency. Merely to state the questions is something of a task. Must the Sumter incident become the appeal to arms? Had the gauntlet been thrown? Was the nation faced with the inescapable challenge that could not be ignored, the irrevocable closing of the door to compromise? Did it have to be war? Should troops be summoned?

On what ground should the summons be based, the putting down of insurrection, or war against a Southern nation? Should reliance be placed upon states—i. e., in practice upon state governors? If so, what states? Should the upper Southern states be expected to respond to a call from a President, a party, and a cause to which they did not adhere? What about Virginia, across the river from Washington? If Virginia should secede, what of the safety of the nation's capital, of the government itself? What of southern Illinois? What of Lincoln's native state, Kentucky? Would precipitate measures not drive wavering states out of the Union?

How far could the fighting spirit, whether in its ardent form or as a reluctant acceptance of war to preserve the nation, be counted on? Would sufficient men join up by choice? If not, the draft was, at the moment, beyond the sphere of practical measures. Not yet did conscription come within the implements available to an American president.

What if Maryland should resist, or balk at the passage of troops?

Was Washington thus to be cut off from the North? What of Baltimore hotheads? Should the President reason with the Maryland authorities, or should he command them? Should it be passive waiting, or action? If he acted, should he go so far as to imprison secessionists in the Maryland legislature? In the cause of liberty and the preservation of democracy, could Lincoln afford to lay himself open to the charge of dictatorship?

Should the actual raising of troops be left with the states, each governor being asked to furnish a stated number of regiments? Should the regiments be uniform? If so, on what pattern? Should it be a national army, or a hodge-podge of military units? How many troops should be called? What number from each state? Should the states bear the cost of raising, equipping, arming, paying, and transporting these regiments? If the governors balked at this, or even if they accepted it and pushed it with zeal, would this not shift too much national authority into the governors' hands and thus weaken the prestige of Washington? Since an army could not be organized overnight, could Washington keep pace with those states which became active and offered more troops than the circumlocution office knew what to do with?

War having been started, a strategic theory of the war would be imperative. The patriarchal attorney general, Edward Bates, even doubted whether war in fact ought to be waged at all. Bates proposed a plan that "would not necessarily lead to the shedding of a drop of blood," yet would be "very *coersive* [*sic*] and very promising of success." [1] Noting that Southerners were an "anomalous people," being agricultural yet unable to live on home products, he would bring them to terms by stopping the mails, closing Southern ports, guarding the Mississippi River, and enforcing a blockade that would offer the "easiest . . . and most humane method" of restraining them.[2] When a nation blunders into war, its leaders in the first phase are likely to promise painless measures, brief sacrifices, and easy victory. But this was not all: what it amounted to was that Bates even after Sumter could not stomach the idea that war was really upon the country.

If this painless theory of the war were not adopted, some military plan would have to be evolved, or rather improvised. The question of a blockade would arise in any case, and with it the danger that

[1] Bates, *Diary*, 184.

[2] *Ibid.*, 182–183.

foreign powers might differ with Washington as to international rights.[3] Should the Confederate States be regarded as a belligerent power, or should its acts of war be treated as piratical, traitorous, and insurrectionary? If the latter theory were chosen, would it be nominally maintained as a matter of status and legality, subject to Olympian revision by the Supreme Court, or would its dire effects upon human beings be envisioned and enforced? When Confederate privateers were captured, should officers and crews be hanged as pirates? What about traitors at home? Could officials of Lincoln's own government be trusted? Should government spies be at once set on foot to combat Confederate or pro-Confederate spies? Should disloyal or suspected employees be imprisoned or merely dismissed? Should arrests be arbitrary? If the slow processes of civil justice were followed, how could arrests be made in such number and with enough swiftness to sustain the government's vital activities?

But the President must not merely decide what action he ought to take; there is the further question what action he *can* take. There are laws, there are legal gaps, and there is Congress to be consulted if new laws are needed. Few American Presidents have got on well with Congress. For Lincoln the question arose, should Congress convene only by schedule? That would have postponed the next meeting to December 1861, by which time, it was devoutly hoped, the trouble would be over. A special session seemed indicated, but would such a session help or hinder a national uprising to meet the crisis? Would not too early a session force the issue in Kentucky to the detriment of the Union? When summoned, would Congress support the President and go forward with him, or would they check his further course while withholding retroactive approval of acts already accomplished?

What appointments should be made? How many major generals should New York have, and what men should be so honored? How could the President resist the pressure for appointments within his own state and among his friends? What of Benjamin F. Butler? How could he be used, yet ruin averted? (This problem, unlike some of the troops trickling in, was to stay with Lincoln "for the duration.") There was the case of General Scott, head of the meager army. He was seventy-five and could not mount a horse. Was he not too old,

[3] For a treatment of foreign affairs in the early stages of the Lincoln administration, see vol. II, 29–53.

too slow and cautious? But who should replace him, or make decisions for him? Would the army not require two heads, some kind of general in chief in the field, in addition to Scott at Washington? There were civil offices, both major and minor. What about the minister to London, to Paris, to scores of other places? And what about the postmastership at Salem, Massachusetts?

II

The firing at Sumter, whose evacuation Lincoln himself admitted to be a military necessity, was taken, whether necessarily or not, as the casting of the die, and Sunday, April 14, 1861, the time of Anderson's formal surrender, was a day of deep anxiety to Lincoln. The necessary papers were phrased on Sunday and on the next day the President issued a far reaching proclamation. There were Federal militia laws of long standing, especially an act passed under Washington (1795) under which provision was made for summoning the militia of the states into Federal service whenever the laws of the United States should be resisted by "combinations too powerful to be suppressed by the ordinary course of judicial proceedings." [1] As if with his finger on this old-time statute and in conscious imitation of similar action by Washington, Lincoln declared, not that states as such were in insurrection, but that "combinations too powerful [etc.]" existed in the states of the lower South, naming the states. In consequence, he called out the militia of the other states to the number of 75,000 "to suppress said combinations, and to cause the laws to be duly executed." For the "extraordinary occasion" he summoned Congress to meet in special session, not, as his reference to the emergency would seem to suggest, at an early date, but on July 4.[2]

This first appeal of Lincoln was greeted with a more vigorous response than some of the later calls. All over the North the air throbbed with mass meetings, rallies, cheers, resolutions, governors' proclamations, special legislative sessions, and parades with Revolutionary fife and drum. Rifle clubs and home guards were formed, arsenals seized, money subscribed, "traitors" arrested, cannon mounted, flags raised, pro-Confederate establishments attacked, companies drilled, camps formed, and the Almighty importuned to wipe the enemy from the face of the earth. So intense was the war excitement

[1] *U. S. Stat. at Large*, I, 424.

[2] *Works*, VI, 246–248.

at Boston, that, as it seemed to Edward Everett, the President might have called out 500,000 men instead of 75,000, and the response would have been equally prompt. Money, he thought, would be tendered as readily as men.[3] There were those in Boston on this fateful week-end who received the news "as a fortunate opening of a contest which . . . [had] been deemed inevitable." [4] To the New York *Times* it seemed that "a heavy burden of anxiety had been suddenly lifted" from the public mind. The "one thing needful" had happened; it was " 'the beginning of the end.' " [5] On the day of Lincoln's proclamation there was but "one sentiment," thought the *Times,* and that was standing by the government. "On every corner, . . . in every car, on board every ferry-boat, in every hotel, in the vestibule of every church, could be heard the remark: 'I am a Democrat . . . ; I voted against Lincoln, but I will stand by . . . my country when assailed . . . .' " [6] In Philadelphia there was equal excitement with keen demand for extras, but there were also "large numbers who refuse[d] . . . to believe that hostilities . . . [had] commenced." [7] Round the country the effect was galvanic: "intense excitement" at Albany where large state appropriations were at once suggested; [8] men with secession cockades chased by crowds in Baltimore; [9] troops tendered at Providence, Rhode Island, Columbus, Ohio, and elsewhere in advance of the call; "profound sensation" in Chicago; bells tolled at Quincy, Illinois, with Orville Browning refusing to believe the "story." [10]

In Washington, where pro-secession men still held office, there were fights and knockdowns. The wildest agitation prevailed, with Union men rejoicing that the issue was made at last. While General Patterson, in command of the troops that guarded the city, thought the capital safe, many feared an immediate Confederate attack while it was inadequately defended. Washington loomed as the great battleground upon which the Confederacy and Virginia would concentrate a force of 100,000 men. Even though not holding the city, Southern leaders were represented as determined that the Lincoln government should be humiliated and driven out.[11]

---

[3] Edward Everett to J. J. Crittenden, April 18, 1861, Crittenden MSS.
[4] G. S. Boutwell to Charles Sumner, April 13, 1861, Sumner MSS.
[5] New York *Times,* April 13, 1861, p. 4, c. 3.
[6] *Ibid.,* April 15, 1861, p. 8, c. 2.
[7] *Ibid.,* April 15, 1861, p. 8, cc. 5–6.
[8] *Ibid.,* April 15, 1861, p. 8, c. 5.
[9] *Ibid.,* p. 8, c. 6.
[10] Browning, *Diary,* I, 462–463.
[11] New York *Herald,* April 19, 1861, p. 6, c. 4; April 25, 1861, p. 1, c. 1.

Yet not all latitudes and corners of the nation rose with equal fervor. In a typical town of southern Illinois the sheriff's feelings were "with the South" and many of the people showed a determination to prevent the formation of companies in the county.[12] From Marion in troubled Williamson County, Illinois, came confidential word to Governor Yates that disunion feeling was promoted by disappointed politicians, including "Logan, Cunningham, Hundley, Pulley and others." These men, Yates was told, had "assisted in getting up a company for the so called 'Southern Confederacy.' "[13] Sympathizers in the region accompanied the secession company to the Ohio River and saw them safely land on the Kentucky side at Paducah to "fite" under General Pillow.[14]

Attention was concentrated upon Virginia, recognized by both sides as a key state. For Virginians the problem had been to promote conciliation and avoid an outbreak. Had this been done, it was expected that they would have been content to remain in the Union in spite of Lincoln. The Union element in the state had been strong, but, as seen in a former chapter, Lincoln's negotiations with Virginia unionists had been neither prompt nor successful. Union sentiment was of the sober, thoughtful variety, but from the noise made it would have been easy to assume that secession and war were popular. Crowds in Richmond kept up a species of secession claque while the Virginia convention deliberated, and when the telegraph carried news of the surrender of Sumter a "wild shout went up and down the streets."[15] Even ten days previous to this a Massachusetts correspondent of Sumner, visiting Richmond, noted processions of secession men marching with bands of music and gaining in numbers with each beat of the drum. It would have been hard, said this writer, for one not on the spot to understand "*the agitation,* the insane excitement" of this city, which was attributed to "the vacillating, uncertain policy

---

[12] "A Unionist" to Governor Yates, Nashville (Washington County), Illinois, April 22, 1861, Yates MSS.

[13] Patrick H. Lang, Marion (Williamson County), Illinois, to Yates, May 28, 1861, Yates MSS. This letter is significant as one of the few extant bits of specific evidence to show the anti-Union attitude of John A. Logan in these early, uncertain days of the war.

[14] Griffin Garland, Attila (Williamson County), Ill., to Governor Yates, May 29, 1861, Yates MSS.

[15] New York *Times,* April 16, 1861, p. 8, c. 1.

of Mr Lincoln." [16] The cure suggested was the adoption by Lincoln of a conciliatory policy toward the South.

On April 17 the Virginia ordinance of secession was passed (one of the most fateful events in American history), and while at the time this act was not understood to be legally binding until ratified by popular vote in a special referendum set for May 23, all the measures of Virginia's government from April 17 on were in terms of adherence to the Southern Confederacy. Indeed on May 16 James M. Mason, who had been Virginia's senator at Washington, wrote an open letter urging that Virginia was already out of the Union and that a pro-Union popular vote on the referendum would amount to betrayal and capture of thousands of soldiers from the lower South who had taken their place on Virginia soil.[17]

The reluctant action of the Old Dominion set the pattern for post-Sumter reaction throughout the upper South. By May 7 Arkansas and Tennessee had followed Virginia out of the Union. In Arkansas, by the familiar device of a "state convention," an "ordinance of secession" was passed on May 6. A different method was used in Tennessee, where the people had decisively rejected the plan to call a convention, at the same time registering their disapproval of secession by 91,803 to 24,749.[18] In direct contravention of this expressed will of the people, the legislature (May 6) framed a declaration of independence and ordinance of secession to be submitted to popular vote on June 8; then, without waiting for this action, the pro-secessionist governor, Isham G. Harris, appointed commissioners who negotiated and signed a military league with the Confederacy, whereupon the compliant legislature "ratified" this league and went so far as to offer Nashville as the capital city for the Confederate States.[19] When it came to the farce of voting on the ordinance of withdrawal (after withdrawal had been made a fact by governor and legislature) "no speeches . . . in favor of the Union were permitted" in large parts of the state.[20]

---

[16] Cornelia Walter Richards to Charles Sumner, Richmond, Virginia, April 3, 1861, Sumner MSS.

[17] Open letter by James M. Mason, Winchester, Va., May 16, 1861, McPherson, *Rebellion*, 7.

[18] James Walter Fertig, *The Secession and Reconstruction of Tennessee*, 20. The date of this election was February 9, 1861.

[19] James Welch Patton, *Unionism and Reconstruction in Tennessee, 1860–1869*, 17–19.

[20] *Offic. Rec.*, 1 ser., LII, pt. 1, 173.

Careful scholars have not regarded the popular vote of June 8 to ratify secession (108,399 to 47,223) as any genuine decision of the people of Tennessee to choose the road of disunion; [21] yet in judging of this subject the severe stresses of the post-Sumter period and the important role of West Tennessee, which was the section most similar to the dominant elements in the Old South, must be borne in mind. Tennessee did not secede till after war began. Its wish to adhere to the Union, however, was fruitless; that wish did not constitute leadership for the Union in the days of critical decision.

In North Carolina the ordinance of secession was passed without a dissenting vote, such was the prostrating effect of April events upon a state whose pre-Sumter attitude was that of resistance to secessionist pressure and preference for Union-preserving compromise.

It was evident that Lincoln's policy—inadequate conciliation, attempted provisioning of Sumter, calling out the militia of the states—had alienated the upper South; some would have said that this resulted not so much from Lincoln's deliberately chosen policy as from the action forced upon him by the course of events. However one might argue about causes, the effect was electric. At one stroke the Washington government lost four important and strategically located commonwealths whose preference for the historic relationship under the old roof had held them within the Union not only under Buchanan, but, if one may use the expression, under Seward—i. e., under the Seward-sponsored program of compromise, avoidance of outbreak, and repetition of the statesmanship of 1850.

In the election of 1860 these states had expressed their preference for the Union. When secession was in the making and the Confederacy forming, they had withheld support from a movement to dismember the nation. With eyes on the uncoercive attitude of Congress and the diplomacy of Seward, they had been led to expect that Lincoln would abandon Fort Sumter, which, they thought, could have been done without loss of face or surrender of principle.

It was not alone the expedition to Sumter and the "first shot" incident that plunged the upper South into secession. It was this, *plus* the appeal to the non-seceding states for troops to be used in "coercing"

---

[21] According to J. W. Fertig (p. 26) the people on June 8 were "no longer free to vote their sentiments." For the strong opposition to secession in East Tennessee, and the abortive effort to form a separate state, see vol. II, 14–15.

sister states. Objective historians are not agreed that Lincoln precipitated the war, but to the upper as well as the lower South it appeared that the President, having unnecessarily, as they thought, chosen a policy of force where conciliation would have worked, was the man upon whom war guilt rested.[22] In all this it was a further count against him in the eyes of the upper South that he had broken promises made through Judge Campbell to Southern negotiators that a Sumter outbreak would be averted. It is true that these negotiators had represented the seceded portion, not the upper South, and had been maneuvering wholly on the basis of a divided nation and an established Confederacy, while Virginians and their sympathizers hoped for union. It is also true, however, that upper Southern devotion to the Union was in terms of not having to fight against brethren of the lower South in order to maintain it. If it came to fighting, if North Carolinian troops would have to be used against South Carolinian neighbors, it was the parting of the ways so far as recognizing Mr. Lincoln was concerned. They might, indeed, detest the haste and precipitateness of South Carolina, and they might have little confidence in the prospect for Southern independence, but to them the day of choice was gone when Lincoln called for troops. Though their answer was in despair and gloom, it had to be an indignant negative.

Such a leader as Jonathan Worth epitomized the plight of the upper South. Worth was a high-minded moderate who had stoutly opposed secession in its earlier stages, but what Lincoln did in April was to Worth a thing for North Carolina to resent and resist. He was doing the unpardonable, seeking to stir up servile insurrection, to destroy the South, in a word to do the vile things which secessionists charged. If in so doing Lincoln had united the North, it was equally true, said Worth, that he had "certainly united North Carolina." [23]

This unity of sentiment in the states of the upper South was evident in the replies which their governors sent in response to Lincoln's requisitions for troops to put down "insurrection." The "militia . . . will not be furnished," wrote Governor Letcher of Virginia.

---

[22] What is stated here is that people in the upper South thought this. The writer by no means places war guilt upon Lincoln, as has been sufficiently indicated in the preceding chapter, but an honest account cannot ignore what the record amply shows—i. e., the resentful verdict of Virginia, North Carolina, *et al.*, that Lincoln had blundered, had precipitated war, and had betrayed Southern Union men.

[23] J. G. de R. Hamilton, *Correspondence of Jonathan Worth*, I, 150–151.

"Your object," continued Letcher, "is to subjugate the southern States . . . ." [24] Ellis of North Carolina professed to doubt the genuineness of the requisition, but stated that "if genuine" the levy of troops "for the purpose of subjugating the . . . South" was a "usurpation of power." [25] Replies from Arkansas and Tennessee were in like vein. The governor of Arkansas said the purpose was to "subjugate the Southern States" and went on to denounce Northern "mendacity and usurpation." [26] Harris of Tennessee sent a curt reply, briefest of all, stating that his state would "not furnish a single man for coercion, but fifty thousand . . . for defence . . . ." [27] Up to July 4, 1861, not one of the slave states except Delaware had supplied a regiment through regular state organization, though some privately recruited units from this area had been taken into the service. Union sentiment in that region, said Lincoln, "was nearly repressed and silenced." [28]

III

So little was the unwieldy American democracy shaped for war making in the hustling days of early recruitment that Lincoln's secretary of war was in a chronic state of being "overwhelmed" by the task of raising 75,000 three-months men among twenty-two million people. Over and over the secretary wrote that he was swamped by the throng offering their services. Often he said he could give no assurances that particular regiments would be accepted. Against the Southern charge that Lincoln planned all along to attack and subjugate them stands the patent fact of the lack of men, facilities, equipment, arms, or even military plans, suitable for so much as a mild policy of Federal defense. Congress, wrote Gideon Welles, "had been inexcusably neglectful" of preparedness, doing nothing itself and failing to confer extraordinary power upon the executive to meet the storm.[1]

It was a half-century prior to the formation of a general staff for the American army, and the unmilitary character of the Federal government in Lincoln's time is an amazing thing for a later day to con-

---

[24] McPherson, *Rebellion*, 114. [25] *Ibid.* [26] *Annual Cyclopaedia*, 1861, 23.

[27] Isham G. Harris to Simon Cameron, April 17, 1861, Misc. Papers, Dep. of State, MSS., Nat. Archives.

[28] *Works*, VI, 305 (July 4, 1861).

[1] Welles to Isaac Arnold, Nov. 27, 1872, photostat of MS., Chicago Hist. Soc.

template. Regulars constituted a mere 13,000 in April 1861, and much of this tiny force was immobilized at various and sundry "posts." What went on in late April, May, and June of 1861 was a disjointed effort to improvise a fighting force with little help from Washington. If fully told, which it cannot be here, the story would reveal spurts of activity among governors, meetings and organizations of citizens tending their services, banks and individuals offering funds (as loans), thousands of common men responding, and, through it all, cross purpose, clumsy administration, and lack of program. Three factors stand out as one makes a study of voluminous government sources: (1) haphazard reliance upon private, impulsive, uncoördinated effort, (2) state activity to the point where governors became little ministers of national defense, and (3) repeated refusal of troops on the part of Secretary Cameron. To select a few bits from Cameron's correspondence, he wrote that the "whole matter of organizing troops . . . [had] been entrusted to the Governors of the Several States," [2] that it was important for Connecticut "to reduce . . . the number [of soldiers], and in no case to exceed it," that if more had been summoned the excess should be discharged,[3] and that he was "obliged [in the case of New York] to hold up . . . acceptance of any more." [4] To an Illinois unit he wrote: ". . . it is impossible for this Department to accept the services of your Company." [5]

After four months of war Governor Yates of Illinois confessed: "I feel cramped when I am in vain begging from Washington for power to do what so evidently ought to be done." [6] When volunteer commanders urged upon him the acceptance of their commands, the President was under great pressure to satisfy them, but constant embarrassment resulted because all these matters belonged to the war department and the President could do little or nothing about them, either by seeking Cameron's coöperation or by going ahead without

[2] Cameron to J. D. Lawyer of Coxsackie, N Y., May 28, 1861, Military Book, War Office, No. 44, p. 189, War Dep. MSS., Nat. Archives. An examination of these archives shows that in the early weeks of the war Cameron frequently confessed that he was overwhelmed by the number offering their services. Often those seeking assurances from him are referred to the governors of their states.

[3] Cameron to Governor W. A. Buckingham of Connecticut, May 16, 1861, *ibid.*, vol. 44, p. 61.

[4] Cameron to Daniel S. Dickinson of Binghamton, N. Y. June 13, 1861, *ibid.*, vol. 44, p. 289.

[5] Cameron to George A. Richmond of Oconee, Ill., May 18, 1861, Yates MSS.

[6] Richard Yates to General John Pope (copy), Aug. 12, 1861, Yates MSS.

consulting him.[7] To Secretary Chase it seemed that the failures were due to the lack of "a strong young head." "Everything [he is reported to have said] goes in confused disorder. Gen. Scott gives an order, Mr. Cameron gives another. Half of both are executed, neutralizing each other." [8]

Against this backdrop it is painful to note the figure of a sorely harassed President pacing the White House floor, glancing toward the enemy on the Virginia side, hearing "feverish rumors about a meditated attack" upon Washington, and wondering whether the troops would ever come. Yet such is the picture etched by John Hay ten days after the fall of Sumter. "This has been a day of gloom and doubt," wrote Hay. On receiving soldiers from Massachuetts at the White House, Lincoln said, "I don't believe there is any North. The Seventh Regiment is a myth. R. Island is not known in our geography any longer. *You* are the only Northern realities." [9]

The picture becomes even more painful when one recalls the prodigious grief involved in getting this small trickle of soldiers through to Washington. The Massachusetts men left Boston on April 17, two days after Lincoln's call, and passed through New York and Philadelphia on the 18th. At Baltimore on the 19th a mob attacked them and a miserable street brawl resulted. Railroad cars bearing the troops had to shift between depots, the cars being drawn by horses on tracks through the streets of this highly wrought city. Though under orders to cause the minimum of annoyance, the troops had to leave the cars because of obstructions on the tracks, put there by angry citizens. Marching at double quick they were assailed with missiles and numerous pistol shots. Police, soldiers, and citizens were at once engaged in a hot battle; approximately nine citizens and four soldiers were killed, several dozen wounded. With better discipline some of the casualties among Baltimoreans might have been averted; according to their own colonel the men were "infuriated beyond control." [10] Under local police escort the troops reached their depot of departure. Arriving at Washington after their baptism of fire, they were quartered in the Senate chamber.

It would be difficult to exaggerate the startling effect of this behind-

[7] New York *Herald,* May 16, 1861, p. 1, c. 2.

[8] Tyler Dennett, ed., *Lincoln . . . in the Diaries . . . of John Hay,* 7. (Chase was so quoted by Hay.)

[9] *Ibid.,* 11.

[10] *Offic. Rec.,* 1 ser., II, 9.

the-lines conflict upon the country and especially within the capital. To Edwin M. Stanton it seemed that "no description could convey . . . the panic that prevailed . . . [in Washington] for several days after the Baltimore riot . . . ." This was increased, he said, "by reports of the trepidation of Lincoln that were circulated through the streets." He added the amazing statement that "Almost every family packed up their effects" and that women and children were sent away in great numbers. Provisions, he said, "advanced to famine prices." [11] River boats were seized for guard duty on the Potomac; buildings in Washington were barricaded; theaters were closed.[12] Through these anxious days an attack upon Washington, and a successful one at that, was feared by residents of the capital, indeed regarded as almost a certainty. Among Southerners in arms against Lincoln the "butchery" of Baltimore citizens was exaggerated and it was asserted on April 20 that Virginia authorities could put seven thousand men in Baltimore in twenty-four hours. In the opinion of a Southern railroad superintendent writing from Petersburg, Virginia, the hour of Southern opportunity had struck. "Lincoln," he wrote, "is in a trap. . . . An hour now is worth years of common fighting. One dash and Lincoln is taken, the country saved, and the leader who does it will be immortalized." [13]

Had the Confederates seized Washington, one cannot doubt that they would have found a great deal of sympathy. The capital was largely a Southern city, and even Baltimore violence met approval by some within its confines. The day after the Baltimore disturbance an anonymous letter was directed from Washington to Charles Sumner advising him never again "to come or stay in this city in *any* capacity; official or private." "To you and your coadjutors," said this writer, ". . . is this . . . people . . . indebted for the terrible events that are imminent." Asserting that the South could never be subjugated, he added: "Even the poor starved slaves . . . will join their *real* friends . . . in repelling the marauders, as they did on friday . . . at Baltimore." [14]

In an emergency loaded with a hundred pressing problems this Maryland situation demanded an amount of attention that was out of all reasonable proportion. Authorities of Maryland and Baltimore

[11] E. M. Stanton to James Buchanan, May 16, 1861, Buchanan MSS.
[12] Nicolay and Hay, *Lincoln*, IV, 140. [13] *Offic. Rec.*, 1 ser., II, 771–772.
[14] Anonymous letter to Sumner, Washington, April 20, 1861, Sumner MSS.

took the ground that movement of army units through Baltimore was "impossible" and that the arrival of further men from the eastern and northern states must be prevented as an "absolute necessity." [15] So earnest a Unionist as Reverdy Johnson told Lincoln the day after the riot that an attempt to bring troops through Maryland to Washington would crush all Union feeling in the state.[16] Railroad bridges on the approaches to Baltimore were accordingly disabled by action of the city authorities, concurred in, said the mayor, by Governor Hicks.[17] In this they professed no disloyalty to the Federal government, yet the effect of their action was, for the moment at least, to let an obstructionist mob have its way in defiance of the United States.

In the first official reaction at Washington national necessity had to bow to Baltimore reality, and a temporary *modus vivendi* was quickly arranged by which troops from the North were shunted off by other routes to avoid Baltimore altogether. Scott and Lincoln agreed to this on the urgent demand of Mayor Brown, Governor Hicks, and prominent citizens. On the 21st a body of Pennsylvania troops was halted at Cockeysville, Maryland, fourteen miles north of Baltimore. A broken bridge would have stopped them in any case, but the men were actually ordered by Secretary Cameron to return to York, Pennsylvania, because the President desired "to gratify the mayor of Baltimore, who . . . [feared] that bloodshed would . . . result from the passage through that city . . . ." [18]

The peak of Lincoln's embarrassment on this Maryland question came on Sunday, April 21, when his cabinet met, not as usual at the White House, but at the navy department. It was a day of "feverish rumors" [19] when it seemed that the capital of the United States was caught in a vise between hostile Virginia and obstructionist Maryland. A series of important orders were prepared and were on the point of being telegraphed. Then came a further shock; insurrectionists at Baltimore had seized the telegraph office. For some days Washington was cut off from communication with New York by rail, mail, and telegraph.[20]

---

[15] *Offic. Rec.*, 1 ser., II, 10.

[16] *Works*, VII, 293 (July 26, 1862); Reverdy Johnson to S. P. Chase, May 8, 1861, Chase MSS., Lib. of Cong.

[17] *Offic. Rec.*, 1 ser., II, 13.

[18] *Ibid.*, 584.

[19] Dennett, ed., *Lincoln . . . in the . . . Diaries of John Hay*, 6.

[20] *Works*, VII, 191 (May 26, 1862).

Inevitably the President's momentary yielding, designed to prevent a bad situation from becoming worse, was made to look like trepidation. In a barrage of committees and delegations, Marylanders descended upon Washington with their complaints, demands, and oracular protestations of loyalty. On April 22 a committee representing the Y. M. C. A. of Baltimore pleaded with the President to pass no more troops through Baltimore or Maryland.[21] They might as well have asked him to give up the government or to remake the face of the earth. As his statements were reported in Baltimore, Lincoln said that he must have the troops and that they had to come through Maryland, since they could not crawl under the earth, nor fly over the state. Carolinians, he pointed out, were at the moment crossing Virginia to assail him. If he yielded, he said, "there would be no Washington . . . , no Jackson . . . , no spunk in that." [22]

Sentiment in Maryland was an uneasy mixture of genuine Union loyalty, outright secessionist sympathy, willingness to recognize the Southern right to secede while avoiding secession for Maryland, distaste and revulsion toward civil war (perhaps chiefly this), and partisan resentment toward Mr. Lincoln and all his works. Admission of Southern "rights" could be expressed on a lofty basis of peace and self determination. This was the tone of that influential paper, the Baltimore *Sun,* which declared on April 22: "Maryland has no quarrel with the North, . . . ; it is . . . not her fault, if she is to be thrust into an unusual conflict which she has no disposition to seek, ... [I]t is . . . with the people to use all their influence for the promotion of peace. Let us, therefore, . . . pending the crisis, demand only the peaceful recognition of Southern rights." Five days later the *Sun* declared that, under Lincoln, the government had "become a vast consolidated despotism."

Avoiding extreme measures, Lincoln's Maryland policy accomplished the two objects sought: assertion of authority, and temporary conciliation to avert further bloodshed inside the lines. Maryland officials and self-constituted delegations were patiently received and tactfully answered. A proposal of Governor Hicks that the President should send no more troops through Maryland and should request

---

21 New York *Herald,* April 25, 1861, p. 1, c. 4.

22 Baltimore *Sun,* April 23, 1861, p. 2, c. 1. Reported also with slight differences in Nicolay and Hay, *Lincoln,* IV, 139–140.

Lord Lyons to serve "as mediator between the contending parties in our country" was diplomatically answered by Seward in the President's name with the explanation that domestic issues could not be "referred . . . to the arbitrament of a European monarchy." [23] A highway was selected which traversed Maryland while avoiding populous cities.[24] Some of the troops were carried by water to Annapolis, thence by land to Washington. Firm measures were taken to reopen broken intercourse. Bridges were repaired. Baltimore cooled off; further riots were avoided. Secessionists went South; withdrawal of the state from the Union, which would have been a supreme menace to Lincoln, was prevented. Governor Hicks, treated with friendliness and understanding of his difficult position, became a factor for loyal Unionism, and succeeded in averting that state convention which was intended as the instrument of secession. In this clearing of the air hundreds of clerks in Washington resigned; higher officials also found this a convenient moment for deciding on which side they stood.[25]

When a Baltimore committee on May 5 went so far as to ask recognition of the independence of the Confederate States, Lincoln replied in strong terms, rebuking them for laying no straw in the way of those who would capture Washington, and asserting that the right of way through Maryland would be maintained "at all hazards." [26] By the 9th of May transit through Baltimore had been reopened and a contingent of Union troops traversed the city unmolested. Less than a month after the April riot a body of Baltimoreans tendered to the secretary of war a thousand volunteers over and above the Maryland quota.[27]

All this was accomplished in spite of the bombast and aggressiveness of General B. F. Butler, who commanded for a time at Annapolis, organized an "expedition against Baltimore," seized Relay House (May 6),[28] occupied Baltimore without authority but with a characteristic blending of flamboyance and maladroitness, issued a proclamation to its people,[29] and produced a series of added irritations in

[23] *Works*, VI, 252–254 (Apr. 22, 1861). [24] *Ibid.*, 253.

[25] Nicolay and Hay, *Lincoln*, IV, 141.

[26] New York *Herald*, May 6, 1861, p. 1, c. 2; Nicolay and Hay, *Lincoln*, IV, 139–140.

[27] New York *Times*, April 16, 1861, p. 1, c. 1.

[28] In Maryland, about nine miles south of Baltimore on the road to Washington.

[29] On May 14, 1861, Winfield Scott sent the following dispatch to Butler: "Your hazardous occupation of Baltimore was . . . without my approbation. It is a Godsend that it was without conflict of arms." At 2:17 next morning came Scott's order to Butler: "Issue no more proclamations." *Offic. Rec.*, 1 ser., II, 28.

sensitive Maryland till superseded by General Banks. Thus displaced, he was praised by Lincoln, who had transferred him to a scene of new vexations at Norfolk.

IV

Amid such imbroglios Lincoln's own preferences could make no claim upon his meager twenty-four hours a day. Executive planning, formulation of policies, phrasing of important papers, and like duties, were so interrupted by official and ceremonial activities as to become almost invisible. Meetings of the cabinet were long and tedious, the secretaries emerging with jaded faces. Once a whole cabinet session seems to have been devoted to General Butler. Again, as reported, the cabinet was "engaged all day in considering promotions and new appointments in the army," with every secretary presenting "a batch of names." [1] At times the President would call in army leaders to confer with the cabinet. Rumors of cabinet differences were in frequent circulation; these were unconvincingly denied in the newspapers "on the highest authority." [2] It is now known that these differences were real and stubborn, and one may doubt whether Lincoln's official family gave him as much assistance and relief as it gave annoyance and worriment.

It was not Lincoln's habit to dodge the time-consuming and often petty occasions of ceremonial duty. When the flag was hoisted over the new general post office building, it had to be Lincoln, flanked by the cabinet, who officiated.[3] Once in mid-May 1861 he was absent from the White House nearly all day, visiting Great Falls (not an easy trip), passing secessionist pickets on the Virginia side, and reconnoitering generally in the vicinity of Washington.[4] If, instead of studio poses, "spot pictures" had been made showing the President as he spent his time, they would have shown him riding up "the Avenue" in

---

[1] New York *Herald,* May 17, 1861, p. 1, c. 1.

[2] "The assertions that the Secretaries of State and of the Navy have differed . . . are without foundation. Equally untrue are the reports . . . that the Secretary of the Treasury differs . . . from the President or other members of the Cabinet. . . . The above is predicated on information from the highest authority." New York *Tribune,* May 6, 1861, p. 5, c. 1. That these differences were only too real is now so well known as to be a commonplace.

[3] New York *Herald,* May 23, 1861, p. 1, c. 2.

[4] *Ibid.,* May 20, 1861, p. 1, c. 1; p. 4, c. 2.

an open barouche with Seward amid manifestations of popular respect, making a tour of observation down the Potomac with Seward and Weed, receiving the First Michigan regiment, exposing himself within range of "rebel" fire, greeting the Kansas "Frontier Guard" in the East Room of the White House, attending the White House funeral of Colonel Ellsworth who fell at Alexandria, visiting the Seventy-first New York to whom he made a short speech, proceeding over Long Bridge in late afternoon with infantry escort to review Union regiments on the Virginia side, appearing at the Capitol to greet and chat with privates and officers, conducting a "grand review" of the "whole Rhode Island brigade," presenting a gold watch and chain to a British ship captain for saving an American crew, or conferring with important men. An example of the latter would be Evarts, Pierrepont, and Vanderpool of New York who were reported as having conveyed to him "the attitude of the North." [5]

Though the newspapers might not know the substance of these consultations, they did know the men with whom they were held or with whom the President appeared. Repeated contact with Seward did not fail to occasion comment. Count Gurowski, a gruff Polish nobleman whose prominence as a social lion contrasted strangely with his unimportant duties in the state department, wrote: ". . . Lincoln is under the tumb [*sic*] of Seward; to a degree allmost ridiculous, Seward brings him out to take airing as were he Lincoln's nurse . . . ." [6] When the Garibaldi Guard marched ceremoniously to the White House the President received them in company with General Scott and Secretary Seward.[7] This was proper enough in view of the circumstances, but the frequency of such occasions tended to give Seward a prominence beyond other secretaries and a position of influence that steadily weakened the Lincoln administration in radical eyes.

A paradox of American democracy appeared in the constant im-

---

[5] These minor incidents are recorded in the New York *Tribune* of May 1 and May 9, 1861, and the *Herald* of the following dates: April 30, May 1, May 14, June 11, June 14, June 25.

[6] Gurowski to Sumner, May 1, 1861, Sumner MSS. Gurowski's diary reveals the quality of this eccentric, picturesque, and violent personality. For a full, documented account, see LeRoy H. Fischer, "Adam Gurowski and the American Civil War: A Radical's Record," *Bulletin*, Polish Institute of Arts and Sciences in America, I, 476–488 (April, 1943).

[7] New York *Herald*, May 31, 1861, p. 1, c. 2.

portance of two opposite factors in the social use of the Executive Mansion: it had to be democratically open to all, yet always a premium was placed upon exclusiveness when groups or individuals were recognized. It is hard to imagine Lincoln lending himself to a function that was not democratic, but news writers delighted in making these affairs seem exclusive. One read in the papers that officers of the regiments in and about Washington were disappointed that White House hospitalities had not been extended to them; [8] four days later the President gave a military reception for the officers. The public was told that this was a "brilliant affair," that the ladies present represented "the elite of Washington," and that "Mrs. Lincoln received with . . . elegance and dignity." The President was "in the best of spirits." Cadets newly graduated from West Point were in attendance, while among the "lions of the occasion" was Major Anderson, who was treated as a "special pet" of the President.[9] When it was a matter of full dress and furbelows the homespun President by no means dispensed with court etiquette. (The man of homespun background usually does not.) Presentations at levees were usually made by that swashbuckling Illinoisan, Colonel Ward Hill Lamon to the President and by some selected "dignitary" to Mrs. Lincoln.[10] The first public reception, held on April 8, 1861, proved at the same time huge and elegant. "The oldest frequenters of White House receptions declared they had never seen so many people pass through the House at any previous time, nor was it ever excelled in brilliancy." [11]

Though White House publicity was not of the "modern" sort, such publicity existed, being composed of close-up accounts of the President or explanatory statements of his policy. In late April it was conjectured that Lincoln would recognize the Confederacy. Later this was denied and it was asserted that the President was at one with the cabinet in vigorously prosecuting measures against the insurrectionary states.[12] A "gentleman, high in the confidence of the President" gave assurance that no truce, pacification or adjustment was intended until "rebellion" was crushed.[13] Southern papers, said the reporters, had no

[8] *Ibid.*, May 6, 1861, p. 1, c. 2.

[9] *Ibid.*, May 10, 1861, p. 1, c. 3.

[10] *Ibid.*, May 29, 1861, p. 1, c. 2.

[11] Virginia Kinnaird, "Mrs. Lincoln as a White House Hostess," *Papers in Ill. Hist.*, 1938, 69–70.

[12] New York *Herald*, April 25, 1861, p. 4, c. 4; April 30, 1861, p. 3, c. 4; May 16, 1861, p. 1, c. 2.

[13] New York *Tribune*, July 1, 1861, p. 5, c. 1.

basis for asserting that the correspondence of the Associated Press was directed by Lincoln.[14] Whatever the President did, or omitted to do, was "news," as when a Washington dispatch stated that pressure of duty required him to deny himself to visitors. Public business compelled him "inflexibly" to decline personal interviews, even members of Congress being refused admittance at the White House while the President's message was in preparation.[15] Journalists mentioned that the message was being prepared; having done so, some of them would make a prediction as to its content, with impressive guesses concerning the "next move" of the military forces.[16] A sizable article could be written on the hoaxes and canards that accompanied all this publicity. An example was the reported resignation of Gideon Welles from the secretaryship of the navy. This brought a letter from a citizen of Illinois who reminded Welles of the "great need for one honest man in the Cabinet" and urged him to remain as an "Argus over such aspirants to the Presidency as Mr. Cameron." [17]

Newspaper editors of the period seemed afflicted with a more or less chronic case of disgruntlement. It was reported that Greeley wanted the office of postmaster general, that Raymond spurned a consulship because he wanted the mission to Italy, that Webb aspired to be minister to England, and that even Bryant was grieved because he received no office.[18] As for Bennett, pungent wrath seemed to be his stock in trade. Whatever the cause or lack of cause, newspapers at an early stage joined in an almost concerted movement to force an overthrow or reconstruction of the cabinet. Pointing out that Lincoln was responsible to the people while the cabinet was moved by selfish motives, the *Herald* harped upon the theme of cabinet change and of "Something Wrong in High Quarters." This paper did not conceal its fear that the administration's "feeble" measures toward the "rebellion" would weaken the Union cause in European eyes.[19] Ridiculing the President's attention to office-seeking appeals, the *Times* queried:

---

[14] New York *Herald,* May 21, 1861, p. 1, c. 2.

[15] New York *Tribune,* June 1, 1861, p. 5, c. 2; June 20, 1861, p. 4, c. 6; New York *Herald,* June 22, 1861, p. 1, c. 2.

[16] New York *Herald,* May 6, 1861, p. 1, c. 1; May 31, 1861, p. 1, c. 2.

[17] George F. Wright to Gideon Welles, Springfield, Ill., July 4, 1861, Welles MSS. The final paragraphs of this letter were devoted to a request for a job in the navy department.

[18] Editorial, New York *Herald,* May 9, 1861, p. 4, c. 4.

[19] *Ibid.,* June 15, 1861, p. 4, c. 5; June 27, p. 1, c. 1.

"And if the old Whigs must not be forgotten, nor the Democrats slighted . . . , why not take equal care of Calvinists and Armenians . . . ?" [20] "It is idle," said the *Times,* "to conceal the fact that the Administration thus far has not met public expectation"; a month after Lincoln's inauguration, things were no better than when Buchanan left Washington.[21] A few weeks later the *Times* discharged an editorial blast under the caption "Wanted—A Leader!" in which it characterized the administration's record as "one continued retreat" and as having "thus far only urged [waged] war upon itself." The spirited uprising of the North was described; then in contrast the *Times* put the question, "Where is the leader of this sublime passion?" [22] Everything in the editorial indicated that to the writer's mind Lincoln was not the man.

In distributing the spoils of victory Lincoln had to recognize those who had "made" him while not wholly ignoring men of the opposite party. He had to consider geographical distribution, claims of eminence, hazards of offending whole groups, and squabbles within Republican ranks. When one adds the factors of cabinet consultation, informal nomination by congressional delegations, senate confirmation, newspaper interference, and volunteer advice, it will be seen that only a sturdy or hard-skinned President could endure the strain. The inquisitive historian, rummaging among the manuscripts and documents of the time, will hardly escape the conclusion that the search and scramble for public favors, if not the party's chief preoccupation, constituted at least the most frequent theme running through the correspondence of statesmen. Half the letters sent out by the President in the first three weeks of May 1861 and included in his collected works dealt with matters of patronage.

Selections for military appointments in the volunteer units were in practice made by governors of the states at least as high as colonelcies; for brigadier- and major-generalships the states had a voice, and state delegations in Congress assumed the function of quasi-nomination to the President. Senator Browning of Illinois wrote of a night caucus of the Illinois delegation (of senators and representatives) in Senator Trumbull's room to "agree upon Brig: Genl[s] for our State." [23] If one takes only the state of Illinois and considers officers of the rank of

---

[20] New York *Times,* April 4, 1861, p. 4, cc. 3–4.
[21] *Ibid.,* April 3, 1861, p. 4, c. 2.
[22] *Ibid.,* Apr. 25, 1861, p. 4, c. 2.
[23] Browning, *Diary,* I, 487.

general, he finds that appointments for Civil War service included one lieutenant general (Grant), ten major generals, eighteen brevet major generals, 53 brigadier generals, and 120 brevet brigadier generals. Thus it will be seen that for one state the appointments to general rank exceeded two hundred.[24] Though recommendations were handed up to him, the President had to "make" each of these appointments.

It is only by laboring through masses of contemporary correspondence that one can glimpse the intrigues and personal jealousies back of these appointments. In the case of Pope a number of bigwigs in Illinois, including Yates, Dubois, Butler, Hatch, and Trumbull, were enlisted in a movement to obtain for him one of the early brigadier generalships, with "command of this State as a separate Military Dept." [25] When, for a time, Pope was passed over though McClernand received a brigadiership, he sent a hot letter of protest to Senator Trumbull in which Pennsylvania appointments were petulantly mentioned and Lincoln was accused of having "departed from his word" as to Pope, while the "personal and political friends of Mr. Cameron" had all been "cared for." His letter went so far as to refer to Lincoln's "failure to comply with his promise." [26]

Thus one might go on from department to department and state to state, taking into view postmasterships, collectorships, marshalships, surveyorships, consulships, diplomatic appointments, et cetera. With state claims, rivalries, and party demands crowding upon him, it was a bit of luck for the President if the public welfare crept into the picture. Under such stress and strain did Lincoln man his ship, sending Charles Francis Adams to England, Cassius M. Clay to St. Petersburg, John Lothrop Motley to Vienna (after Anson Burlingame had been rejected as *persona non grata* by the Austrian government because he favored Hungarian independence), William L. Dayton as minister to Paris, John Bigelow to the important Paris consulship, Thomas H. Dudley as consul to Liverpool, Thomas Corwin to Mexico, and George Perkins Marsh, erudite Vermont Whig, as the first United States minister to the Kingdom of Italy.

---

[24] *Report of the Adj. Gen. of . . . Ill.* (revised, 1886), I, 170–173. (In 1866 Grant attained the title of general; his highest title during the war was that of lieutenant general.)

[25] John Pope to Lyman Trumbull, June 16, 1861, Trumbull MSS.

[26] *Ibid.*

V

By his emergency acts and his wide use of executive power in the months just following the outbreak of war, Lincoln set a pattern for his whole administration. It was the pattern of a President who did not as a rule depend upon, or work with, the Congress, but hewed out his own path, assumed executive power even when he questioned its legality, reached his own decisions (not without vacillation), and, on rare occasions, turned to Congress for *post facto* approval. Usually he did not even seek this ratification after the fact.

In the days of late April, May, and June of 1861, while human slaughter was deferred because neither side was in fighting fettle, Lincoln took purely executive steps of far-reaching importance. To his critics it seemed that he "started" the war; at least it was Lincoln who determined both the policy and the legal forms in which the challenge at Sumter was met. Accepting war as the consequence of the Sumter incident was the essential policy (some thought this unnecessary), while legal molds were chosen which gave the conflict, technically, the aspect of an intramural rather than an international affair. That is to say, the enemies whose challenge he met were regarded in theory, not as a foreign nation or a continuing, permanent government, but as rebellious or insurrectionary groups within the United States. In this light Lincoln's executive acts in April 1861 had at least five important aspects: (1) they inaugurated for the nation a state of war where there had been peace; (2) they set up a legal front in terms of theory and status; (3) they equally set the pattern for the President's own theory of executive measures with regard to Congress; (4) they launched a military policy (reliance upon "militia" and upon action by the states rather than upon national army expansion); (5) finally, these measures fixed the mold into which the government's policy was to be cast in its relations with foreign nations.

The proclamation of April 15 summoning the militia was followed by two proclamations (April 19 and April 27) setting on foot a blockade of Southern ports in pursuance both of United States law and international law. An order of April 27 to General Scott repeated the declaration that the business in hand was "suppressing an insurrection" and authorized a regional suspension of the habeas corpus privilege, this power to be exercised either personally by the commanding general of the whole army (Scott) or by subordinate officers where resistance might occur.[1] This action applied to the military line between Philadelphia and Washington; later (May 10) the line was extended to New York, then Florida was subjected to the suspension, and the order was given to remove suspected persons from United States forts.[2] Deeming state authorities in Missouri unreliable, the President, through the adjutant general, directed that a close watch be kept upon their activities, and that any hostile movement be put down.[3] On May 3 Lincoln made an important supplementary call for troops, summoning 42,000 volunteers to serve for three years "unless sooner discharged" (instead of three months as indicated in April), and directing that additional regiments be added to the regular army.[4] This increase of the size of the regular army by executive action without even consulting Congress was most unusual. Those who remembered the American tradition for legislative control of the military machine, and the specific constitutional provisions for congressional authority in building and paying for the army, regarded this act as a very questionable proceeding. It is doubtful whether even Lincoln's supporters would have wished it to become a precedent for later administrations. It has not so become; in this respect Lincoln's assumption of power stands by itself. There was less question of the President's act when he required all army officers, except those who had entered the service after April 1, to renew their oaths of allegiance to the United States. This action was taken amid reports of disloyalty in the service and of "plenty of spies in the very midst of the federal troops." [5]

Other emergency acts fell equally into the category of independent executive measures. A series of such steps was taken on April 21, when the President had an urgent conference with his cabinet at the Navy Office. By unanimous agreement at this conference the President directed an armed revenue cutter to operate for the protection of inbound California treasure ships.[6] Other ships were purchased or chartered by presidential direction and armed for public defense with

---

[1] *Works*, VI, 258.

[2] *Ibid.*, VI, 271.

[3] *Ibid.*, VI, 288–289 (May 27, 1861).

[4] *Ibid.*, VI, 263–265.

[5] New York *Herald*, May 11, 1861, p. 1, c. 2; May 13, 1861, p. 1, c. 2.

[6] Lincoln himself reported this conference to Congress. *Works*, VII, 190 (May 26, 1862).

special attention to the water communications of Washington. New York notables were empowered to act for the government in forwarding troops and supplies during a temporary interruption of communication between Washington and New York. Men who were not Federal officials were thus given large governmental powers, while two million dollars from the Federal treasury was advanced to a kind of informal committee of three (John A. Dix, George Opdyke, and R. M. Blatchford) who spent the money without bond and without the constitutional prerequisite of congressional appropriation. Lincoln himself stated that the civil service contained so many disloyal persons that he had to go outside the field of officialdom and confide governmental duties to chosen citizens who were "known for . . . ability, loyalty, and patriotism." [7] The sequel to this episode, coming in 1862, was to be bound up with the President's necessity of getting rid of Cameron as secretary of war. In this sequel the President gave the war secretary a foreign assignment, the House of Representatives condemned him, the Senate gave evidence of formidable opposition to him, and the Supreme Court uttered a stern rebuke concerning his methods. Lincoln, however, showed a magnanimous willingness to take the blame upon himself.[8]

VI

Lincoln's relation to Douglas, which had begun in the eighteen-thirties at Vandalia and had increased in rivalry through the decades, now reached its final phase. In the last months of his life Douglas showed a patriotic disregard of partisanship which no American leader has surpassed. In the critical days when the nation faced dissolution, men had looked to him both for avoidance of war and for preservation of national integrity. ". . . I know the hopes of many patriot hearts are looking to you to save us if possible," wrote a Vir-

---

[7] *Ibid.*, VII, 192.

[8] The unfortunate complication here was that Lincoln's assumption of emergency powers at the outset of the war was later brought into the picture by the President himself as a way of shielding Cameron even after his forced withdrawal, and as a means of magnanimously transferring blame to the President's own shoulders. Yet in reality the questionable acts were not those associated with Lincoln's emergency executive measures as such—e. g., with the New York committee of three—but with Cameron's administrative looseness. This whole matter is reserved for later treatment. See vol. II, 59–60.

ginia leader.[1] "Your friends . . . throughout the Union look again to you in this hour of need," wrote a Louisianan.[2] "You are *the* Statesman of the time," wrote another Louisiana friend; "let us have . . . the greatest speech you ever made." [3] The large vote for Douglas, both in the North and the South, had been above all pro-Union. At both extremes it was the uncompromising radicals who had opposed him most keenly. His role was thus cast for him; it was the role of conciliation, and he played it with all his skill and force. Nor should it be supposed that because secession and war occurred, Douglas's efforts had gone for naught. "I have watched your course in the Senate during the final struggle," wrote an opponent on March 7, 1861, "and . . . I am satisfied that but for you, Mason and Dixon's line wo[ul]d now be the boundary of the Southern Confederacy. I have been your political opponent but feel it to be a sacred duty to thank you for your noble & patriotic course & to assure you that this universal sentiment pervades all classes of good men in the country." [4]

Constantly Douglas was consulted; always he spoke the language of loyalty to the United States. When certain senators in March 1861 assailed Lincoln's policy as expressed in his inaugural, Douglas spoke "boldly in defense of Mr. Lincoln." [5] This was one of the most significant efforts of Douglas's life. "While I expect to oppose the Administration upon all the political issues of the day," he said, "I trust I shall never hesitate to do justice to those who, by their devotion to the Constitution and the Union, . . . love their country more than their party." Noting that Lincoln's policy would be "peaceful and not aggressive," Douglas declared that he found "much cause . . . for encouragement" in the President's inaugural.[6] When challenged in debate by Mason of Virginia, he replied that he "must refer him . . . to those who have been intrusted by the American people according to the Constitution with the decision" as to national troubles.[7] Lincoln was represented as highly "elated" because Douglas had joined in defense of his administration; this was said to be the chief topic of

---

[1] John S. Carlile to Douglas, Clarksburg, Va., December 6, 1860, Douglas MSS.
[2] A. Lafargne to Douglas, Marksville, Parish of Avoyelles, La., December 9, 1860, *ibid.*
[3] Alfred Goodwill to Douglas, Minden, La., December 18, 1860, *ibid.*
[4] Britton A. Hill to Douglas, Washington, March 7, 1861, *ibid.*
[5] Blaine, *Twenty Years of Congress*, I, 288.
[6] *Cong. Globe*, 36 Cong., 2 sess., 1438 (March 6, 1861).
[7] *Ibid.*, 36 Cong., 2 sess., 1445.

his conversation with visitors to the White House.[8]

Shortly before the outbreak at Sumter Douglas met Gideon Welles on the street and had an earnest talk with him, making it clear that he was "for the Union and would stand by the Administration . . . regardless of party." The Little Giant was greatly saddened by events. "He had tried to rally the Democracy, but the party was broken up." He considered Buchanan feeble and incompetent, had no faith in Seward, and put his trust in a kind of vague hope that Lincoln would be independent of his "premier." [9] On Sunday, April 14, the day of the formal surrender at Sumter, Douglas had an interview with President Lincoln. There are various reports of this meeting. According to the account by George Ashmun, Douglas was requested by Ashmun to go at once to the President's and make an open declaration of a determination to sustain him.

"I well remember his first reply [wrote Ashmun]: 'Mr. Lincoln has dealt hardly with me, in removing some of my friends from office, and I don't know as he wants my advice or aid.' " On persuasion, however, Douglas called on Lincoln, finding the President alone and "most cordial in his welcome." Preparing the way for friendly conversation, Lincoln drew from a drawer and read the proclamation he meant to issue next day. Rising from his chair, Douglas spoke in great earnestness, saying that he concurred in "every word" of the proclamation, except that he would have called out 200,000 men instead of 75,000. Stepping to a map in the President's room he gave strategic suggestions for the coming contest. He found Lincoln "an earnest and gratified listener," and "no two men [thought Ashmun] . . . parted that night with a more cordial feeling of a united, friendly, and patriotic purpose than Mr. Lincoln and Mr. Douglas." [10]

A statement which Douglas prepared was given to the press and was read next day all over the North: "Mr. Douglas called on the President this evening and had an interesting conversation on the present condition of the country. The substance of the conversation was that while Mr D[ouglas] was . . . opposed to the administration on all its political issues, he was prepared to sustain the President in the exercise of all his constitutional functions to preserve the

---

[8] E. M. Stanton to James Buchanan, March 12, 1861, Buchanan MSS.

[9] Welles, *Diary*, I, 32–35.

[10] Washington *Daily Morning Chronicle*, October 26, 1864, p. 2, c. 5.

Union, . . . maintain the government, and defend the Federal capital. . . . He spoke of the present and future, without reference to the past." [11]

Realizing that his service could nowhere be better performed than in vigorous support of the Union in his own state, Douglas traveled back to Illinois, made contact with many friends there, urged firm support of the Lincoln government, and delivered a notable speech before a joint session of the Illinois legislature, together with "a great audience of citizens" at Springfield on April 25.[12] Speaking as one who had "omitted no opportunity, to secure a peaceful solution of all these troubles," Douglas denounced the "[h]ostile armies . . . marching upon the Federal Capitol" to promote a "war of aggression." Deriding the alleged cause of the conflict, he declared: "For the first time in the history of this Republic, there is no prohibitory act of Congress upon the institution of slavery, anywhere within the limits of the United States." Showing that no cause for rebellion could be found either in the territorial or the fugitive-slave question, he asked: "Can any man tell me of any one act of aggression . . . since the . . . election, that justifies this violent disruption of the . . . Union?" If Breckinridge had been elected, he said, and if Republicans had rebelled against him, "you would have found me tendering my . . . energies to . . . Breckinridge to put down the Republican rebels." "The first duty of an American citizen," he said, "is obedience to the constitution and laws of his country." Yet he favored no war upon the rights of the Southern states, no bloody triumph over his countrymen. Avoiding vengeance, he asked that the spirit of moderation and justice should prevail. Mindful of the world significance of the struggle, he urged that "whatever we may do must be the result of . . . the duty that we owe to ourselves, to our posterity and to the friends of . . . self-government throughout the world." [13]

The speaker of the Illinois lower house on this occasion records that Douglas spoke "with great earnestness, & power," and adds that never before was he "so impressed by the power of a man talking to

---

[11] *Ibid.*

[12] S. M. Cullom to I. N. Arnold, Springfield, March 19, 1883, Arnold MSS., Chicago Hist. Soc.

[13] *Speech of Senator Douglas, before the Legislature of Illinois, April 25, 1861* (contemporary pamphlet).

an audience." [14] Douglas made a similar speech on May 1, in Chicago, speaking at the National Hall, the old wigwam in which Lincoln had been nominated.[15]

Not all approved of Douglas's support of Lincoln; some denounced him as a traitor to his party [16] and as joining the hell hounds of Black Republicanism.[17] Such scurrilous attacks seem untypical; they are of interest chiefly as showing that it cost something for the Democratic leader to take the stand he did.

Shortly after his Chicago speech Douglas fell ill, borne down by financial embarrassments and the exhaustion of overwork. On June 3 he died, Adele, his wife, at his bedside. In token of popular mourning bells were rung, cannon boomed, business was suspended in Chicago, and public buildings were draped. The President denied himself to visitors,[18] and an army order was issued from the war department directing appropriate recognition of a "national calamity." [19]

---

[14] S. M. Cullom to Arnold, Springfield, Mar. 19, 1883, Arnold MSS., Chicago Hist. Soc.

[15] All the arrangements—the committee of welcome, procession, and the like—indicate that this was a big event in Chicago. The *Tribune* spoke of Douglas's magnificent ovation and warmly praised his speech "in which the necessity of sustaining the Government and the honor of the flag was eloquently enforced." It was added that Republicans and Democrats united to do him honor. Chicago *Tribune,* May 2, 1861.

[16] Referring to men who denounced the North as the aggressor, a pseudonymous writer stated that such men (in Southern Illinois) "voted for Douglas but when Douglas declared for the perpetuity of the Union they denounced him as a traitor to his party." "Leonidas," Fayette Co., Ill., to Richard Yates, Aug. 15, 1861, Yates MSS.

[17] T. N. Lawrence (of Golconda, Ill.) to S. Maynard, May 22, 1861, Yates MSS.

[18] New York *Herald,* June 8, 1861, p. 1, cc. 2–3.

[19] Major Donald B. Sanger, discussing the army order of June 4, 1861, directing that military ceremonies be held in honor of Douglas, tentatively suggests that this order may be traceable to Lincoln as author. For this conjecture (which Major Sanger properly presents as such) the present writer has found no confirmation. The slipshod wording of the order would suggest that Lincoln did not write or edit it. *Transactions,* Ill. State Hist. Soc., 1933, 67–79.

CHAPTER XIV

DEMOCRACY'S TESTING

WHEN Congress met on July 4, 1861, after eighty days of almost bloodless war, Lincoln faced a bitter mixture of frustration and grief. The coming months were to bring radical interference, military debacle, broken lines at home, and embroilment abroad. No one could tell how far the war would reach; yet there was no turning back; or, if one wanted to play upon words, there was nothing in sight except turning back—back from peace and normal relations to an unknowable future in which the only sure prospects were slaughter and destruction. For the addled sections to have recovered the pre-Sumter status would have been to go notably forward; this was psychologically impossible. July was vastly more distant from mid-April than the eighty days that intervened.

Lincoln had now reached a point of significant transition. He could go forward (if it was forward) only in terms of prosecuting the war in earnest; yet this presaged a storm of unpredictable hazards. The muddle had started as a little war, a mere sequel to the Sumter incident, the kind of trouble that short-service militia, and only a few at that, could "suppress." But when wars start they seldom give notice of the proportions they will assume or the course they will take. Rarely indeed can a war leader control a war. The month of July 1861 was to mark the transition from a short, little, unplanned war to a prolonged and vastly extended struggle in which organization and preparation would count heavily. Lincoln thought that the existing struggle was to prove whether democracy could survive not only on these shores but anywhere. No one felt more keenly the enormous values at hazard. If this nation broke into pieces, it was a serious question whether any nation based on popular rule could succeed. A major battle with the Confederacy was soon to be fought which would throw this whole question into doubt. In addition, there was opposition brewing within the North, and within Lincoln's party ranks, which was to throw into question the ability of a democracy to maintain its own governmental lines. As if this were not enough, an international crisis of terrible possibilities lay not far ahead.

I

The message which Lincoln presented to the called session of Congress stands as one of his most elaborate and carefully prepared papers. It comprised a history of events, a report of stewardship, a constitutional argument, and an exalted commentary on fundamentals. In these latter days of ghost writers and aides with a passion for anonymity it is worth recording that the message was Lincoln's own. For weeks, as above indicated, reporters had been noting that the President was denying himself to visitors while preparing his address; in style and reasoning the address is unmistakably Lincolnian.

Though best studied in the distinguished original, the message must be given here in brief paraphrase. Here, said the President, was the situation faced by the present administration. Here was my duty; these were my measures; here is what they mean in national survival and broad human destiny; further things are now recommended which rest with Congress. In March, he said, governmental functions were suspended in seven states. Arsenals and forts had been seized, armed forces assembled. An illegal organization "in the character of confederate States" had been set up. The Union was declared severed. The problem was to prevent the consummation of disunion while still preserving peace; the method proposed and inaugurally announced was to exhaust all peaceful measures before resorting to "any stronger ones." The purpose was "only to hold" Federal property. No disturbance of the Southern people in their rights was intended. Pledges were given against such disturbance. In the waiting period of March and early April the administration sought only to collect the revenue, continue the mails, and to forbear "everything . . . without which it was believed possible to keep the government on foot." [1]

To hold Sumter, said Lincoln in retrospect, was militarily impossible. Twenty thousand troops were needed; they were not available.

[1] *Works*, VI, 299–300.

The military task was to remove the garrison. But that by itself, with no collateral measure to point up the government's policy of Federal maintenance, would have been ruinous. Friends of the Union would not have understood "the necessity under which it was . . . done." National destruction would have been consummated. "This could not be allowed." [2] What then? There was a peaceful way out. Starvation was not yet upon the garrison. Let Pickens be firmly yet peaceably held, and the country might accept the evacuation of Fort Sumter as a military necessity. A Pickens expedition was sent to accomplish this peace-promoting mission, but because of conflicting influences the troops were not landed. Till then, the Sumter expedition, tentatively prepared, had been withheld. It was now sent, but with full notice that no attack from Sumter was intended. There was no reason to mistake the government's purpose. The other side "well knew that the [Sumter] garrison . . . could by no possibility commit aggression upon them." The government was keeping the garrison there "not to assail them," but "to maintain visible possession, and thus to preserve the Union," trusting to "the ballot-box for final adjustment." They "assailed . . . the fort for precisely the reverse object—to . . . force it [the Union] to immediate dissolution." [3]

If America failed, thought Lincoln, in its experiment of free government—if it fell apart from some seemingly inherent defect—the loss would be tragic and world-wide. It was more than these United States that were at stake; the whole experiment of democracy as an example to the world was on trial. Thus early expressed, this concept was to be Lincoln's central idea of the significance of America's tragedy. Over and again the President was to return to the theme in his mental searching and in public address, notably at Gettysburg.[4]

Such was the President's approach. In developing his report to the nation Lincoln commented upon the anti-Union action of Virginia and the upper South, and recounted his own calls for troops and other emergency executive measures. Suspension of a few of the laws, he said, was necessary lest the government itself go to pieces and all the laws fail. In a vigorous passage the President denounced the attempt to make secession seem legal; such an attempt he considered only a

---

[2] *Ibid.*, VI, 301. [3] *Ibid.*, VI, 303.

[4] It is best to deal with this theme in connection with Gettysburg; see vol. II, 317 ff.

"sophism" to conceal what amounted to rebellion. The states, he said, "have their status in the Union, and they have no other legal status." Secession is "disintegration." "Whatever concerns the whole should be confided to the whole . . . ." [5]

"This," he said, "is essentially a people's contest. On the side of the Union it is a struggle . . . to elevate the condition of men—to lift artificial weights from all shoulders; . . . to afford all an unfettered start, and a fair chance in the race of life." [6] If free government succeeded in preventing dissolution of the nation, he argued, it would be "a great lesson of peace: . . . teaching all the folly of being the beginners of a war." Even as a private citizen, he said, the present Executive could not consent "that these institutions shall perish; much less could he, in betrayal of so vast . . . a trust as the free people have confided to him." [7]

According to later practice the message would have been delivered by the President in person before House and Senate in joint session. With this possibility of public delivery by the President in view, it is of interest to re-read the message. In its turning of epigrammatic phrases and its restrained yet exalted eloquence it was well adapted to such an occasion; it would have sounded the better for its noticeable lack of emotional denunciation.

At noon on July 3 the message was reviewed by the cabinet. That night, at about nine o'clock, Orville H. Browning of Illinois called at the White House. When told that Lincoln was busy, he turned to pay his respects to Mrs. Lincoln. The President "heard my voice [wrote Browning] and wished to see me. I went to his room, and as he had just finished his message, he said he wished to read it to me, and did so. . . . I remained . . . in conversation . . . when the reading was concluded." [8] Not the larger public, not the assembled Congress, the press, and galleries, but one lone senator, heard Lincoln's oral delivery. He also heard the President's off-the-record comments which accompanied and interpreted the message. In perfunctory manner the message was communicated to Congress as a formal public document one day after the convening. Thus undramatically presented, it attracted inadequate notice. For opening oratory the House

---

[5] *Works*, VI, 314–316.
[6] *Ibid.*, VI, 321.
[7] *Ibid.*, VI, 322, 324.
[8] Browning, *Diary*, I, 475–476.

had to listen to the "inaugural" of Galusha A. Grow, newly elected speaker. "It was a pretty thing," wrote Browning, "but on the Star spangled banner order." [9]

II

In terms of popular demand and press agitation the emphasis was upon intensified war effort. Up to July 1861 the clashes at arms had nowhere reached the point of a sizable engagement. They had been confined to rioting in Baltimore and in Missouri, minor though well advertised battles under McClellan in western Virginia, and small incidents elsewhere in Virginia, as at Harpers Ferry, Vienna, and Big Bethel. To the 75,000 asked for in April (instead of the 200,000 suggested by Douglas [1] or the 300,000 deemed necessary by Scott [2]) Lincoln had added a request for an additional 42,000 in May.[3] Now in July he asked for 400,000 men and 400 millions of money. He estimated that this number was "about one tenth of those of proper ages within the regions where, apparently, all are willing to engage." [4] At the same time he revealed the weakness of governmental organization by adding that one of the greatest perplexities was to avoid receiving troops faster than they could be provided for.

To the military historian the delay in active operations would occasion no surprise. New troops need drilling; major battles require elaborate preparation. In the American Civil War, however, those who had the least military understanding were loudest in their advice, and the radicals especially, men who were to become an increasing nuisance to Lincoln, were most insistent in demanding a quick movement "On to Richmond." As early as May 24 Sumner informed Governor Andrew of great pressure upon the administration for "active aggressive measures" and predicted a "collision soon." [5] In early June a member of Lincoln's cabinet wrote: "Matters are approaching a crisis & we will very probably soon have a fight." [6]

Urged on by an intense political demand, the Union army under

---

[9] *Ibid.*, 476.

[1] Above, p. 377.

[2] R. M. Johnston, *Bull Run: Its Strategy and Tactics*, 18. See also 68.

[3] Proclamation of May 3, 1861, *Works*, VI, 263–265.

[4] Message of July 4, 1861, *ibid.*, VI, 311.

[5] Sumner to Andrew, May 24, 1861, Andrew MSS.

[6] Caleb B. Smith to R. W. Thompson, June 10, 1861, MS., Lincoln Nat. Life Foundation, Ft. Wayne, Ind.

McDowell stepped daily closer to the hour of attack. To read of those anxious days is almost to watch the ticking of an irresponsible time bomb; the approaching crisis was less a matter of controlled preparation than of fate. Wagons had been drawn from the main arena, subsistence was interrupted, artillery horses and trains were delayed, men were sent forward "without having been together before in a brigade." [7] The Union troops were "unaccustomed to marching . . . and not used to carrying even the load of 'light marching order.'" [8] It is true that the Confederate troops were also raw, but they had the advantages of timely reënforcement, superior generalship, and, chiefly, the less hazardous task of defense as contrasted with difficult assault by exhausted men inadequately held together in battle command.

With miscalculation and unfulfilled plans the Moving Finger brought the army to the oppressive Sunday of July 21. Then a part of the Union force tardily crossed Bull Run (near Manassas, about twenty miles southwest of Washington) and struck the enemy under Beauregard and Johnston. That the moment of attack found the forces of these two important Confederate generals united, constituted one of the main points of Union miscalculation. Joseph E. Johnston had been in the Winchester–Harpers-Ferry region facing Robert Patterson, but had been permitted to slip away and join Beauregard at Manassas on July 20, the day before the battle; his operations on July 21 were an indispensable factor in Confederate victory.

The work of the Union army was not as badly done as has often been inferred. For a time some of the Confederates were driven back; indeed at an advanced stage of the battle it was supposed that "a complete [Union] victory had been won." [9] With all their lack of discipline, Union artillery and infantry had achieved an attack by which it seemed that the battle had been "virtually . . . lost" by the Confederates, and Richmond was shaken by "tales of a Confederate *débâcle*." [10] A difficult assault had been carried off well and the Confederates seemed broken after four hours of fighting. Beauregard's lines had been pushed back and in hot contest the Yankees had taken enemy positions and repulsed counter attacks until they thought the business was concluded.

---

[7] *Offic. Rec.*, 1 ser., II, 324. [8] *Ibid.*
[9] Johnston, *Bull Run*, 195; *Offic. Rec.*, 1 ser., II, 320.
[10] D. S. Freeman, *R. E. Lee*, I, 537–538.

Then the tide turned. Retreating Southern troops were rallied, reserves and reënforcements were thrown in, weak spots were found in the over-extended Union lines. McDowell's men had been up since two o'clock in the morning, and it was now mid-afternoon. They had marched weary miles, had in some cases gone into battle without food, and had done a great deal of heavy and prolonged fighting. By the time the Confederates launched their final counter attack with strong reënforcements some of the Yankees were already out of ranks. They had done much, but not enough. They could not stand against "an enemy ably commanded, superior in numbers, who had but a short distance to march, and who acted on his own ground on the defensive . . . under cover," while the Union troops "were of necessity out on the open fields." [11]

Contrary to the general impression the conclusion of this battle was not a Confederate walk-over nor a complete Union rout. Some of the Federal brigades held firm, covering an orderly withdrawal, so that the lack of Confederate pursuit had a valid reason. The men under Louis Blenker and Israel B. Richardson, to mention examples, did not run. Confusion did not pervade the whole army. Yet the Union line had been broken; part of the army did become a disorganized mass; control over some of the troops was lost in a mêlée of spectators, soldiers, and congressmen; there was a certain amount of panic long after the main fighting was over; and the portion of the retreat that journalists noted at a considerable distance back of the lines, including stragglers who had not been in the fight, did take on the nature of a stampede.

The disorganized retreat to Washington is not to be denied; neither is it to be regarded as the most significant part of the story of that battle. It was, unfortunately, the phase which, alike in contemporary newspapers and in stereotyped history, has received most of the emphasis. According to R. M. Johnston, who has competently studied the whole campaign, it was "a mere incident of a not abnormal character." [12] Conditions productive of the stampede began, writes Johnston, even before the Union advance, when "the columns were kept standing long hours in the sun and the officers proved unable to prevent their men from going off into the woods after blackberries; . . . or even when Lincoln proclaimed that only the common soldier

[11] *Offic. Rec.*, 1 ser., II, 322.

[12] Johnston, *Bull Run*, 272.

could be trusted and his officer was a leader not entitled to confidence." [13]

The reference is to Lincoln's statement in his message of July 4 that "not one common soldier or common sailor is known to have deserted his flag." In contrast, said Lincoln, ". . . in this, the government's hour of trial, large numbers" of the officers in the army and navy "have resigned and proved false to the hand which had pampered them . . . ." [14] It was felt that those officers who stayed with the army and handled the difficult tasks of command under Scott and McDowell deserved better recognition, and these words of Lincoln had been denounced as the appeal of a demagogue who sought popular approval by putting the patriotism of privates above that of their officers.[15] In retrospect it does appear that Lincoln's pardonable censure of officers who left the service ought to have been accompanied with commensurate praise for those who remained. Though in the democratic Union army a private was as good as an officer, this principle was misapplied if it meant, as it did in July 1861 (not particularly because of Lincoln), that privates could disregard or disobey their officers.

In truth the outcome at Bull Run was an uncommanded retreat where, to withstand powerful Confederate counter attack, there should have been orderly withdrawal to a point, perhaps Centerville, where the army could re-form and stand formidably in a new position. In essence it was a lack of military cohesion among some of the troops of an army that, in the main, had fought well and had almost won the day. With all the Yankee panic and disorganization the Southern army failed to follow up its success. This brought Southern disapprobation upon Johnston who defended himself with the statement that all the military conditions known to him forbade an attempt upon Washington. The Confederate army, he said, "was more disorganized by victory than that of the United States by defeat." [16]

Yet in the North and abroad the Union rout was played up as evidence of Yankee cowardice, moblike inefficiency, and unmanly weakness. The most devastating rhetoric was that of William Howard Russell in the *Times* of London. In haughty and scornful passages, not unpleasing to Tory readers, Russell wrote of the "disgraceful con-

---

[13] *Ibid.*, 272–273.

[14] *Works*, VI, 321.

[15] Johnston, *Bull Run*, 70–71.

[16] *Battles and Leaders of the Civil War*, I, 252.

duct" of the Union troops. The retreat, he said, was a "cowardly rout —a miserable, causeless panic." "Such scandalous behaviour . . . I should have considered impossible" he added, though he admitted that of his own knowledge he could only assert that the disorganization extended to "more than one regiment." It was not Sir William's fault. In letters and conversation he had indicated the seriousness of the task, "but in the state of [Union] arrogance . . . one might as well have preached to the Pyramid of Cheops."

In a crescendo of devastating journalism Russell filled in the details. The complete Federal repulse was due to a "little skirmish at Bull's Run." About forty casualties were magnified into fifteen hundred. General Scott was but "the mouthpiece of the more violent civilians of the Government." A "Babel of tongues" revealed a mass of Union men "in good spirits"; these were Pennsylvania troops headed for home.[17] "Men literally screamed with rage and fright when their way was blocked up. . . . Faces black and dusty, tongues out in the heat, eyes staring—it was a most wonderful sight." [18] Warming to his theme, Russell emphasized the perfection of the Southern troops (drawing upon notes prior to the battle); yet he revealed the difficulty of the Union task as he expatiated upon the zigzag fortification, angles, salients, abundance of food, perfection of communication, and admirable disposition of the Confederate forces.[19]

In a follow-up letter three days after the battle Russell generalized as to the whole Union cause, for which he could see only the gloomiest prospect. The Lincoln government would be beaten, he thought, if they should "yield to the fanatics and fight battles against the advice of their officers." [20] He questioned whether "the men and the money [would] be forthcoming . . . to continue the war of aggression . . . against the Seceded States." [21]

When, about a month after the battle, the *Times* account arrived on these shores, Sir William's narrative was "received with execration" [22] and so great was the outcry against "Bull Run Russell" that the correspondent's usefulness had virtually ended. Having fallen ill, he recovered from "a state of powder and mint julep" [23] to find himself threatened with tar and feathers and even assassination.[24]

---

[17] *The Times*, London, August 6, 1861, p. 7.
[18] *Ibid.*, p. 8, c. 1.
[19] *Ibid.*, p. 7, c. 5.
[20] *Ibid.*, Aug. 10, 1861, p. 9, c. 3.
[21] *Ibid.*
[22] John Black Atkins, *Life of Sir William Howard Russell*, II, 68.
[23] *Ibid.*, II, 67.
[24] *Ibid.*, II, 73.

Yet his biographer says that he "helped Englishmen to . . . see that the Federal cause was the cause of justice and truth." [25] In American comments on Russell's lurid description it was noted that he was not within musket shot of the enemy, that he was quietly eating his lunch at the moment of hottest fighting, and that he "only saw the rout." [26] Yet for admission of failure and dramatization of disaster one did not need to turn to the foreign press. One quotation, out of a vast literature of description, must suffice here. "Every account that comes [wrote John Russell Young], comes filled with disaster. . . . *We have sent into Virginia the best . . . of our grand army, we have fought the greatest battle ever fought on the continent, and we have been not only beaten, but our army has been routed, and many of its best regiments wholly demoralized.*" [27]

III

North of the Potomac the effect of Bull Run followed a complex pattern. The grave and reverend, as well as lesser folk, fell into a quagmire of despair. There was bickering against the government, doubt of Lincoln, and indignant demand for a scapegoat, but that was not all. In addition there was grim realization of the reality of war, with renewed determination to carry on. Even the latter sentiment, however, did not necessarily work in Lincoln's favor. In modern slang the Lincoln administration was "on the spot." "The truth is," wrote Lyman Trumbull, "there is a lack of . . . positive action & business talent in the cabinet. Lincoln though a most excellent & an honest man lacks these qualities." After several months it was on the Union side still a defensive war and Trumbull expressed the fear that "the men at the head of our affairs do not realize our condition and are not equal to the occasion." [1] Common themes of the time were distrust of commanders, lack of confidence in the cabinet, fear of imminent attack upon Washington (this continued for weeks), clamor for peace, and a determination to have no more trifling.[2] In this phase a kind of patronizing compliment to Lincoln, though many

---

[25] *Ibid.*, I, preface, vii.

[26] Moore, *Rebellion Record* (Doc.), II, 63.

[27] *Ibid.* (Doc.), II, 376.

[1] Lyman Trumbull to Judge Doolittle of Wisconsin, Lakeside, Conn., Aug. 31, 1861, MS., Ill. State Hist. Lib.

[2] New York *Herald*, July 27, 1861, p. 4, c. 4.

refused even this, would be balanced by denunciation of influences surrounding him. Lincoln, admitted the *Herald,* was "an honest . . . amiable man," but he should not trust "everything to his Cabinet, to his party and to Providence." [3] He should ferret out the ones responsible for the blunder at Bull Run and act at once. Next day the *Herald* put the blame upon the abolitionists and secondarily upon Lincoln for permitting abolition influence to defeat the Crittenden compromise.[4] When offering advice this paper could deliver a broadside of criticism, as when it stated that Lincoln's duty was to achieve a cabinet "superior to all Presidential cliques and intriguers, rising above all temptations for jobs and contracts, and spoils and plunder, renouncing all abolition vagaries, and discarding the delusion that the patience of the country will cover all delinquencies." [5] It was further asserted that Lincoln's first duty was to "cease to be the politician, and perform the duties of the statesman." [6]

To the President himself the news of Bull Run had come with a ruder shock because it had been preceded by a steady accumulation of convincing assurances. Lincoln spent this eventful Sunday at church, at the White House, and at the war department. While at the war building his interest was in the telegraph office where he "waited with deep anxiety for each succeeding despatch." [7] These despatches were encouraging, and Lincoln was led to believe "that Beauregard was being pushed back." [8] "At supper [wrote Browning] the news was that . . . our army had forced the batteries at Bulls run and driven the enemy back upon Manassas . . . ." [9] Feeling that the news of Union victory had been confirmed, the President went for his usual drive. By the time he returned, the telegraph had announced that McDowell was in full retreat, that the day was lost, and that it was a matter of saving Washington with the remnants of a broken army.[10] In factual manner Browning recorded the stunned bewilderment at Washington. It was thought that the fight was over with the Unionists "in possession of the field." Then, "in some unaccountable manner, our troops were seized with a panic, and fled. They were not pursued. . . . How it happened no body seems to know." [11]

---

[3] *Ibid.,* July 25, 1861, p. 4, c. 3.
[4] *Ibid.,* July 26, 1861, p. 4, c. 3.
[5] *Ibid.,* Aug. 2, 1861, editorial, p. 4, c. 4.
[6] *Ibid.,* Aug. 17, 1861, editorial, p. 4, c. 4.
[7] David H. Bates, *Lincoln in the Telegraph Office,* 88.
[8] *Ibid.,* 91.
[9] Browning, *Diary,* I, 484.
[10] *Offic. Rec.,* 1 ser., II, 747.
[11] Browning, *Diary,* I, 485.

In all this painful frustration it was a kind of human necessity to put the blame somewhere, the blame of ordering "a battle before our troops were prepared for it." [12] General Scott's comment was given in a remarkable conversation with Lincoln, Cameron, and a group of Illinois men. In mock self-condemnation Scott called himself "the greatest coward in America" because he had fought this battle against his judgment. Lincoln is said to have remarked: "Your conversation seems to imply that I forced you to fight this battle," to which Scott replied that no President had been "kinder" to him than Lincoln.[13]

The problem of responsibility in the premises is more than a question of whether Lincoln "forced" the battle. A congressional opponent, W. A. Richardson of Illinois, though assailing the Republican administration, disclaimed any implication that Lincoln had compelled Scott to fight at this stage. Lincoln's friend Francis P. Blair, Jr., asserted that Lincoln, on learning that Johnston had joined Beauregard, suggested to Scott the propriety of waiting, but that Scott was determined to attack and disregarded the suggestion.[14] Lincoln's secretaries do not so easily relieve the President of at least partial responsibility, for they record that, at a council summoned by the President (June 29), the generals were of opinion that simultaneous victories could be won at Manassas and Winchester, that Scott preferred delay until autumn, and that "the President and the Cabinet, as political experts" intervened on the ground that the public could not brook delay. The secretaries assert flatly that "the Administration was responsible for the forward movement." [15] A good deal of this whole discussion was animated by a purpose to discredit Lincoln's cabinet and advisers. Lincoln was even complimented by some who were damning his administration. Yet the President and his cabinet seem to have been in no serious disagreement on this point.

At least two factors of a fortuitous nature had acted powerfully against the Union side in this battle: the failure of Patterson and the falling off of three-months volunteers. An essential link in the strategy of Scott and McDowell was General Robert Patterson, in command at Winchester. His task was to keep Johnston busy and prevent him from joining Beauregard at Manassas when McDowell's blow should fall.

---

[12] Remarks of Francis P. Blair in House of Representatives, August 1, 1861, *Cong. Globe*, 37 Cong., 1 sess., 388.

[13] Quoted in remarks of W. A. Richardson, July 24, 1861, *ibid.*, 246.

[14] August 1, 1861, *ibid.*, 387.

[15] Nicolay and Hay, *Lincoln*, IV, 360.

This he failed to do. Authorities are pretty well agreed that this failure made all the difference;[16] yet Union high command could not be blamed for this unforeseen factor. So also with the aggravating circumstance that the battle came just at the time when the service of three-months militia was expiring. According to McDowell's own words he could neither push on faster nor delay. "A large and the best part . . . of my forces [he said] were three-months' volunteers, whose terms . . . were about expiring, but who were sent forward as having long enough to serve for the purpose of the expedition." "In the next few days [he added], day by day I should have lost ten thousand of the best armed, drilled, officered, and disciplined troops in the Army. In other words, every day which added to the strength of the enemy made us weaker."[17] If the President was responsible for this amazing situation at the time of a major campaign, it was in introducing the three-months limitation in the first place, or in not correcting it before the moment of advance.

It was a case of a war leader suffering when unsuccessful, whatever the cause. Before the battle it seemed reasonable to hope that the Union campaign, not badly planned, might succeed. It was not so much Lincoln, or Scott, or the cabinet, or McDowell, but unforeseeable happenings, together with the unmilitary emphasis of the American democracy, that had produced a failure which to Browning seemed "unaccountable."

IV

More significant than post-mortem recrimination was the forward look which showed an unshaken government backed by a people that could close ranks, re-form lines, and push grimly on. If Lincoln was hurt and stunned, his resilience was equally manifest. The night after Bull Run he "did not go to his bed,"[1] but began some pencil jottings which two days later (July 23) had been elaborated into "memoranda of military policy suggested by the Bull Run defeat." In brief his policy was: push the blockade, drill the forces at Fort Monroe and vicinity, hold Baltimore, strengthen "Patterson or Banks" (in the Winchester area), push forward in Missouri (this was Frémont's job),

---

[16] *Battles and Leaders of the Civil War*, I, 175, 230.

[17] *Offic. Rec.*, 1 ser., II, 325.

[1] Nicolay and Hay, *Lincoln*, IV, 355.

reorganize the main force in and near Washington, discharge those three-months men who declined longer service (a bitter lesson had been learned here), bring up new volunteers as fast as possible, seize and hold suitable points in Virginia, then advance with a coördinated movement on western fronts.[2]

For the new program a new commander was needed. Not that McDowell had served so badly; it was rather that this unfortunate commander bore the imprimatur of defeat and that conditions of army morale and popular feeling demanded a change. The name of George B. McClellan was in favor because of a minor but skillfully advertised campaign in western Virginia (June and July, 1861). In an address to his troops ("Soldiers of the Army of the West") he had dramatically acclaimed the achievements of his men; this address, whose publication was not neglected, was dated only five days before McDowell's defeat.[3] More than this, McClellan had real qualities. Training at West Point had been followed by regular army duty, Mexican War service, military surveys, observation in the Crimean War (perfectly reported and published by the United States government), and executive experience with the Illinois Central Railroad.

On July 27, 1861, McClellan formally assumed his duties in command of the Union army with headquarters at Washington.[4] No time had been lost in putting him there. His summons to Washington came the day after Bull Run (July 22);[5] the order assigning him to his new "department" was dated July 25.[6] This, the first important change in army command traceable to the fortunes of war, was less a presidential than a war-department affair; at any rate Lincoln's part in the business does not appear in the documents. Scott loyally accepted the new commander, though his biographer states that he was "slightly irritated . . . that McClellan had been invited to confer with the President and Cabinet on the afternoon of the 27th—a conference to which the General-in-Chief [Scott] had apparently not been summoned."[7]

Months of friction ensued between the General in Chief and the Young Napoleon, due in part to overlapping duties and in part to temperamental reasons on both sides. Meanwhile, for supporting the government he had served all his life, Scott was denounced by fellow

---

[2] *Works*, VI, 331–333.
[3] *Offic. Rec.*, 1 ser., II, 236.
[4] *Ibid.*, 766.
[5] *Ibid.*, 753.
[6] *Ibid.*, 763.
[7] Elliott, *Scott*, 733.

Virginians as a traitor and compared to Benedict Arnold.[8] The followers of "General Greeley" assailed him from a quite different quarter as an inefficient dotard.[9] The old warrior grew weaker and could no longer remain awake during working hours. Behind the scenes the President tried to ease matters between his top commanders. It was of no use; McClellan considered that Scott was in his way and was determined to "force the issue." [10] In cabinet meeting it was agreed (October 18) that Scott could "*command* no longer." [11] Here was a situation calling for presidential tact. Lincoln handled it with deferential respect to the distinguished septuagenarian, and with that added element of personal kindness to which the old general had already gratefully alluded. The President read in cabinet "a draft of a letter to Gen S.[cott] (delicately and handsomely written) importing that . . . [Scott] had expressed a wish to be retired, . . . that he would no longer object— That he would still . . . need his advice . . . and was disposed to deal generously by the Genl.'s military family." [12]

On October 31 Scott wrote asking formal retirement under existing law. In accepting his request (November 1) Lincoln paid him the compliment of a personal visit of himself and full cabinet to the general's headquarters. There was a "touching interview" at which the President made a "neat and feeling address." [13] The army order recognizing the retirement was drawn by Lincoln; it was "done chastely and in excellent taste." [14] In a published letter the President took note of the nation's sympathy for the retiring commander and its recognition of his "long and brilliant career." [15] McClellan was directed to "assume the command of the Army of the United States." This did not mean that he was accorded Scott's rank of Lieutenant General, yet he was appointed in his stead and Lincoln referred to him as "general-in-chief of the army." [16] In effect McClellan took the places of both Scott and McDowell. Stating that there was no difference of opinion as to the person to be appointed, Lincoln paid McClellan a handsome compliment in his annual message to Congress.[17]

---

[8] *Ibid.*, 725. [9] *Ibid.*, 731–732. [10] *McClellan's Own Story*, 170.
[11] Bates, *Diary*, 196. [12] *Ibid.*, 196–197. [13] *Ibid.*, 199.
[14] *Ibid.* [15] *Works*, VII, 13–14 (Nov. 1, 1861).
[16] Annual message to Congress, Dec. 3, 1861, *Works*, VII, 55. (On November 1, 1861, Lincoln in a formal order directed that McClellan "assume command of the army of the United States." *Ibid.*, VII, 14.)
[17] *Ibid.*, VII, 55 (Dec. 3, 1861).

Thus did Winfield Scott lay down his duties after heavy overtime service. Writers have customarily emphasized his age, inadequacy, and pompous fussiness; yet this veteran, at the outset of the war, had embodied in his massive person a large share of such professional competence as belonged to the tiny army which Lincoln inherited. His biographer states that, except Scott and Wool, both over-age, "the Regular Army did not carry on its rolls a single officer who had directed, in peace or war, the evolutions of a brigade." [18] The unmilitary democracy that had stumbled into war had looked to the old general for organization and strategy far beyond the tools at his disposal. Experience of a half-century, reaching back to the days of Van Rensselaer's ineffective New York militia, when press and public were "howling for action," [19] had given him a low opinion of volunteers. Tiny as the professional army was, Scott felt that it ought to be the nucleus of the organization that would fight battles. On this point his advice was not followed. Instead of being expanded from a trained nucleus, the new army was a kind of emergency hodge-podge. As to high strategy, Scott's master plan—a broad, slow blockade and encirclement dubbed "Scott's anaconda" [20]—was likewise disregarded.

In a long lull of military operations McClellan concerned himself with replenishment and elaborate reconditioning of the force which, he knew, would face a task of major proportions in its campaign of 1862 against Richmond. This was a period when Washington saw much of the magnetic Young Napoleon who was "courted . . . as few men in our history have been." [21] His prolonged presence in Washington was a constant reminder that the war was at a standstill. Before he was on the march Lincoln was to undergo some of the most bothersome and menacing episodes of his administration.

---

18 Elliott, *Scott*, 718.

19 *Ibid.*, 54.

20 *Ibid.*, 722–724.

21 Nicolay and Hay, *Lincoln*, IV, 444.

3 5282 00484 8415